INTERTWINED

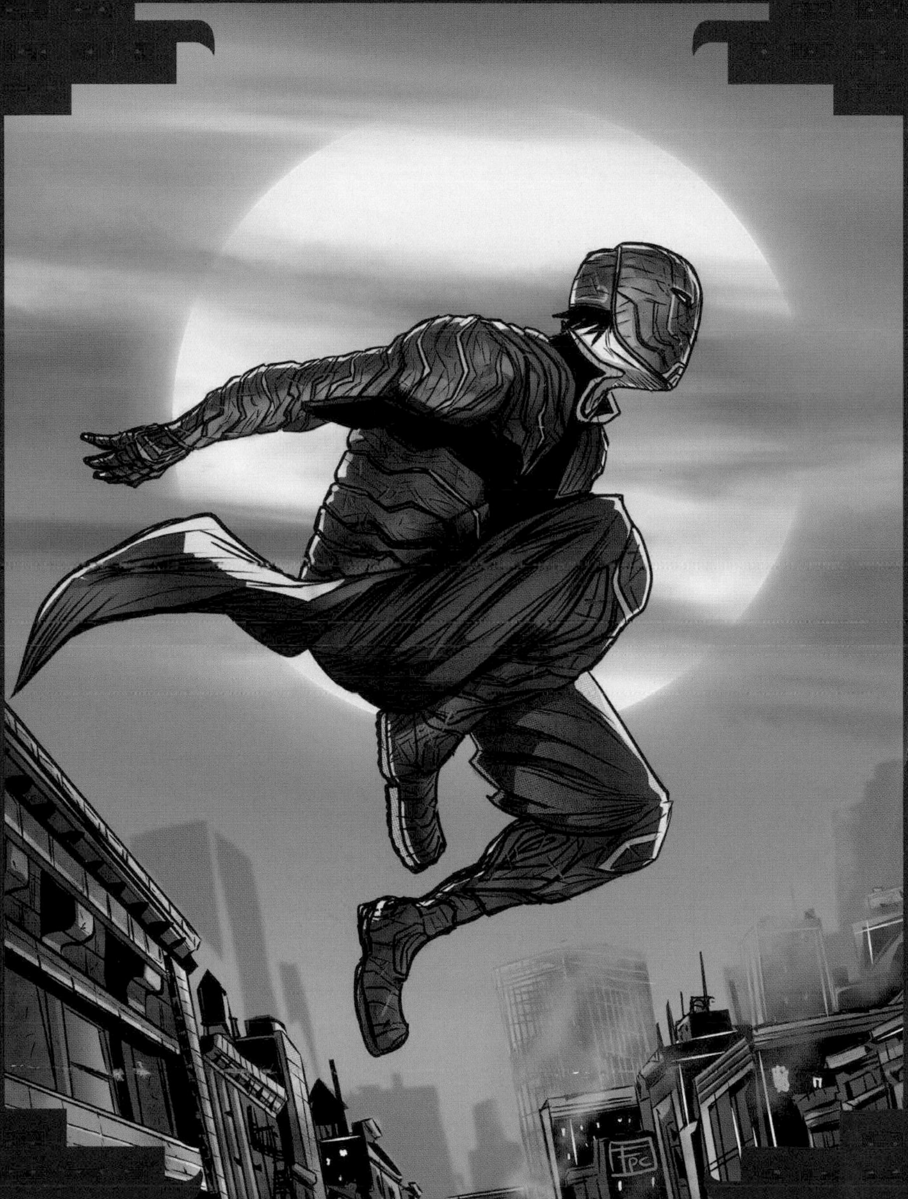

DYNAMITE

THE INTERTWINED TEAM WISHES TO THANK
The Kickstarter backers who were
instrumental in making this book a reality.
Thanks for your unconditional support (and
your patience).
Rich Young, Juan Collado, Anthony Marques,
Matt Humphreys, Keith Davidsen, Pat
O'Connell and all the DYNAMITE COMICS
team!

Fred's thank yous:
Merci à mon père, la team INTW: mon frère
d'armes Fabrice, Veronica, Heather. Alex
mon bro, ma famille, Laurence, mon fils, mes
amis, Dynamite, Chris, Pierrick, Elsa, Mark,
Maxime, Jull, Philou, Pierro, Mateus, Olivier,
Roland tous les backers, ma kung fu family
et tous les gens qui croient en moi, sans qui
Intertwined ne serait pas !

Fabrice's thank yous:
First, my family for tolerating and
encouraging my passion for comics:
Keren, Ethan and Dana, my awesome mom,
my brothers and sisters, my sister in law Xin
Wang (thanks for the translations too!).
My BFFs: E. David B., Raphy and the Schkopi
Gang, Xavier Fournier, Piero Bisson, Lise
Benkemon, Justin "Moritat" Norman, Joe
Keatinge, El Torres, Will Torres, Ramon Gil.

Special shoutout to Anthony Kavanagh for
being a part of this and to Aiken Zhu who
invited me to Beijing early 2015 (it definitely
played a part in the creation of this story).

All the wonderful creators I respect and
admire in the business and that I'm happy
to call my friends (so many to name but you
know who you are).

Veronica and our "Hawesome" editor: we did
it thanks to you too! M. this is for you.

DYNAMITE®

Nick Barrucci, CEO / Publisher
Juan Collado, President / COO

Joe Rybandt, Executive Editor
Matt Idelson, Senior Editor
Anthony Marques, Associate Editor
Matt Humphreys, Assistant Editor
Kevin Ketner, Assistant Editor

Jason Ullmeyer, Art Director
Geoff Harkins, Senior Graphic Designer
Cathleen Heard, Graphic Designer
Alexis Persson, Production Artist
Chris Caniano, Digital Associate
Rachel Kilbury, Digital Assistant

Brandon Dante Primavera, V.P. of IT and Operations
Rich Young, Director of Business Development

Alan Payne, V.P. of Sales and Marketing
Keith Davidsen, Marketing Director
Pat O'Connell, Sales Manager

ISBN: 978-1-5241-0347-7
First Printing   10 9 8 7 6 5 4 3 2 1

Online at   www.DYNAMITE.com
Facebook   /Dynamitecomics
Instagram /Dynamitecomics
Tumblr   dynamitecomics.tumblr.com
Twitter   @dynamitecomics
YouTube   /Dynamitecomics

PARENTAL
ADVISORY
EXPLICIT COMICS

VOLUME I
COMING TO AMERICA

FABRICE SAPOLSKY and FRED PHAM CHUONG
CREATORS & STORYTELLERS

VERÓNICA R. LÓPEZ
COLOR ARTIST

FRED PHAM CHUONG
COVER

RAMON GIL
GUEST CO-WRITING (P.119-121)

GUEST STARRING
YUKI NISHIMURA *AS YUKI*
ALEX PHAM CHUONG *AS THE SPIRIT OF FIRE*
LUCA HERZOG *AS LUCA*
DAVID BENAYM *AS DETECTIVE DAVID BEE*

AND

ANTHONY KAVANAGH *AS ANTWAN*

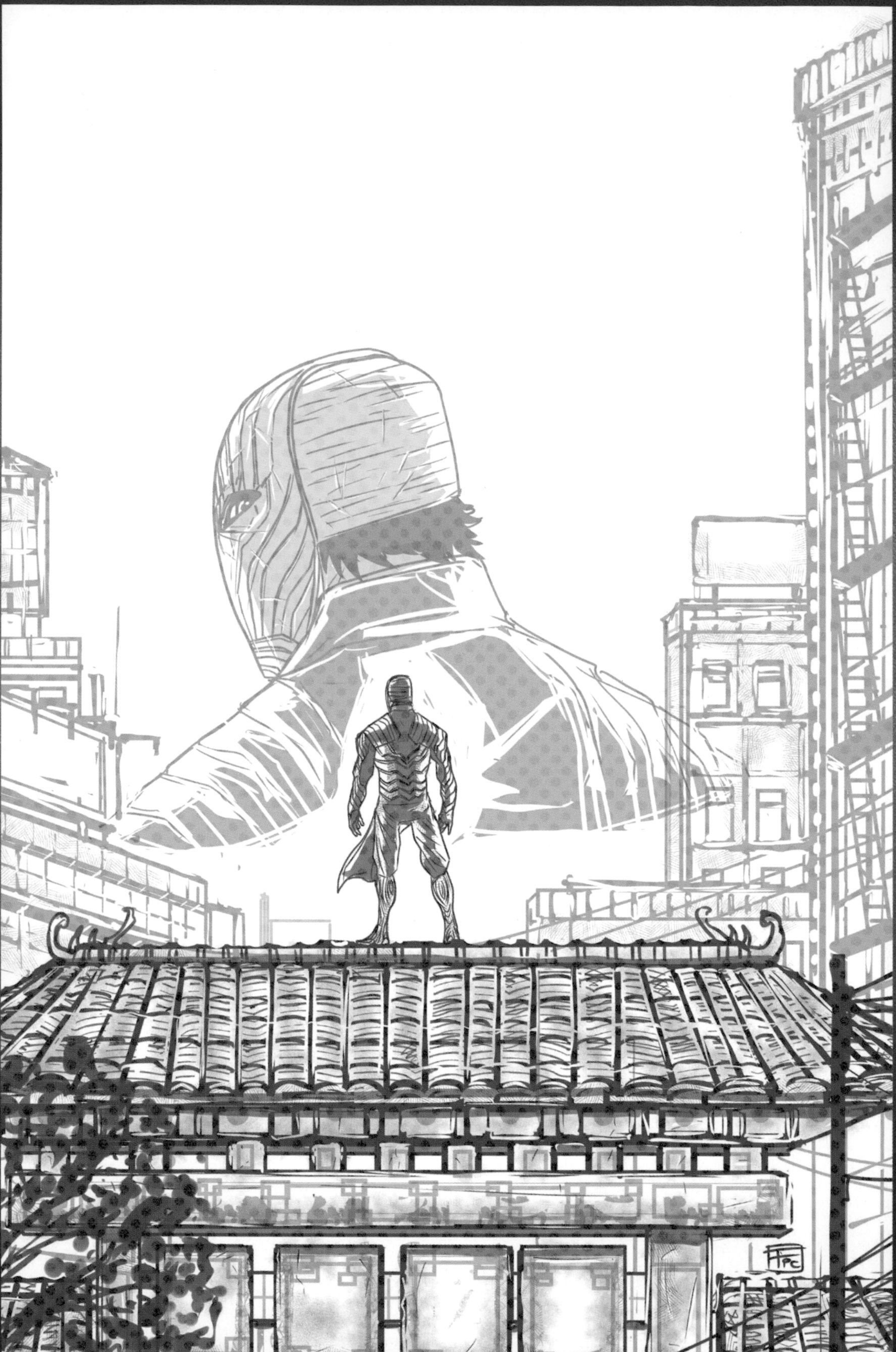

INTERTWINED #1 - KICKSTARTER EXCLUSIVE COVER - ART BY FRED PHAM CHUONG

THE WU XING

五行

The Five Elements
– or cycles – that rule
the universe according
to Chinese philosophy.

Metal. Water. Wood. Fire. Earth.

The balance between those five elements has been
preserved for millennia. But not anymore.

The fall began in New York City, where every one of
those elements and every community is no
longer just mixing with one another.

They are...INTERTWINED

FOREWORD

FABRICE
SAPOLSKY
FRED
PHAM CHUONG
KUNG FU
NOIR
COMES TO COMICS!
MARVEL

It's the story of two French guys making comics, loving Kung-Fu and determined to share their passion with the world.
It all started in February 2015 with a trip to China for an ambitious comic book project (that never happened). That trip opened my eyes. I was a few weeks from relocating from Paris to New York when I went to Beijing. And, at the time, I was collecting a lot of ideas for Spider-Man Noir, in case Dave Hine and myself woud be brought back for more issues after *Edge of Spider-Verse* (but Marvel had other plans). It struck me that had Peter Parker been an immigrant, his life would have been radically different. After a week in Beijing, I saw and heard a lot of things that impacted me greatly. On the plane back to Paris, I wrote an outline for a story called 'The Spirit of the Earth'. There was Kung-Fu and super-powers already. A philosophical and mystical Chinese background was included, but something was missing there too. And when it appeared that I wouldn't go back to writing Spider-Man Noir anytime soon, a whole bunch of my ideas morphed into the project that would be called *Intertwined.*

FABRICE SAPOLSKY'S
INTERTWINED
WHERE WOULD YOU GO TO CARRY YOUR LEGACY?
AN ONGOING COMIC BOOK SERIES
PARENTAL ADVISORY EXPLICIT COMICS

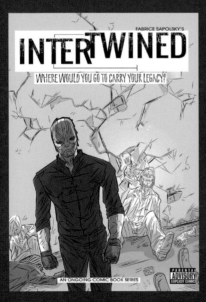

In May I started scouting for an artist to embark on that journey with me. I wanted somebody who loved and understood Kung Fu. Fred came by accident (or was it fate?). I liked one of his drawings on Facebook– I think it was a Hellboy– and he wrote me he was very happy that I did. We started chatting. We didn't know each other before. But he said : *"If you ever have a project for me, I'm in".*

Well, a few weeks later, I asked Fred to test for *Intertwined.* I gave very little information and I warned him he'd be competing with an American and a Chinese artist. He was very happy. And hungry for the project like I've never seen an artist hungry before. It took me two test pages and a couple of sketches to understand Fred was not only the right man for the job, he was born to draw *Intertwined.* And he's not just a terrific young artist. He also practices Kung-Fu. His father was even a Kung-Fu master.

The third member of our team, Veronica, came on board courtesy of my friend El Torres, spanish horror writer extraordinaire and Editor in Chief of Amigo Comics (you should all check them in your LCS). He introduced me to Veronica and she immediately loved the project. Veronica is not just a colorist. She's a color artist. She did miracles on so many pages over the course of our series.

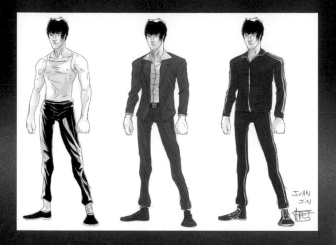

Last but not least, I hired an editor to help me with the story. This was a first for me. When we met, she said : *"what do you expect from me?"* And I replied: *"to kick my ass and help me make my comics better"*. Boy… She did exactly that! But I coudn't be happier. All of us put our little project on Kickstarter on February 2nd, 2016. And the campaign exceeded our expectations. A few days after it ended, Dynamite Comics offered us a contract. We had some kind of a gentleman's agreement. At New York Comic Con 2015, I pitched the series to a few publisher. Rich Young, at Dynamite, was clearly the most enthusiastic of them all. The Kickstarter was already on our minds. He said: *"Get yourself funded and we sign you."* We succeeded and…the rest is history.

I asked the first issue of *Intertwined* to be released on October 5th, 2016. At that point, we knew we'd go to New York Comic Con and it seemed like a good idea to have Fred and myself promote the book at the show. We sold an impressive 120 copies of issue #1 at the show! Proving that there was an apetite for the genre we call Kung Fu Noir. Unfortunately, that month, the market started to soften and the biggest publishers chose that time to issue even more books on top of their already impressive line-up. Bad news for Intertwined? Yes and No. Sure, the single issues didn't perform as well as we'd hope. But it gave us even more motivation to tour and show that Intertwined is a project like no other.

Where in comics do you see characters like ours? A bunch of immigrants, unsung heroes, saving the day. A series showcasing many minorities in a positive way while appealing to everyone. *Intertwined* is a love letter to melting pot. To that unique mix of cultures and individuals who walk, breathe and love through streets the city I chose to live in: New York.

Fred, Veronica and myself put our blood, sweat and tears into this project. As much as I loved working on *Spider-Man Noir* and *One-Hit Wonder*, *Intertwined* is special. It's my most personal story to date. We finished the series a few weeks ago and I can't wait to get back to it. Hopefully, with your help we'll be able to tell all the stories we have in store for Juan Jin, Long Huo and the Spirits of Wu Xing.

In the meantime, welcome to the Kung Fu Noir revolution.

Fabrice Sapolsky
04.15.2017

PREVIOUS PAGE: First (rejected) designs for Intertwined. Fred did that based on the pitch. The logo was also weaker.

ABOVE: Final designs for Juan Jin and the Spirit of the Earth. From the first pitch, Fabrice knew the costume wasn't made of leather or wood. Most of it is made from Lyocell (a fiber made from wood pulp), Coir (a coarse made from coconut shells) and Flax (fibers extracted from the stems of the plant Linum usitatissimum).

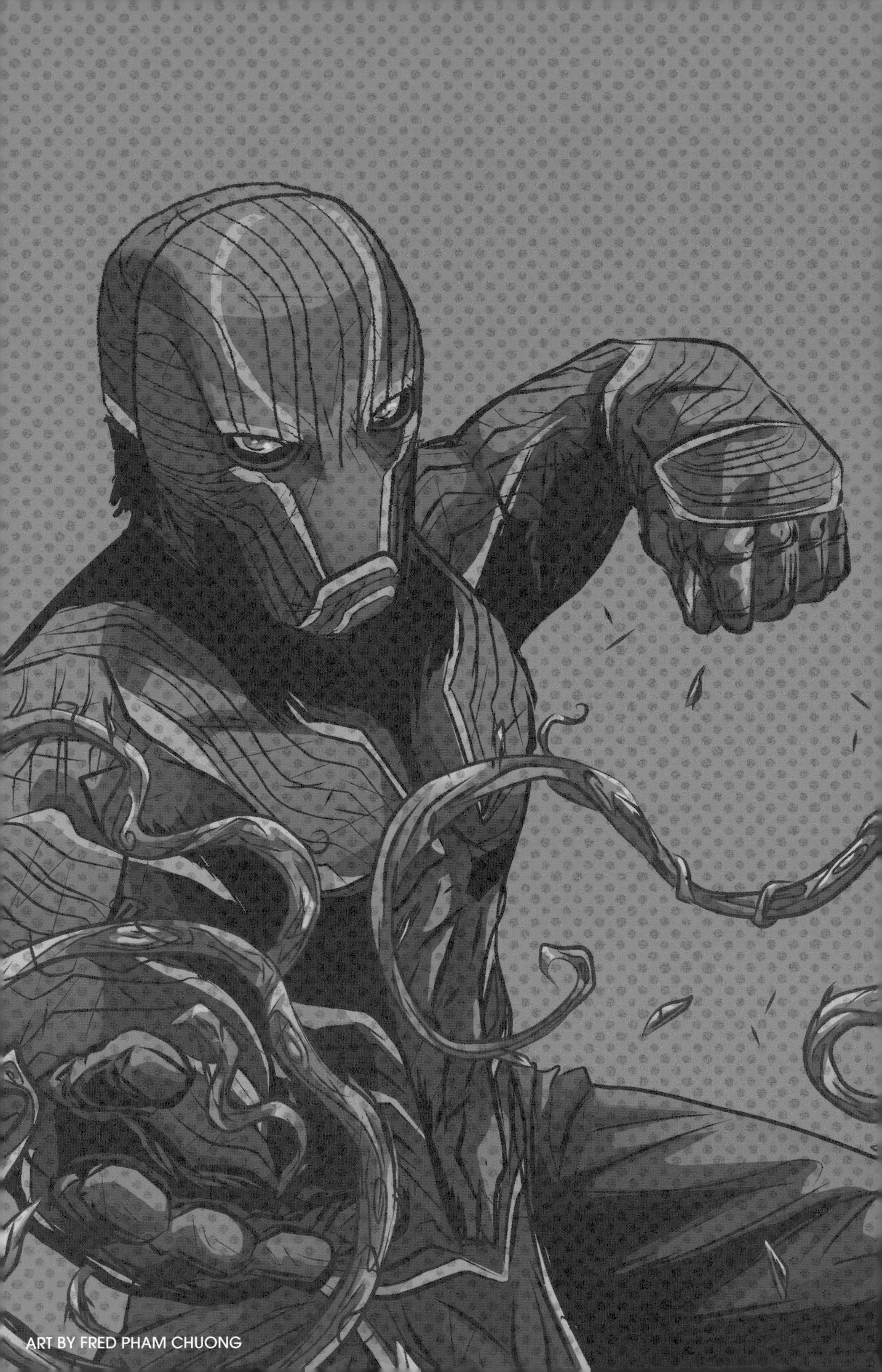
ART BY FRED PHAM CHUONG

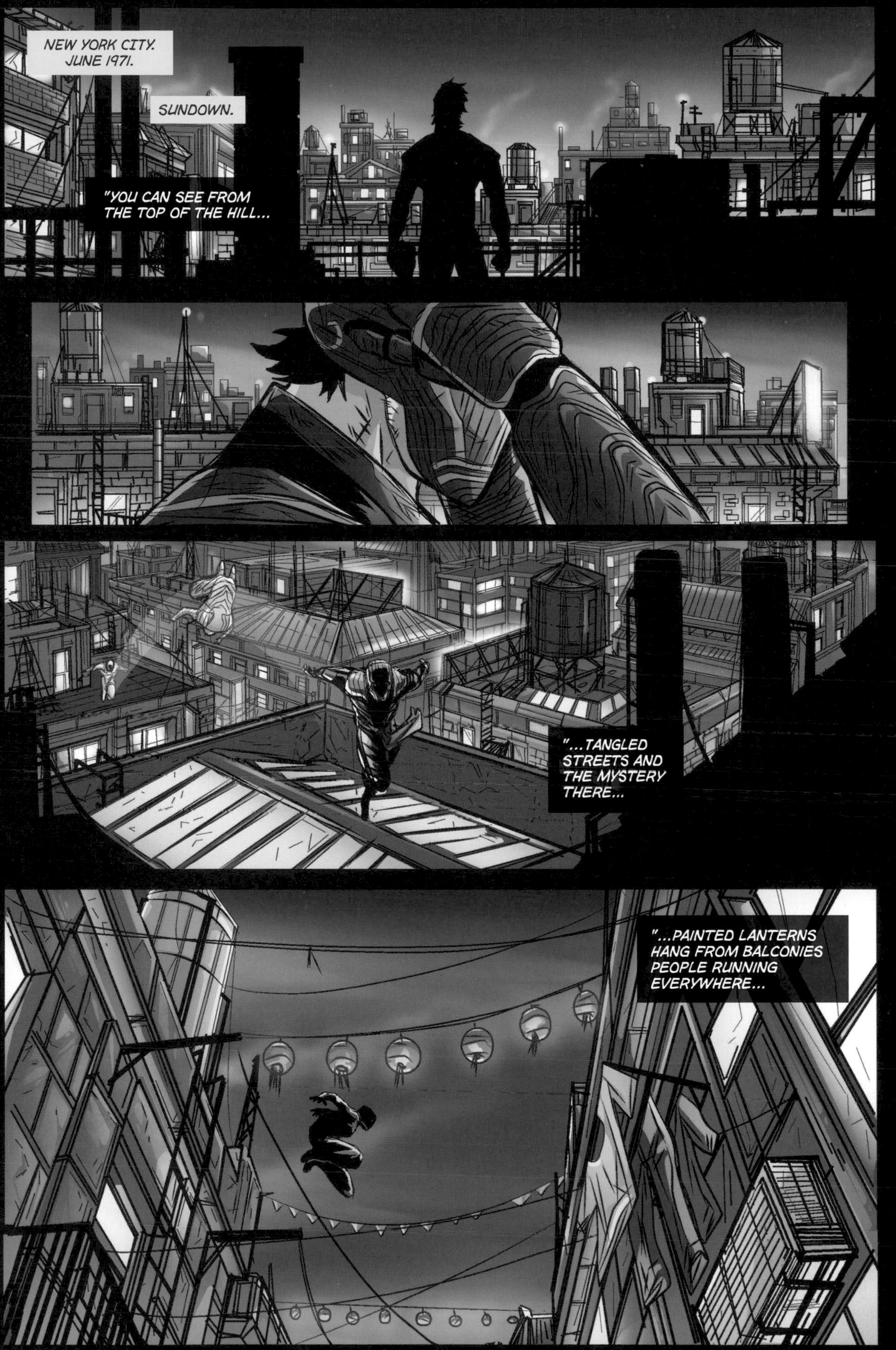
NEW YORK CITY. JUNE 1971.
SUNDOWN.
"YOU CAN SEE FROM THE TOP OF THE HILL...
"...TANGLED STREETS AND THE MYSTERY THERE...
"...PAINTED LANTERNS HANG FROM BALCONIES PEOPLE RUNNING EVERYWHERE...

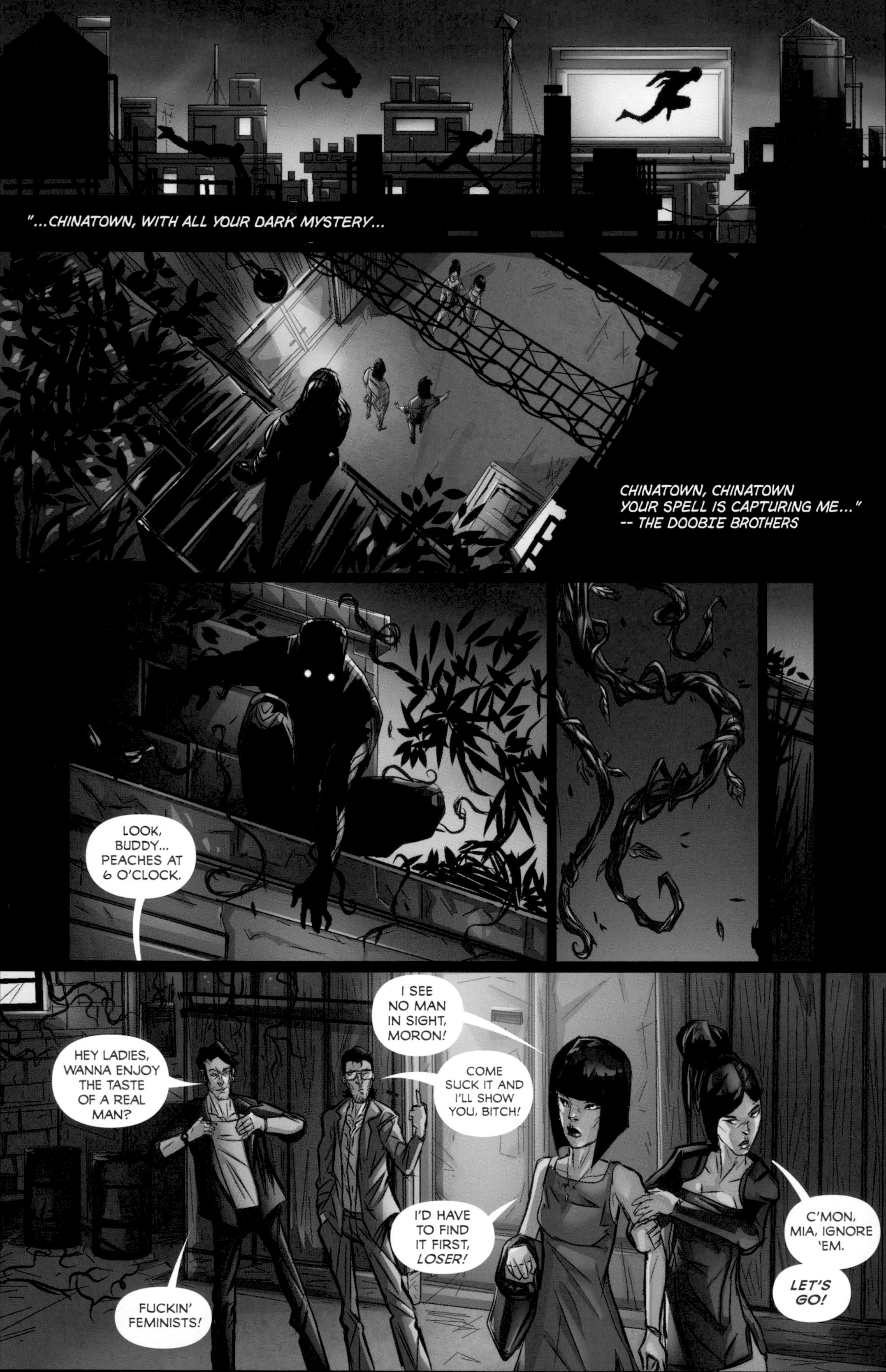
"...CHINATOWN, WITH ALL YOUR DARK MYSTERY...
CHINATOWN, CHINATOWN
YOUR SPELL IS CAPTURING ME..."
-- THE DOOBIE BROTHERS
LOOK, BUDDY... PEACHES AT 6 O'CLOCK.
HEY LADIES, WANNA ENJOY THE TASTE OF A REAL MAN?
I SEE NO MAN IN SIGHT, MORON!
COME SUCK IT AND I'LL SHOW YOU, BITCH!
I'D HAVE TO FIND IT FIRST, *LOSER!*
C'MON, MIA, IGNORE 'EM.
LET'S GO!
FUCKIN' FEMINISTS!

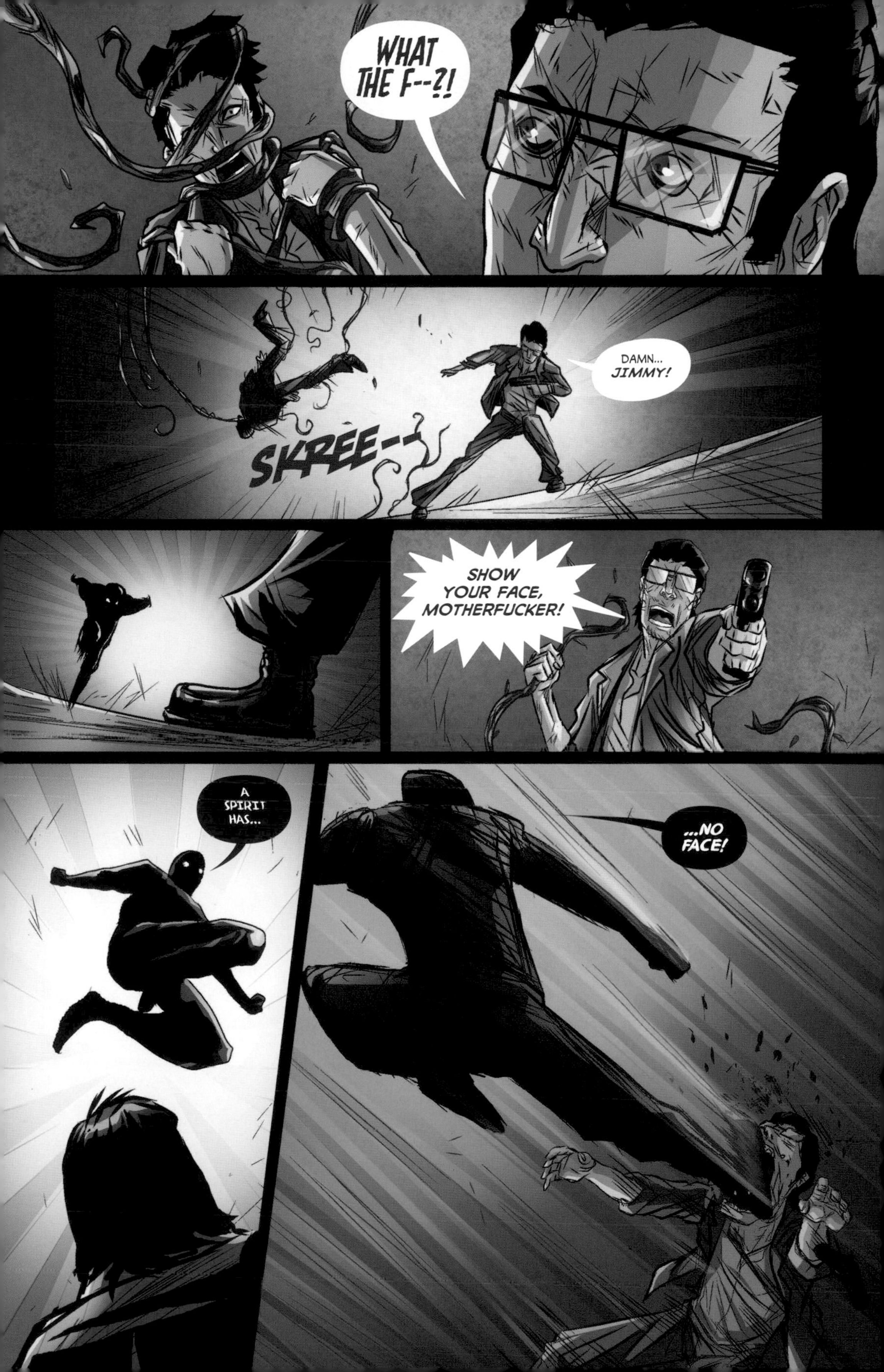
WHAT THE F--?!
DAMN... JIMMY!
SKREE--
SHOW YOUR FACE, MOTHERFUCKER!
A SPIRIT HAS...
...NO FACE!

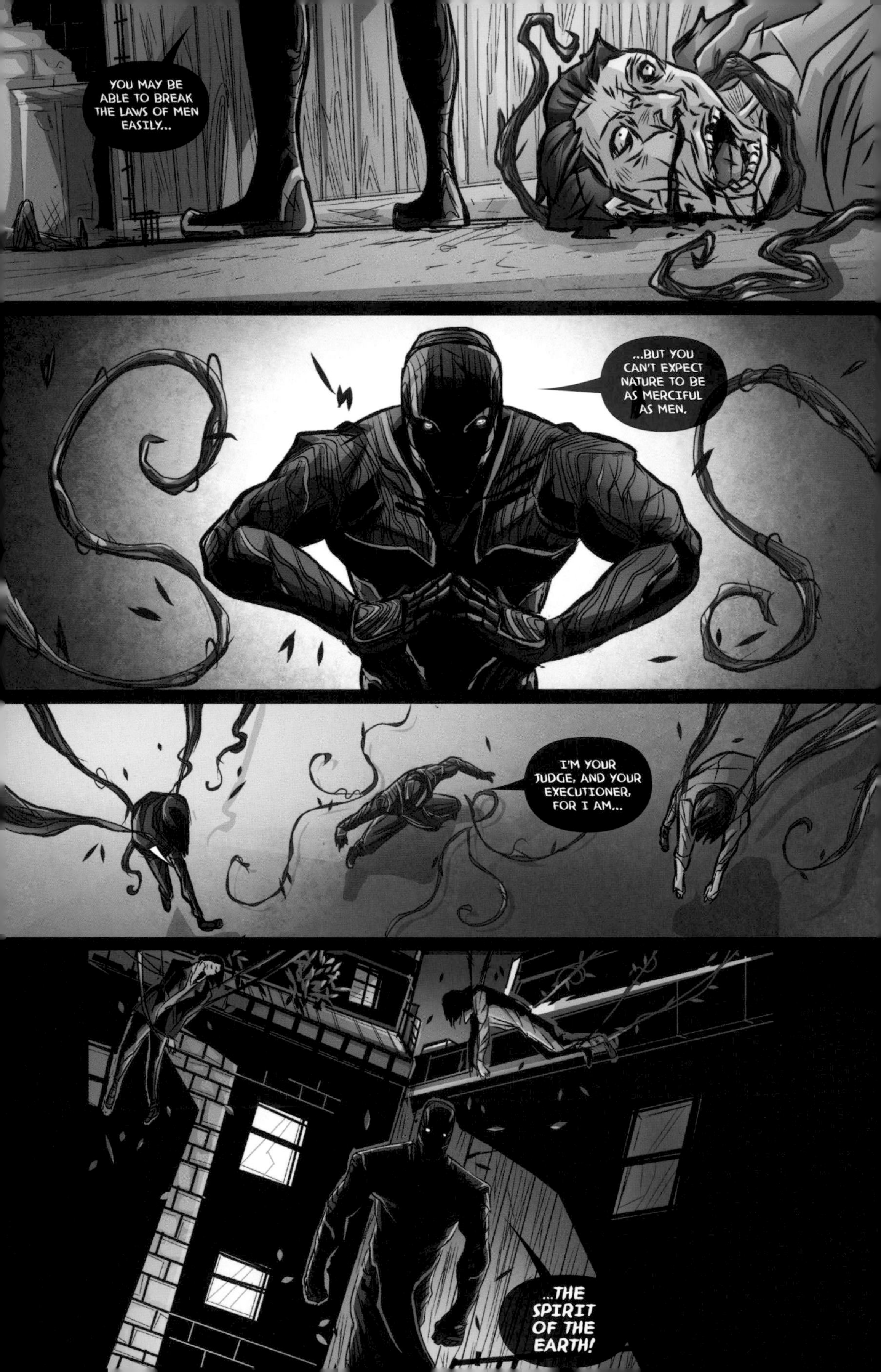
YOU MAY BE ABLE TO BREAK THE LAWS OF MEN EASILY...
...BUT YOU CAN'T EXPECT NATURE TO BE AS MERCIFUL AS MEN.
I'M YOUR JUDGE, AND YOUR EXECUTIONER, FOR I AM...
...THE SPIRIT OF THE EARTH!

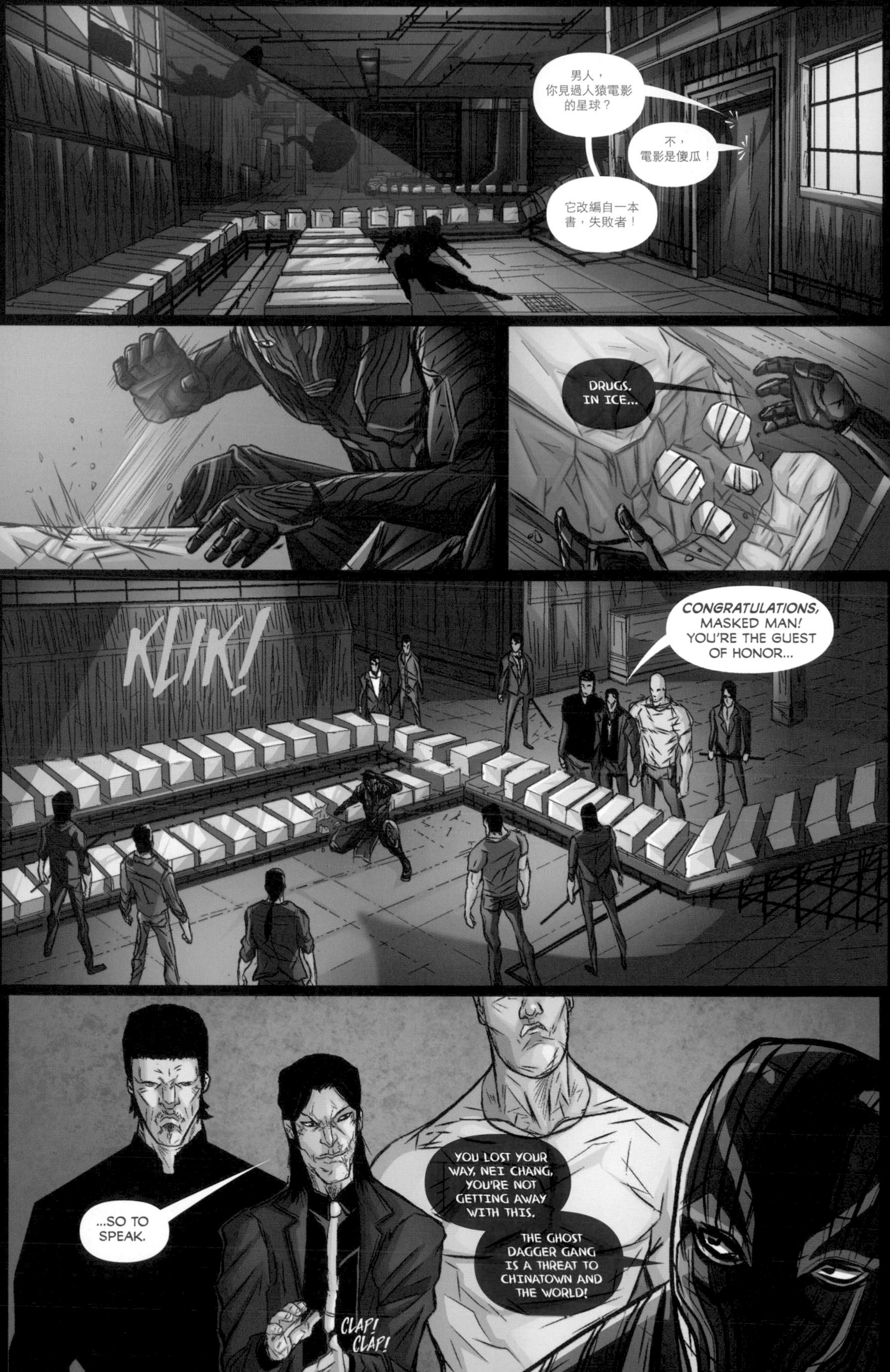
男人，
你見過人猿電影
的星球？
不，
電影是傻瓜！
它改編自一本
書，失敗者！
DRUGS.
IN ICE...
KLIK!
CONGRATULATIONS, MASKED MAN! YOU'RE THE GUEST OF HONOR...
...SO TO SPEAK.
YOU LOST YOUR WAY, NEI CHANG. YOU'RE NOT GETTING AWAY WITH THIS.
THE GHOST DAGGER GANG IS A THREAT TO CHINATOWN AND THE WORLD!
CLAP! CLAP!

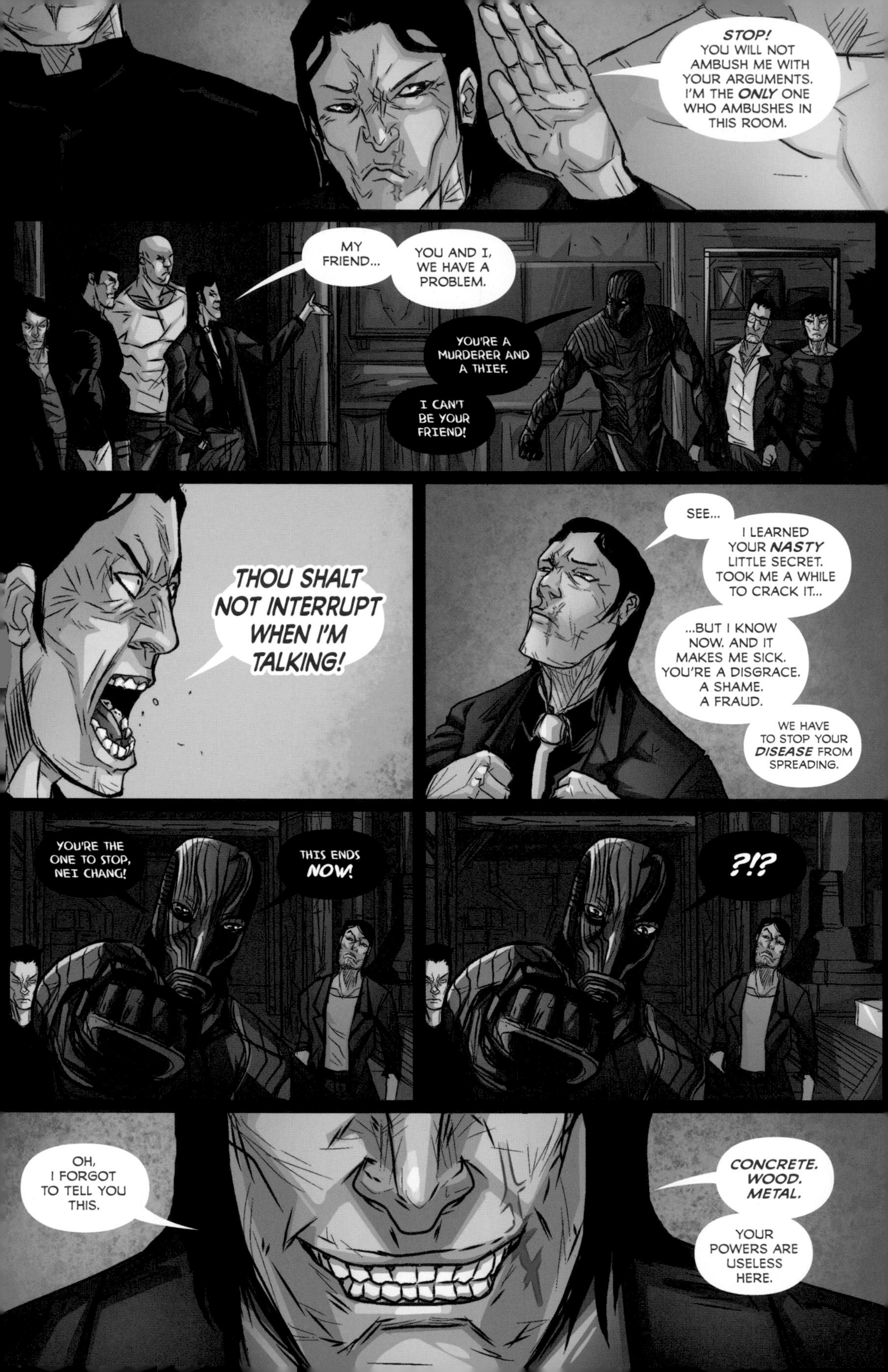
STOP! YOU WILL NOT AMBUSH ME WITH YOUR ARGUMENTS. I'M THE ONLY ONE WHO AMBUSHES IN THIS ROOM.
MY FRIEND...
YOU AND I, WE HAVE A PROBLEM.
YOU'RE A MURDERER AND A THIEF.
I CAN'T BE YOUR FRIEND!
THOU SHALT NOT INTERRUPT WHEN I'M TALKING!
SEE...
I LEARNED YOUR NASTY LITTLE SECRET. TOOK ME A WHILE TO CRACK IT...
...BUT I KNOW NOW. AND IT MAKES ME SICK. YOU'RE A DISGRACE. A SHAME. A FRAUD.
WE HAVE TO STOP YOUR DISEASE FROM SPREADING.
YOU'RE THE ONE TO STOP, NEI CHANG!
THIS ENDS NOW!
?!?
OH, I FORGOT TO TELL YOU THIS.
CONCRETE. WOOD. METAL.
YOUR POWERS ARE USELESS HERE.

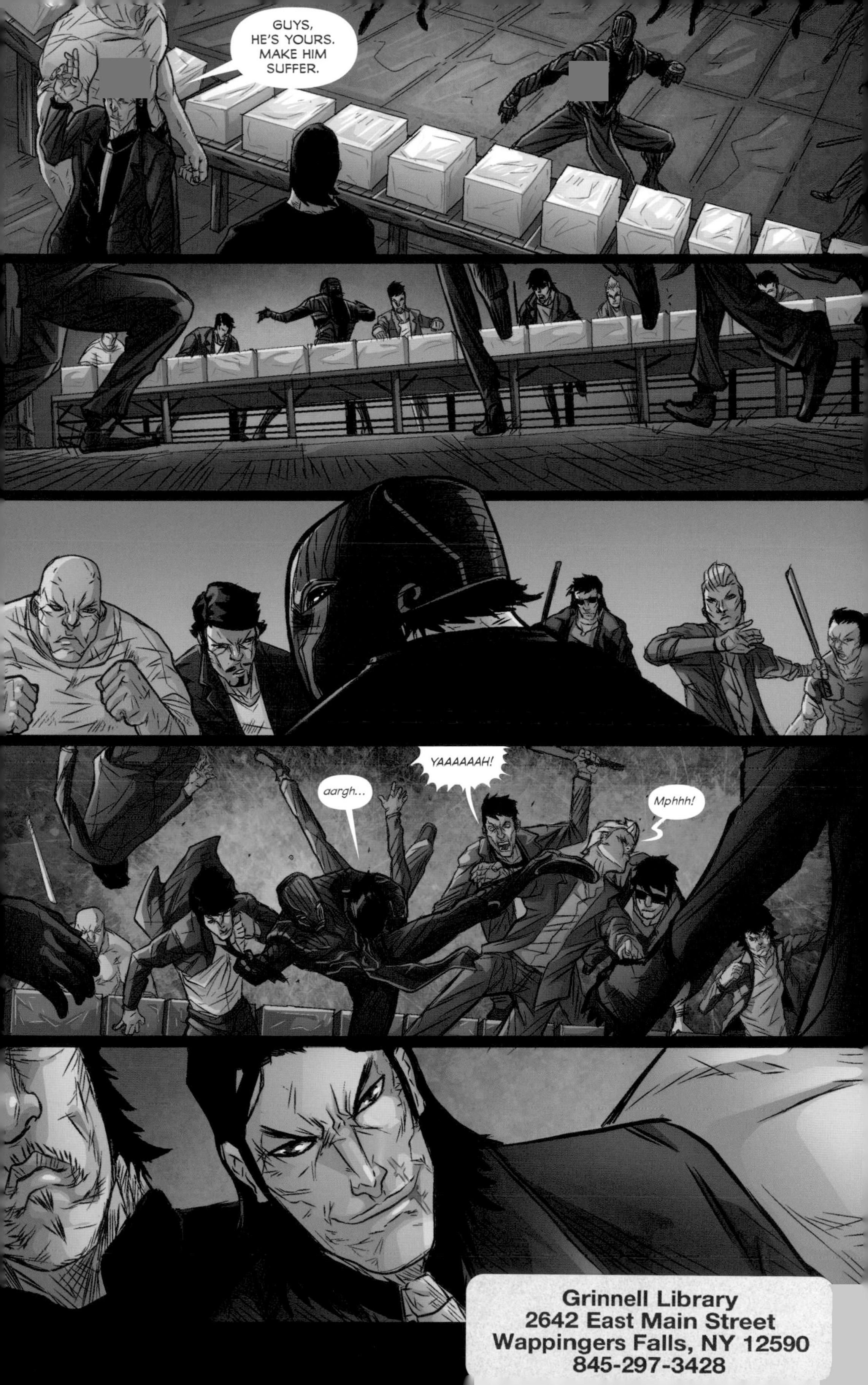
GUYS, HE'S YOURS. MAKE HIM SUFFER.
aargh...
YAAAAAAH!
Mphhh!

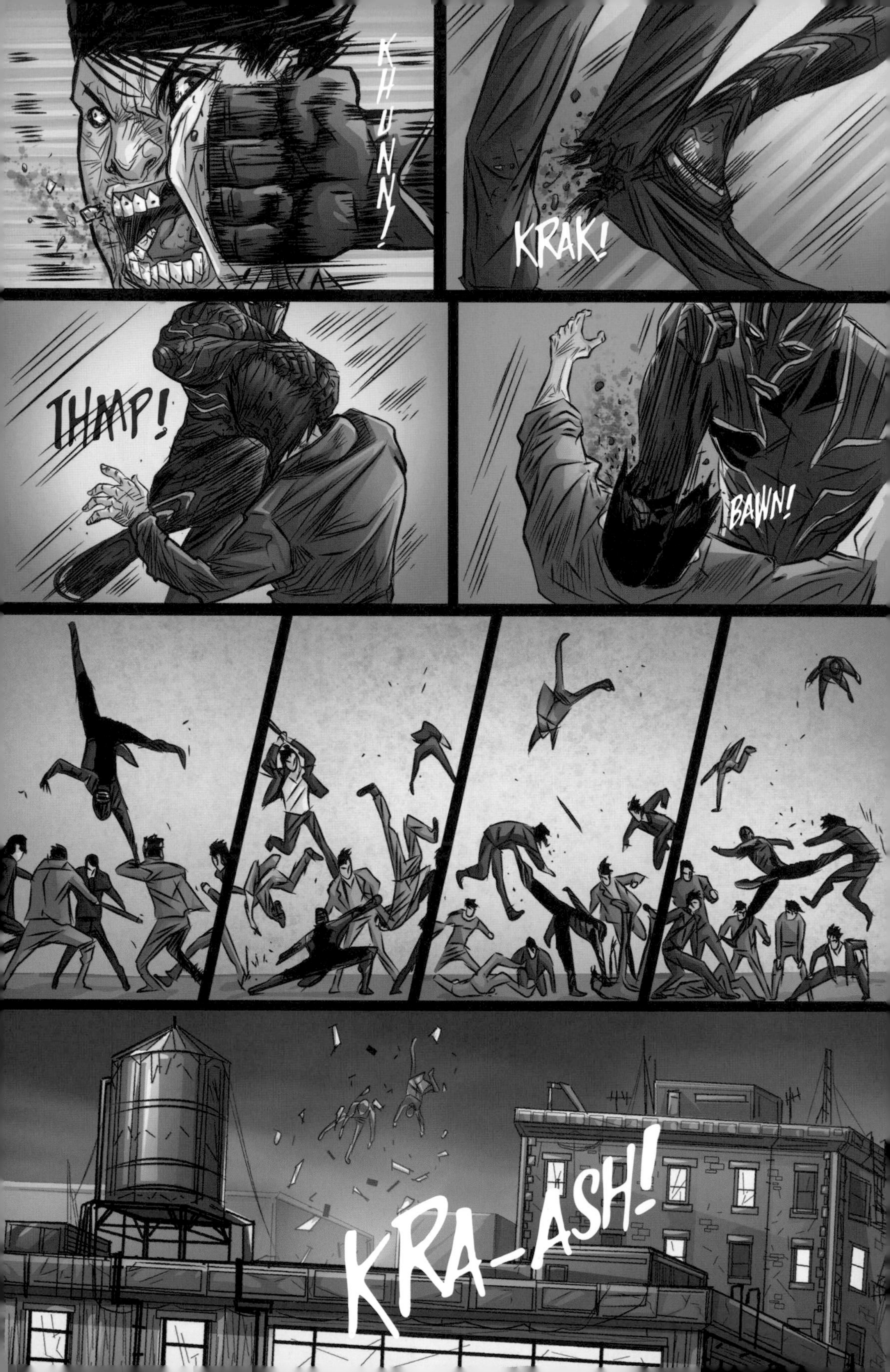
KHUNNN!
KRAK!
THMP!
BAWN!
KRA-ASH!

UHHHH... UHHHH... UHHHHHH...
YOU DID IT! *ALMOST* AGAINST ALL ODDS. YOU'RE SUCH AN ENTERTAINER!
SIGH... I- I KILLED ALL YOUR MEN... I DON'T UNDERSTAND.
NNNG...
FIRST, YOU JUST MADE ME RICHER!
ALL THIS WAS PLANNED... ***STAGED***. I GOT ALL THE BOOKMAKERS BET AGAINST YOU WHILE I BET THE OTHER WAY.
AND SECOND... YOU LOOK TIRED. YOUR HEART'S FAILING YOU. YOU'VE BEEN WEARING THAT MASK FOR WHAT...
...25... 30 YEARS NOW? YOU'VE BEEN AROUND FOR A LONG TIME.
BUT I HAVE GOOD NEWS FOR YOU...

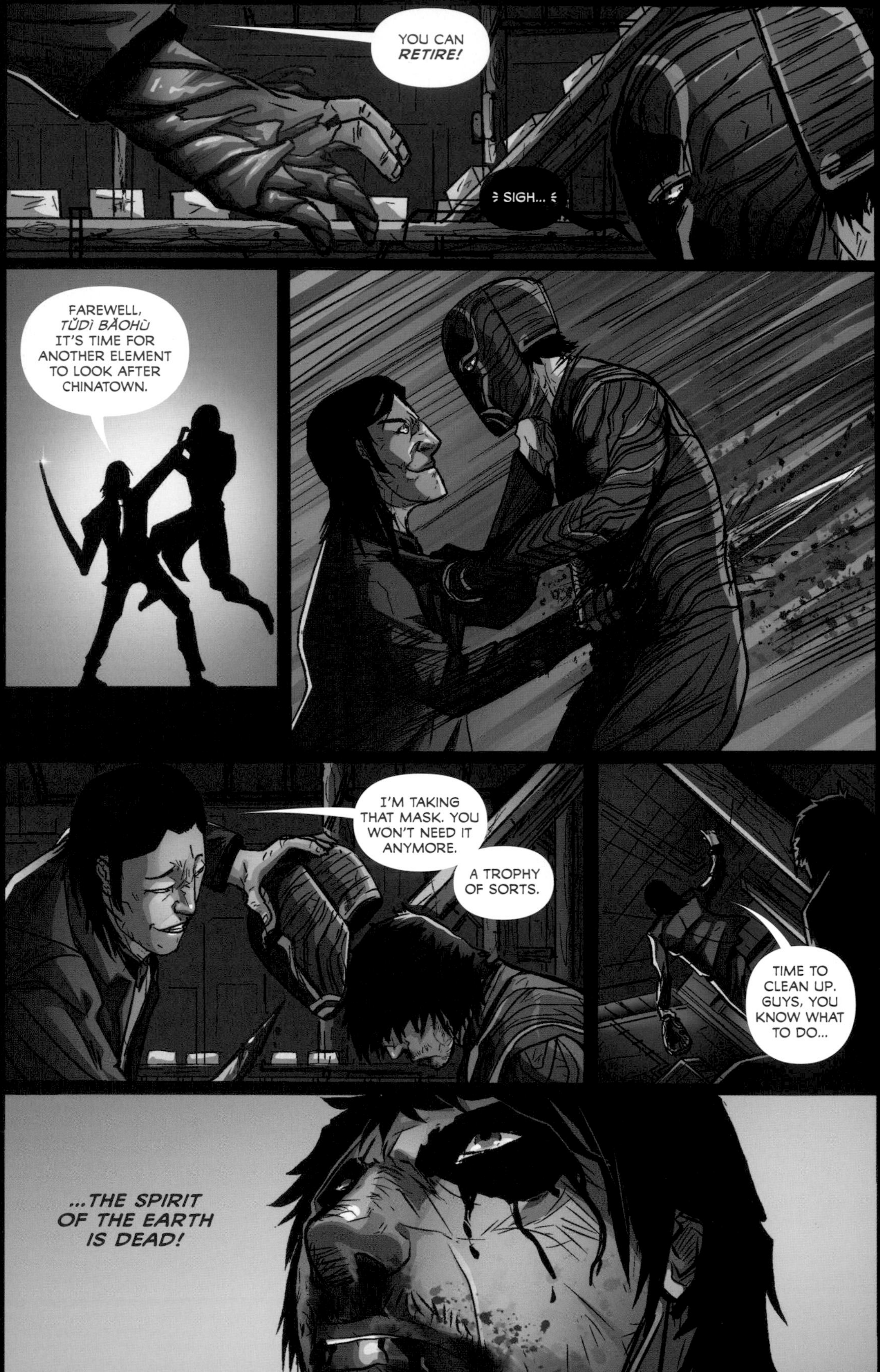
YOU CAN *RETIRE!*
SIGH...
FAREWELL, *TŬDÌ BǍOHÙ* IT'S TIME FOR ANOTHER ELEMENT TO LOOK AFTER CHINATOWN.
I'M TAKING THAT MASK. YOU WON'T NEED IT ANYMORE.
A TROPHY OF SORTS.
TIME TO CLEAN UP. GUYS, YOU KNOW WHAT TO DO...
...THE SPIRIT OF THE EARTH IS DEAD!

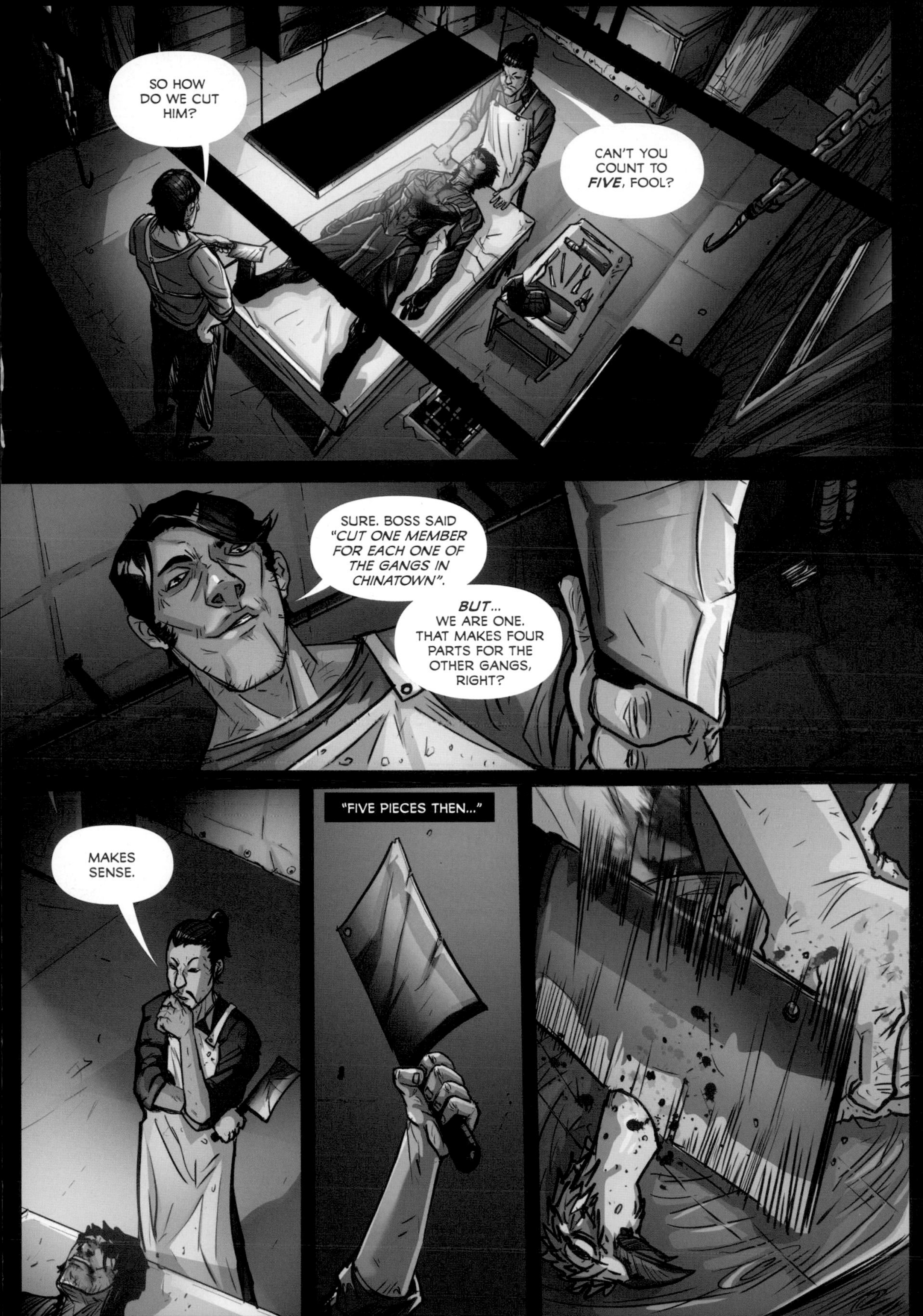
SO HOW DO WE CUT HIM?
CAN'T YOU COUNT TO *FIVE*, FOOL?
SURE. BOSS SAID *"CUT ONE MEMBER FOR EACH ONE OF THE GANGS IN CHINATOWN".*
BUT... WE ARE ONE. THAT MAKES FOUR PARTS FOR THE OTHER GANGS, RIGHT?
MAKES SENSE.
"FIVE PIECES THEN..."

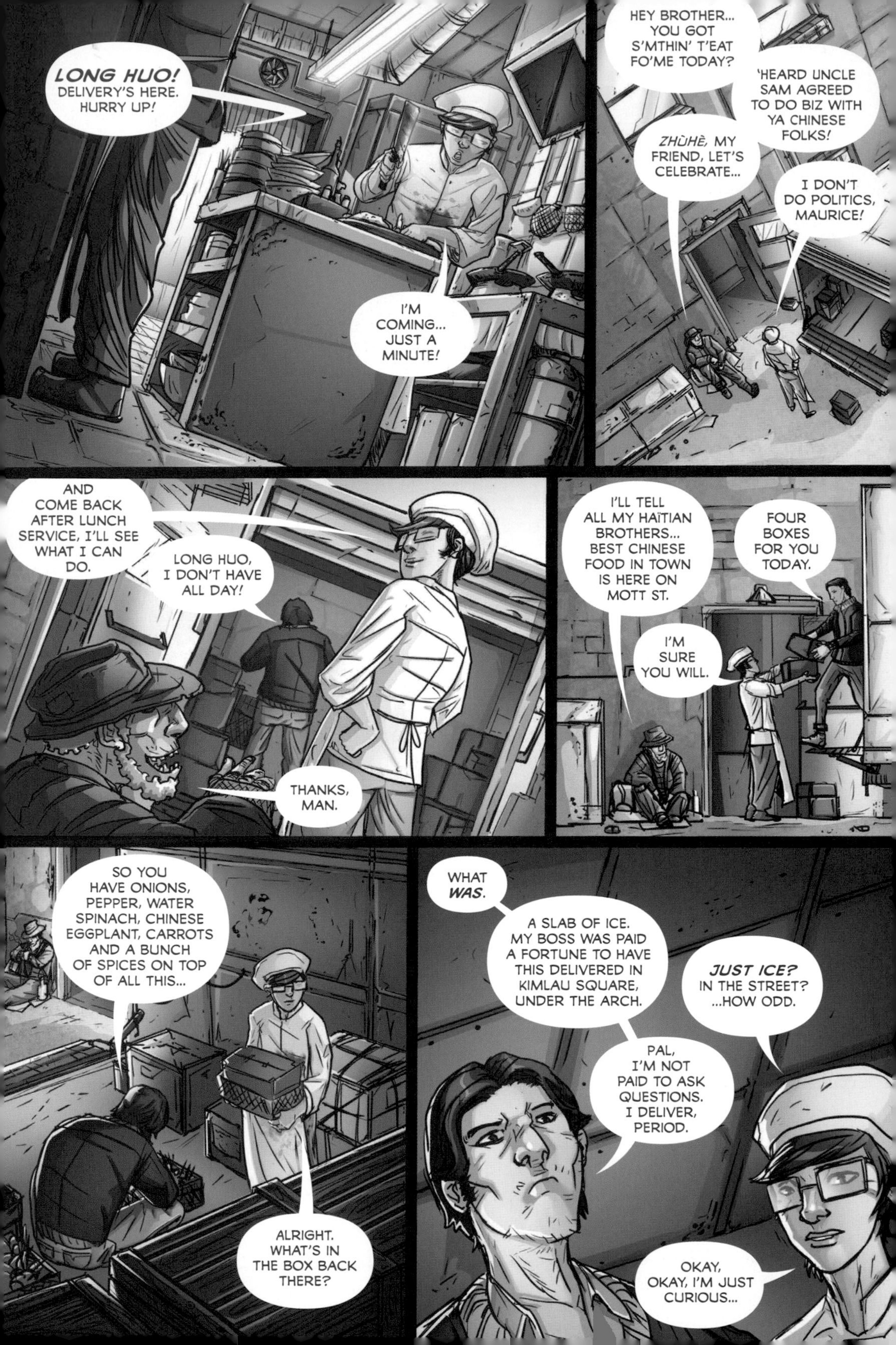
LONG HUO! DELIVERY'S HERE. HURRY UP!
I'M COMING... JUST A MINUTE!
HEY BROTHER... YOU GOT S'MTHIN' T'EAT FO'ME TODAY?
'HEARD UNCLE SAM AGREED TO DO BIZ WITH YA CHINESE FOLKS!
ZHÙHÈ, MY FRIEND, LET'S CELEBRATE...
I DON'T DO POLITICS, MAURICE!
AND COME BACK AFTER LUNCH SERVICE, I'LL SEE WHAT I CAN DO.
LONG HUO, I DON'T HAVE ALL DAY!
THANKS, MAN.
I'LL TELL ALL MY HAÏTIAN BROTHERS... BEST CHINESE FOOD IN TOWN IS HERE ON MOTT ST.
FOUR BOXES FOR YOU TODAY.
I'M SURE YOU WILL.
SO YOU HAVE ONIONS, PEPPER, WATER SPINACH, CHINESE EGGPLANT, CARROTS AND A BUNCH OF SPICES ON TOP OF ALL THIS...
ALRIGHT. WHAT'S IN THE BOX BACK THERE?
WHAT WAS.
A SLAB OF ICE. MY BOSS WAS PAID A FORTUNE TO HAVE THIS DELIVERED IN KIMLAU SQUARE, UNDER THE ARCH.
JUST ICE? IN THE STREET? ...HOW ODD.
PAL, I'M NOT PAID TO ASK QUESTIONS. I DELIVER, PERIOD.
OKAY, OKAY, I'M JUST CURIOUS...

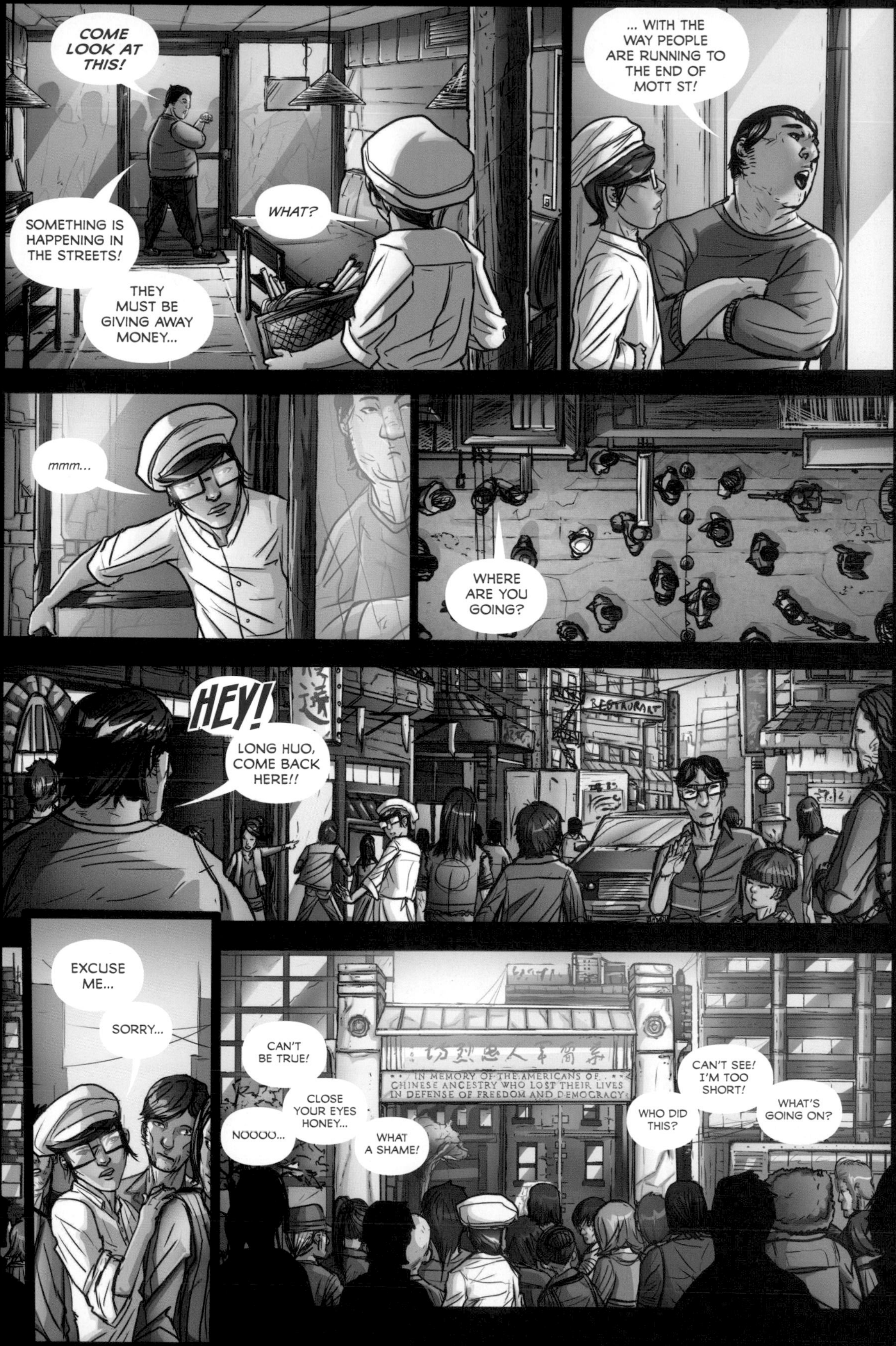
COME LOOK AT THIS!
SOMETHING IS HAPPENING IN THE STREETS!
THEY MUST BE GIVING AWAY MONEY...
WHAT?
... WITH THE WAY PEOPLE ARE RUNNING TO THE END OF MOTT ST!
mmm...
WHERE ARE YOU GOING?
HEY!
LONG HUO, COME BACK HERE!!
RESTAURANT
EXCUSE ME...
SORRY...
IN MEMORY OF THE AMERICANS OF CHINESE ANCESTRY WHO LOST THEIR LIVES IN DEFENSE OF FREEDOM AND DEMOCRACY
CAN'T BE TRUE!
CLOSE YOUR EYES HONEY...
NOOOO...
WHAT A SHAME!
CAN'T SEE! I'M TOO SHORT!
WHO DID THIS?
WHAT'S GOING ON?

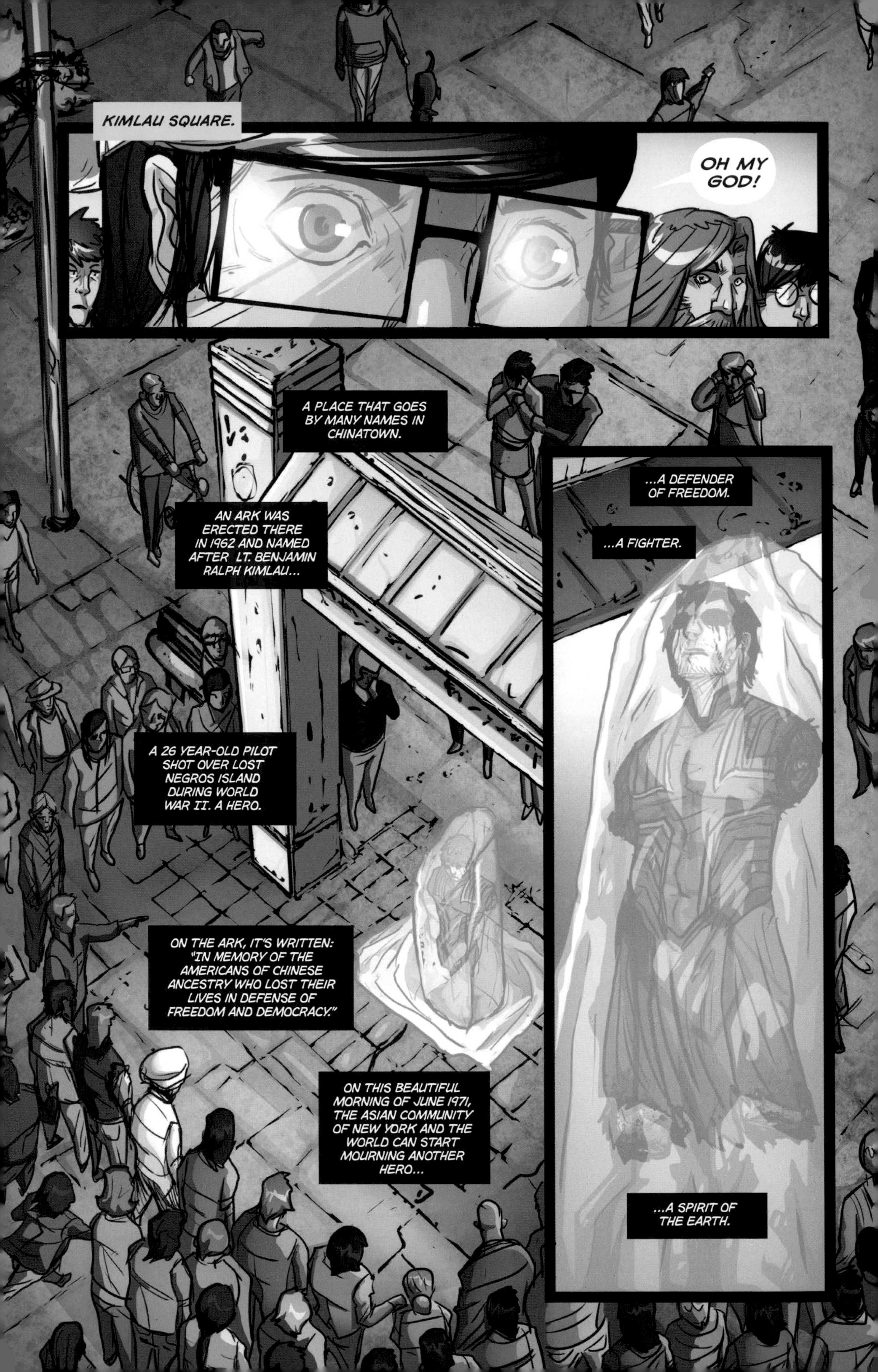
KIMLAU SQUARE.
OH MY GOD!
A PLACE THAT GOES BY MANY NAMES IN CHINATOWN.
AN ARK WAS ERECTED THERE IN 1962 AND NAMED AFTER LT. BENJAMIN RALPH KIMLAU...
A 26 YEAR-OLD PILOT SHOT OVER LOST NEGROS ISLAND DURING WORLD WAR II. A HERO.
ON THE ARK, IT'S WRITTEN: "IN MEMORY OF THE AMERICANS OF CHINESE ANCESTRY WHO LOST THEIR LIVES IN DEFENSE OF FREEDOM AND DEMOCRACY."
ON THIS BEAUTIFUL MORNING OF JUNE 1971, THE ASIAN COMMUNITY OF NEW YORK AND THE WORLD CAN START MOURNING ANOTHER HERO...
...A DEFENDER OF FREEDOM.
...A FIGHTER.
...A SPIRIT OF THE EARTH.

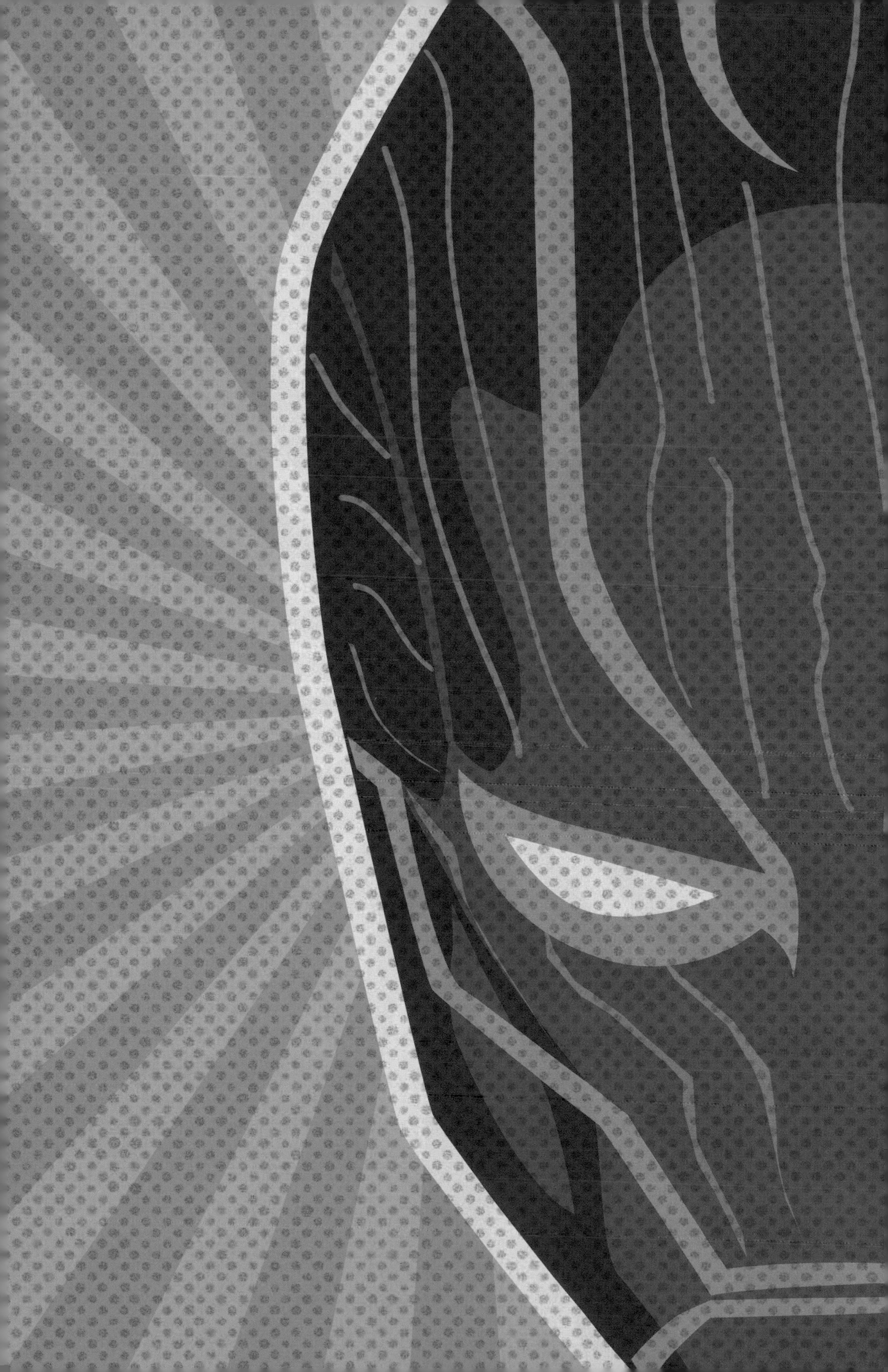

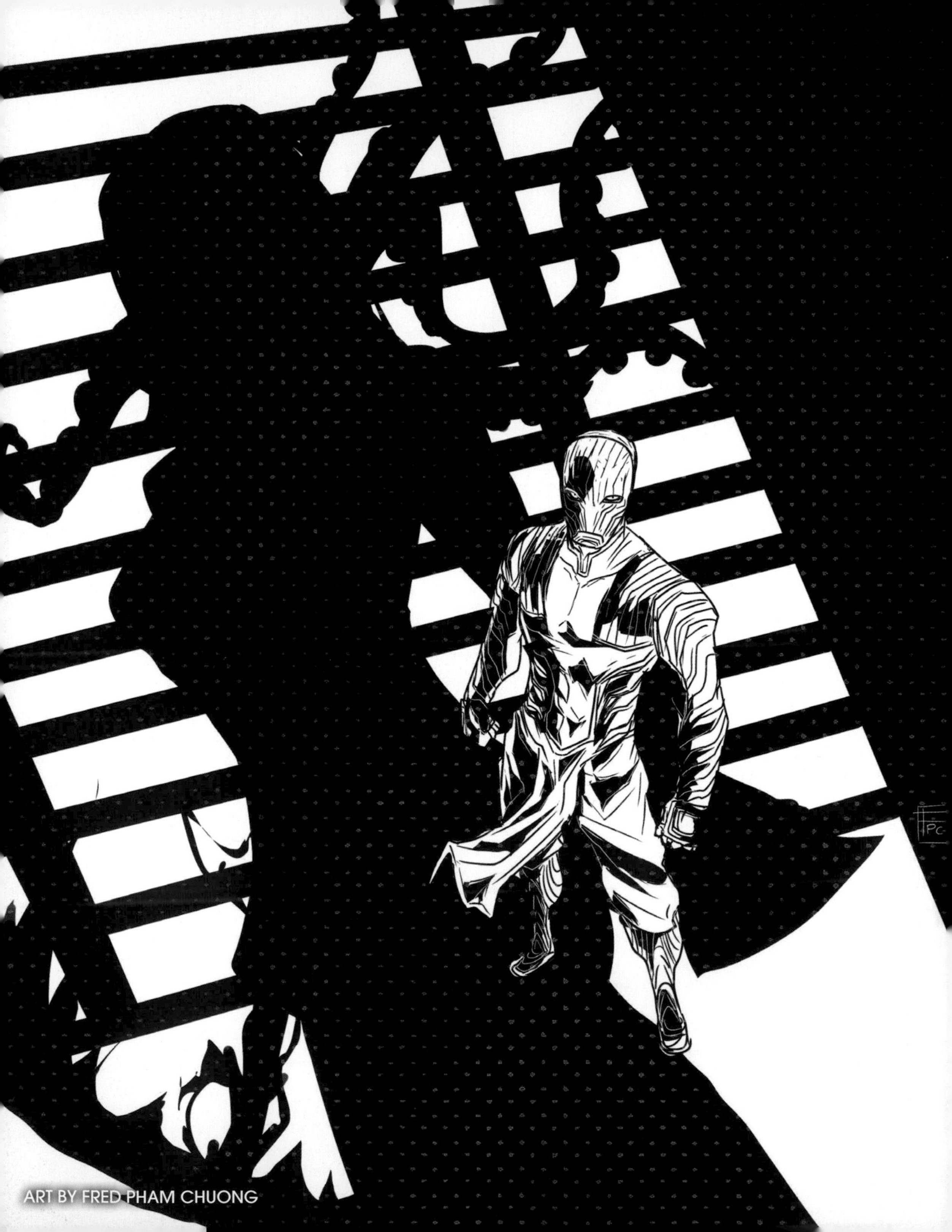

ART BY FRED PHAM CHUONG

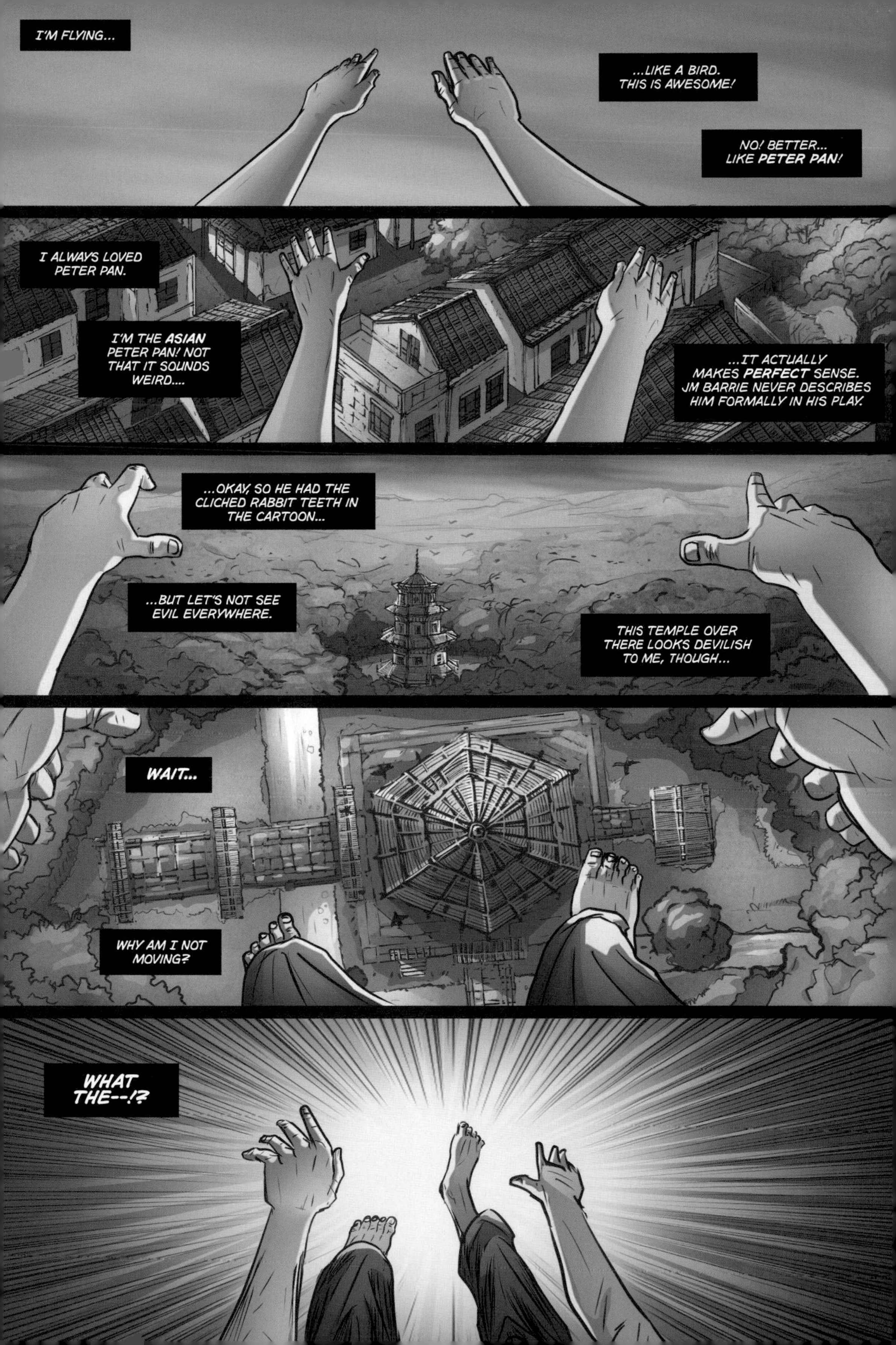
I'M FLYING...
...LIKE A BIRD. THIS IS AWESOME!
NO! BETTER... LIKE PETER PAN!
I ALWAYS LOVED PETER PAN.
I'M THE ASIAN PETER PAN! NOT THAT IT SOUNDS WEIRD....
...IT ACTUALLY MAKES PERFECT SENSE. JM BARRIE NEVER DESCRIBES HIM FORMALLY IN HIS PLAY.
...OKAY, SO HE HAD THE CLICHED RABBIT TEETH IN THE CARTOON...
...BUT LET'S NOT SEE EVIL EVERYWHERE.
THIS TEMPLE OVER THERE LOOKS DEVILISH TO ME, THOUGH...
WAIT...
WHY AM I NOT MOVING?
WHAT THE--!?

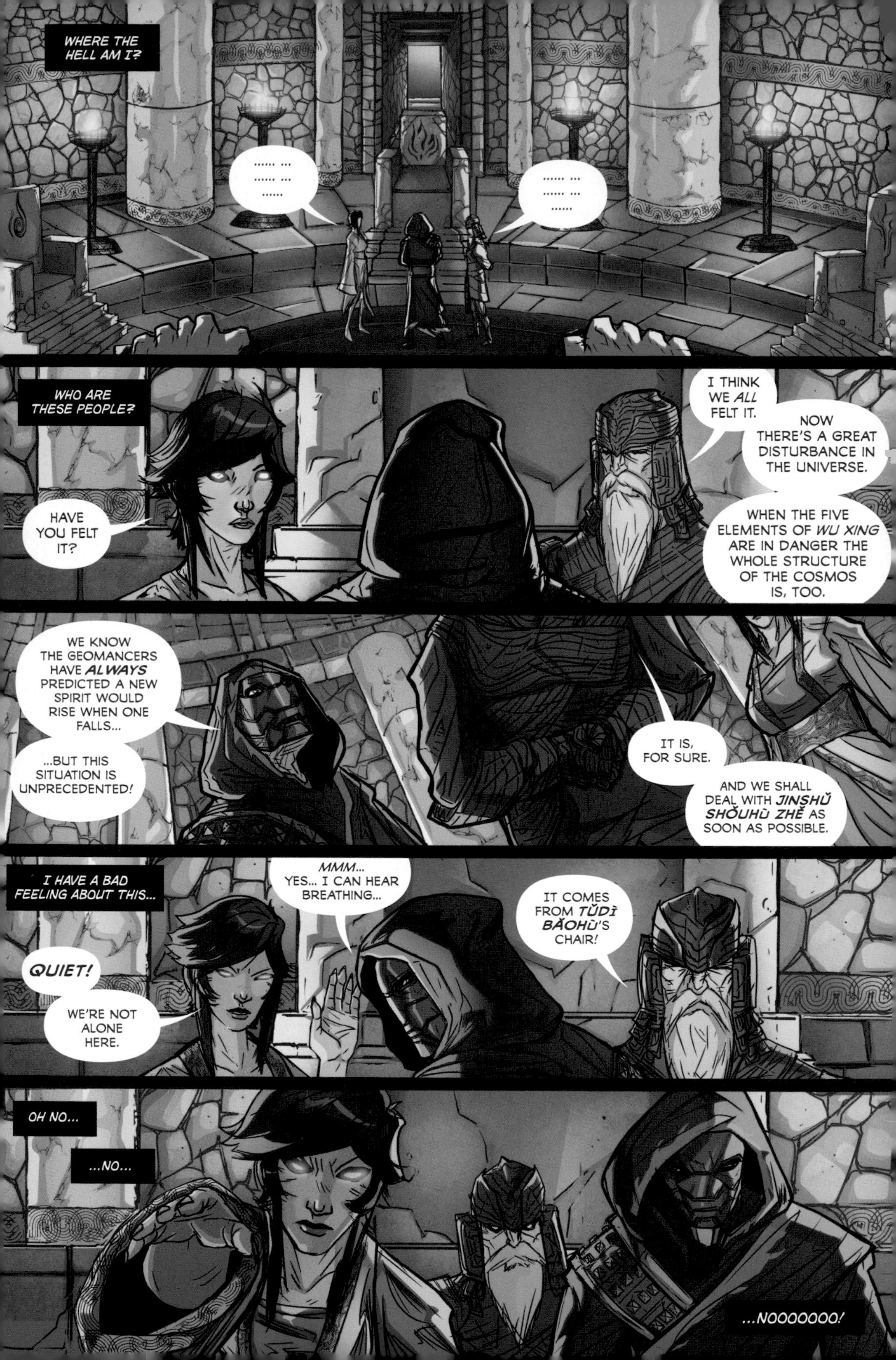
WHERE THE HELL AM I?
....
....
WHO ARE THESE PEOPLE?
HAVE YOU FELT IT?
I THINK WE *ALL* FELT IT.
NOW THERE'S A GREAT DISTURBANCE IN THE UNIVERSE.
WHEN THE FIVE ELEMENTS OF *WU XING* ARE IN DANGER THE WHOLE STRUCTURE OF THE COSMOS IS, TOO.
WE KNOW THE GEOMANCERS HAVE ***ALWAYS*** PREDICTED A NEW SPIRIT WOULD RISE WHEN ONE FALLS...
...BUT THIS SITUATION IS UNPRECEDENTED!
IT IS, FOR SURE.
AND WE SHALL DEAL WITH ***JINSHǓ SHǑUHÙ ZHĚ*** AS SOON AS POSSIBLE.
I HAVE A BAD FEELING ABOUT THIS...
MMM... YES... I CAN HEAR BREATHING...
IT COMES FROM ***TǓDÌ BǍOHÙ***'S CHAIR!
QUIET!
WE'RE NOT ALONE HERE.
OH NO...
...NO...
...NOOOOOOO!

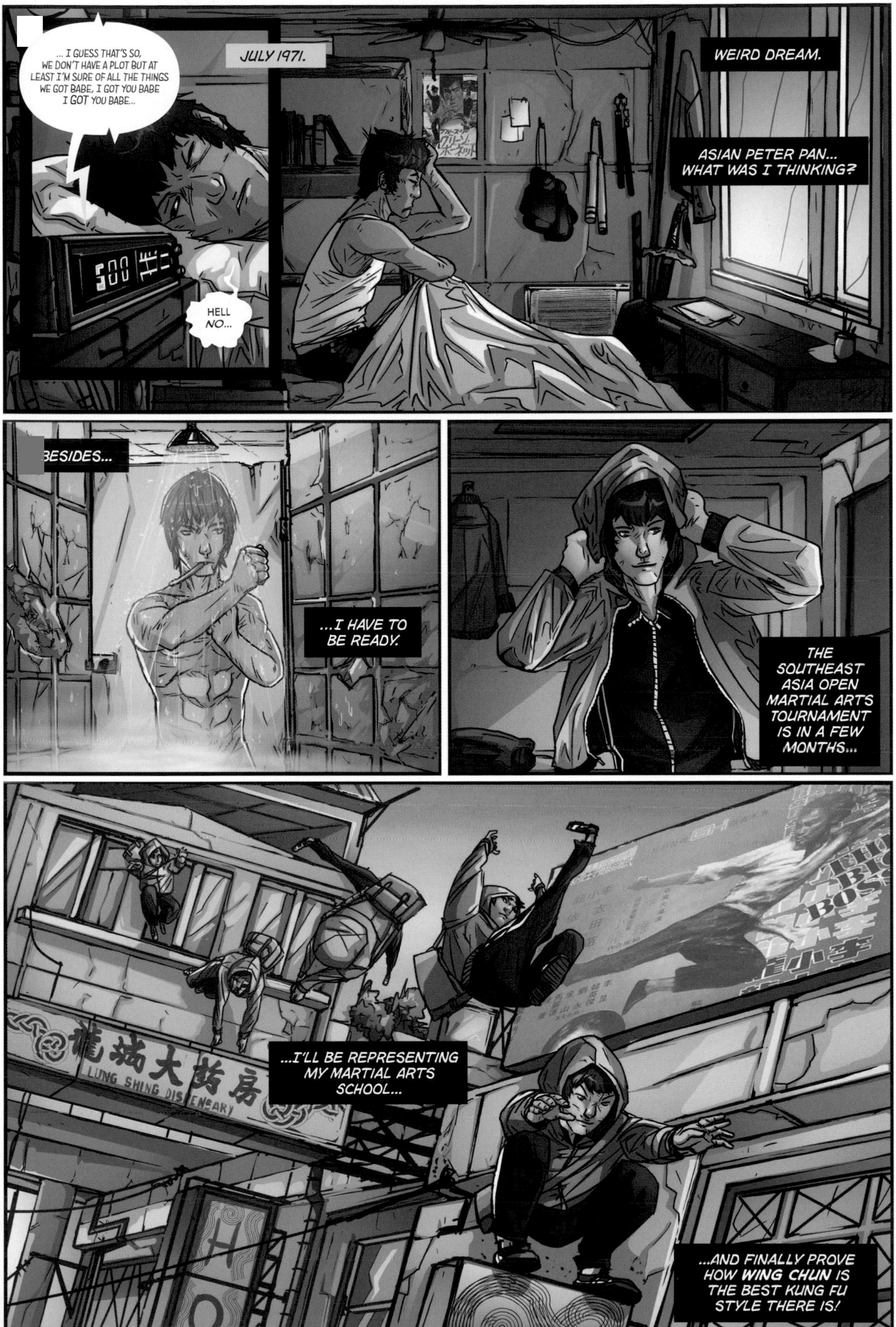

... I GUESS THAT'S SO, WE DON'T HAVE A PLOT BUT AT LEAST I'M SURE OF ALL THE THINGS WE GOT BABE, I GOT YOU BABE I GOT YOU BABE...
HELL NO...
JULY 1971.
WEIRD DREAM.
ASIAN PETER PAN... WHAT WAS I THINKING?
BESIDES...
...I HAVE TO BE READY.
THE SOUTHEAST ASIA OPEN MARTIAL ARTS TOURNAMENT IS IN A FEW MONTHS...
...I'LL BE REPRESENTING MY MARTIAL ARTS SCHOOL...
...AND FINALLY PROVE HOW WING CHUN IS THE BEST KUNG FU STYLE THERE IS!

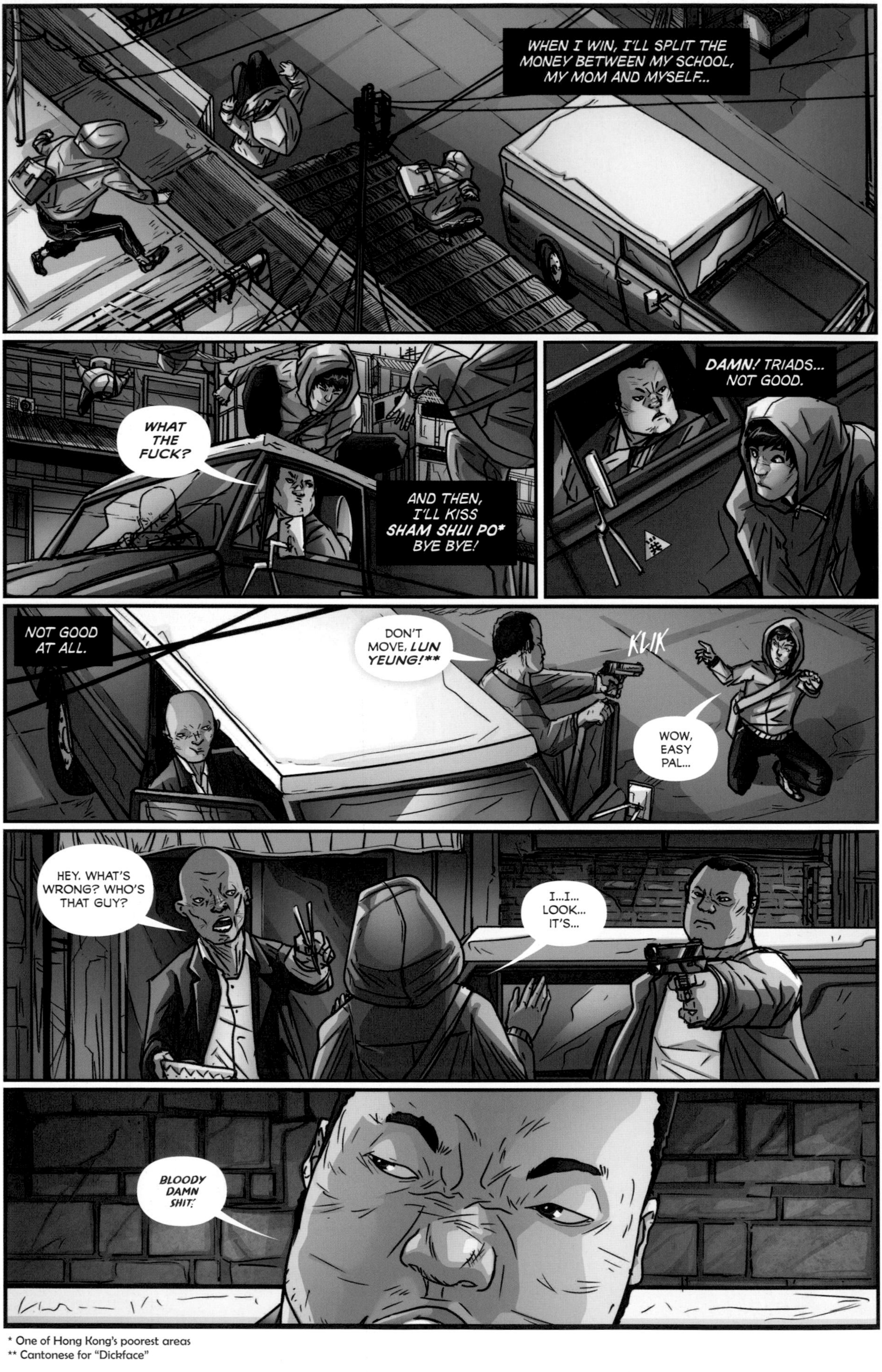
WHEN I WIN, I'LL SPLIT THE MONEY BETWEEN MY SCHOOL, MY MOM AND MYSELF...
WHAT THE FUCK?
AND THEN, I'LL KISS SHAM SHUI PO* BYE BYE!
DAMN! TRIADS... NOT GOOD.
NOT GOOD AT ALL.
DON'T MOVE, LUN YEUNG!**
KLIK
WOW, EASY PAL...
HEY. WHAT'S WRONG? WHO'S THAT GUY?
I...I... LOOK... IT'S...
BLOODY DAMN SHIT!

* One of Hong Kong's poorest areas

** Cantonese for "Dickface"

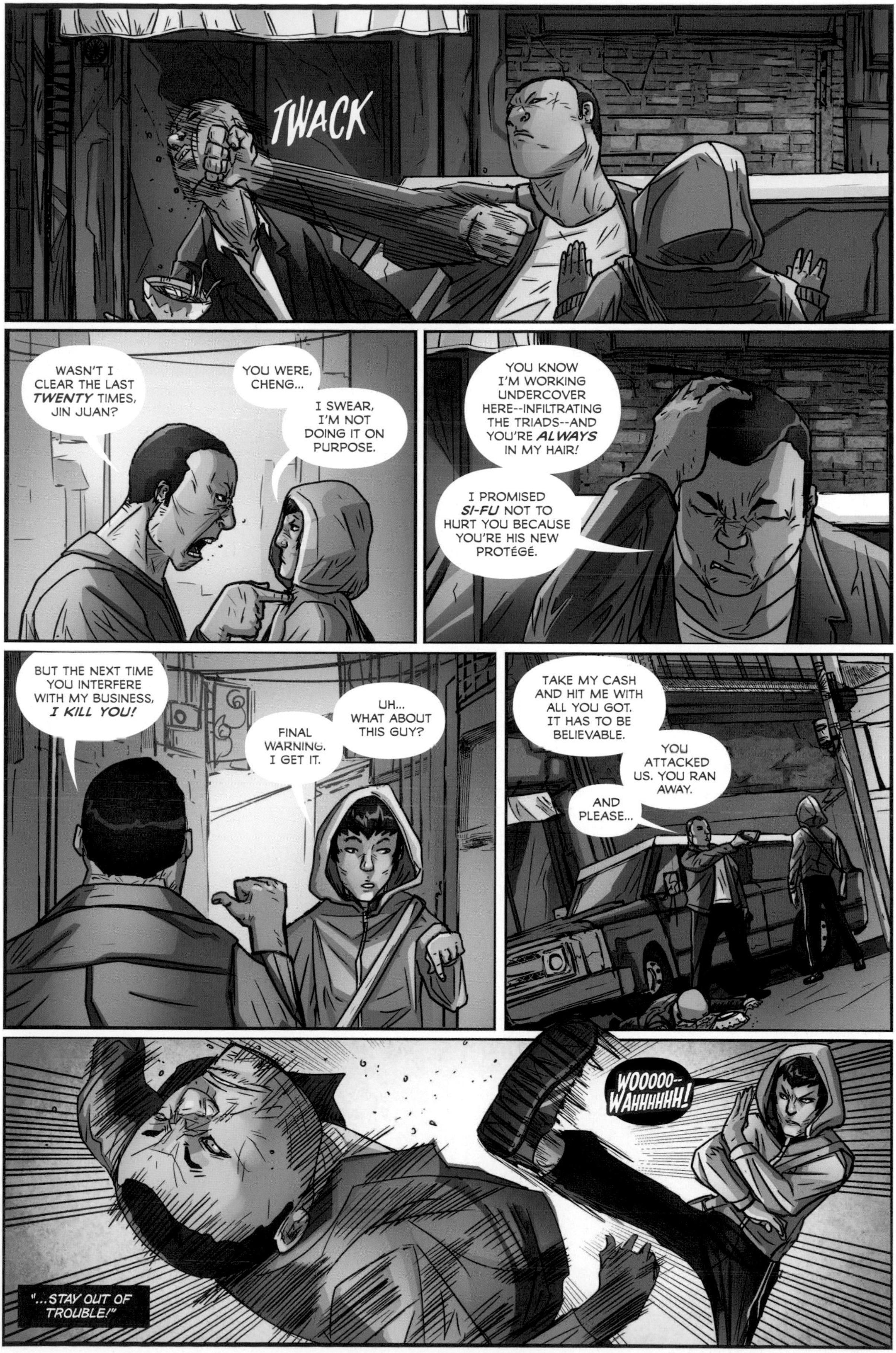
TWACK
WASN'T I CLEAR THE LAST TWENTY TIMES, JIN JUAN?
YOU WERE, CHENG...
I SWEAR, I'M NOT DOING IT ON PURPOSE.
YOU KNOW I'M WORKING UNDERCOVER HERE--INFILTRATING THE TRIADS--AND YOU'RE ALWAYS IN MY HAIR!
I PROMISED SI-FU NOT TO HURT YOU BECAUSE YOU'RE HIS NEW PROTÉGÉ.
BUT THE NEXT TIME YOU INTERFERE WITH MY BUSINESS, I KILL YOU!
FINAL WARNING. I GET IT.
UH... WHAT ABOUT THIS GUY?
TAKE MY CASH AND HIT ME WITH ALL YOU GOT. IT HAS TO BE BELIEVABLE.
YOU ATTACKED US. YOU RAN AWAY.
AND PLEASE...
WOOOOO-WAHHHHHH!
"...STAY OUT OF TROUBLE!"

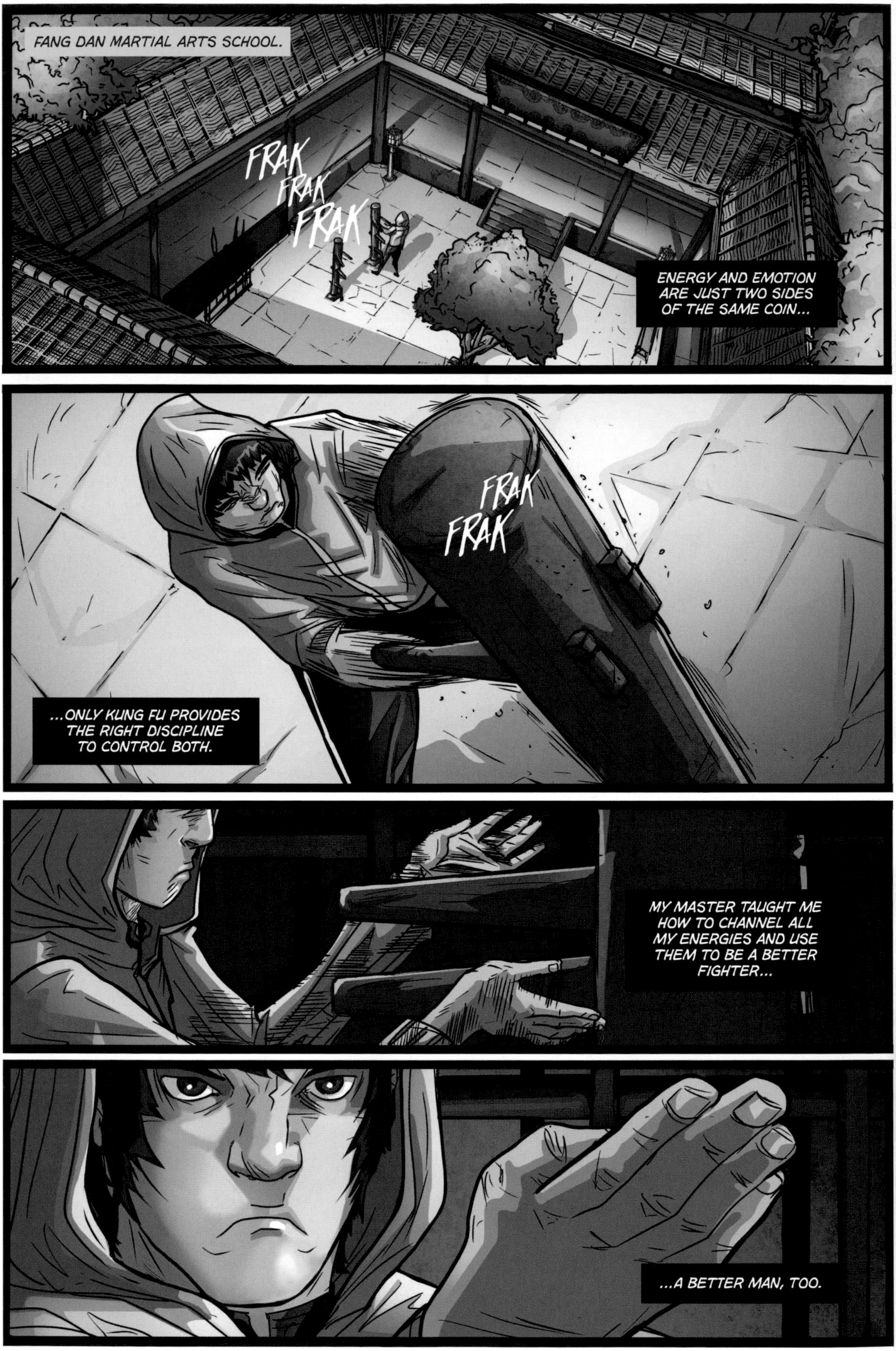
FANG DAN MARTIAL ARTS SCHOOL.
FRAK
FRAK
FRAK
ENERGY AND EMOTION ARE JUST TWO SIDES OF THE SAME COIN...
FRAK
FRAK
...ONLY KUNG FU PROVIDES THE RIGHT DISCIPLINE TO CONTROL BOTH.
MY MASTER TAUGHT ME HOW TO CHANNEL ALL MY ENERGIES AND USE THEM TO BE A BETTER FIGHTER...
...A BETTER MAN, TOO.

WELL...I MAY NOT BE THERE YET. BUT I'M WORKING ON IT.

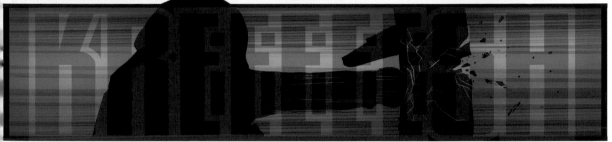

KRRKTTTH

JIN JUAN!

DO YOU THINK YOU'RE GOING TO ACHIEVE ANYTHING IN *WING CHUN* BY BREAKING A WOODEN DUMMY?

NO, SI-FU.

WING CHUN REQUIRES *PATIENCE*, YOUNG APPRENTICE.

HAY, SI FU!

AND *CONTROL*.

HAY, SI FU!

ARE YOU GOING TO AGREE TO EVERYTHING I SAY...

...ONLY TO COME HERE EARLY EVERY MORNING AND *DESTROY* MY PROPERTY?

I'LL PAY FOR THAT, SI FU. I PROMISE!

THAT'S WHAT YOU SAID THE *LAST* TIME.

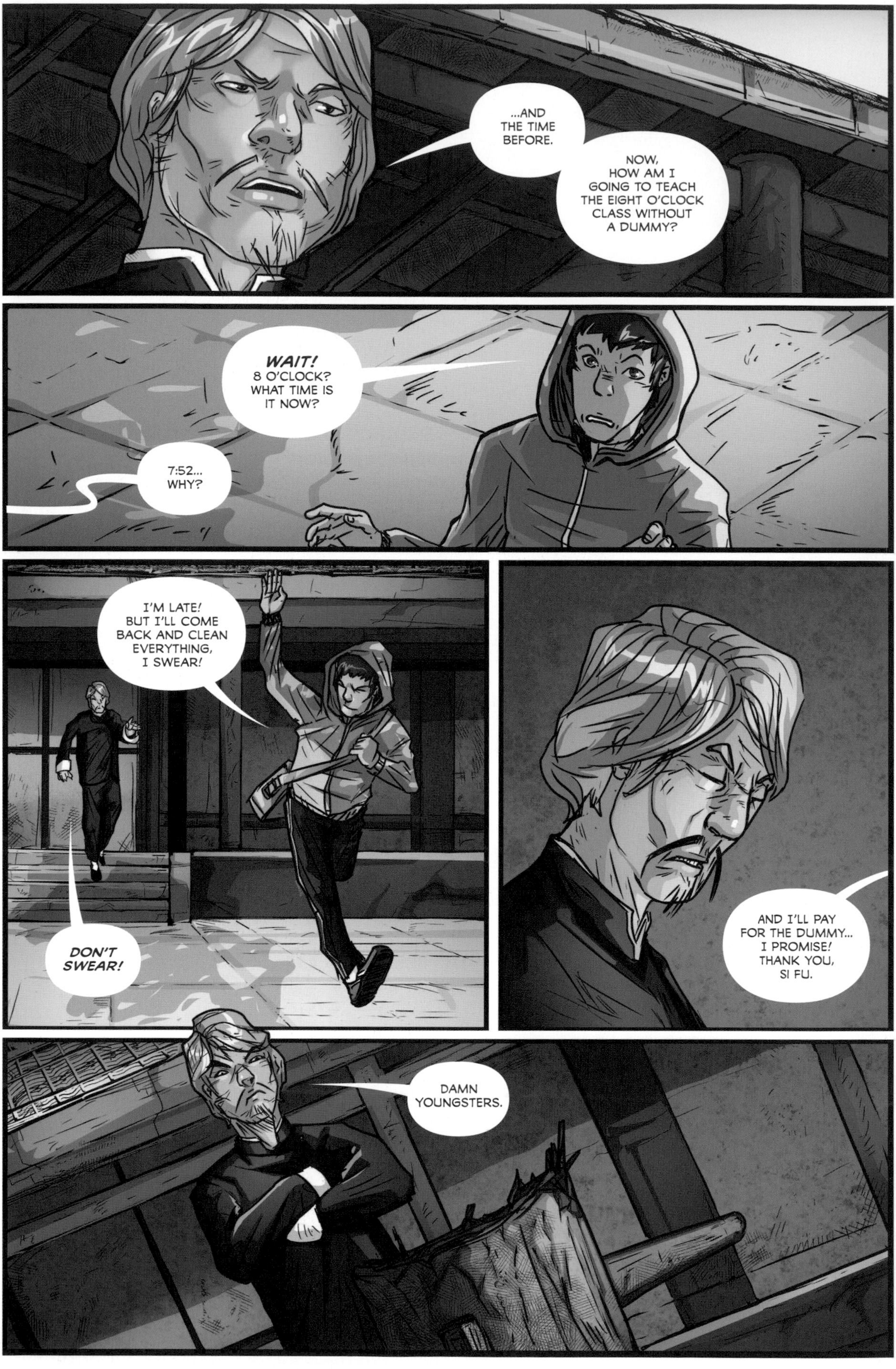
...AND THE TIME BEFORE.
NOW, HOW AM I GOING TO TEACH THE EIGHT O'CLOCK CLASS WITHOUT A DUMMY?
WAIT! 8 O'CLOCK? WHAT TIME IS IT NOW?
7:52... WHY?
I'M LATE! BUT I'LL COME BACK AND CLEAN EVERYTHING, I SWEAR!
DON'T SWEAR!
AND I'LL PAY FOR THE DUMMY... I PROMISE! THANK YOU, SI FU.
DAMN YOUNGSTERS.

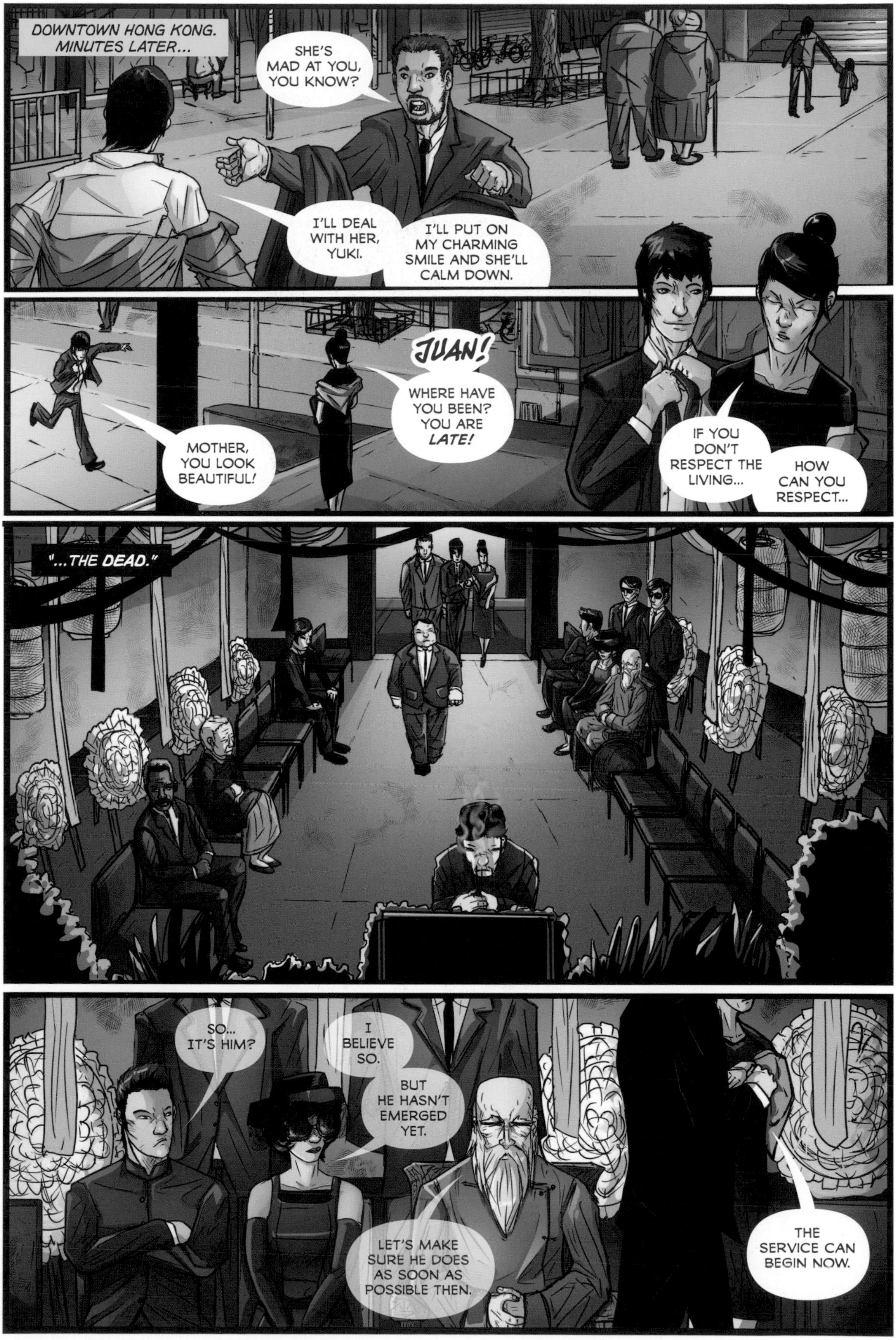
DOWNTOWN HONG KONG. MINUTES LATER...
SHE'S MAD AT YOU, YOU KNOW?
I'LL DEAL WITH HER, YUKI.
I'LL PUT ON MY CHARMING SMILE AND SHE'LL CALM DOWN.
MOTHER, YOU LOOK BEAUTIFUL!
JUAN!
WHERE HAVE YOU BEEN? YOU ARE LATE!
IF YOU DON'T RESPECT THE LIVING...
HOW CAN YOU RESPECT...
"...THE DEAD."
SO... IT'S HIM?
I BELIEVE SO.
BUT HE HASN'T EMERGED YET.
LET'S MAKE SURE HE DOES AS SOON AS POSSIBLE THEN.
THE SERVICE CAN BEGIN NOW.

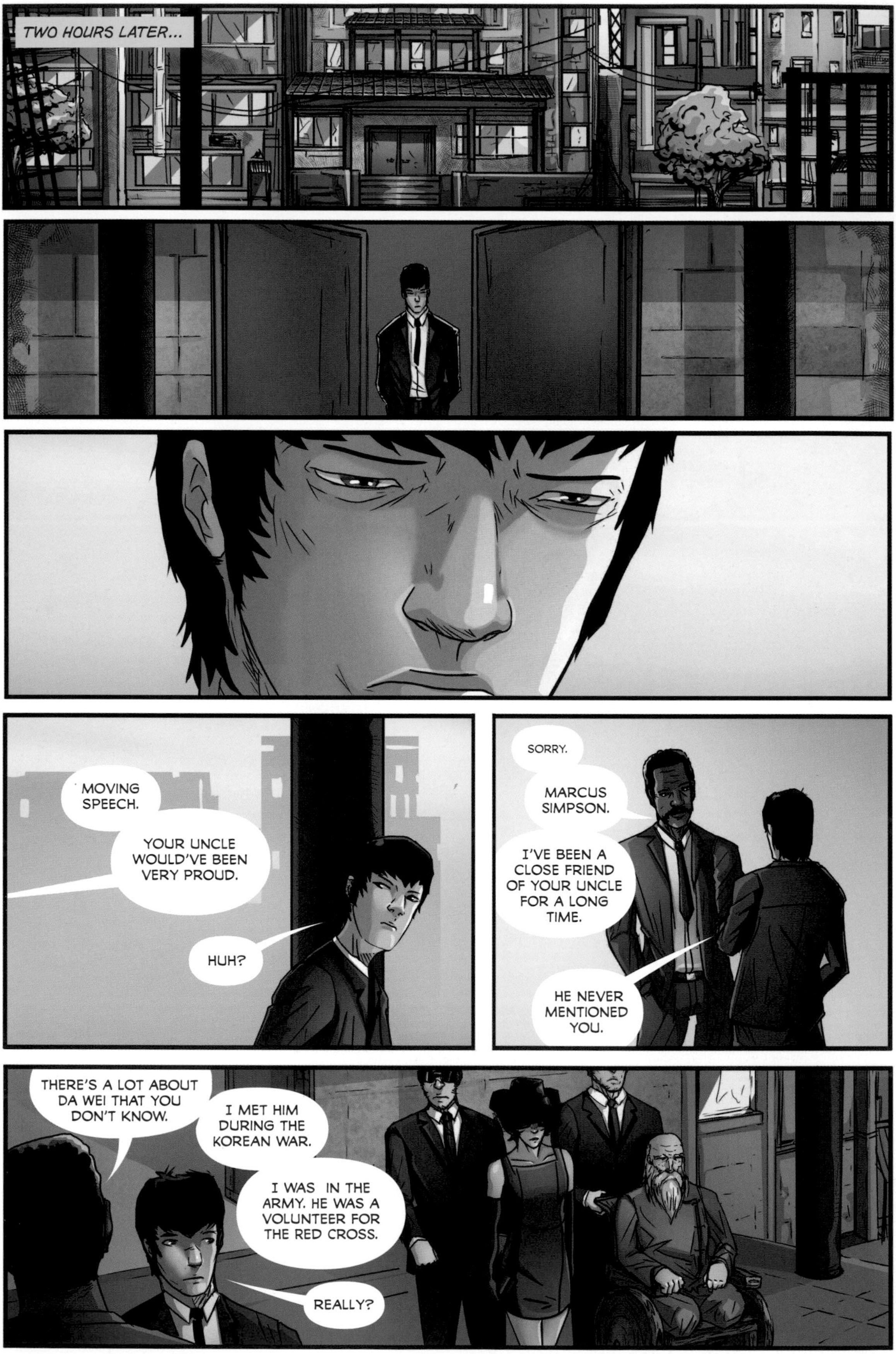
TWO HOURS LATER...
MOVING SPEECH.
YOUR UNCLE WOULD'VE BEEN VERY PROUD.
HUH?
SORRY.
MARCUS SIMPSON.
I'VE BEEN A CLOSE FRIEND OF YOUR UNCLE FOR A LONG TIME.
HE NEVER MENTIONED YOU.
THERE'S A LOT ABOUT DA WEI THAT YOU DON'T KNOW.
I MET HIM DURING THE KOREAN WAR.
I WAS IN THE ARMY. HE WAS A VOLUNTEER FOR THE RED CROSS.
REALLY?

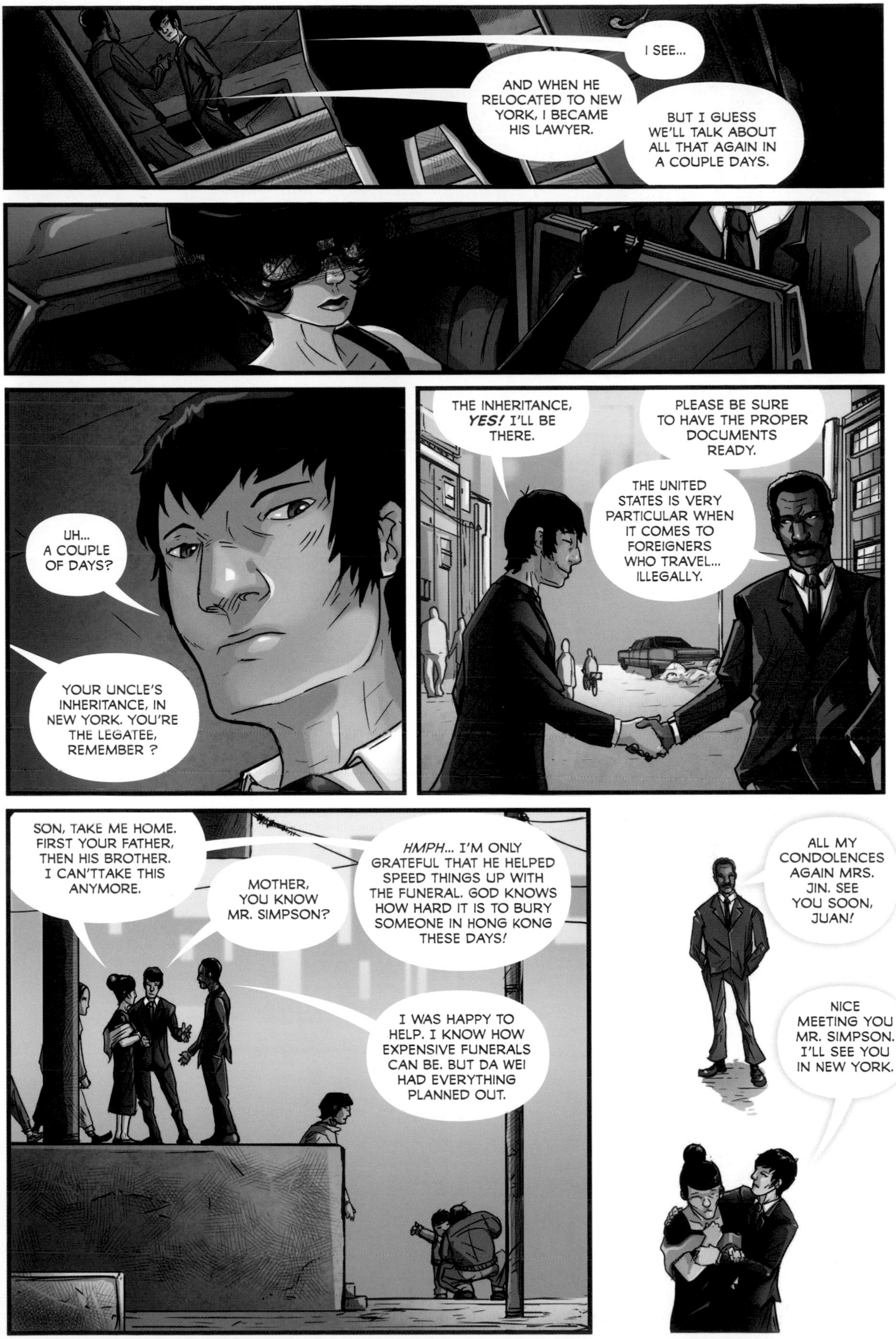
I SEE...
AND WHEN HE RELOCATED TO NEW YORK, I BECAME HIS LAWYER.
BUT I GUESS WE'LL TALK ABOUT ALL THAT AGAIN IN A COUPLE DAYS.
UH... A COUPLE OF DAYS?
YOUR UNCLE'S INHERITANCE, IN NEW YORK. YOU'RE THE LEGATEE, REMEMBER ?
THE INHERITANCE, YES! I'LL BE THERE.
PLEASE BE SURE TO HAVE THE PROPER DOCUMENTS READY.
THE UNITED STATES IS VERY PARTICULAR WHEN IT COMES TO FOREIGNERS WHO TRAVEL... ILLEGALLY.
SON, TAKE ME HOME. FIRST YOUR FATHER, THEN HIS BROTHER. I CAN'TTAKE THIS ANYMORE.
MOTHER, YOU KNOW MR. SIMPSON?
HMPH... I'M ONLY GRATEFUL THAT HE HELPED SPEED THINGS UP WITH THE FUNERAL. GOD KNOWS HOW HARD IT IS TO BURY SOMEONE IN HONG KONG THESE DAYS!
I WAS HAPPY TO HELP. I KNOW HOW EXPENSIVE FUNERALS CAN BE. BUT DA WEI HAD EVERYTHING PLANNED OUT.
ALL MY CONDOLENCES AGAIN MRS. JIN. SEE YOU SOON, JUAN!
NICE MEETING YOU MR. SIMPSON. I'LL SEE YOU IN NEW YORK.

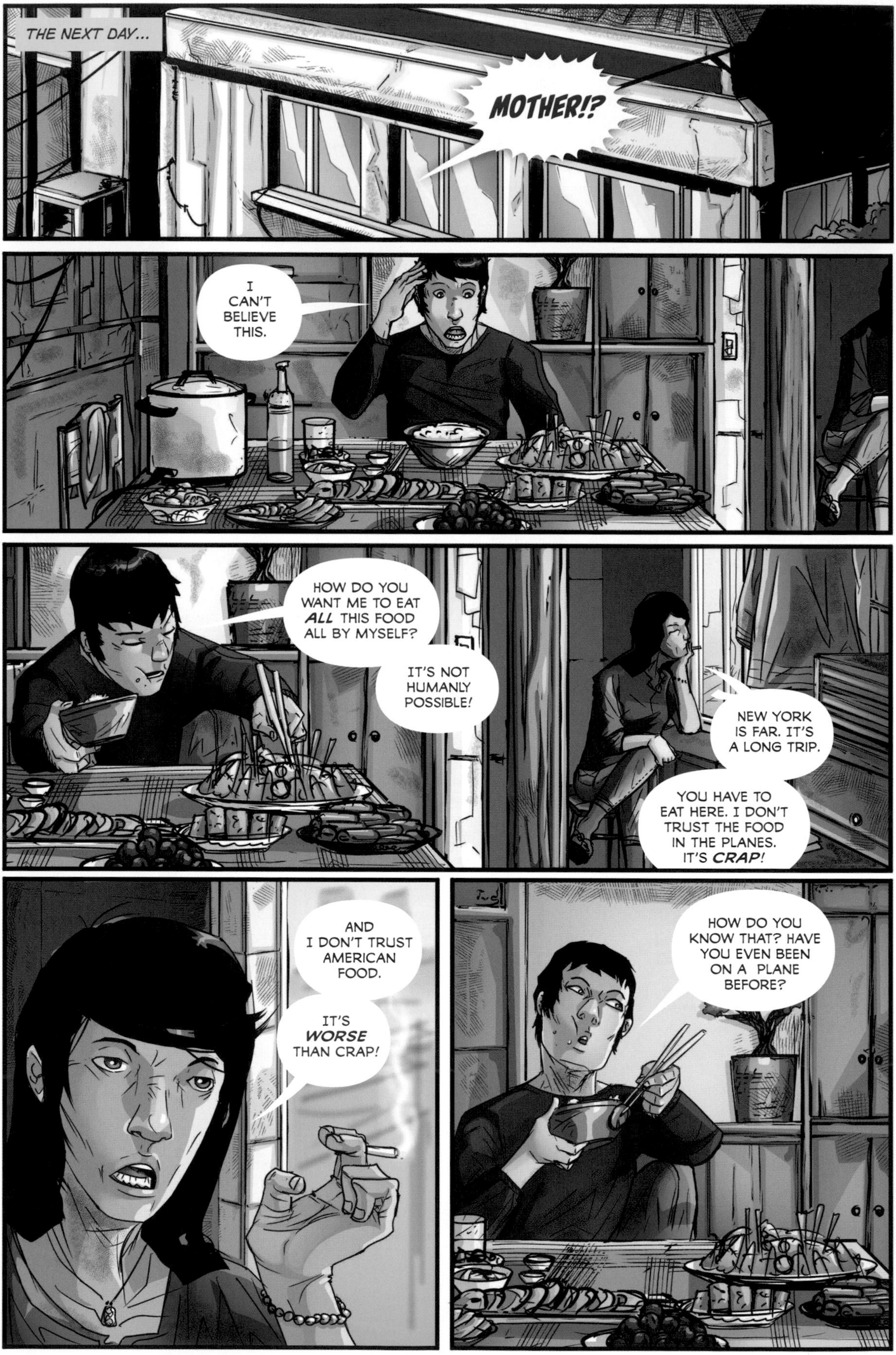
THE NEXT DAY...
MOTHER!?
I CAN'T BELIEVE THIS.
HOW DO YOU WANT ME TO EAT *ALL* THIS FOOD ALL BY MYSELF?
IT'S NOT HUMANLY POSSIBLE!
NEW YORK IS FAR. IT'S A LONG TRIP.
YOU HAVE TO EAT HERE. I DON'T TRUST THE FOOD IN THE PLANES. IT'S *CRAP!*
AND I DON'T TRUST AMERICAN FOOD.
IT'S *WORSE* THAN CRAP!
HOW DO YOU KNOW THAT? HAVE YOU EVEN BEEN ON A PLANE BEFORE?

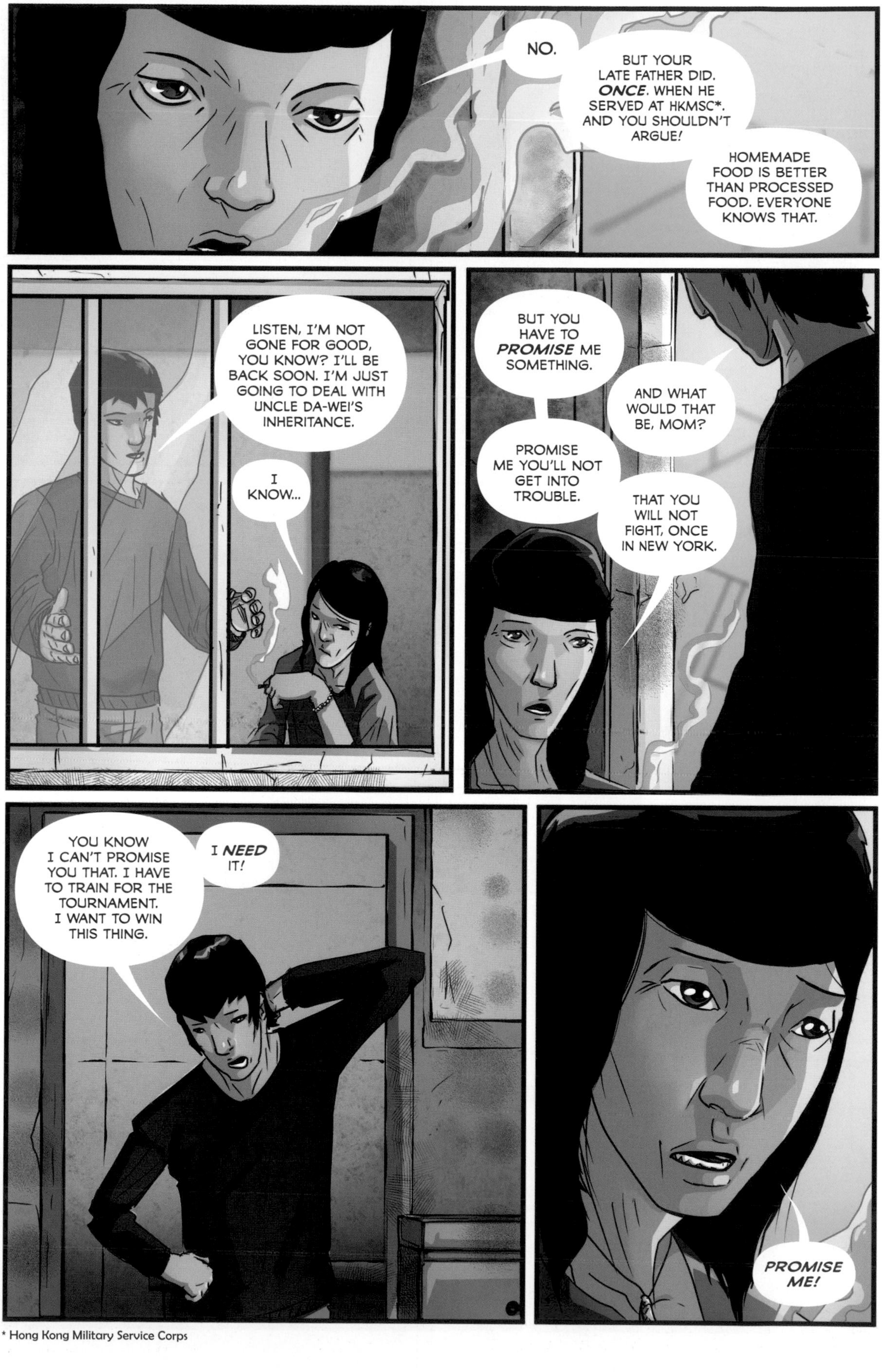
NO.
BUT YOUR LATE FATHER DID. ONCE. WHEN HE SERVED AT HKMSC*. AND YOU SHOULDN'T ARGUE!
HOMEMADE FOOD IS BETTER THAN PROCESSED FOOD. EVERYONE KNOWS THAT.
LISTEN, I'M NOT GONE FOR GOOD, YOU KNOW? I'LL BE BACK SOON. I'M JUST GOING TO DEAL WITH UNCLE DA-WEI'S INHERITANCE.
I KNOW...
BUT YOU HAVE TO PROMISE ME SOMETHING.
AND WHAT WOULD THAT BE, MOM?
PROMISE ME YOU'LL NOT GET INTO TROUBLE.
THAT YOU WILL NOT FIGHT, ONCE IN NEW YORK.
YOU KNOW I CAN'T PROMISE YOU THAT. I HAVE TO TRAIN FOR THE TOURNAMENT. I WANT TO WIN THIS THING.
I NEED IT!
PROMISE ME!

* Hong Kong Military Service Corps

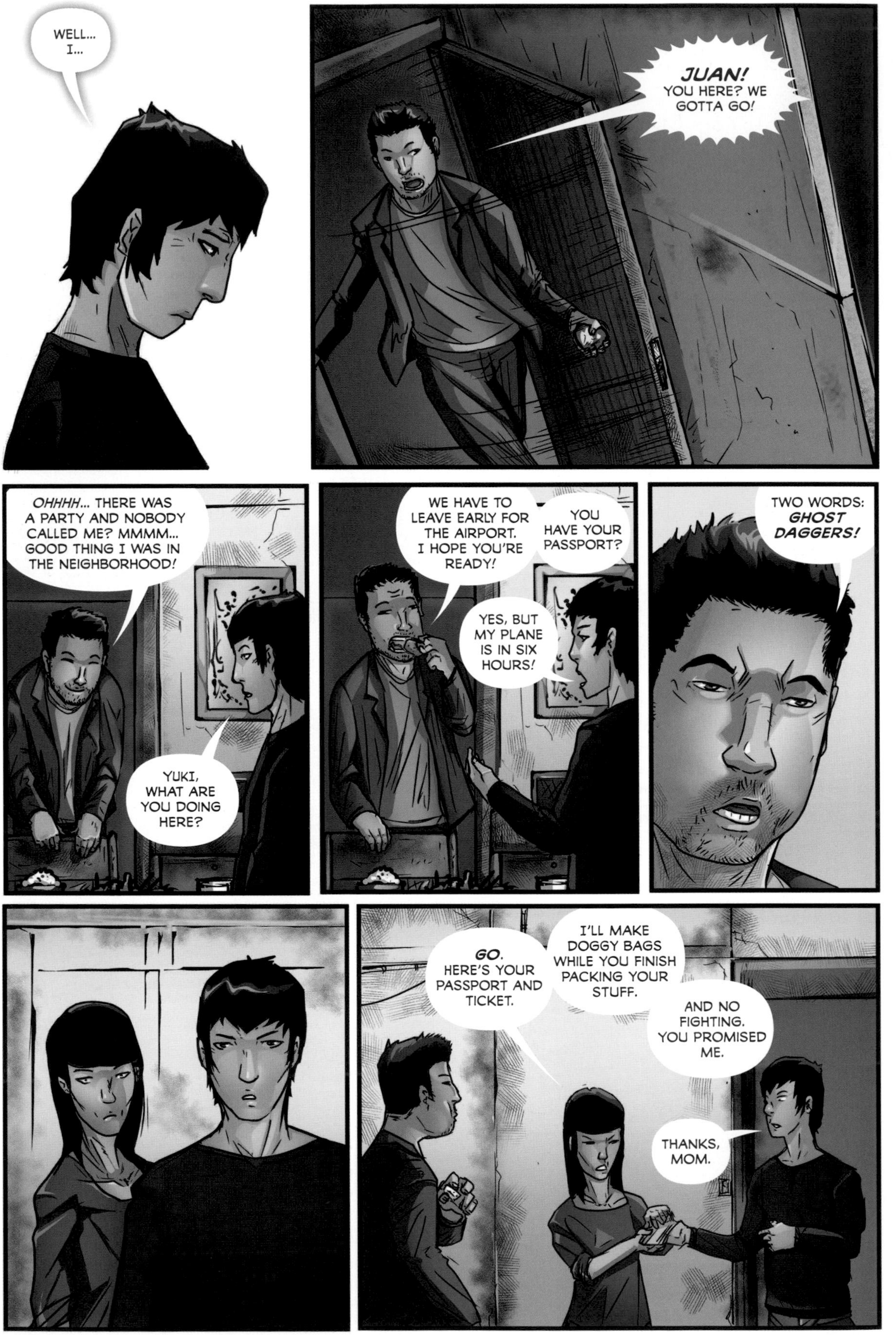
WELL... I...
JUAN! YOU HERE? WE GOTTA GO!
OHHHH... THERE WAS A PARTY AND NOBODY CALLED ME? MMMM... GOOD THING I WAS IN THE NEIGHBORHOOD!
YUKI, WHAT ARE YOU DOING HERE?
WE HAVE TO LEAVE EARLY FOR THE AIRPORT. I HOPE YOU'RE READY!
YOU HAVE YOUR PASSPORT?
YES, BUT MY PLANE IS IN SIX HOURS!
TWO WORDS: GHOST DAGGERS!
GO. HERE'S YOUR PASSPORT AND TICKET.
I'LL MAKE DOGGY BAGS WHILE YOU FINISH PACKING YOUR STUFF.
AND NO FIGHTING. YOU PROMISED ME.
THANKS, MOM.

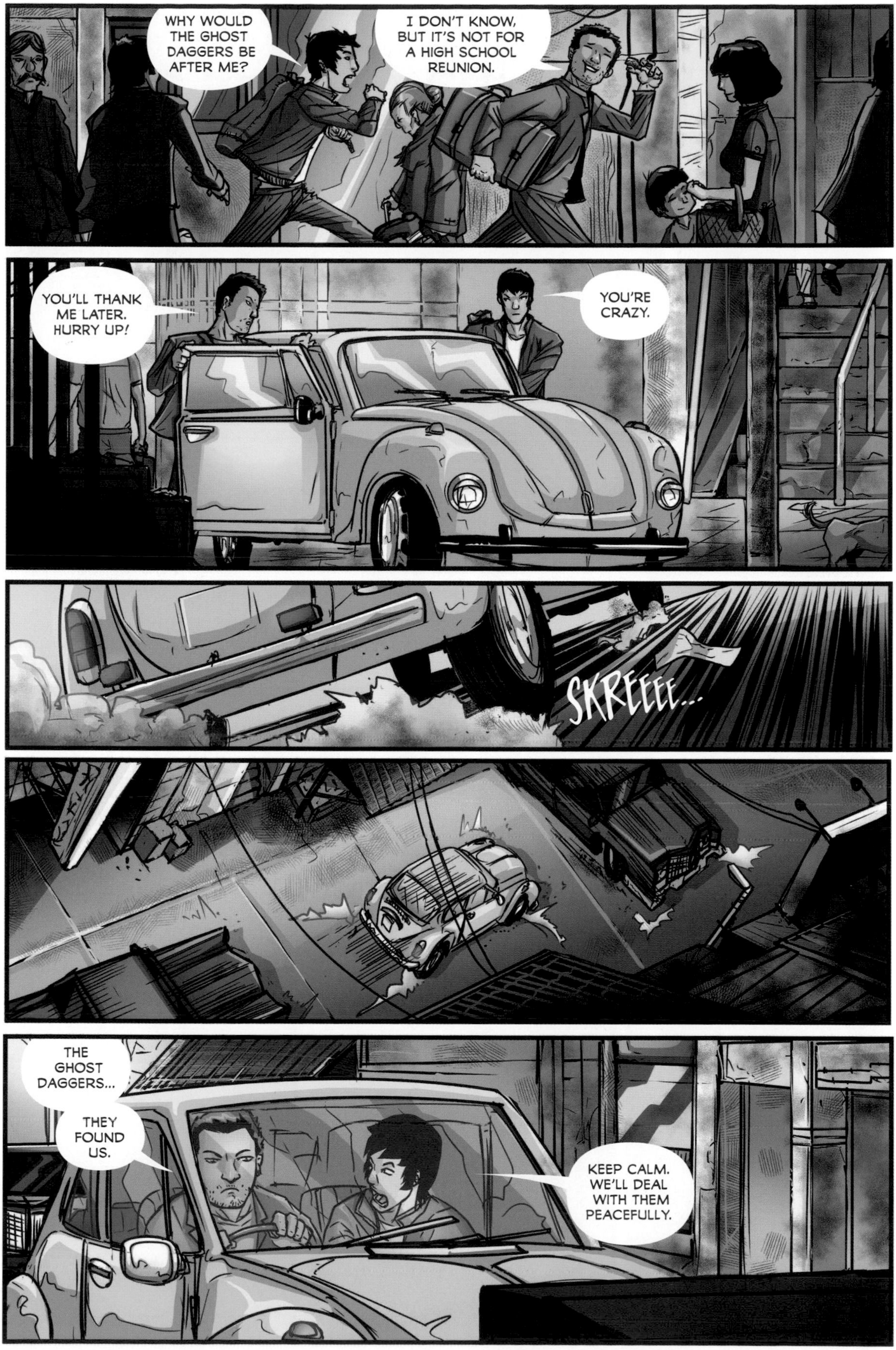
WHY WOULD THE GHOST DAGGERS BE AFTER ME?
I DON'T KNOW, BUT IT'S NOT FOR A HIGH SCHOOL REUNION.
YOU'LL THANK ME LATER. HURRY UP!
YOU'RE CRAZY.
SKREEEE...
THE GHOST DAGGERS...
THEY FOUND US.
KEEP CALM. WE'LL DEAL WITH THEM PEACEFULLY.

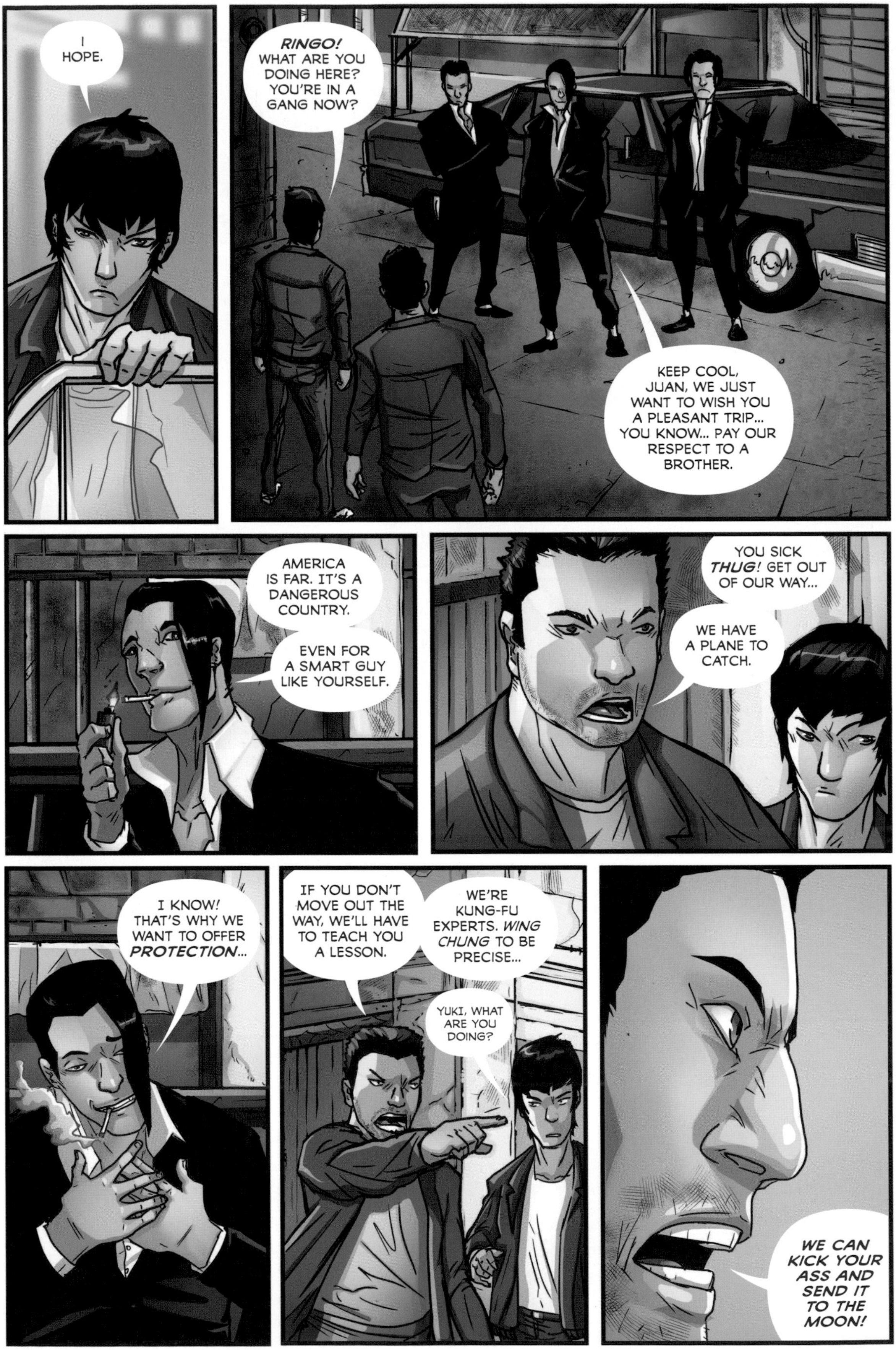

I HOPE.
RINGO! WHAT ARE YOU DOING HERE? YOU'RE IN A GANG NOW?
KEEP COOL, JUAN, WE JUST WANT TO WISH YOU A PLEASANT TRIP... YOU KNOW... PAY OUR RESPECT TO A BROTHER.
AMERICA IS FAR. IT'S A DANGEROUS COUNTRY.
EVEN FOR A SMART GUY LIKE YOURSELF.
YOU SICK THUG! GET OUT OF OUR WAY...
WE HAVE A PLANE TO CATCH.
I KNOW! THAT'S WHY WE WANT TO OFFER PROTECTION...
IF YOU DON'T MOVE OUT THE WAY, WE'LL HAVE TO TEACH YOU A LESSON.
WE'RE KUNG-FU EXPERTS. WING CHUNG TO BE PRECISE...
YUKI, WHAT ARE YOU DOING?
WE CAN KICK YOUR ASS AND SEND IT TO THE MOON!

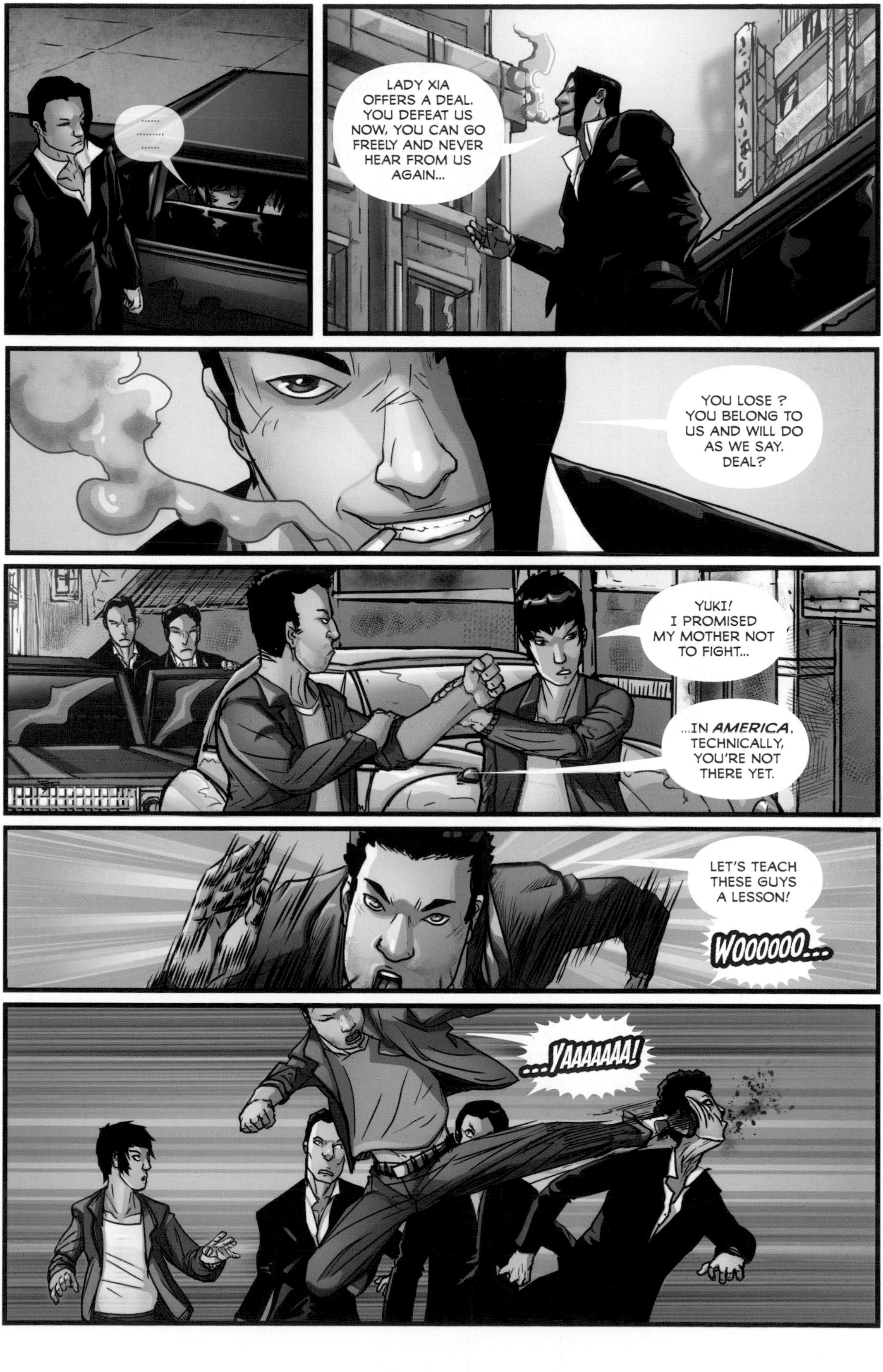
......
....
......
LADY XIA OFFERS A DEAL. YOU DEFEAT US NOW, YOU CAN GO FREELY AND NEVER HEAR FROM US AGAIN...
YOU LOSE ? YOU BELONG TO US AND WILL DO AS WE SAY. DEAL?
YUKI! I PROMISED MY MOTHER NOT TO FIGHT...
...IN AMERICA. TECHNICALLY, YOU'RE NOT THERE YET.
LET'S TEACH THESE GUYS A LESSON!
WOOOOOO...
...YAAAAAAA!

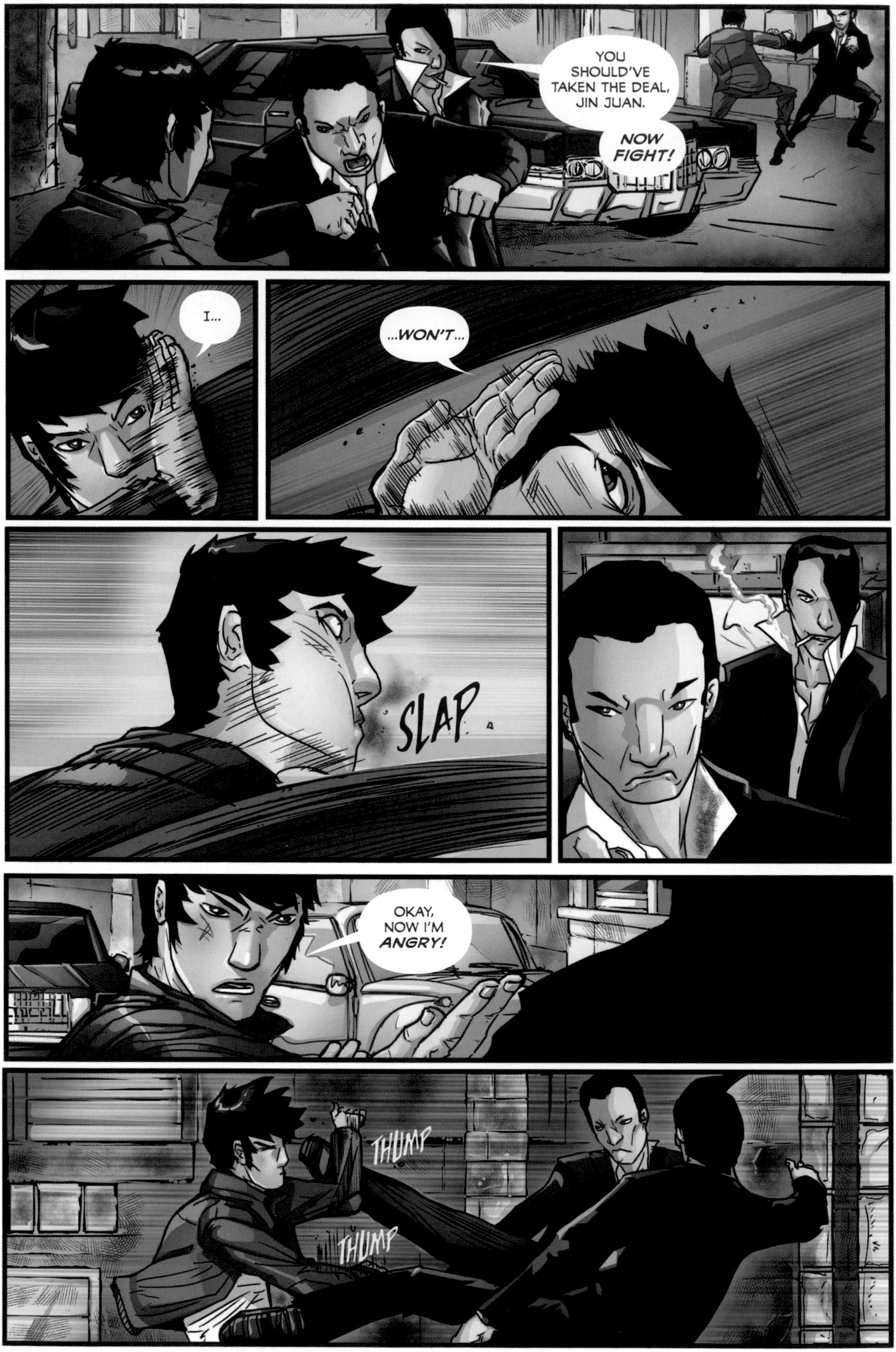
YOU SHOULD'VE TAKEN THE DEAL, JIN JUAN.
NOW FIGHT!
I...
...WON'T...
SLAP
OKAY, NOW I'M ANGRY!
THUMP
THUMP

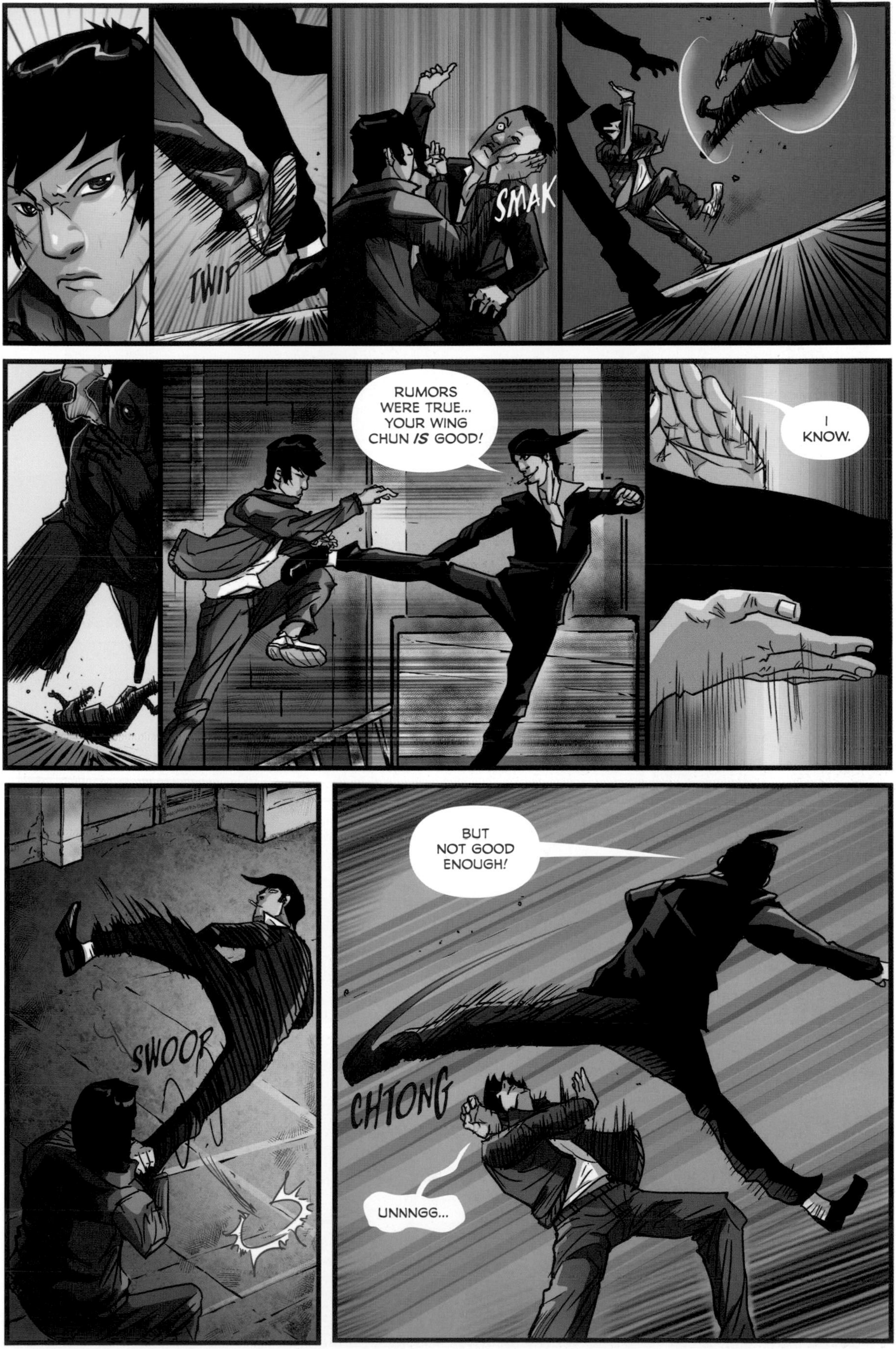
TWIP
SMAK
RUMORS WERE TRUE... YOUR WING CHUN *IS* GOOD!
I KNOW.
SWOOR
BUT NOT GOOD ENOUGH!
CHTONG
UNNNGG...

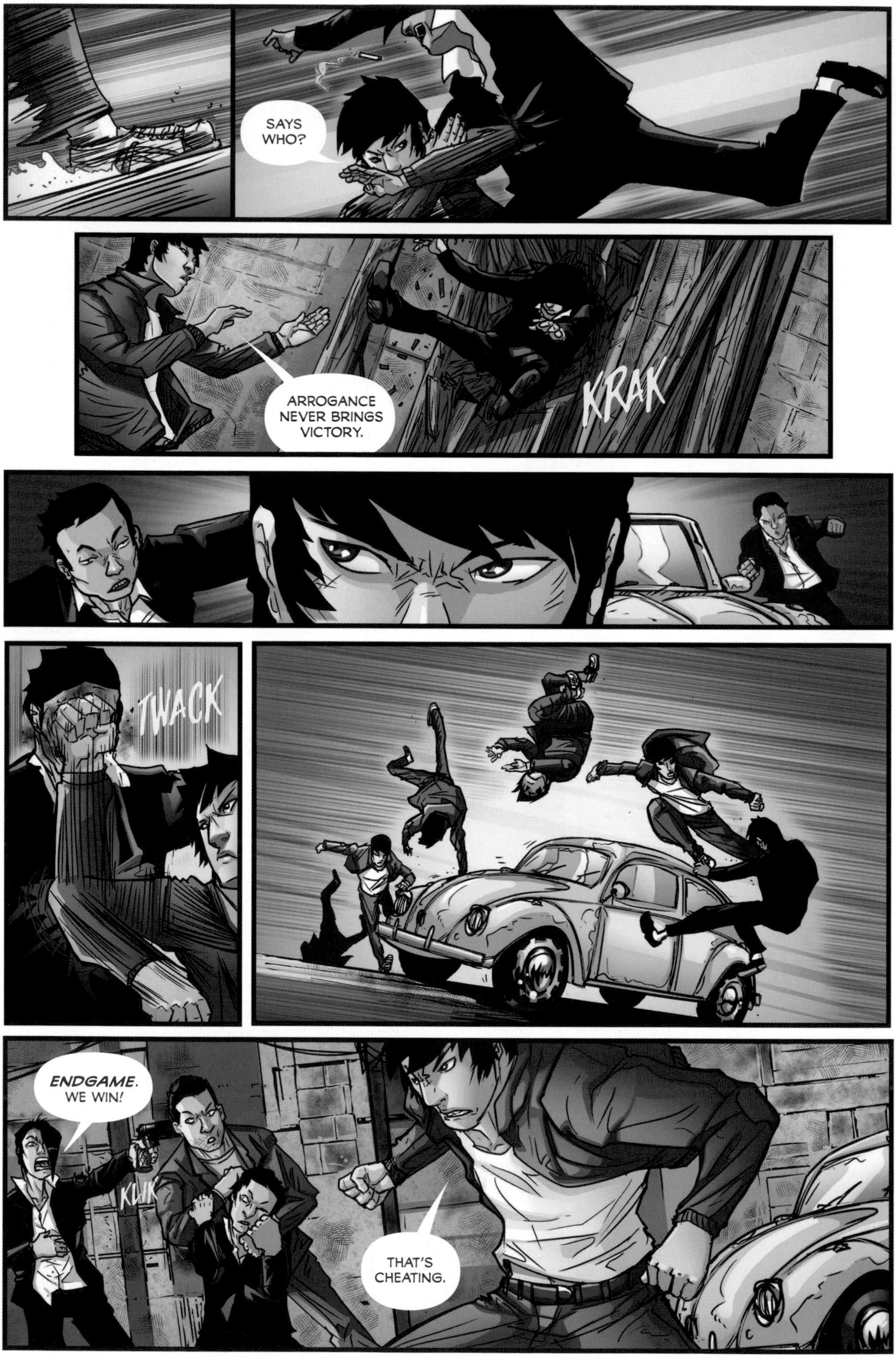
SAYS WHO?
ARROGANCE NEVER BRINGS VICTORY.
KRAK
TWACK
ENDGAME. WE WIN!
KLIK
THAT'S CHEATING.

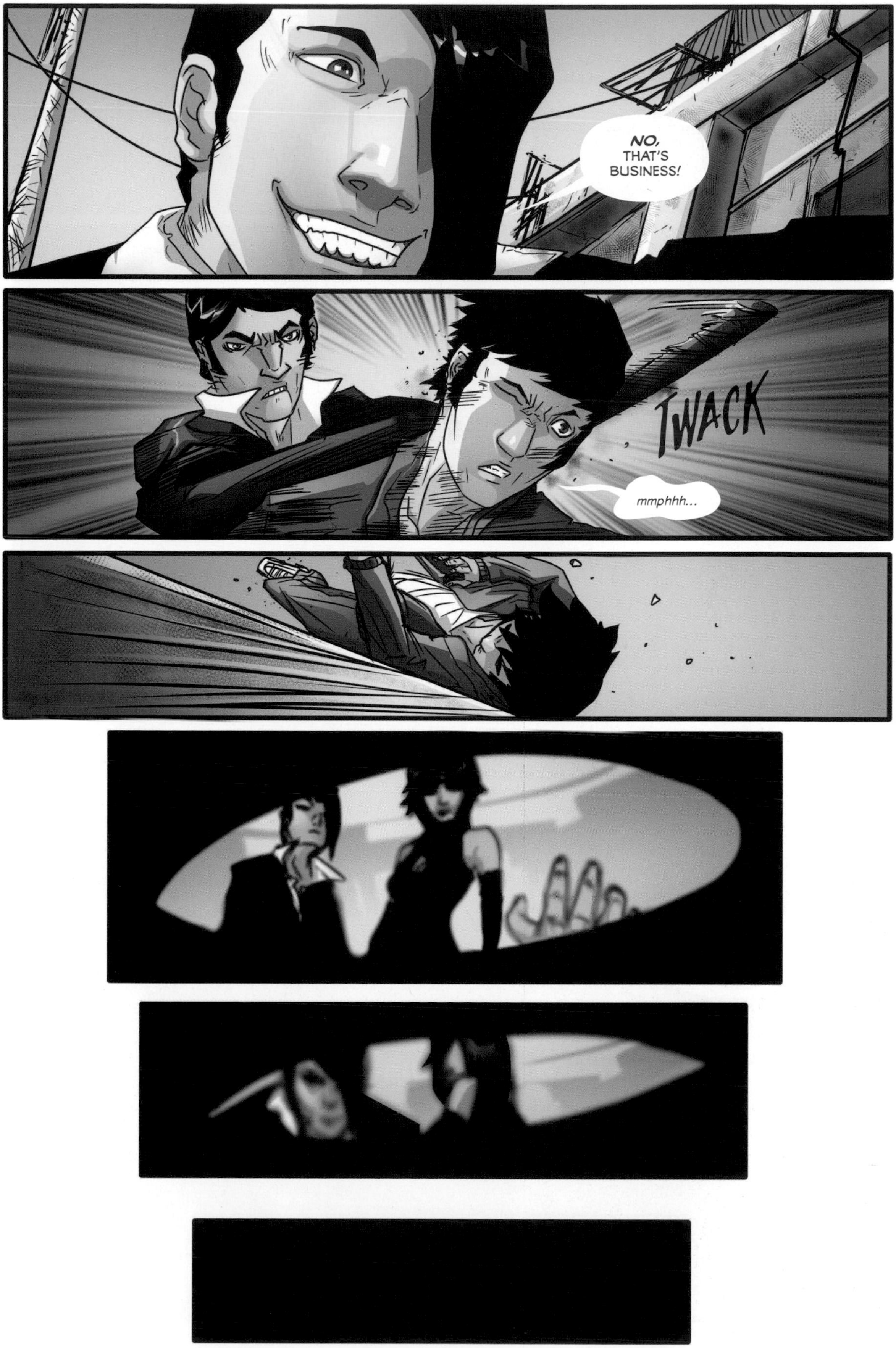
NO, THAT'S BUSINESS!
TWACK
mmphhh...

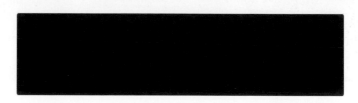

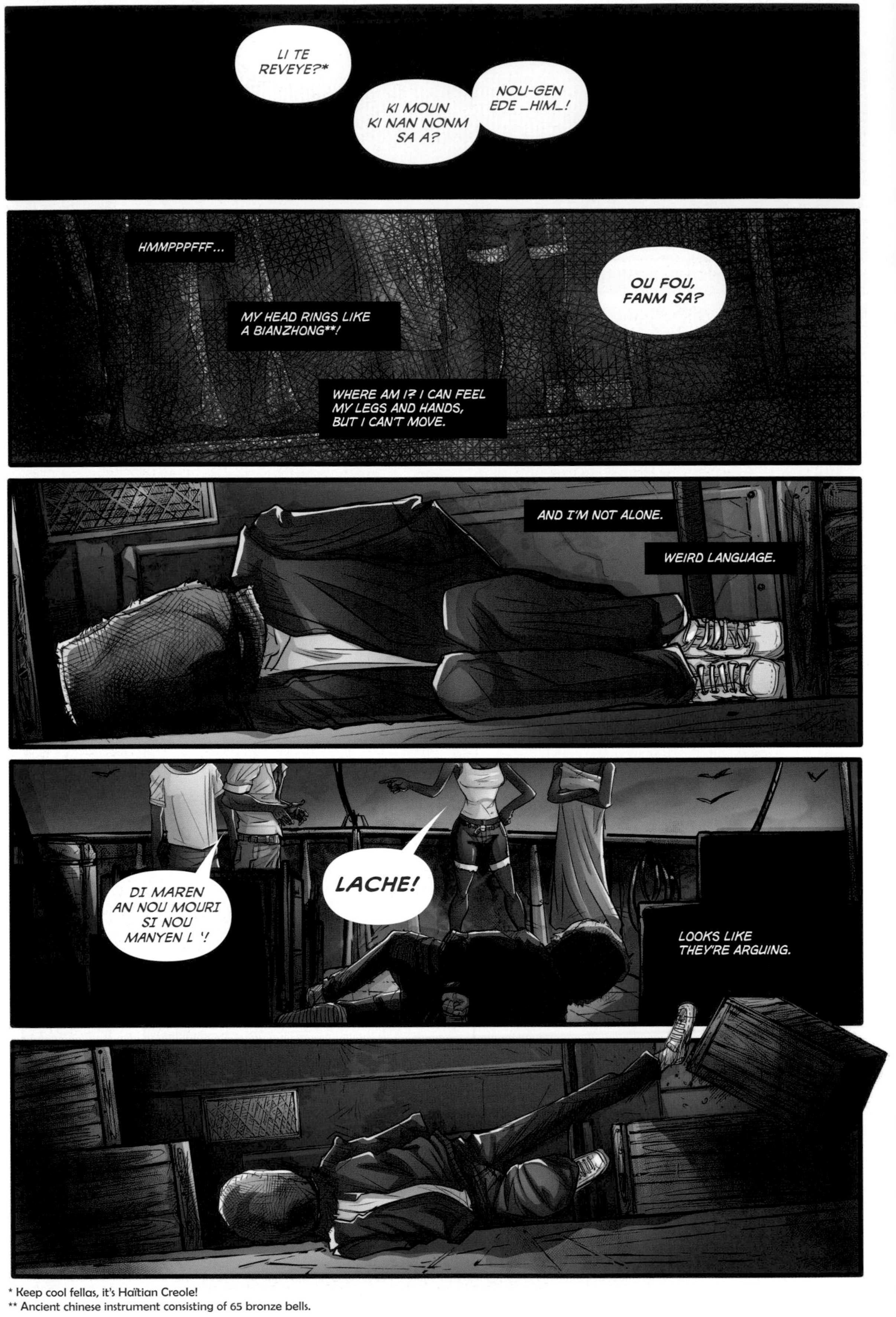
LI TE REVEYE?*
KI MOUN KI NAN NONM SA A?
NOU-GEN EDE _HIM_!
HMMPPPFFF...
MY HEAD RINGS LIKE A BIANZHONG**!
WHERE AM I? I CAN FEEL MY LEGS AND HANDS, BUT I CAN'T MOVE.
OU FOU, FANM SA?
AND I'M NOT ALONE.
WEIRD LANGUAGE.
DI MAREN AN NOU MOURI SI NOU MANYEN L '!
LACHE!
LOOKS LIKE THEY'RE ARGUING.

* Keep cool fellas, it's Haïtian Creole!

** Ancient chinese instrument consisting of 65 bronze bells.

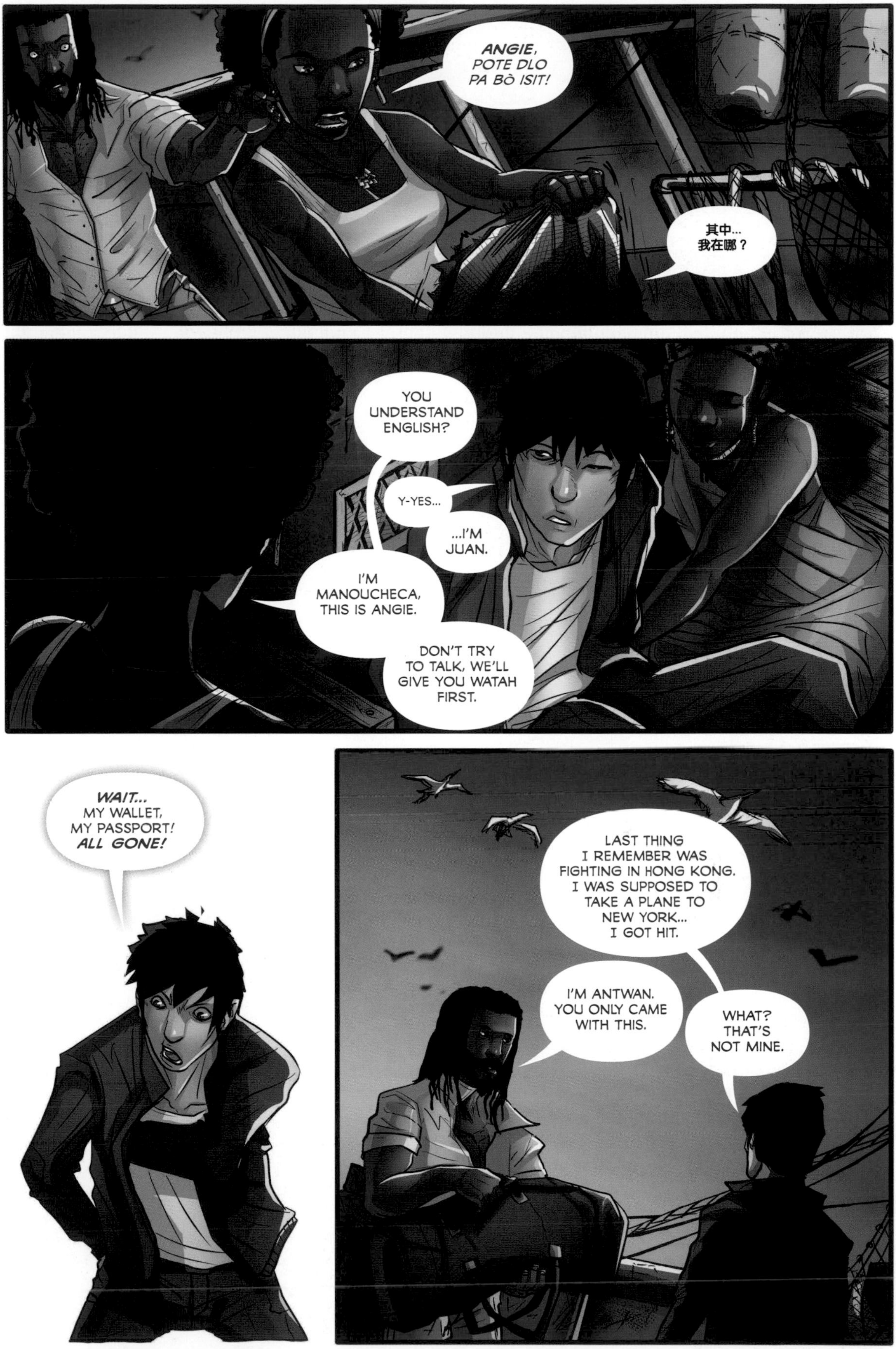
ANGIE, POTE DLO PA BÒ ISIT!
其中...
我在哪？
YOU UNDERSTAND ENGLISH?
Y-YES...
...I'M JUAN.
I'M MANOUCHECA, THIS IS ANGIE.
DON'T TRY TO TALK, WE'LL GIVE YOU WATAH FIRST.
WAIT... MY WALLET, MY PASSPORT! ALL GONE!
LAST THING I REMEMBER WAS FIGHTING IN HONG KONG. I WAS SUPPOSED TO TAKE A PLANE TO NEW YORK... I GOT HIT.
I'M ANTWAN. YOU ONLY CAME WITH THIS.
WHAT? THAT'S NOT MINE.

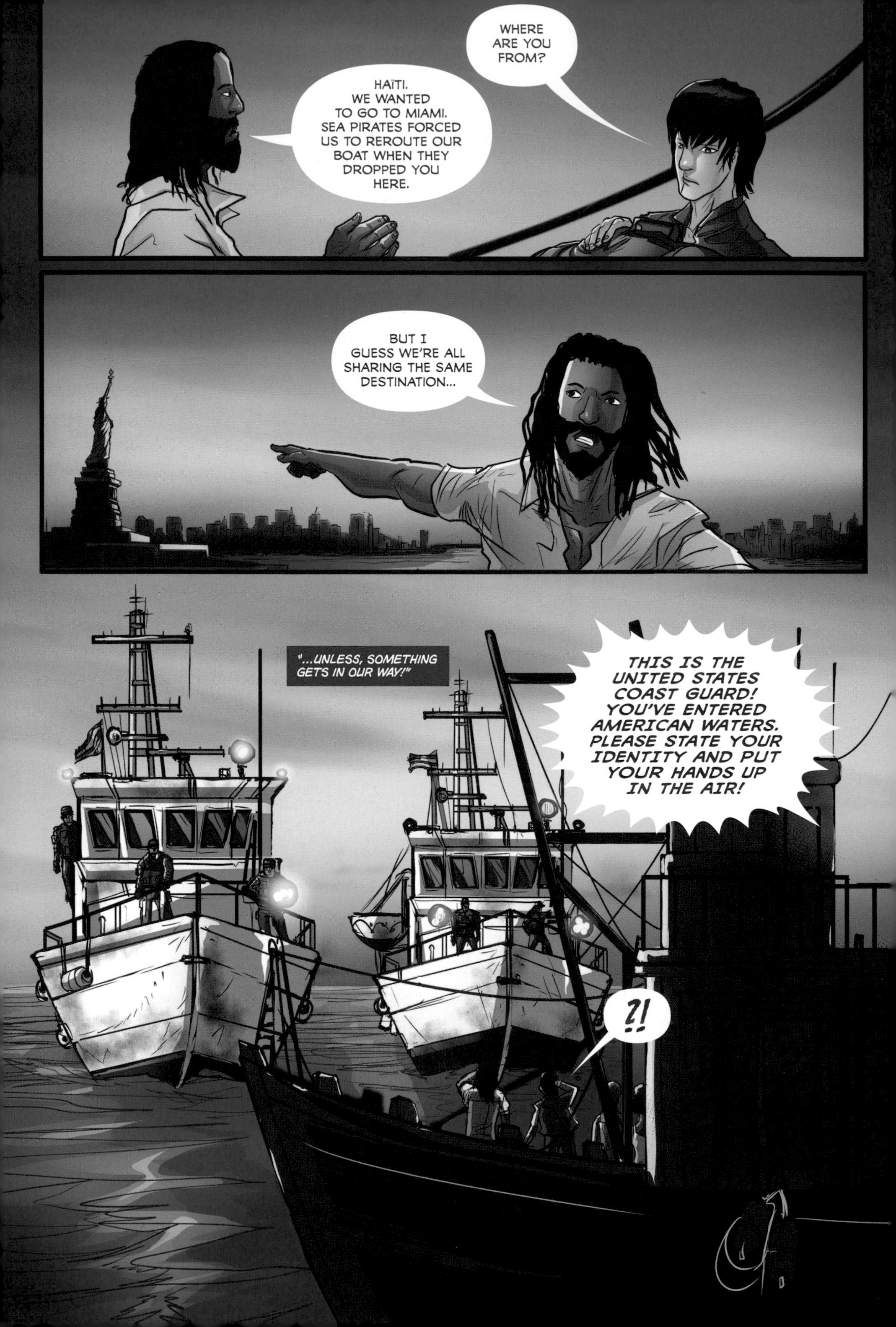
WHERE ARE YOU FROM?
HAÏTI. WE WANTED TO GO TO MIAMI. SEA PIRATES FORCED US TO REROUTE OUR BOAT WHEN THEY DROPPED YOU HERE.
BUT I GUESS WE'RE ALL SHARING THE SAME DESTINATION...
"...UNLESS, SOMETHING GETS IN OUR WAY!"
THIS IS THE UNITED STATES COAST GUARD! YOU'VE ENTERED AMERICAN WATERS. PLEASE STATE YOUR IDENTITY AND PUT YOUR HANDS UP IN THE AIR!
?!

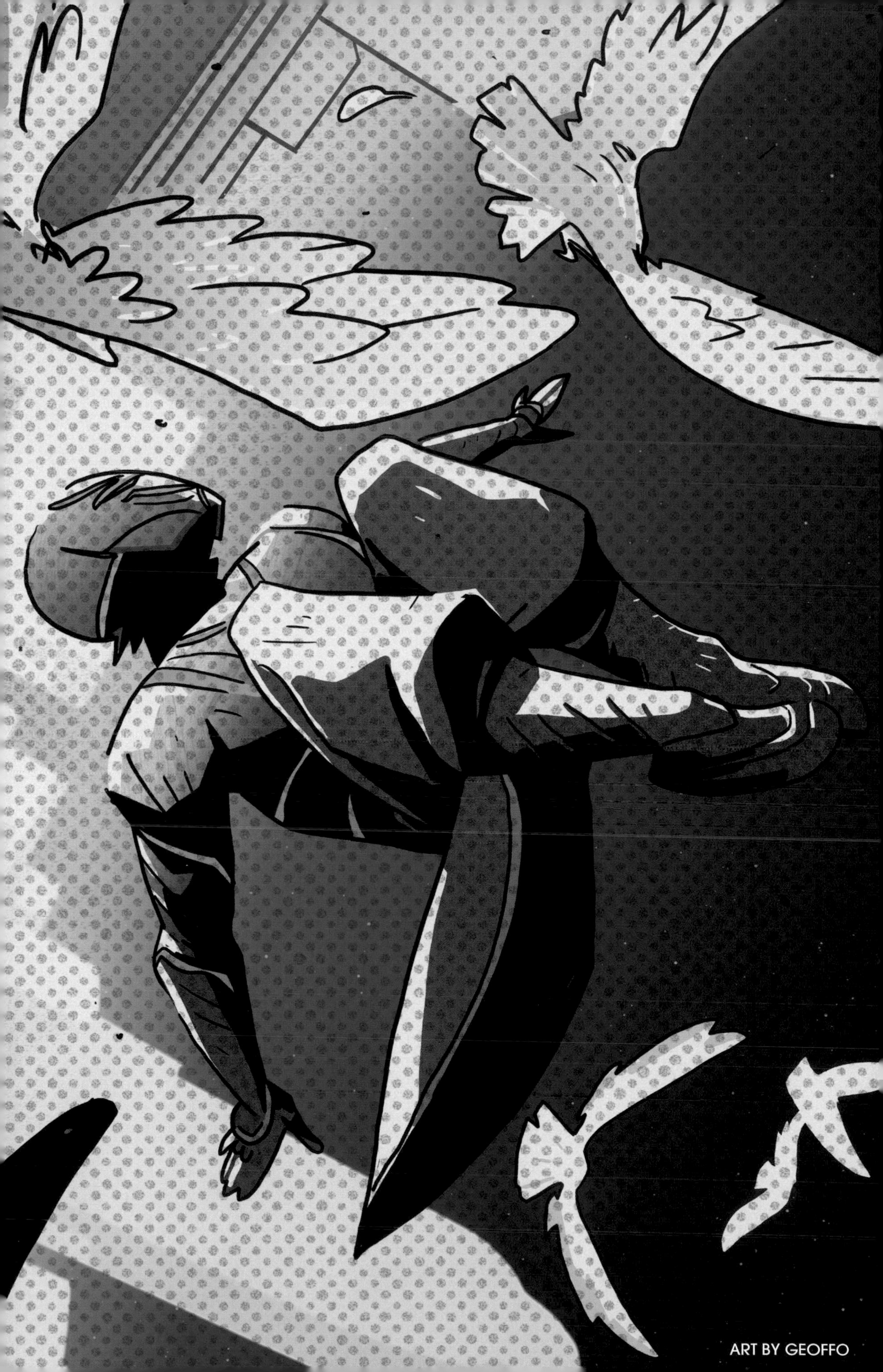

ART BY GEOFFO

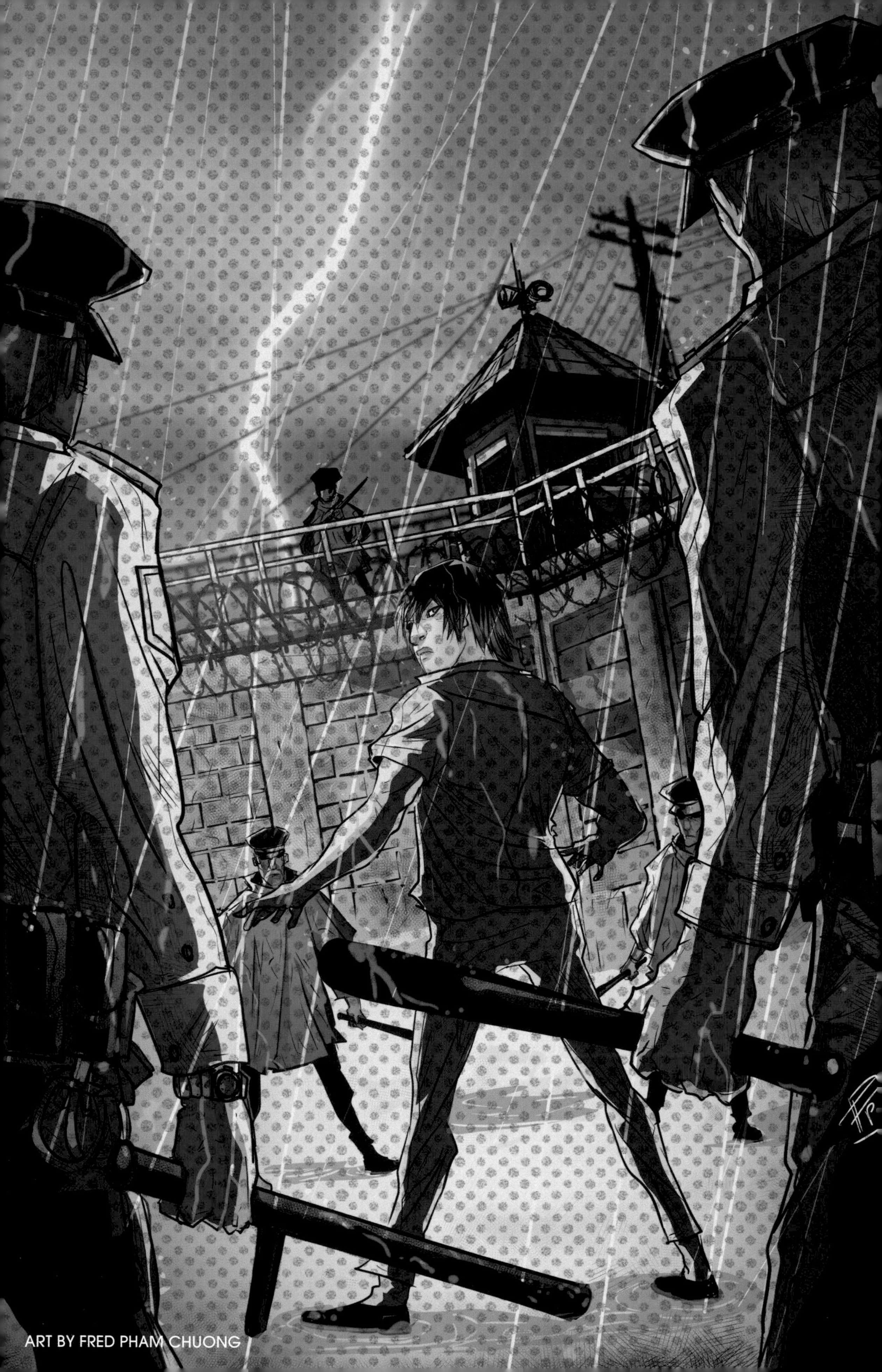

ART BY FRED PHAM CHUONG

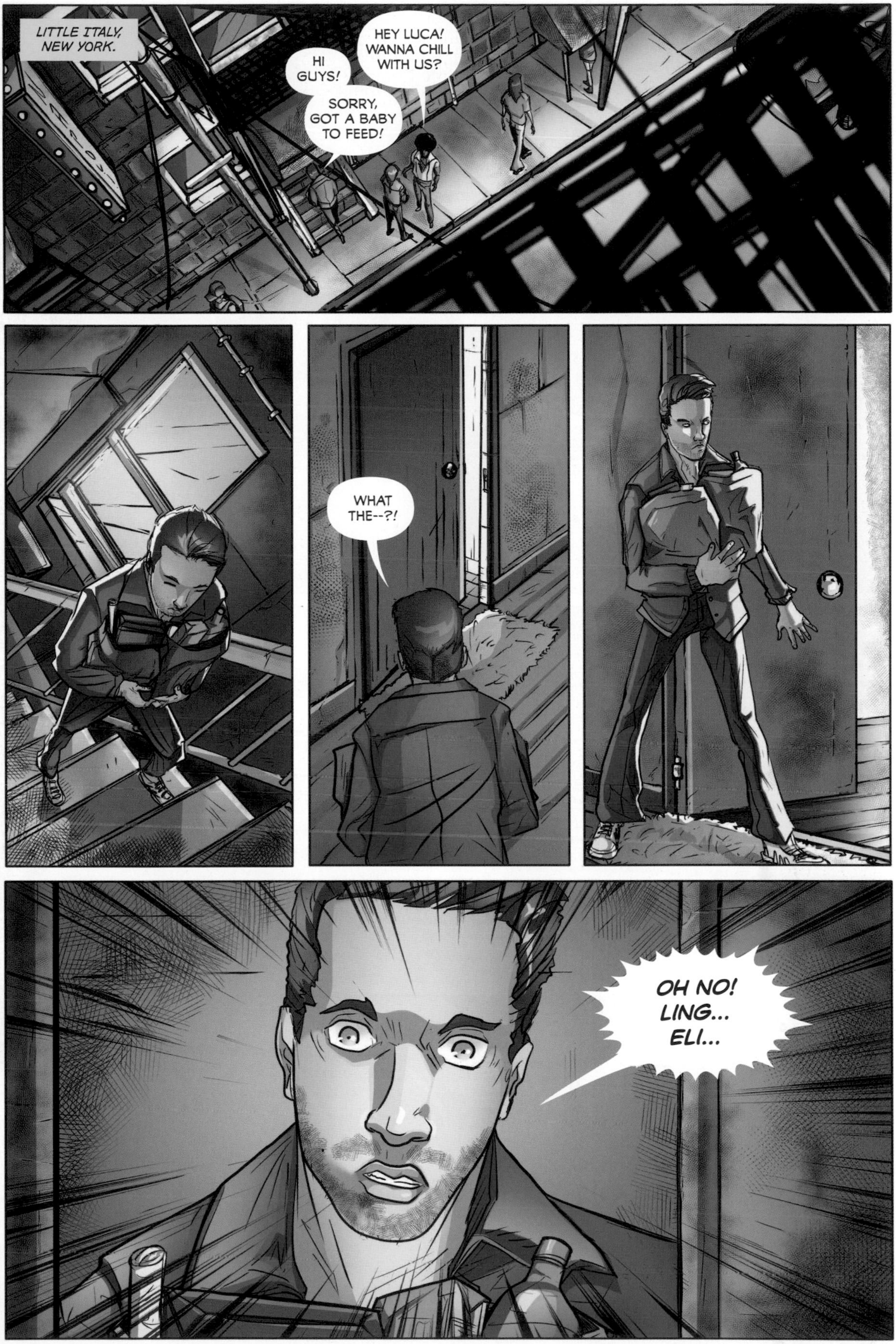

LITTLE ITALY, NEW YORK.
HI GUYS!
HEY LUCA! WANNA CHILL WITH US?
SORRY, GOT A BABY TO FEED!
WHAT THE--?!
OH NO! LING... ELI...

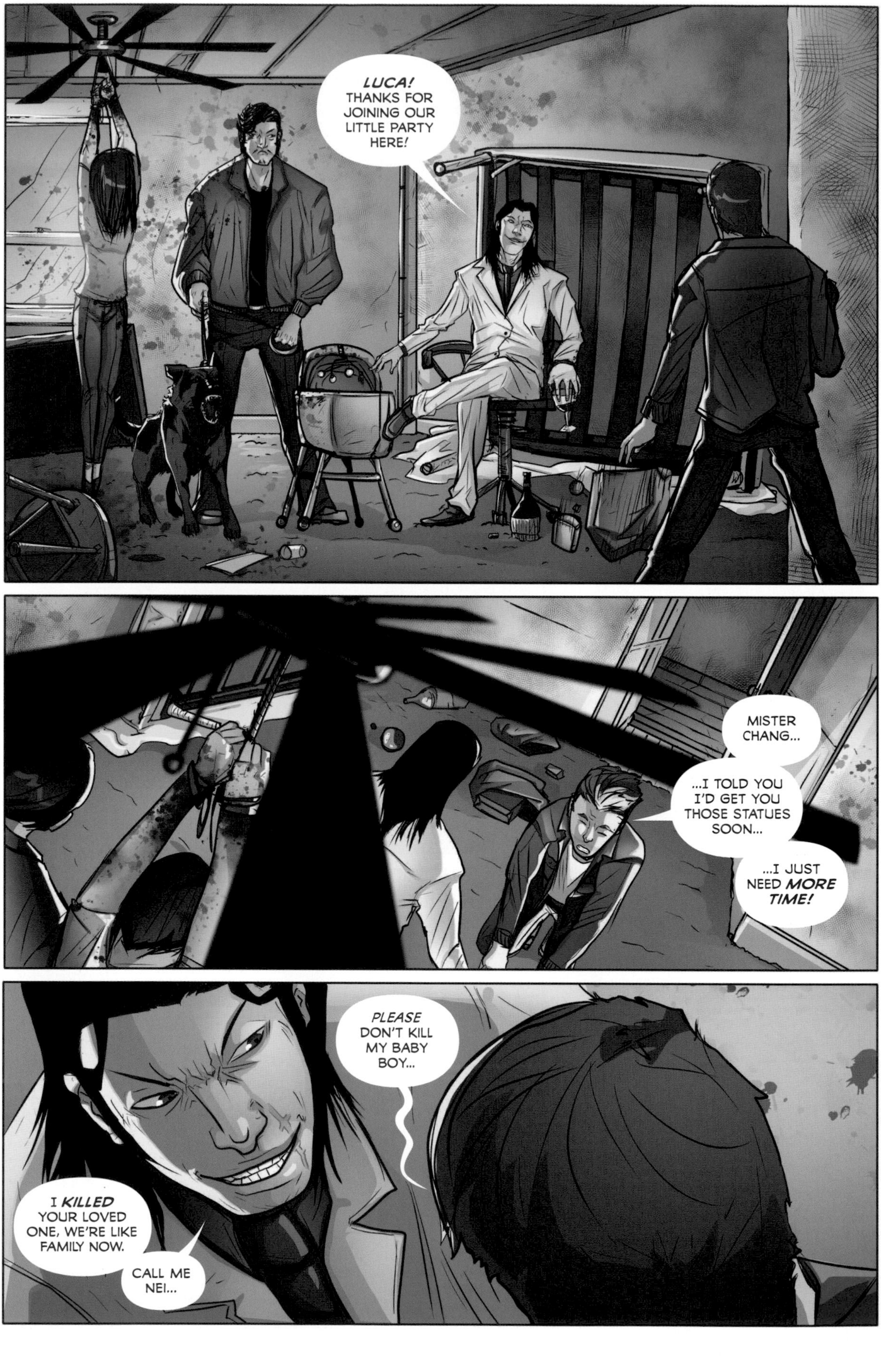
LUCA! THANKS FOR JOINING OUR LITTLE PARTY HERE!
MISTER CHANG...
...I TOLD YOU I'D GET YOU THOSE STATUES SOON...
...I JUST NEED MORE TIME!
PLEASE DON'T KILL MY BABY BOY...
I KILLED YOUR LOVED ONE, WE'RE LIKE FAMILY NOW.
CALL ME NEI...

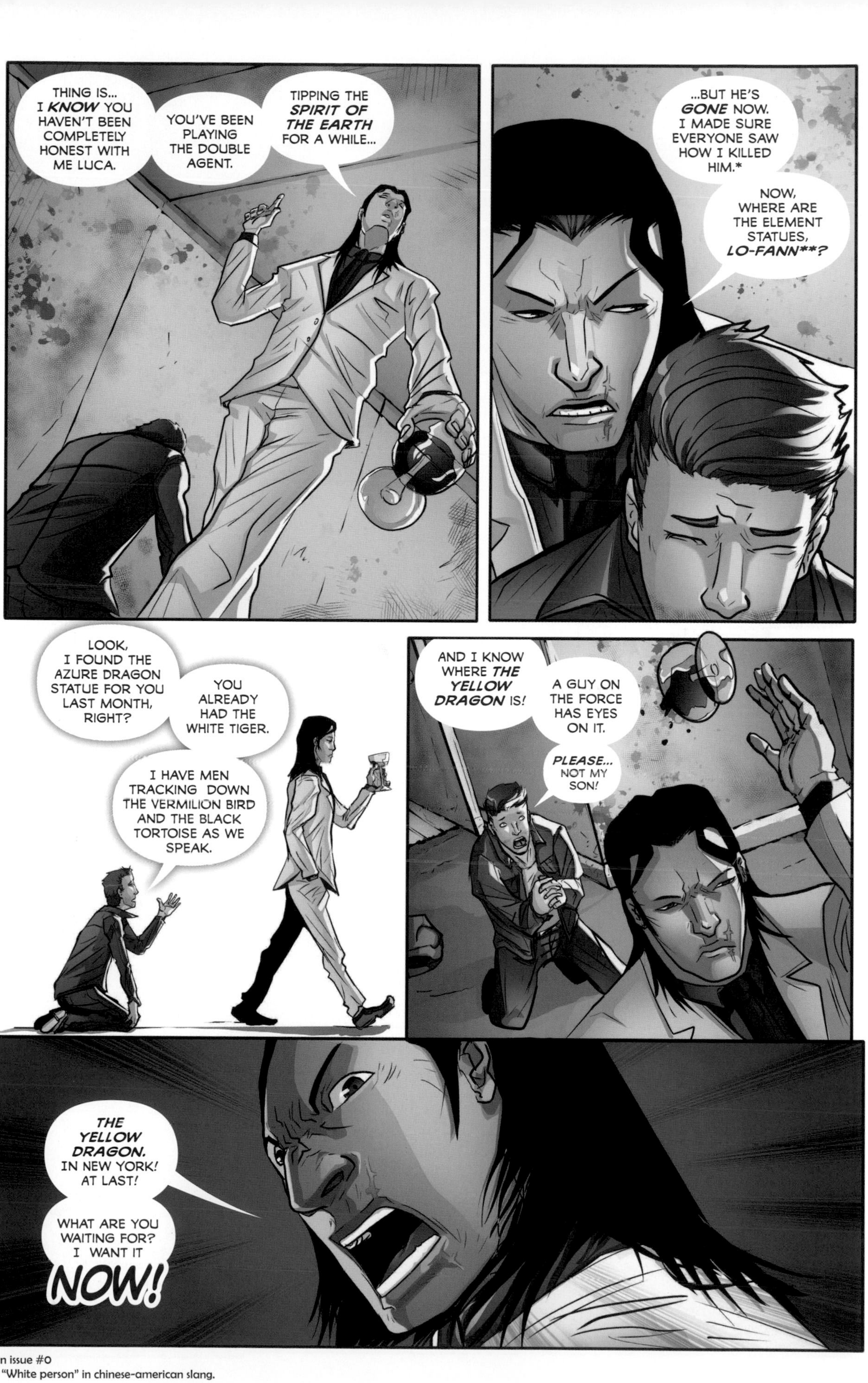
THING IS... I KNOW YOU HAVEN'T BEEN COMPLETELY HONEST WITH ME LUCA.
YOU'VE BEEN PLAYING THE DOUBLE AGENT.
TIPPING THE SPIRIT OF THE EARTH FOR A WHILE...
...BUT HE'S GONE NOW. I MADE SURE EVERYONE SAW HOW I KILLED HIM.*
NOW, WHERE ARE THE ELEMENT STATUES, LO-FANN**?
LOOK, I FOUND THE AZURE DRAGON STATUE FOR YOU LAST MONTH, RIGHT?
YOU ALREADY HAD THE WHITE TIGER.
I HAVE MEN TRACKING DOWN THE VERMILION BIRD AND THE BLACK TORTOISE AS WE SPEAK.
AND I KNOW WHERE THE YELLOW DRAGON IS!
A GUY ON THE FORCE HAS EYES ON IT.
PLEASE... NOT MY SON!
THE YELLOW DRAGON. IN NEW YORK! AT LAST!
WHAT ARE YOU WAITING FOR? I WANT IT
NOW!

* In issue #0

** "White person" in chinese-american slang.

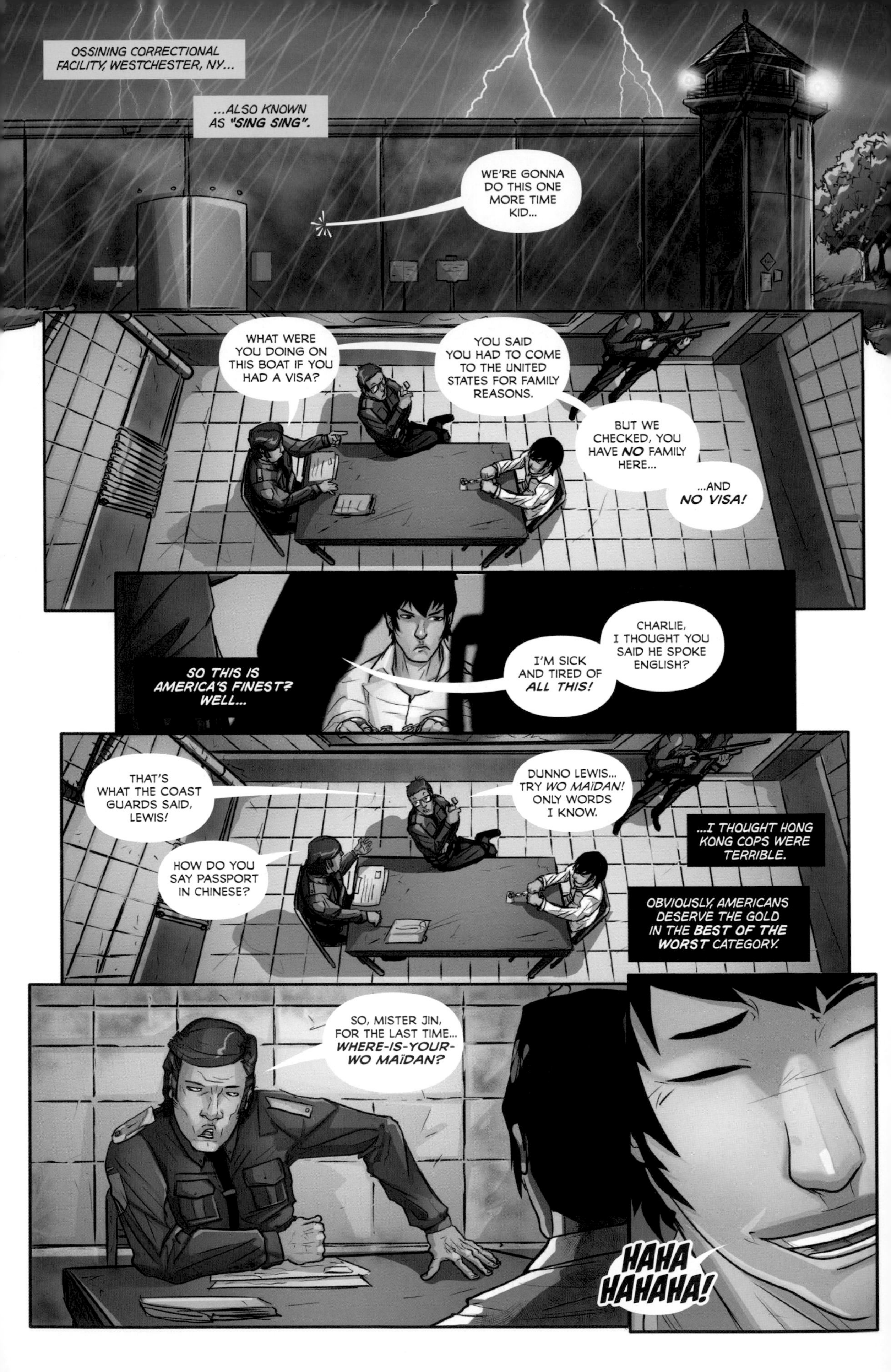

OSSINING CORRECTIONAL FACILITY, WESTCHESTER, NY...
...ALSO KNOWN AS "SING SING".
WE'RE GONNA DO THIS ONE MORE TIME KID...
WHAT WERE YOU DOING ON THIS BOAT IF YOU HAD A VISA?
YOU SAID YOU HAD TO COME TO THE UNITED STATES FOR FAMILY REASONS.
BUT WE CHECKED, YOU HAVE NO FAMILY HERE...
...AND NO VISA!
SO THIS IS AMERICA'S FINEST? WELL...
I'M SICK AND TIRED OF ALL THIS!
CHARLIE, I THOUGHT YOU SAID HE SPOKE ENGLISH?
THAT'S WHAT THE COAST GUARDS SAID, LEWIS!
DUNNO LEWIS... TRY WO MAÏDAN! ONLY WORDS I KNOW.
HOW DO YOU SAY PASSPORT IN CHINESE?
...I THOUGHT HONG KONG COPS WERE TERRIBLE.
OBVIOUSLY, AMERICANS DESERVE THE GOLD IN THE BEST OF THE WORST CATEGORY.
SO, MISTER JIN, FOR THE LAST TIME... WHERE-IS-YOUR-WO MAÏDAN?
HAHA HAHAHA!

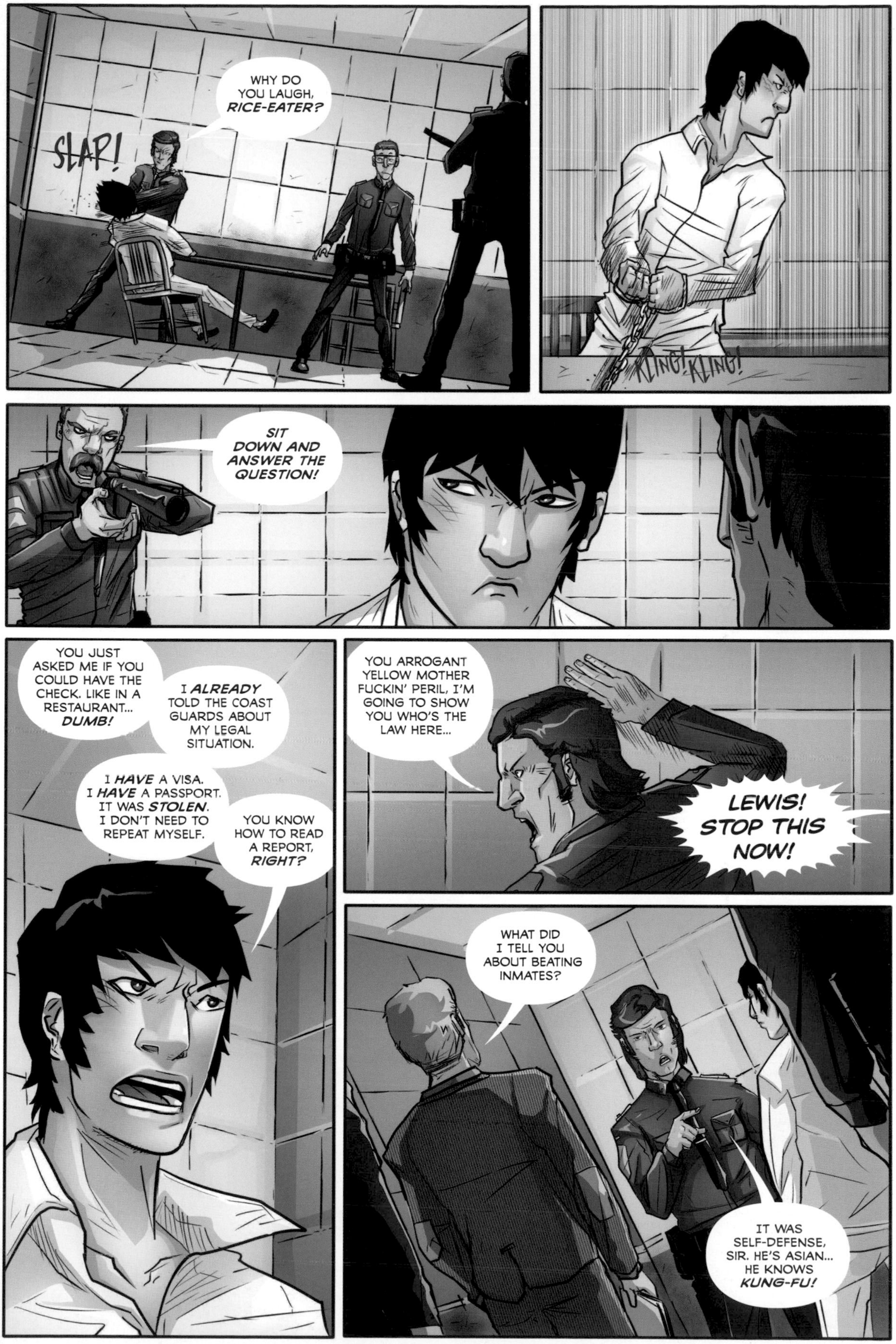
WHY DO YOU LAUGH, RICE-EATER?
SLAP!
KLING! KLING!
SIT DOWN AND ANSWER THE QUESTION!
YOU JUST ASKED ME IF YOU COULD HAVE THE CHECK. LIKE IN A RESTAURANT... DUMB!
I ALREADY TOLD THE COAST GUARDS ABOUT MY LEGAL SITUATION.
I HAVE A VISA. I HAVE A PASSPORT. IT WAS STOLEN. I DON'T NEED TO REPEAT MYSELF.
YOU KNOW HOW TO READ A REPORT, RIGHT?
YOU ARROGANT YELLOW MOTHER FUCKIN' PERIL, I'M GOING TO SHOW YOU WHO'S THE LAW HERE...
LEWIS! STOP THIS NOW!
WHAT DID I TELL YOU ABOUT BEATING INMATES?
IT WAS SELF-DEFENSE, SIR. HE'S ASIAN... HE KNOWS KUNG-FU!

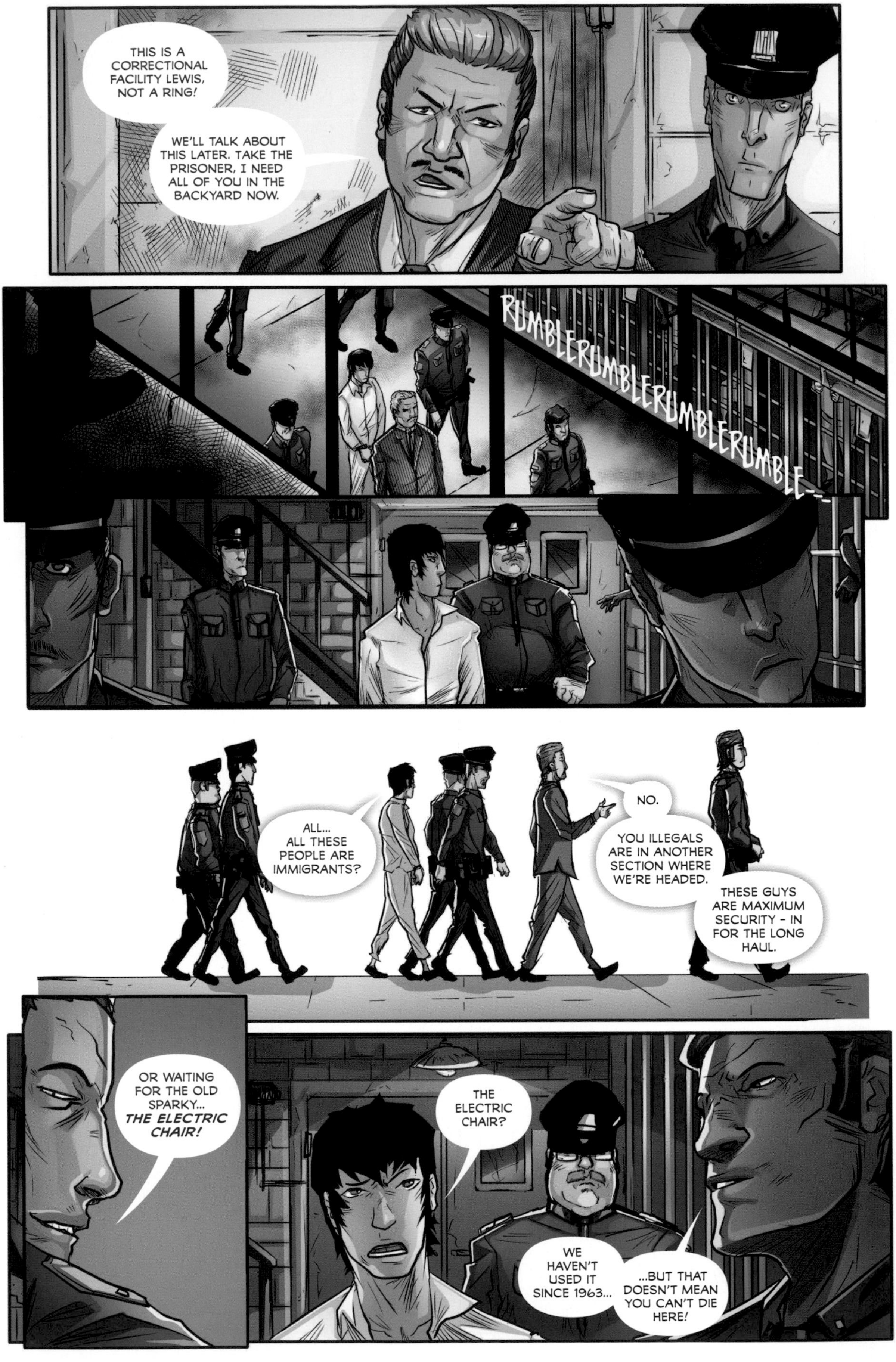

THIS IS A CORRECTIONAL FACILITY LEWIS, NOT A RING!
WE'LL TALK ABOUT THIS LATER. TAKE THE PRISONER, I NEED ALL OF YOU IN THE BACKYARD NOW.
RUMBLERUMBLERUMBLERUMBLERUMBLE---
ALL... ALL THESE PEOPLE ARE IMMIGRANTS?
NO.
YOU ILLEGALS ARE IN ANOTHER SECTION WHERE WE'RE HEADED.
THESE GUYS ARE MAXIMUM SECURITY - IN FOR THE LONG HAUL.
OR WAITING FOR THE OLD SPARKY... *THE ELECTRIC CHAIR!*
THE ELECTRIC CHAIR?
WE HAVEN'T USED IT SINCE 1963...
...BUT THAT DOESN'T MEAN YOU CAN'T DIE HERE!

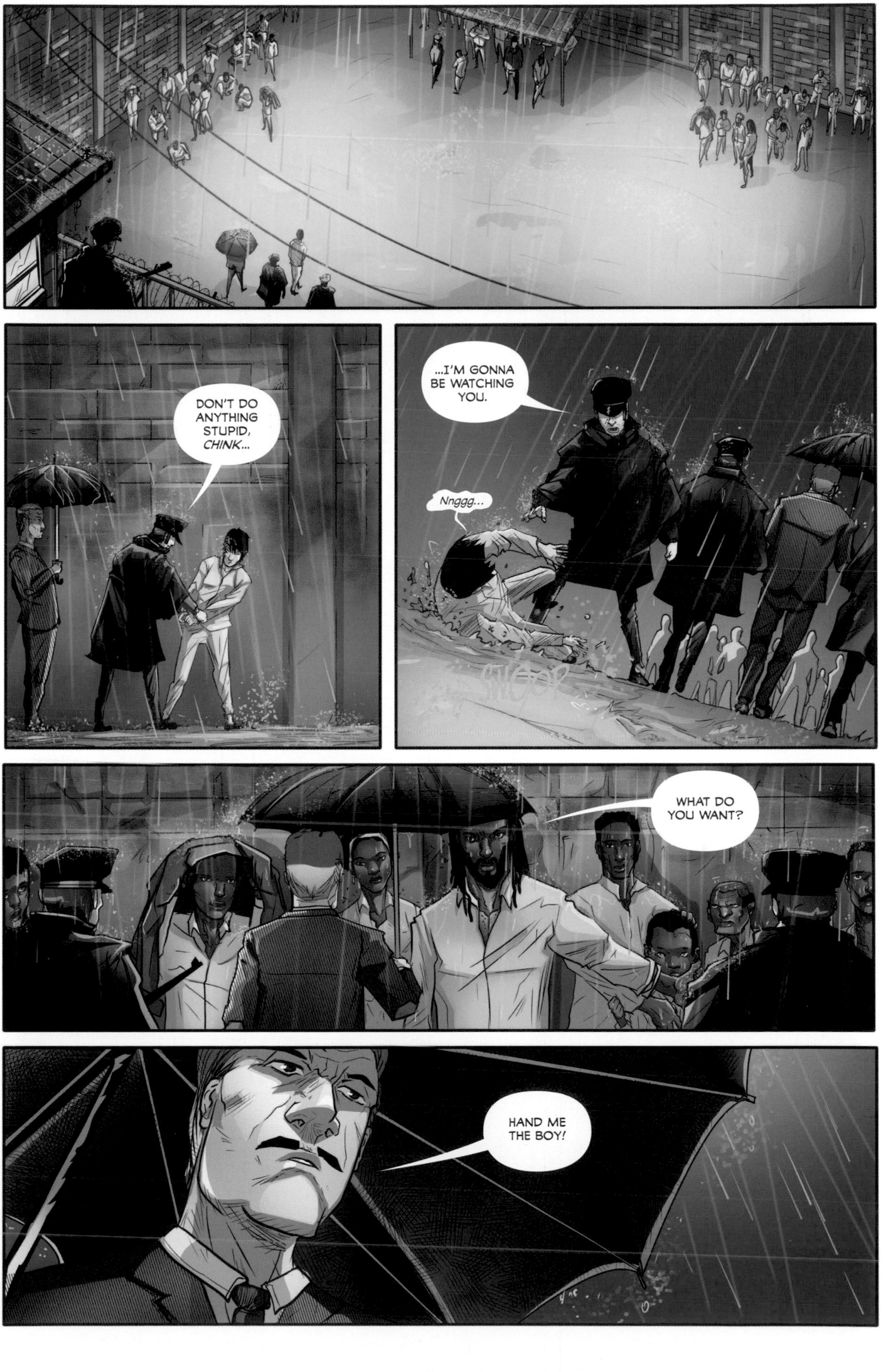
DON'T DO ANYTHING STUPID, *CHINK*...
...I'M GONNA BE WATCHING YOU.
Nnggg...
WHAT DO YOU WANT?
HAND ME THE BOY!

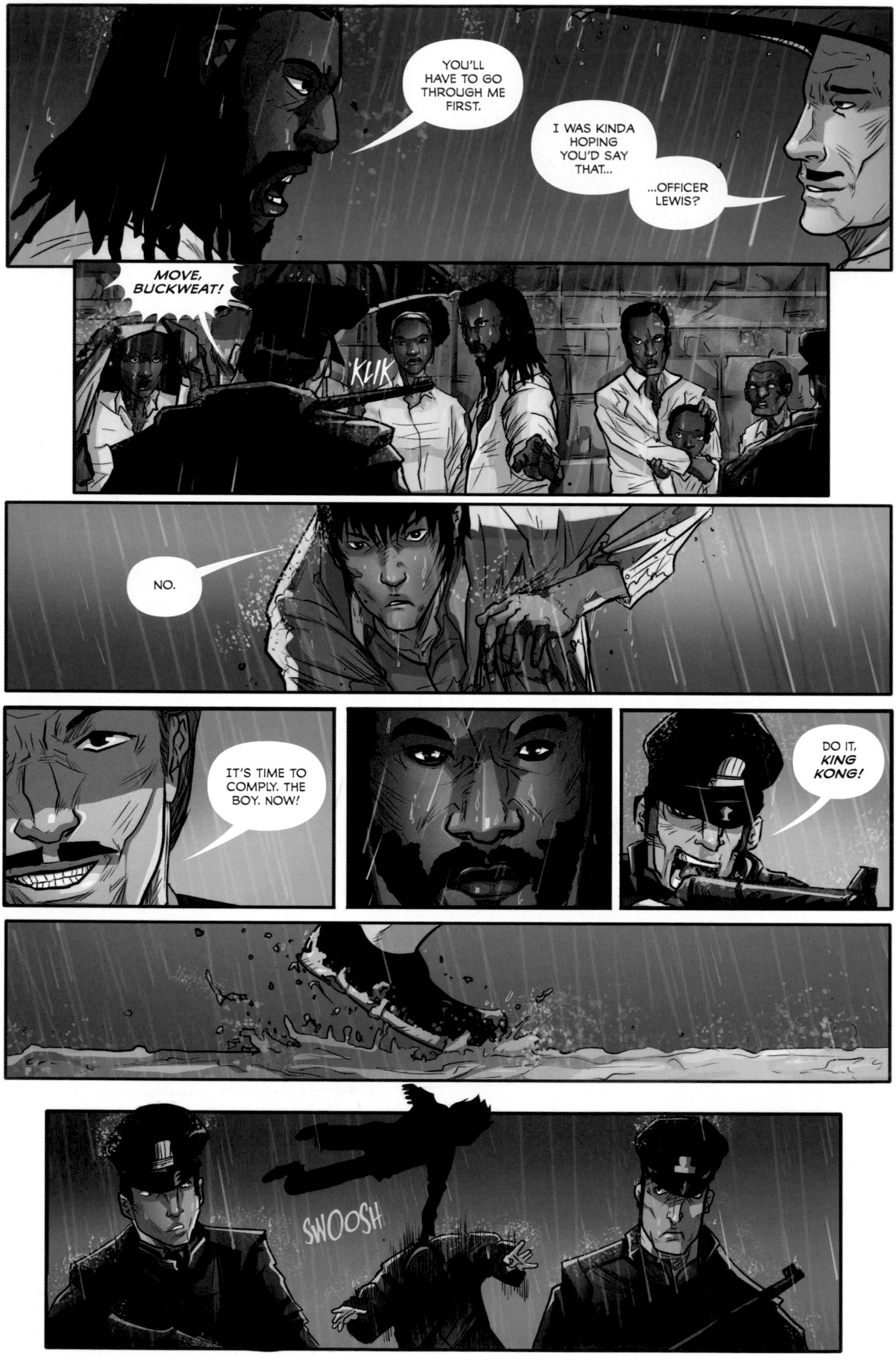

YOU'LL HAVE TO GO THROUGH ME FIRST.
I WAS KINDA HOPING YOU'D SAY THAT...
...OFFICER LEWIS?
MOVE, BUCKWEAT!
KLIK
NO.
IT'S TIME TO COMPLY. THE BOY. NOW!
DO IT, KING KONG!
SWOOSH

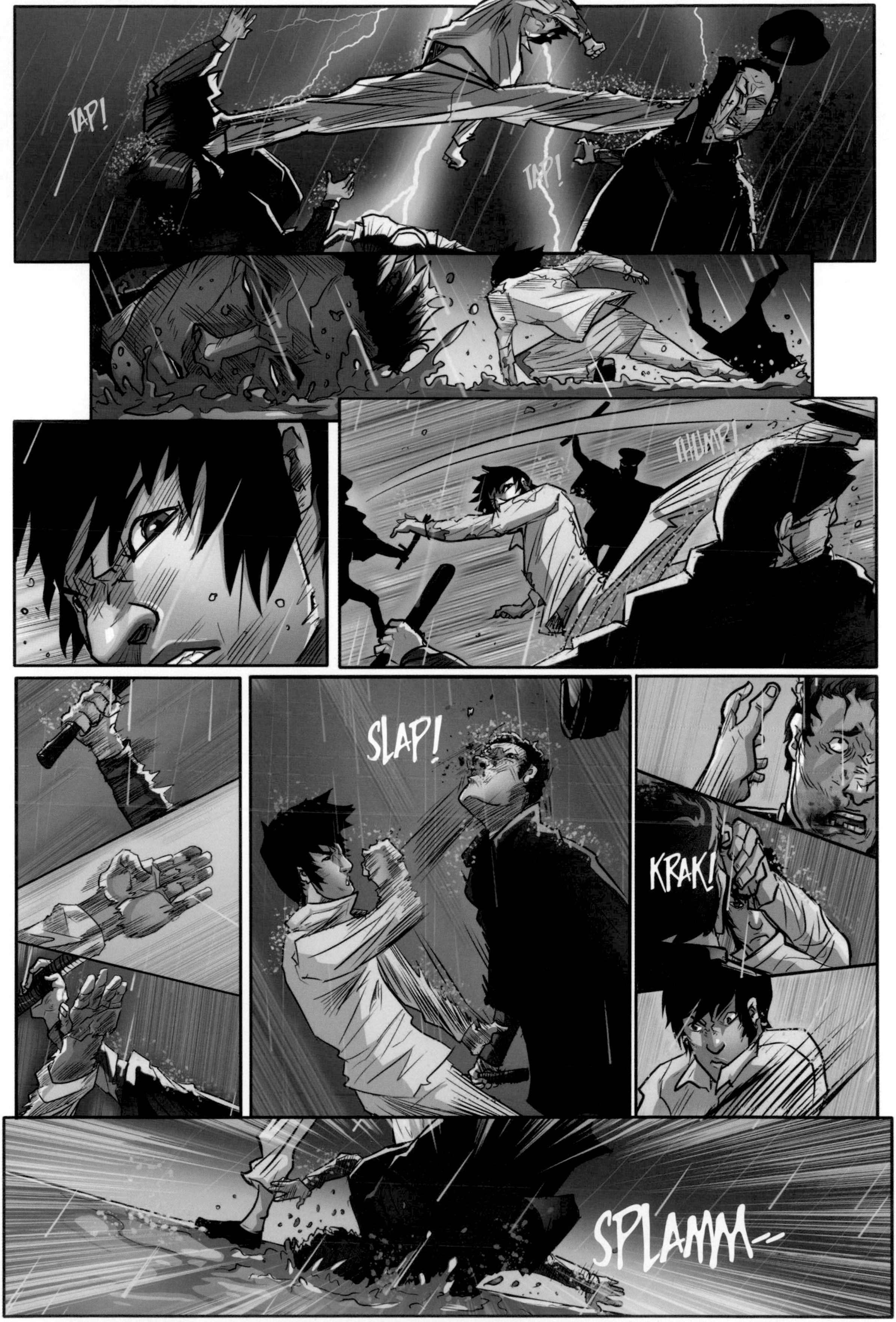
TAP!
TAP!
THUMP!
SLAP!
KRAK!
SPLAMM--

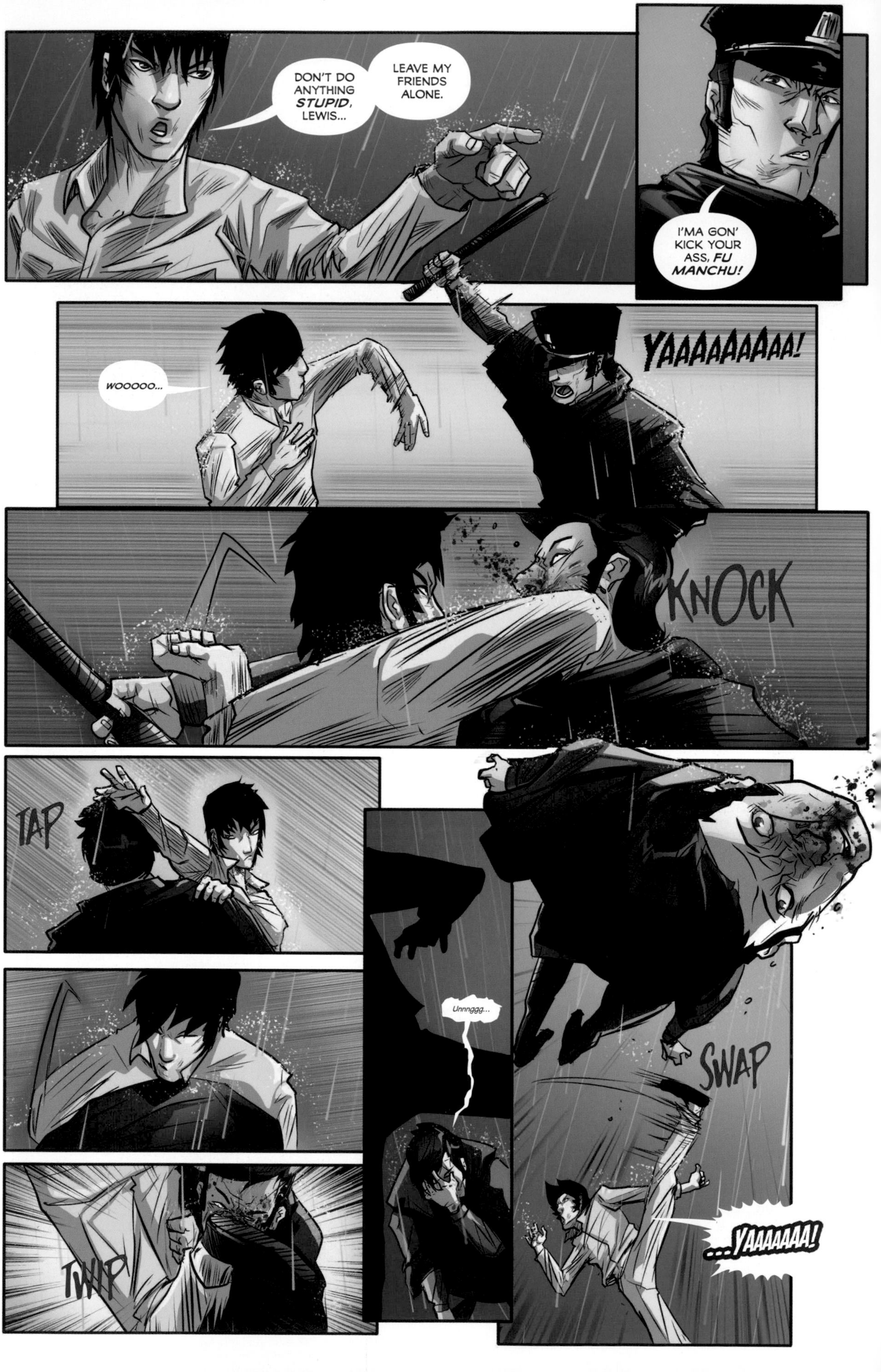

DON'T DO ANYTHING STUPID, LEWIS...
LEAVE MY FRIENDS ALONE.
I'MA GON' KICK YOUR ASS, FU MANCHU!
WOOOOO...
YAAAAAAAAA!
KNOCK
TAP
TWIP
Unnnggg...
SWAP
...YAAAAAAA!

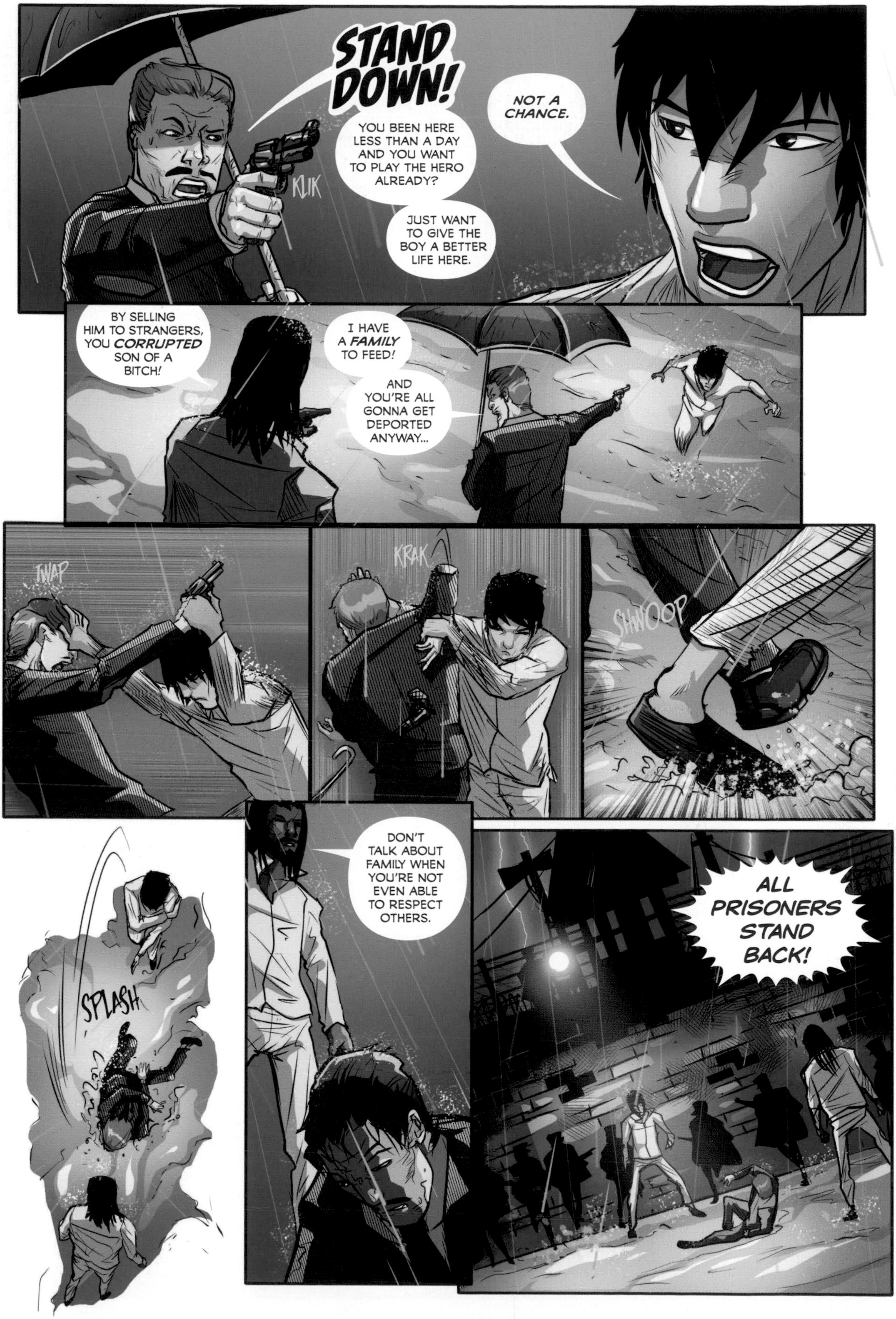
STAND DOWN!
KLIK
YOU BEEN HERE LESS THAN A DAY AND YOU WANT TO PLAY THE HERO ALREADY?
NOT A CHANCE.
JUST WANT TO GIVE THE BOY A BETTER LIFE HERE.
BY SELLING HIM TO STRANGERS, YOU CORRUPTED SON OF A BITCH!
I HAVE A FAMILY TO FEED!
AND YOU'RE ALL GONNA GET DEPORTED ANYWAY...
TWAP
KRAK
SHWOOP
SPLASH
DON'T TALK ABOUT FAMILY WHEN YOU'RE NOT EVEN ABLE TO RESPECT OTHERS.
ALL PRISONERS STAND BACK!

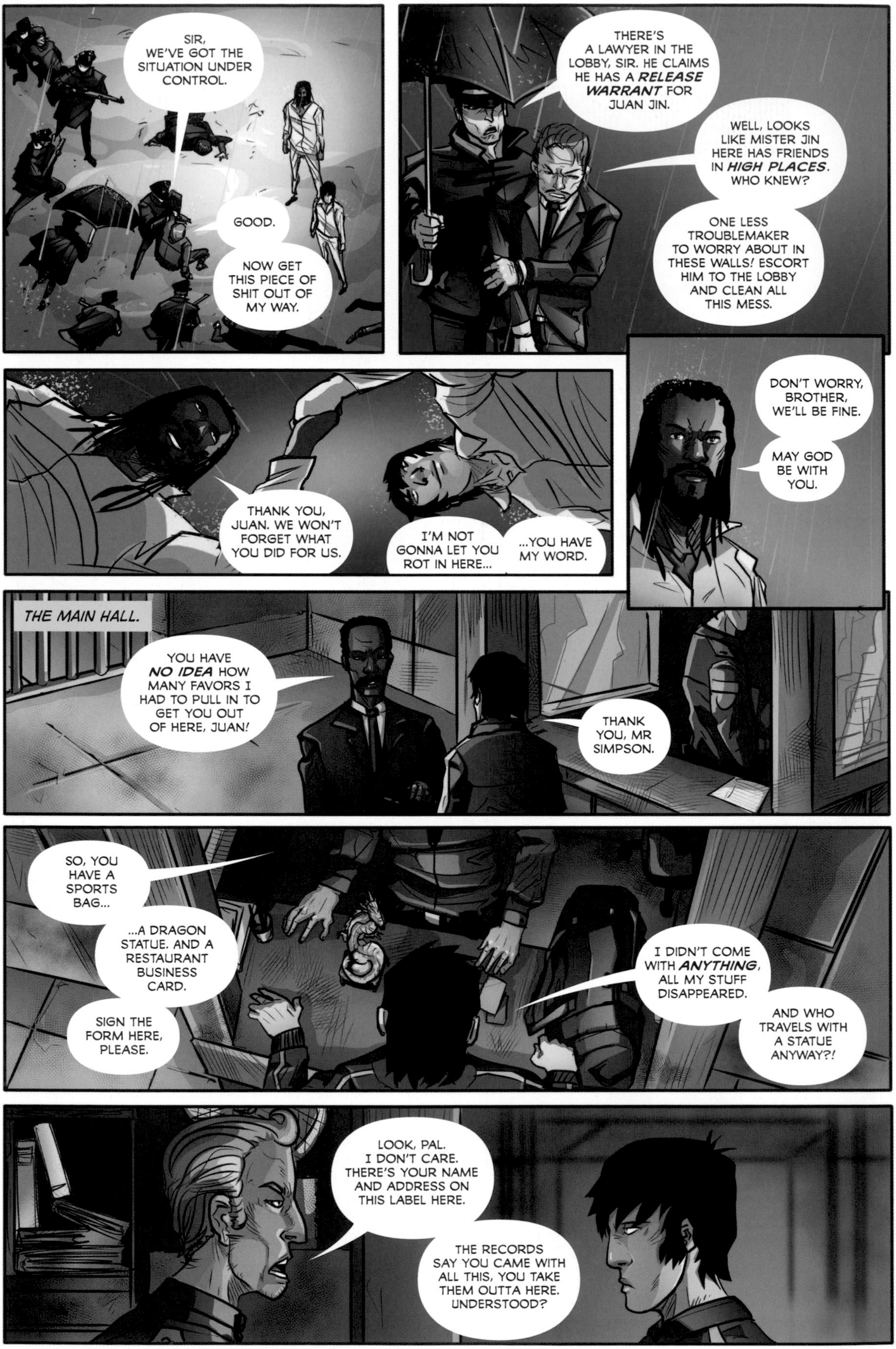
SIR, WE'VE GOT THE SITUATION UNDER CONTROL.
GOOD.
NOW GET THIS PIECE OF SHIT OUT OF MY WAY.
THERE'S A LAWYER IN THE LOBBY, SIR. HE CLAIMS HE HAS A **RELEASE WARRANT** FOR JUAN JIN.
WELL, LOOKS LIKE MISTER JIN HERE HAS FRIENDS IN **HIGH PLACES**. WHO KNEW?
ONE LESS TROUBLEMAKER TO WORRY ABOUT IN THESE WALLS! ESCORT HIM TO THE LOBBY AND CLEAN ALL THIS MESS.
THANK YOU, JUAN. WE WON'T FORGET WHAT YOU DID FOR US.
I'M NOT GONNA LET YOU ROT IN HERE...
...YOU HAVE MY WORD.
DON'T WORRY, BROTHER, WE'LL BE FINE.
MAY GOD BE WITH YOU.
THE MAIN HALL.
YOU HAVE **NO IDEA** HOW MANY FAVORS I HAD TO PULL IN TO GET YOU OUT OF HERE, JUAN!
THANK YOU, MR SIMPSON.
SO, YOU HAVE A SPORTS BAG...
...A DRAGON STATUE. AND A RESTAURANT BUSINESS CARD.
SIGN THE FORM HERE, PLEASE.
I DIDN'T COME WITH **ANYTHING**, ALL MY STUFF DISAPPEARED.
AND WHO TRAVELS WITH A STATUE ANYWAY?!
LOOK, PAL. I DON'T CARE. THERE'S YOUR NAME AND ADDRESS ON THIS LABEL HERE.
THE RECORDS SAY YOU CAME WITH ALL THIS, YOU TAKE THEM OUTTA HERE. UNDERSTOOD?

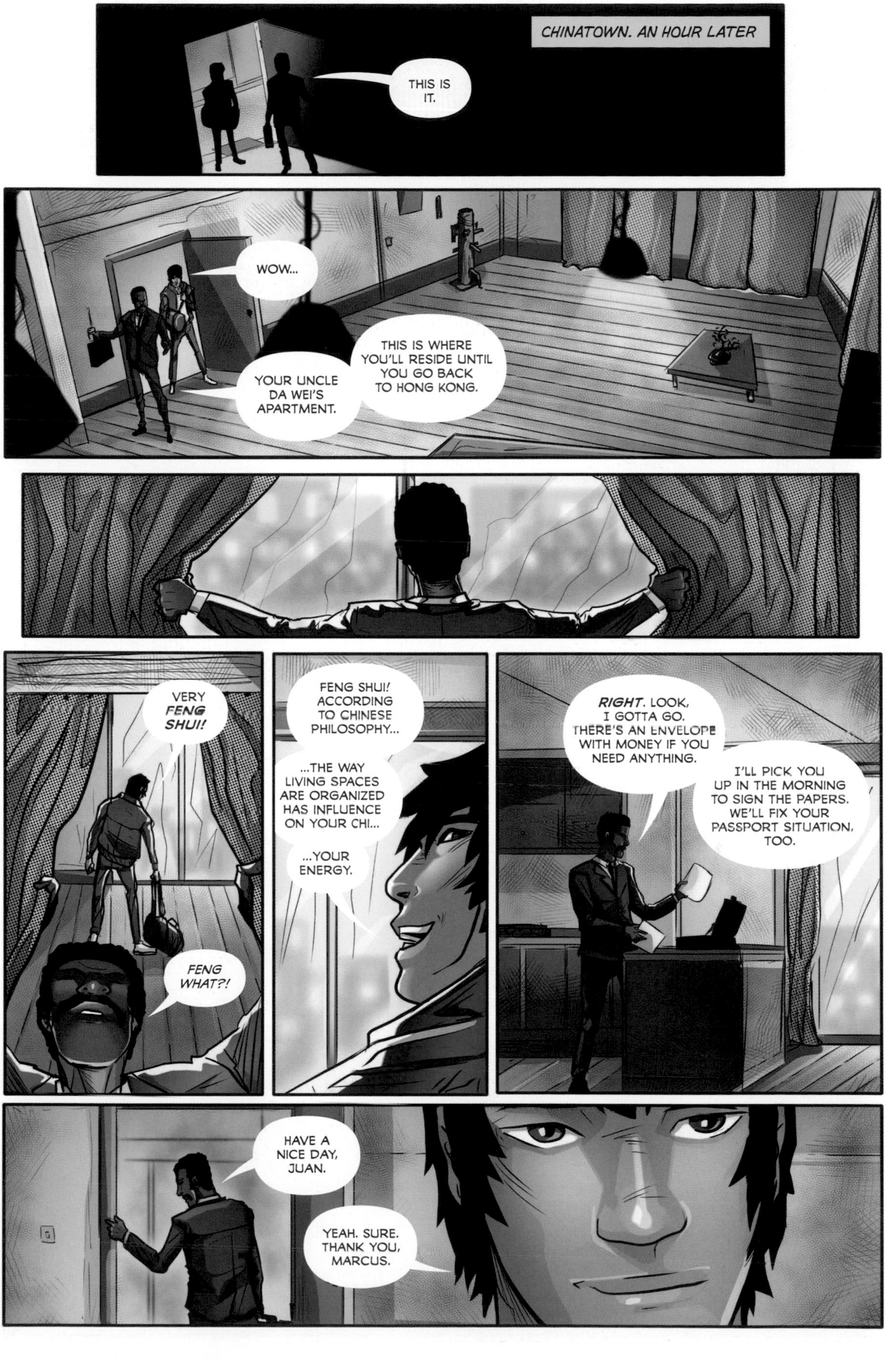
CHINATOWN. AN HOUR LATER
THIS IS IT.
WOW...
YOUR UNCLE DA WEI'S APARTMENT.
THIS IS WHERE YOU'LL RESIDE UNTIL YOU GO BACK TO HONG KONG.
VERY *FENG SHUI!*
FENG WHAT?!
FENG SHUI! ACCORDING TO CHINESE PHILOSOPHY...
...THE WAY LIVING SPACES ARE ORGANIZED HAS INFLUENCE ON YOUR CHI...
...YOUR ENERGY.
RIGHT. LOOK, I GOTTA GO. THERE'S AN ENVELOPE WITH MONEY IF YOU NEED ANYTHING.
I'LL PICK YOU UP IN THE MORNING TO SIGN THE PAPERS. WE'LL FIX YOUR PASSPORT SITUATION, TOO.
HAVE A NICE DAY, JUAN.
YEAH. SURE. THANK YOU, MARCUS.

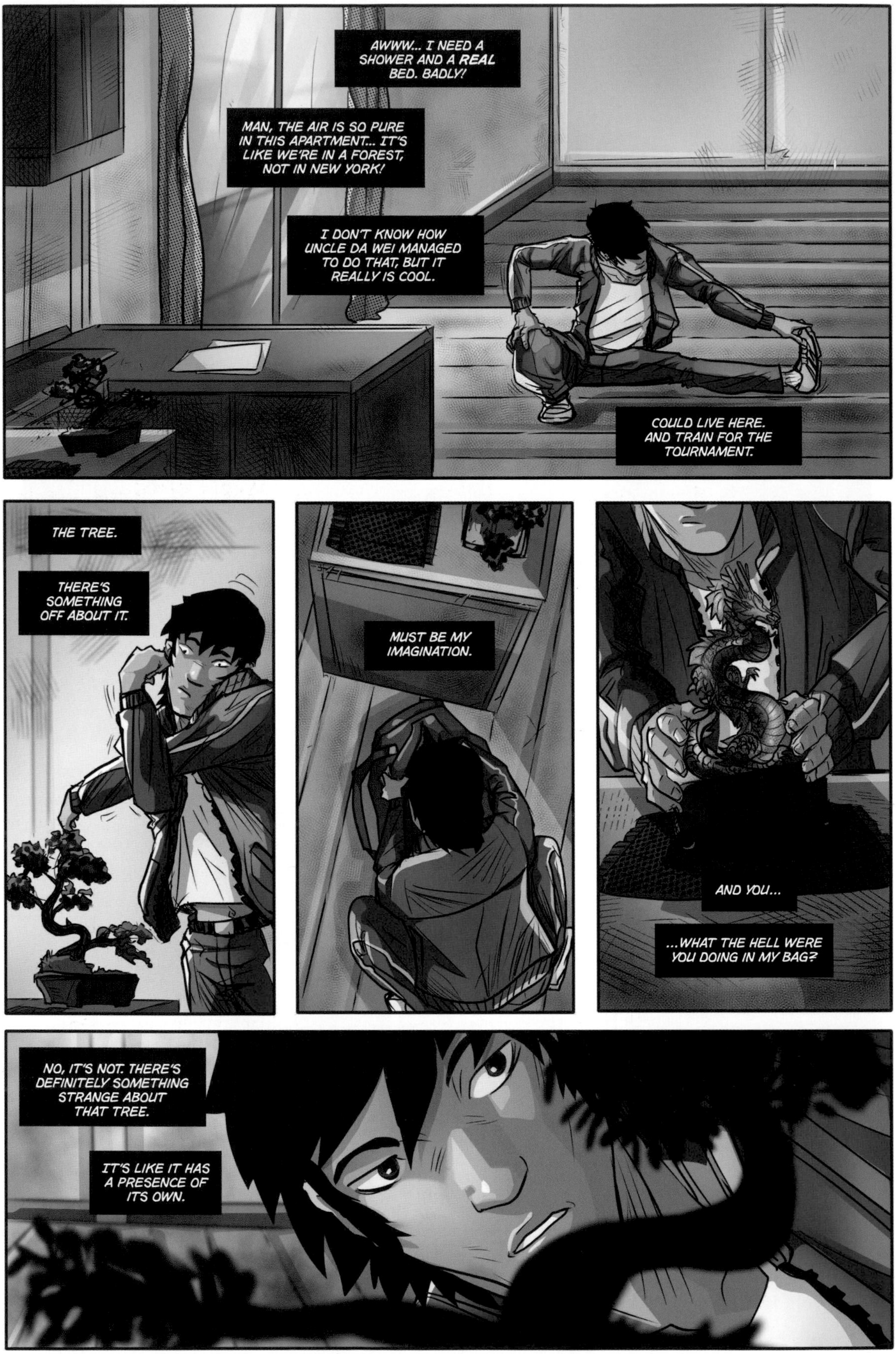
AWWW... I NEED A SHOWER AND A **REAL** BED. BADLY!
MAN, THE AIR IS SO PURE IN THIS APARTMENT... IT'S LIKE WE'RE IN A FOREST, NOT IN NEW YORK!
I DON'T KNOW HOW UNCLE DA WEI MANAGED TO DO THAT, BUT IT REALLY IS COOL.
COULD LIVE HERE. AND TRAIN FOR THE TOURNAMENT.
THE TREE.
THERE'S SOMETHING OFF ABOUT IT.
MUST BE MY IMAGINATION.
AND YOU...
...WHAT THE HELL WERE YOU DOING IN MY BAG?
NO, IT'S NOT. THERE'S DEFINITELY SOMETHING STRANGE ABOUT THAT TREE.
IT'S LIKE IT HAS A PRESENCE OF ITS OWN.

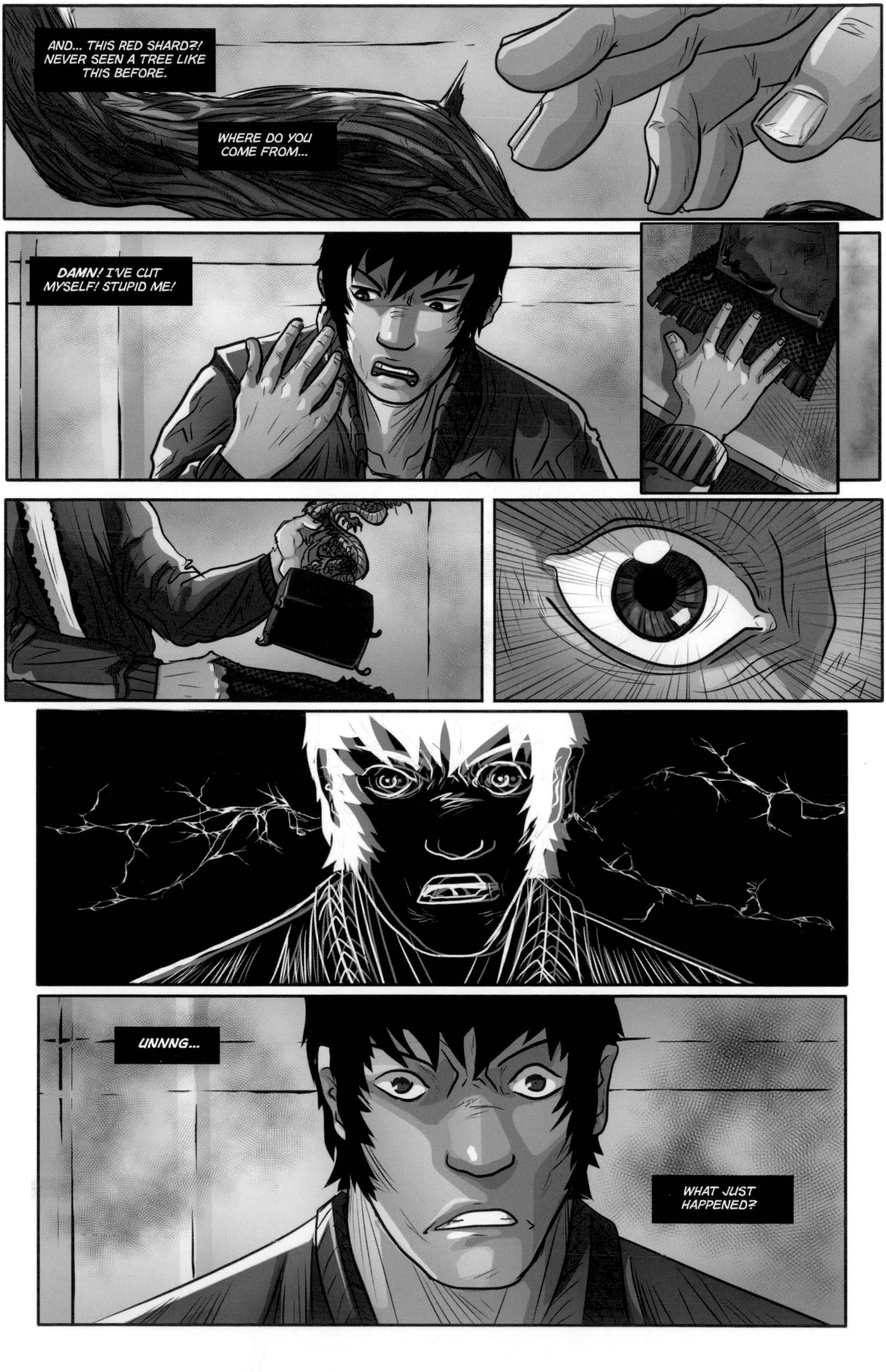
AND... THIS RED SHARD?! NEVER SEEN A TREE LIKE THIS BEFORE.
WHERE DO YOU COME FROM...
DAMN! I'VE CUT MYSELF! STUPID ME!
UNNNG...
WHAT JUST HAPPENED?

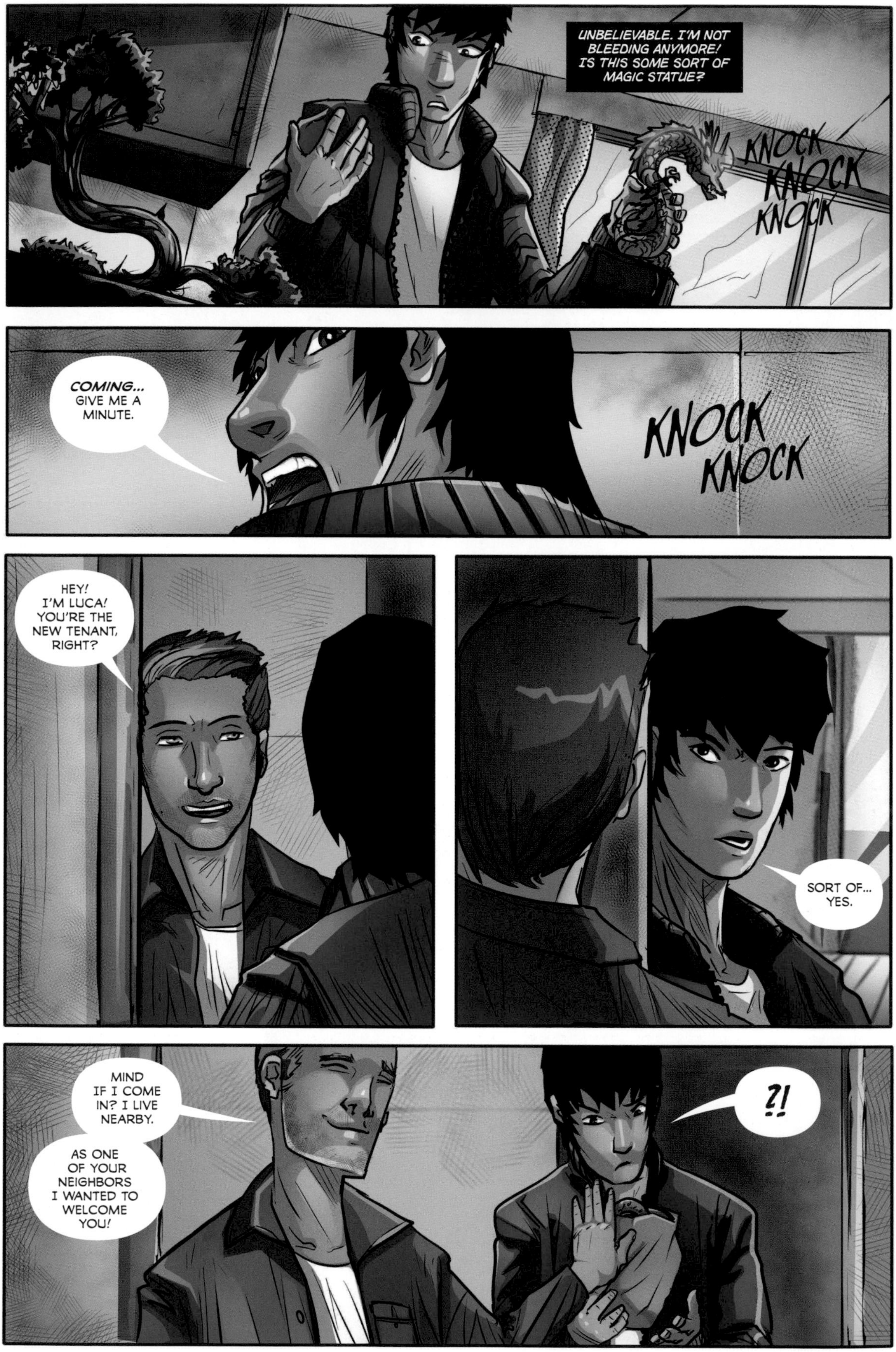
UNBELIEVABLE. I'M NOT BLEEDING ANYMORE! IS THIS SOME SORT OF MAGIC STATUE?
KNOCK KNOCK KNOCK
COMING... GIVE ME A MINUTE.
KNOCK KNOCK
HEY! I'M LUCA! YOU'RE THE NEW TENANT, RIGHT?
SORT OF... YES.
MIND IF I COME IN? I LIVE NEARBY.
AS ONE OF YOUR NEIGHBORS I WANTED TO WELCOME YOU!
?!

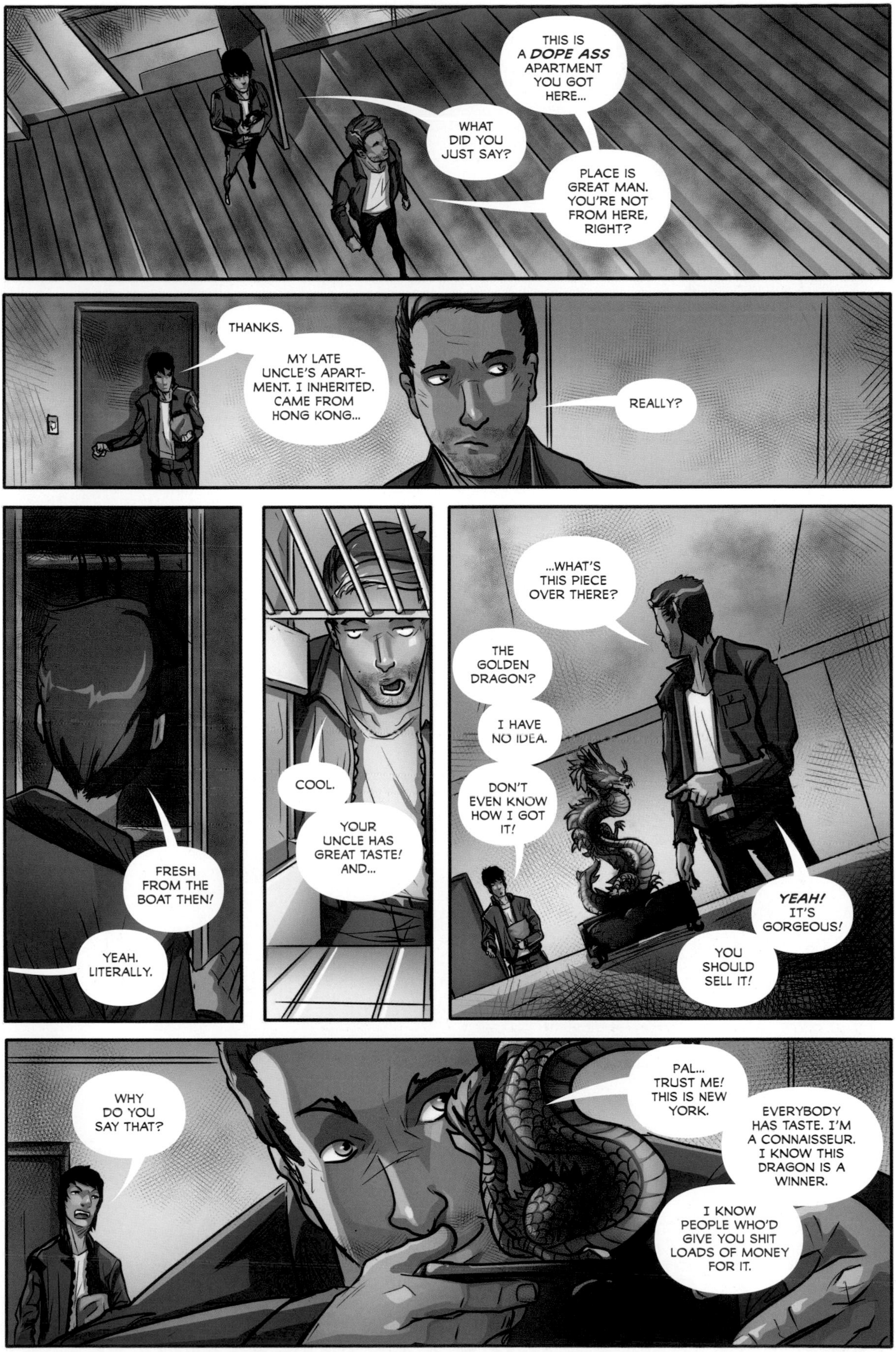
THIS IS A DOPE ASS APARTMENT YOU GOT HERE...
WHAT DID YOU JUST SAY?
PLACE IS GREAT MAN. YOU'RE NOT FROM HERE, RIGHT?
THANKS.
MY LATE UNCLE'S APART- MENT. I INHERITED. CAME FROM HONG KONG...
REALLY?
FRESH FROM THE BOAT THEN!
YEAH. LITERALLY.
COOL.
YOUR UNCLE HAS GREAT TASTE! AND...
...WHAT'S THIS PIECE OVER THERE?
THE GOLDEN DRAGON?
I HAVE NO IDEA.
DON'T EVEN KNOW HOW I GOT IT!
YEAH! IT'S GORGEOUS!
YOU SHOULD SELL IT!
WHY DO YOU SAY THAT?
PAL... TRUST ME! THIS IS NEW YORK.
EVERYBODY HAS TASTE. I'M A CONNAISSEUR. I KNOW THIS DRAGON IS A WINNER.
I KNOW PEOPLE WHO'D GIVE YOU SHIT LOADS OF MONEY FOR IT.

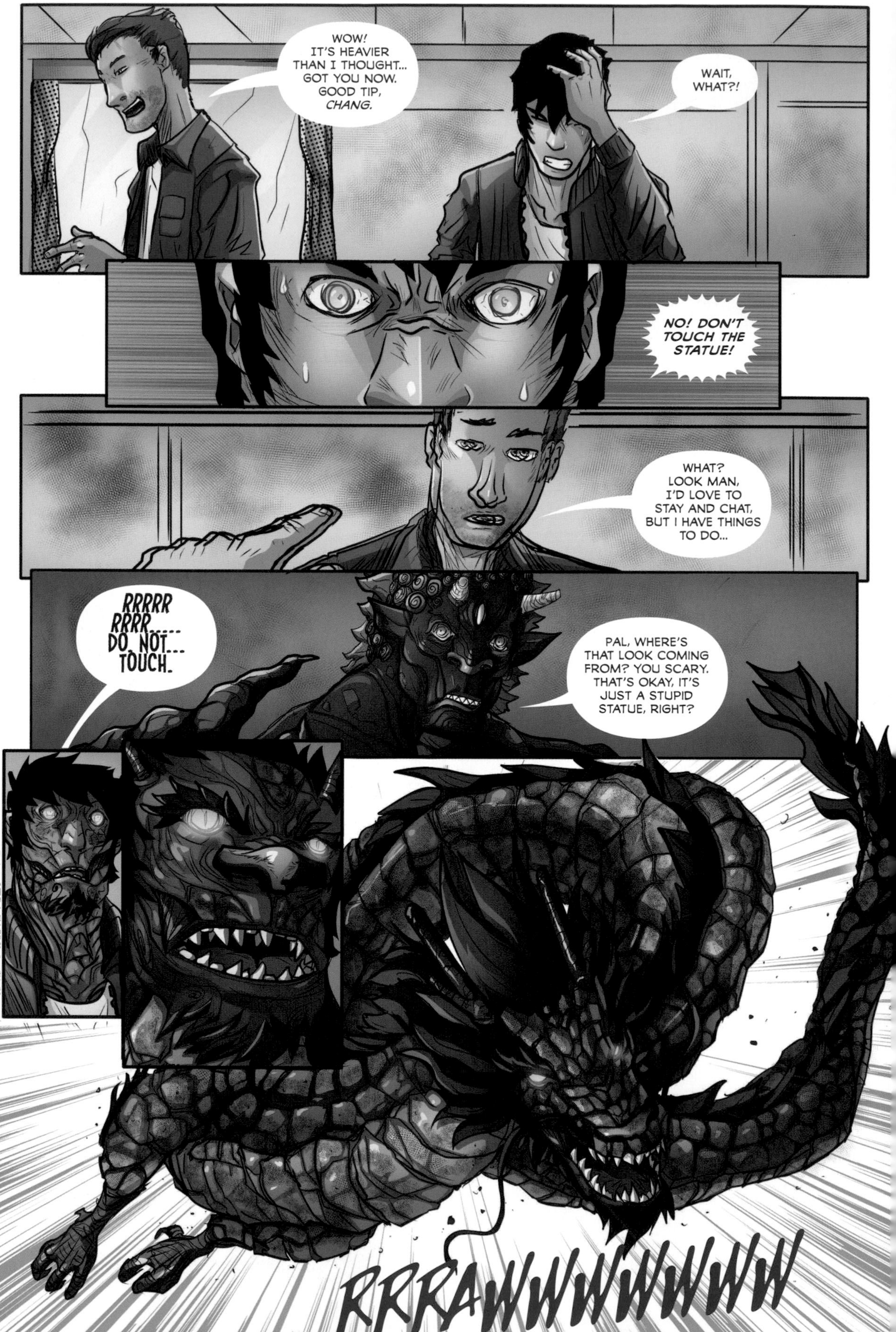
WOW! IT'S HEAVIER THAN I THOUGHT... GOT YOU NOW. GOOD TIP, *CHANG.*
WAIT, WHAT?!
NO! DON'T TOUCH THE STATUE!
WHAT? LOOK MAN, I'D LOVE TO STAY AND CHAT, BUT I HAVE THINGS TO DO...
RRRRR RRRR..... DO. NOT... TOUCH.
PAL, WHERE'S THAT LOOK COMING FROM? YOU SCARY. THAT'S OKAY, IT'S JUST A STUPID STATUE, RIGHT?
RRRAWWWWWWWW

RHAAAAA...

MAN, I'M SORRY,
YOU'RE PROBABLY
A GOOD GUY, BUT
I NEED THIS STATUE...
NEI CHANG'S GONNA
KILL MY SON IF I
DON'T BRING IT!

KLINK

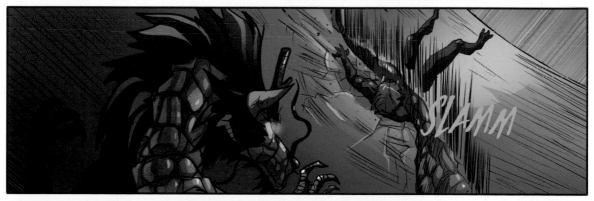

SLAMM

DUDE,
LEMME
GO...

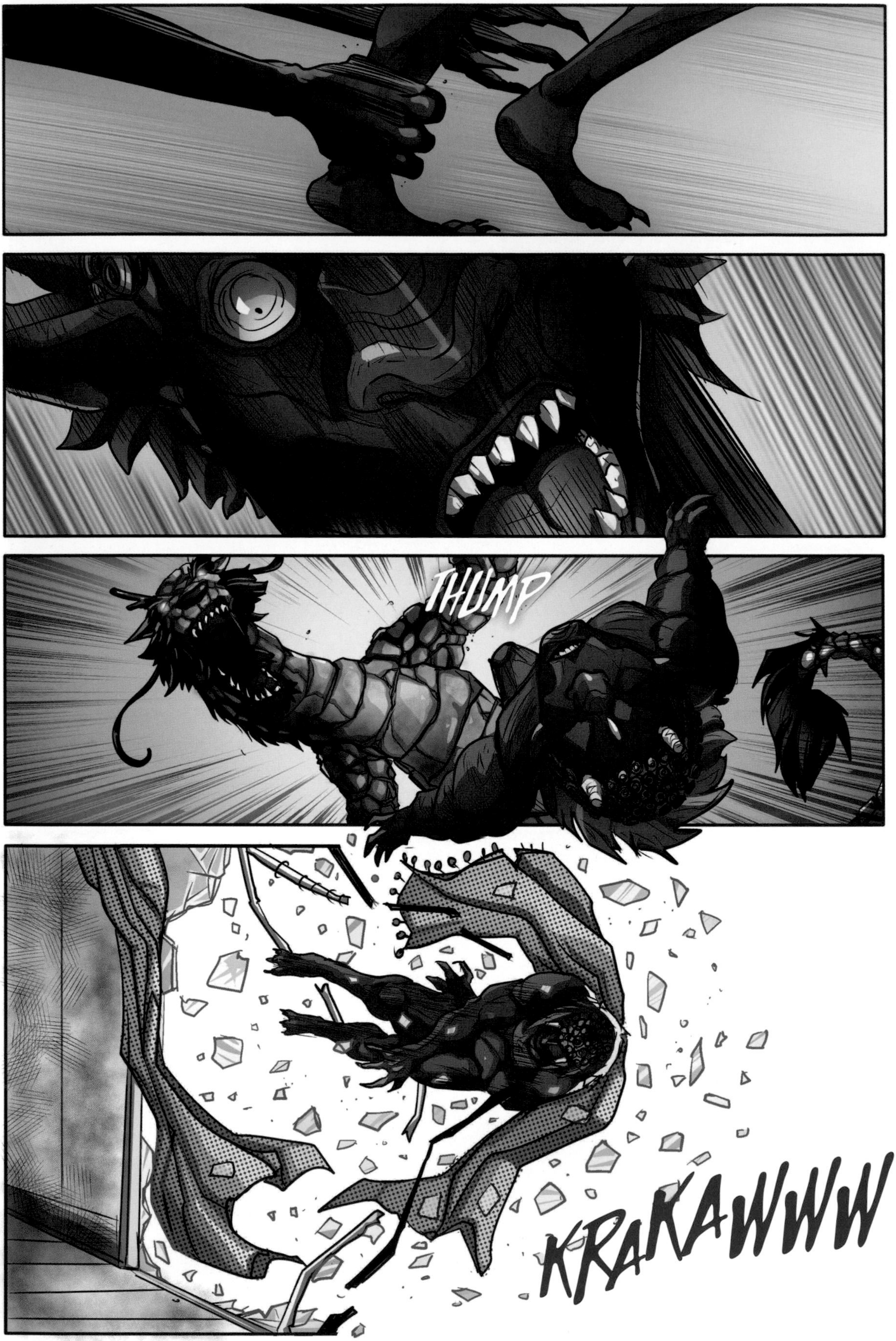
THUMP
KRAKAWWW

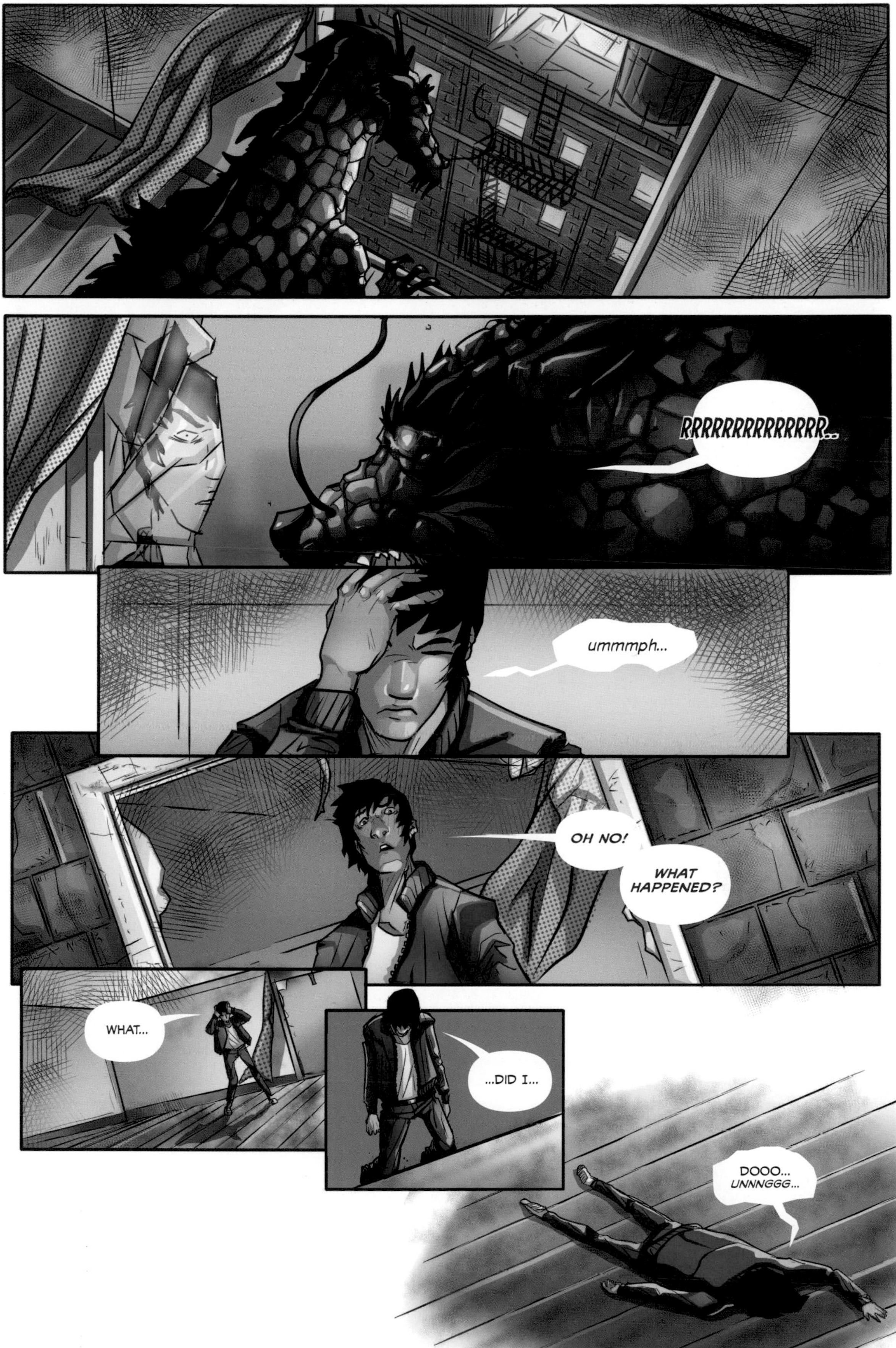
RRRRRRRRRRRRRR...
ummmph...
OH NO!
WHAT HAPPENED?
WHAT...
...DID I...
DOOO...
UNNNGGG...

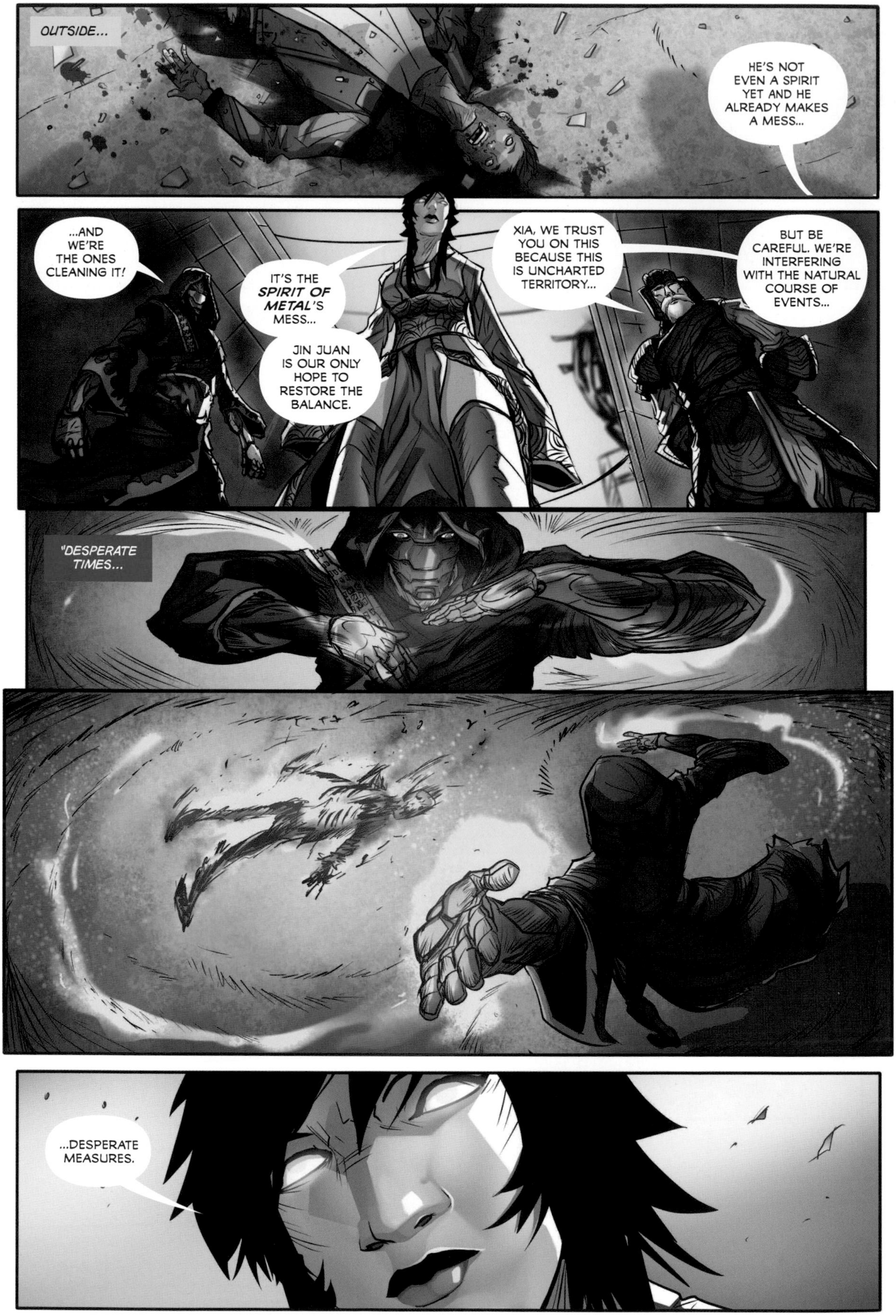
OUTSIDE...
HE'S NOT EVEN A SPIRIT YET AND HE ALREADY MAKES A MESS...
...AND WE'RE THE ONES CLEANING IT!
IT'S THE SPIRIT OF METAL'S MESS...
JIN JUAN IS OUR ONLY HOPE TO RESTORE THE BALANCE.
XIA, WE TRUST YOU ON THIS BECAUSE THIS IS UNCHARTED TERRITORY...
BUT BE CAREFUL. WE'RE INTERFERING WITH THE NATURAL COURSE OF EVENTS...
"DESPERATE TIMES...
...DESPERATE MEASURES.

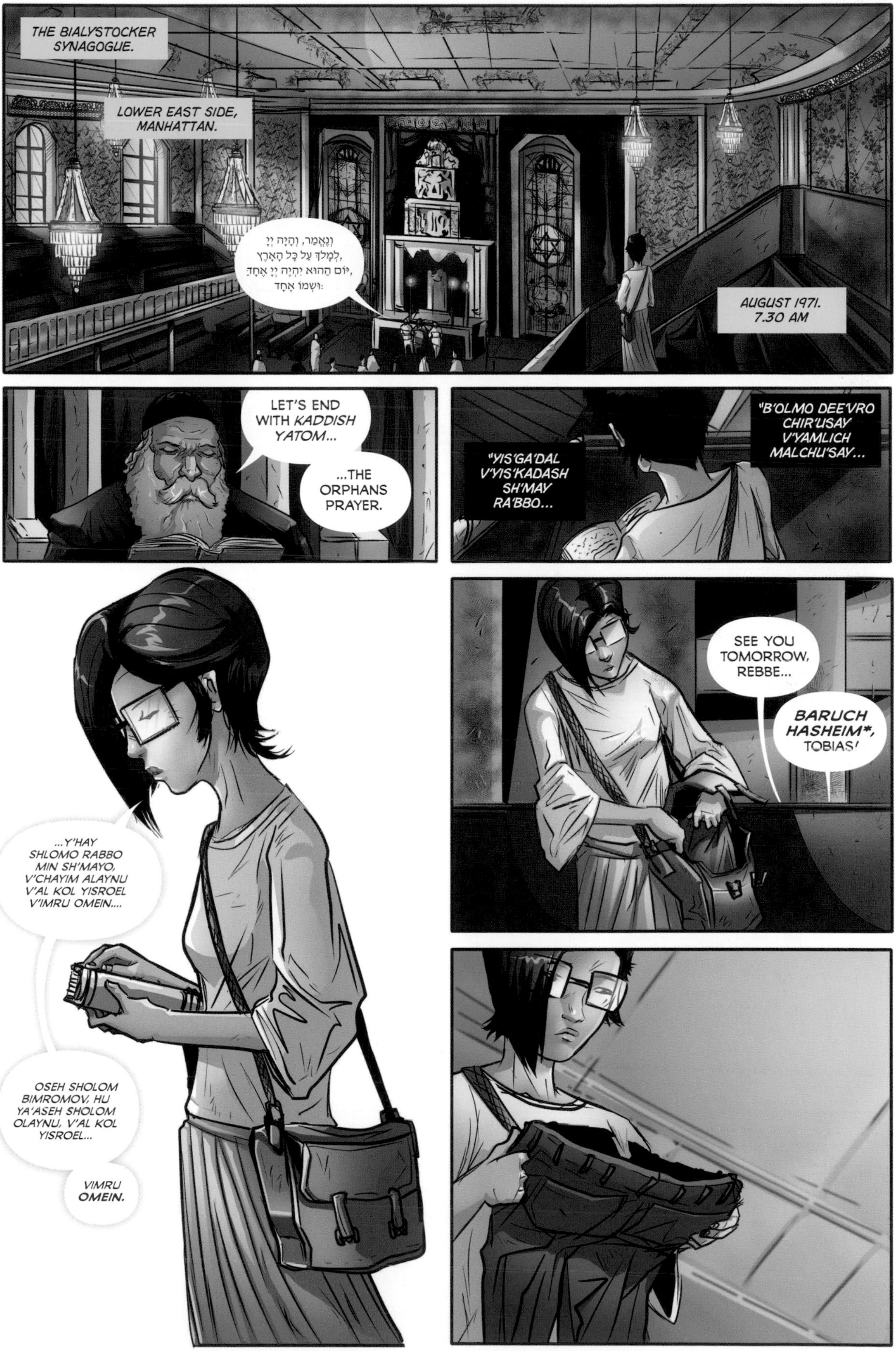
THE BIALYSTOCKER SYNAGOGUE.
LOWER EAST SIDE, MANHATTAN.
וְנֶאֱמַר, וְהָיָה יְיָ לְמֶלֶךְ עַל כָּל הָאָרֶץ, בַּיּוֹם הַהוּא יִהְיֶה יְיָ אֶחָד, וּשְׁמוֹ אֶחָד:
AUGUST 1971. 7.30 AM
LET'S END WITH KADDISH YATOM...
...THE ORPHANS PRAYER.
"YIS'GA'DAL V'YIS'KADASH SH'MAY RA'BBO...
"B'OLMO DEE'VRO CHIR'USAY V'YAMLICH MALCHU'SAY...
...Y'HAY SHLOMO RABBO MIN SH'MAYO, V'CHAYIM ALAYNU V'AL KOL YISROEL V'IMRU OMEIN....
OSEH SHOLOM BIMROMOV, HU YA'ASEH SHOLOM OLAYNU, V'AL KOL YISROEL...
VIMRU OMEIN.
SEE YOU TOMORROW, REBBE...
BARUCH HASHEIM*, TOBIAS!

* "Thank G.od" in Hebrew, folks.

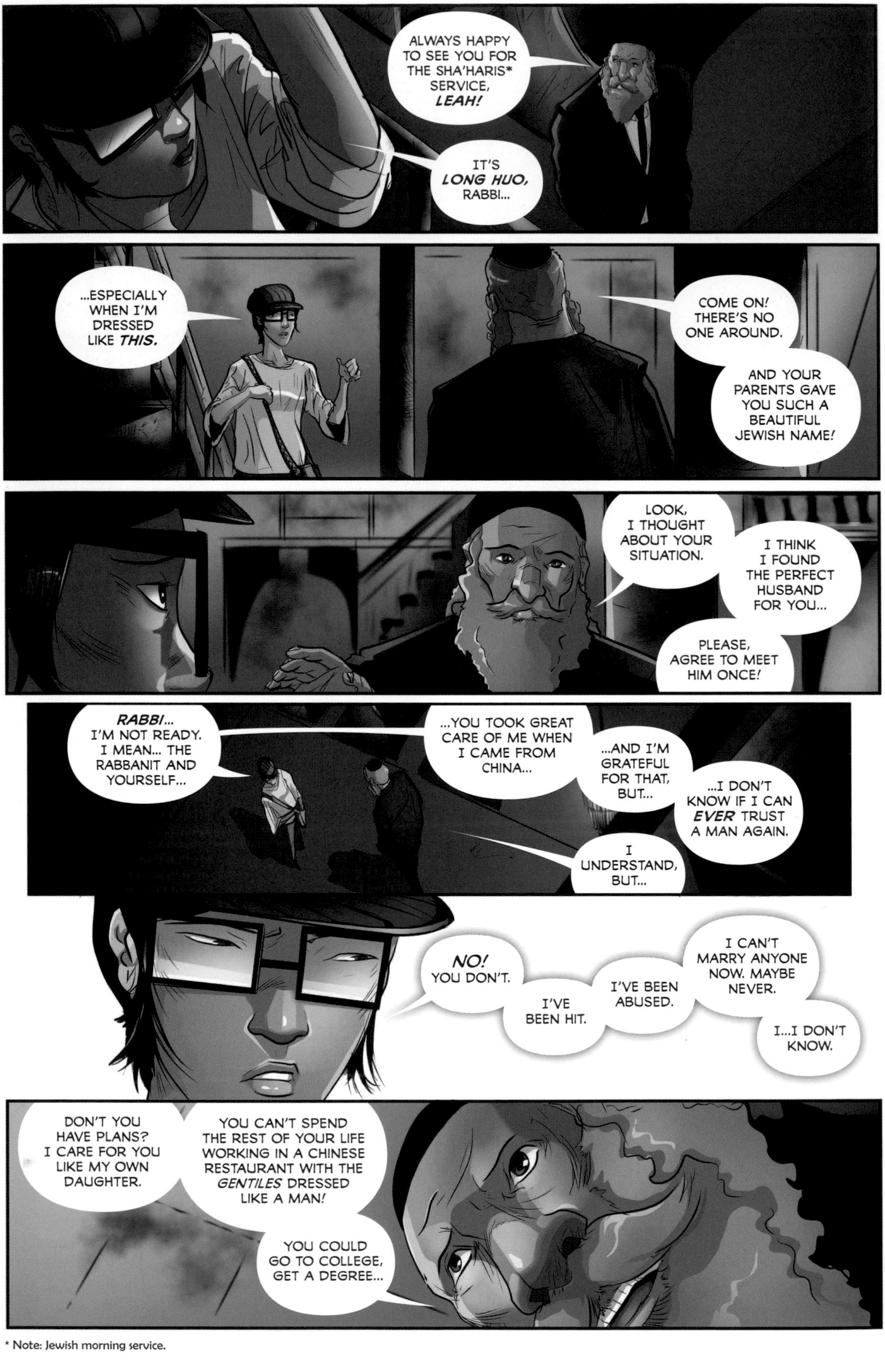
ALWAYS HAPPY TO SEE YOU FOR THE SHA'HARIS* SERVICE, **LEAH!**
IT'S ***LONG HUO,*** RABBI...
...ESPECIALLY WHEN I'M DRESSED LIKE ***THIS.***
COME ON! THERE'S NO ONE AROUND.
AND YOUR PARENTS GAVE YOU SUCH A BEAUTIFUL JEWISH NAME!
LOOK, I THOUGHT ABOUT YOUR SITUATION.
I THINK I FOUND THE PERFECT HUSBAND FOR YOU...
PLEASE, AGREE TO MEET HIM ONCE!
RABBI... I'M NOT READY. I MEAN... THE RABBANIT AND YOURSELF...
...YOU TOOK GREAT CARE OF ME WHEN I CAME FROM CHINA...
...AND I'M GRATEFUL FOR THAT, BUT...
...I DON'T KNOW IF I CAN ***EVER*** TRUST A MAN AGAIN.
I UNDERSTAND, BUT...
NO! YOU DON'T.
I'VE BEEN HIT.
I'VE BEEN ABUSED.
I CAN'T MARRY ANYONE NOW. MAYBE NEVER.
I...I DON'T KNOW.
DON'T YOU HAVE PLANS? I CARE FOR YOU LIKE MY OWN DAUGHTER.
YOU CAN'T SPEND THE REST OF YOUR LIFE WORKING IN A CHINESE RESTAURANT WITH THE *GENTILES* DRESSED LIKE A MAN!
YOU COULD GO TO COLLEGE, GET A DEGREE...

* Note: Jewish morning service.

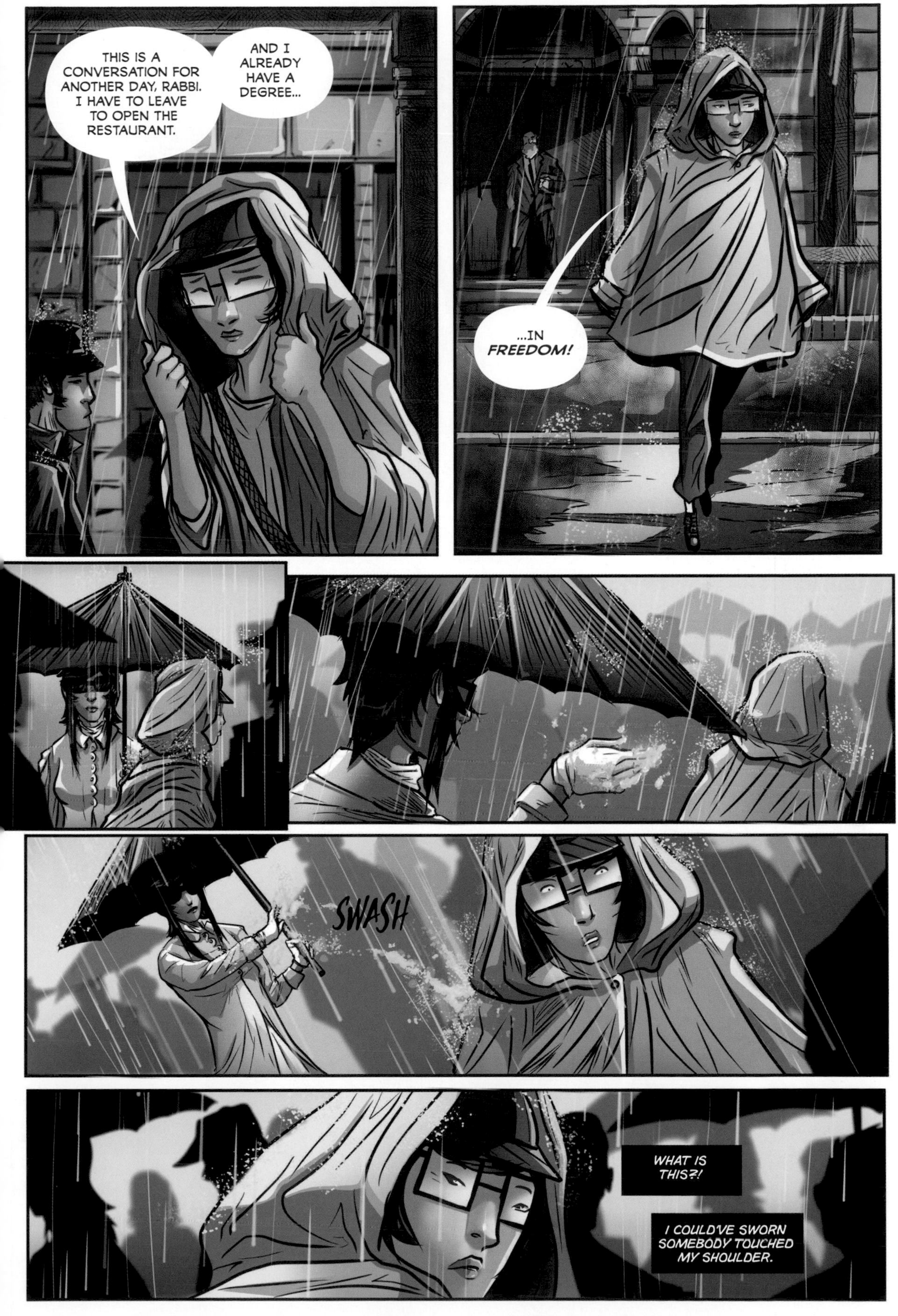
THIS IS A CONVERSATION FOR ANOTHER DAY, RABBI. I HAVE TO LEAVE TO OPEN THE RESTAURANT.
AND I ALREADY HAVE A DEGREE...
...IN *FREEDOM!*
SWASH
WHAT IS THIS?!
I COULD'VE SWORN SOMEBODY TOUCHED MY SHOULDER.

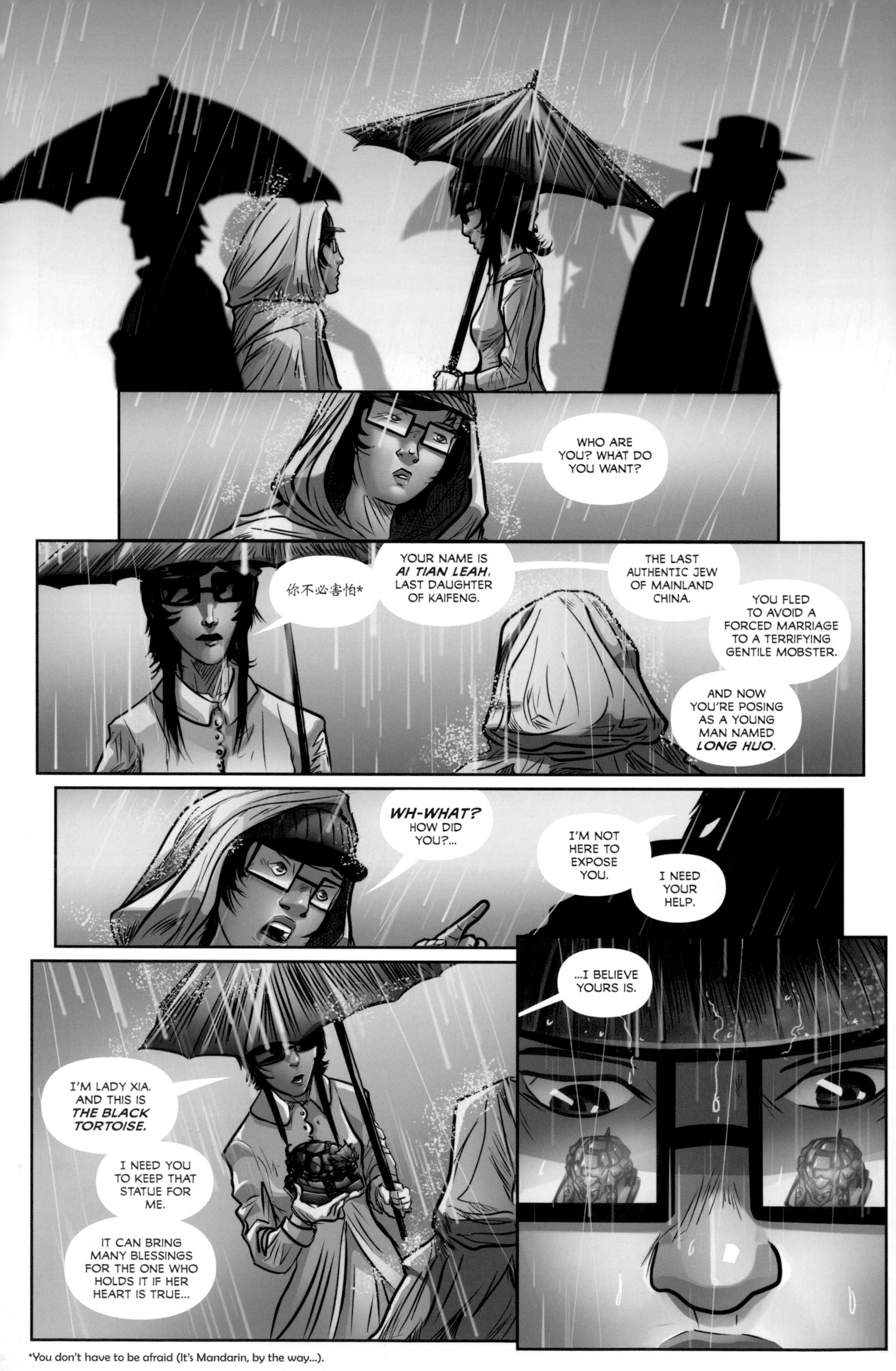
WHO ARE YOU? WHAT DO YOU WANT?
你不必害怕*
YOUR NAME IS AI TIAN LEAH, LAST DAUGHTER OF KAIFENG.
THE LAST AUTHENTIC JEW OF MAINLAND CHINA.
YOU FLED TO AVOID A FORCED MARRIAGE TO A TERRIFYING GENTILE MOBSTER.
AND NOW YOU'RE POSING AS A YOUNG MAN NAMED LONG HUO.
WH-WHAT? HOW DID YOU?...
I'M NOT HERE TO EXPOSE YOU.
I NEED YOUR HELP.
I'M LADY XIA. AND THIS IS THE BLACK TORTOISE.
I NEED YOU TO KEEP THAT STATUE FOR ME.
IT CAN BRING MANY BLESSINGS FOR THE ONE WHO HOLDS IT IF HER HEART IS TRUE...
...I BELIEVE YOURS IS.

*You don't have to be afraid (It's Mandarin, by the way...).

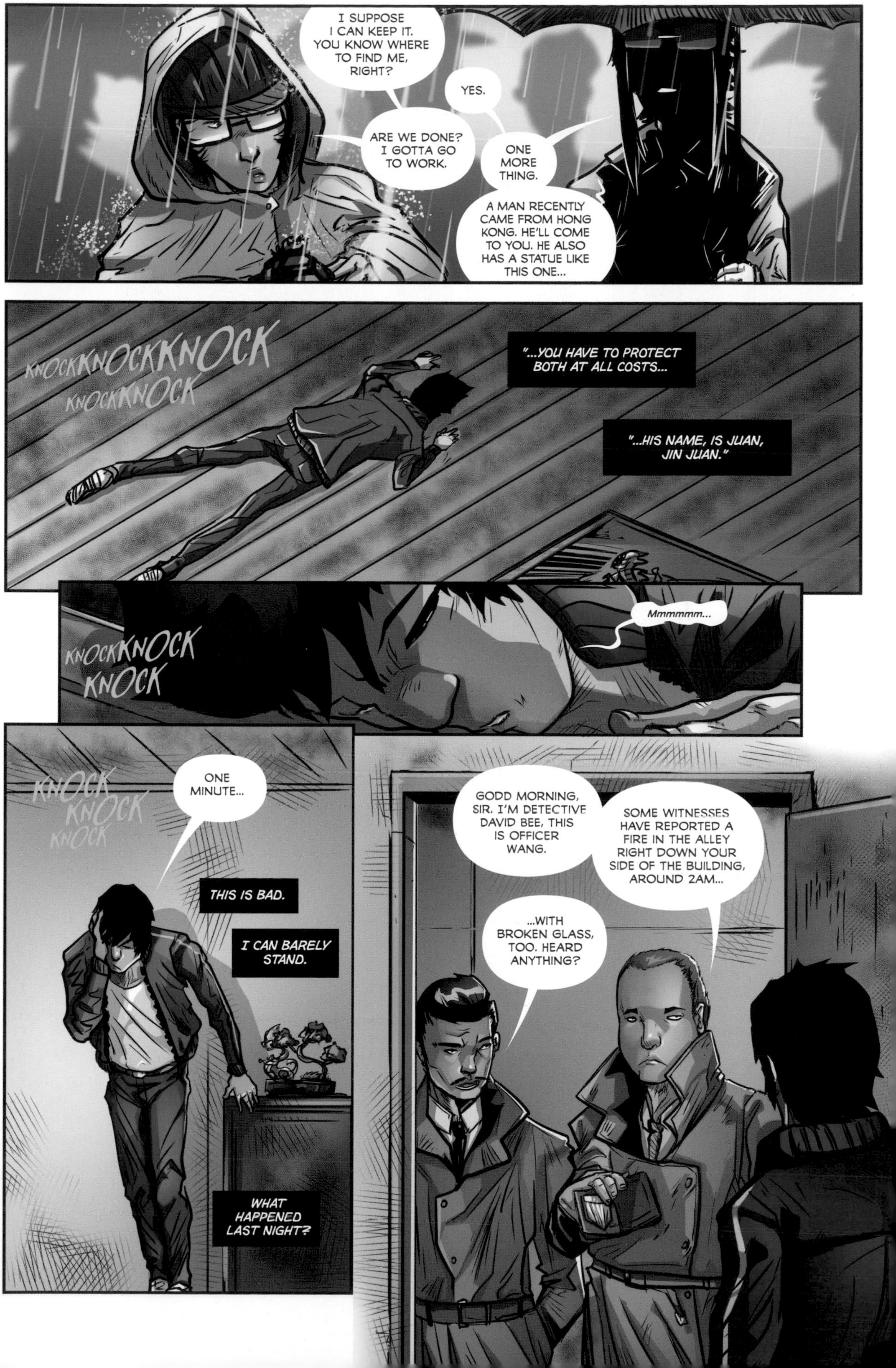

I SUPPOSE I CAN KEEP IT. YOU KNOW WHERE TO FIND ME, RIGHT?
YES.
ARE WE DONE? I GOTTA GO TO WORK.
ONE MORE THING.
A MAN RECENTLY CAME FROM HONG KONG. HE'LL COME TO YOU. HE ALSO HAS A STATUE LIKE THIS ONE...
KNOCKKNOCKKNOCK
KNOCKKNOCK
"...YOU HAVE TO PROTECT BOTH AT ALL COSTS...
"...HIS NAME, IS JUAN, JIN JUAN."
KNOCKKNOCK
KNOCK
Mmmmmm...
KNOCK
KNOCK
KNOCK
ONE MINUTE...
THIS IS BAD.
I CAN BARELY STAND.
WHAT HAPPENED LAST NIGHT?
GODD MORNING, SIR. I'M DETECTIVE DAVID BEE, THIS IS OFFICER WANG.
SOME WITNESSES HAVE REPORTED A FIRE IN THE ALLEY RIGHT DOWN YOUR SIDE OF THE BUILDING, AROUND 2AM...
...WITH BROKEN GLASS, TOO. HEARD ANYTHING?

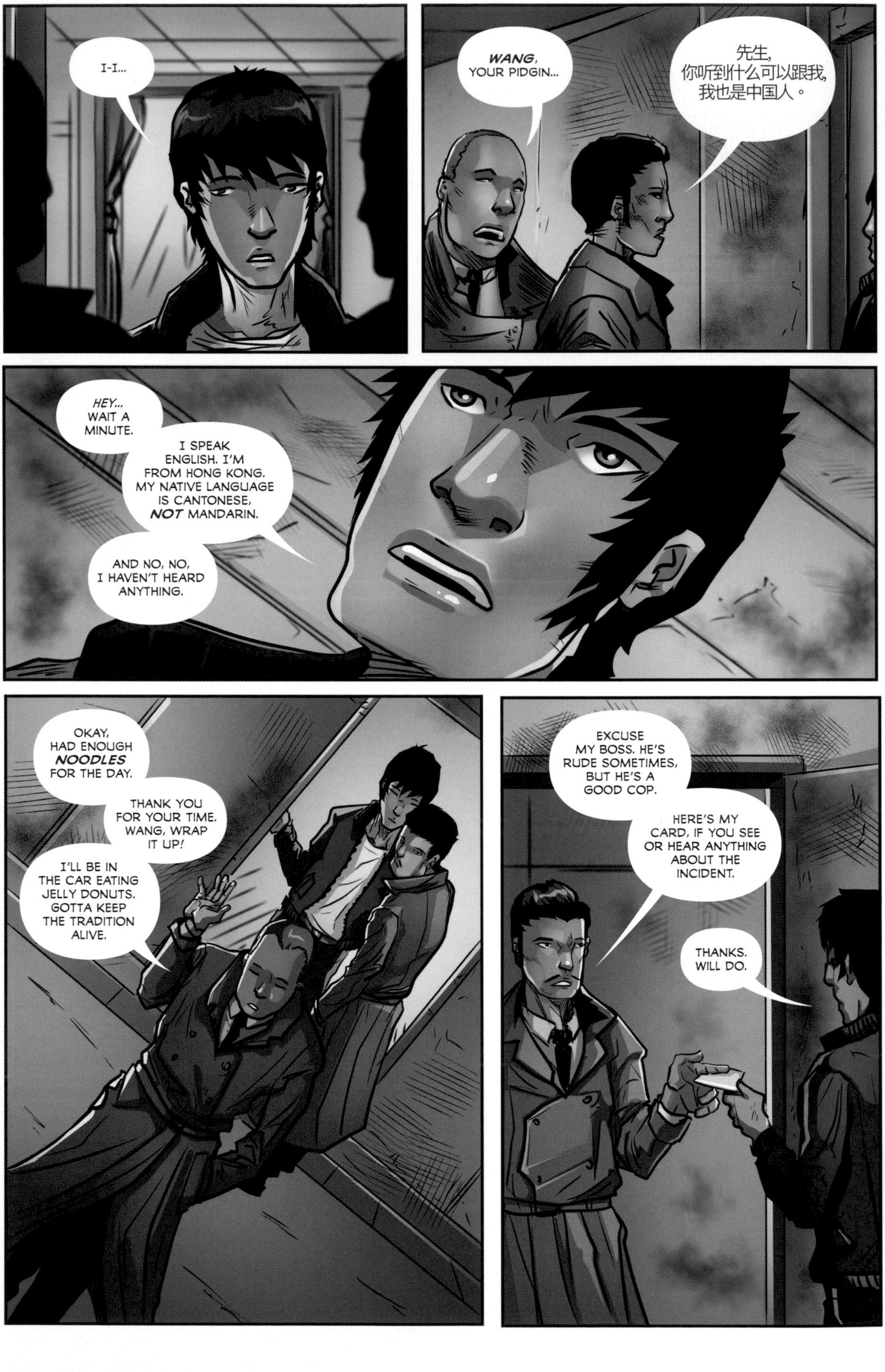
I-I...
WANG, YOUR PIDGIN...
先生,
你听到什么可以跟我,
我也是中国人。
HEY... WAIT A MINUTE.
I SPEAK ENGLISH. I'M FROM HONG KONG. MY NATIVE LANGUAGE IS CANTONESE, NOT MANDARIN.
AND NO, NO, I HAVEN'T HEARD ANYTHING.
OKAY, HAD ENOUGH NOODLES FOR THE DAY.
THANK YOU FOR YOUR TIME. WANG, WRAP IT UP!
I'LL BE IN THE CAR EATING JELLY DONUTS. GOTTA KEEP THE TRADITION ALIVE.
EXCUSE MY BOSS. HE'S RUDE SOMETIMES, BUT HE'S A GOOD COP.
HERE'S MY CARD, IF YOU SEE OR HEAR ANYTHING ABOUT THE INCIDENT.
THANKS. WILL DO.

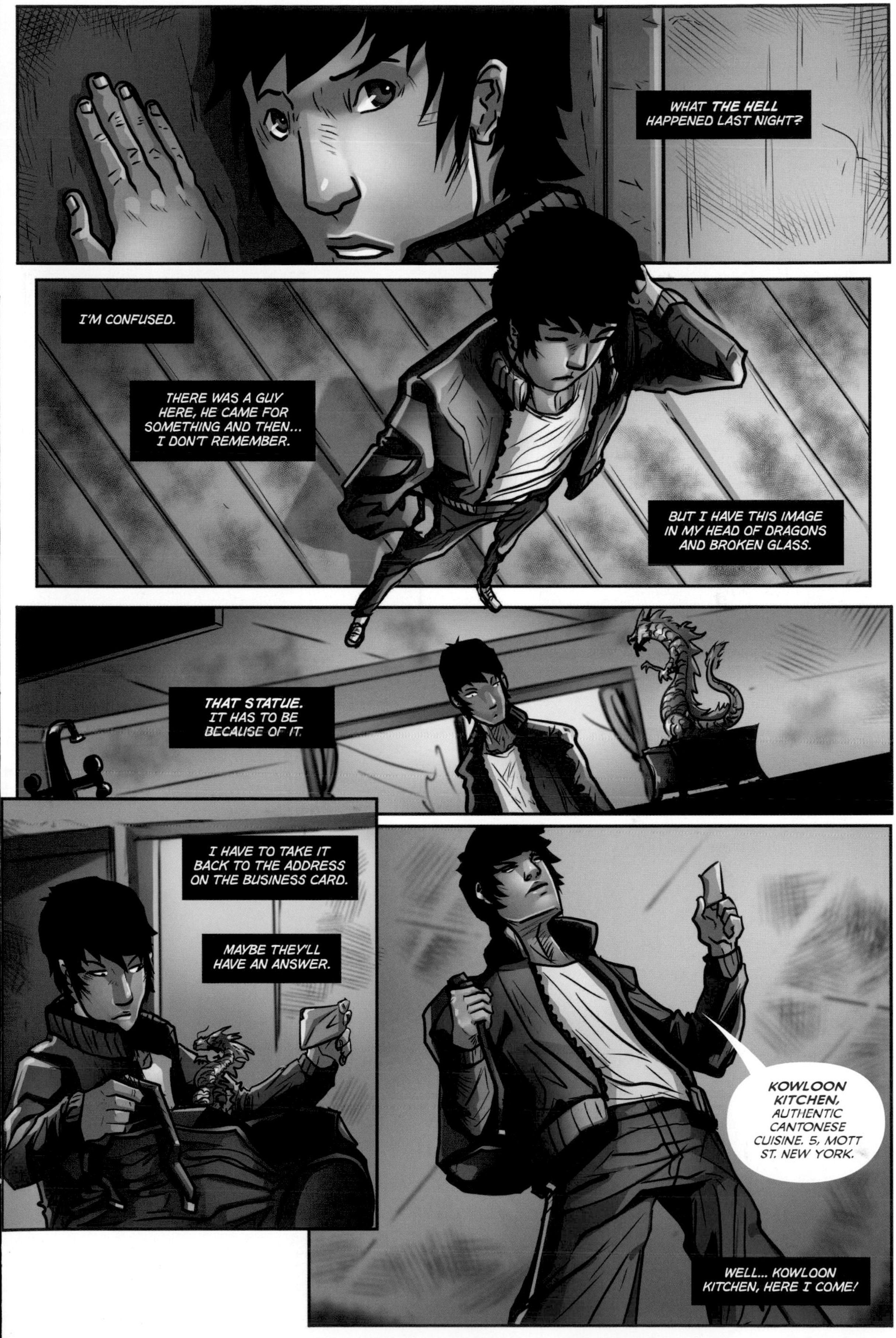
WHAT THE HELL HAPPENED LAST NIGHT?
I'M CONFUSED.
THERE WAS A GUY HERE, HE CAME FOR SOMETHING AND THEN... I DON'T REMEMBER.
BUT I HAVE THIS IMAGE IN MY HEAD OF DRAGONS AND BROKEN GLASS.
THAT STATUE. IT HAS TO BE BECAUSE OF IT.
I HAVE TO TAKE IT BACK TO THE ADDRESS ON THE BUSINESS CARD.
MAYBE THEY'LL HAVE AN ANSWER.
KOWLOON KITCHEN, AUTHENTIC CANTONESE CUISINE. 5, MOTT ST. NEW YORK.
WELL... KOWLOON KITCHEN, HERE I COME!

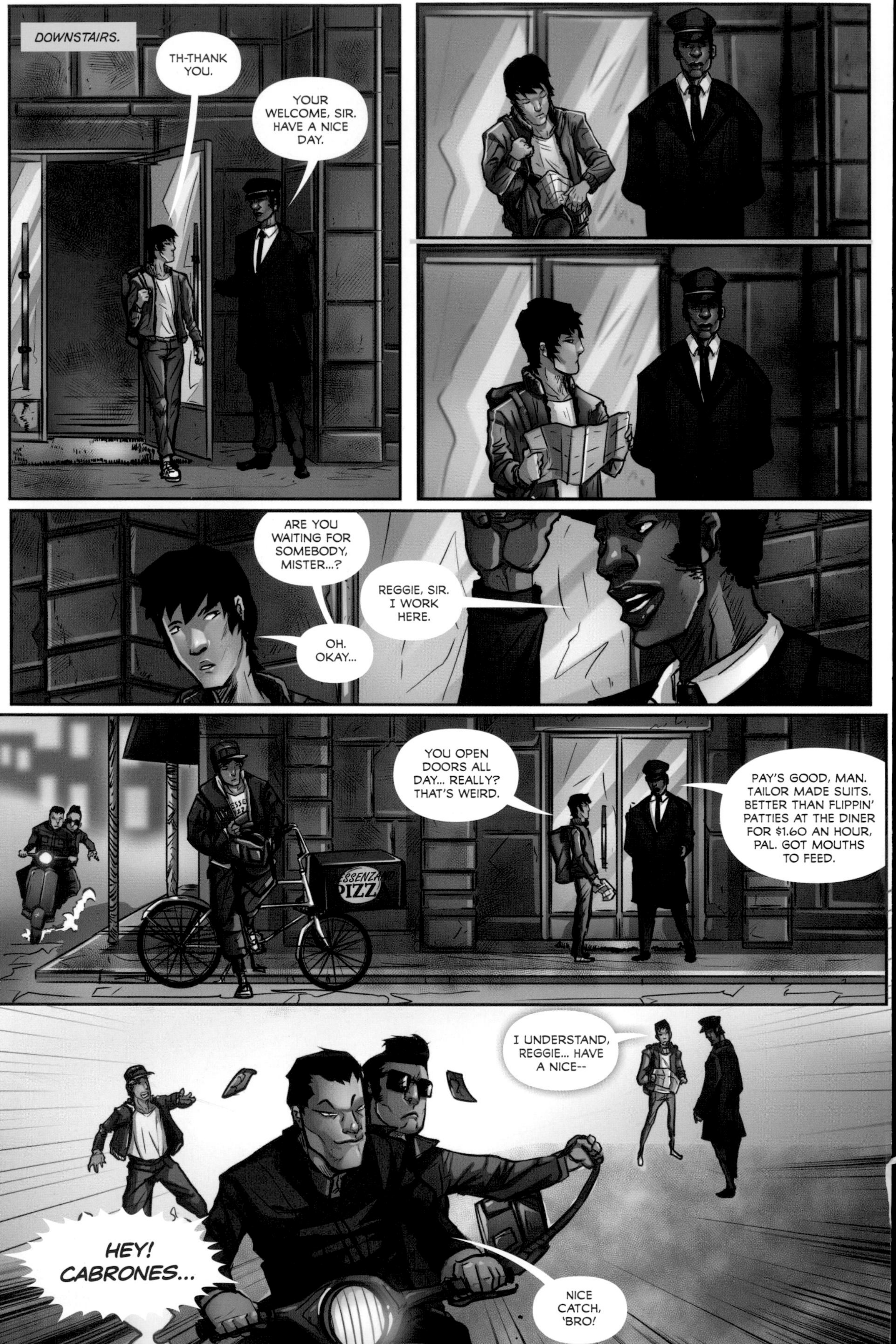
DOWNSTAIRS.
TH-THANK YOU.
YOUR WELCOME, SIR. HAVE A NICE DAY.
ARE YOU WAITING FOR SOMEBODY, MISTER...?
REGGIE, SIR. I WORK HERE.
OH. OKAY...
YOU OPEN DOORS ALL DAY... REALLY? THAT'S WEIRD.
PAY'S GOOD, MAN. TAILOR MADE SUITS. BETTER THAN FLIPPIN' PATTIES AT THE DINER FOR $1.60 AN HOUR, PAL. GOT MOUTHS TO FEED.
I UNDERSTAND, REGGIE... HAVE A NICE--
HEY! CABRONES...
NICE CATCH, 'BRO!

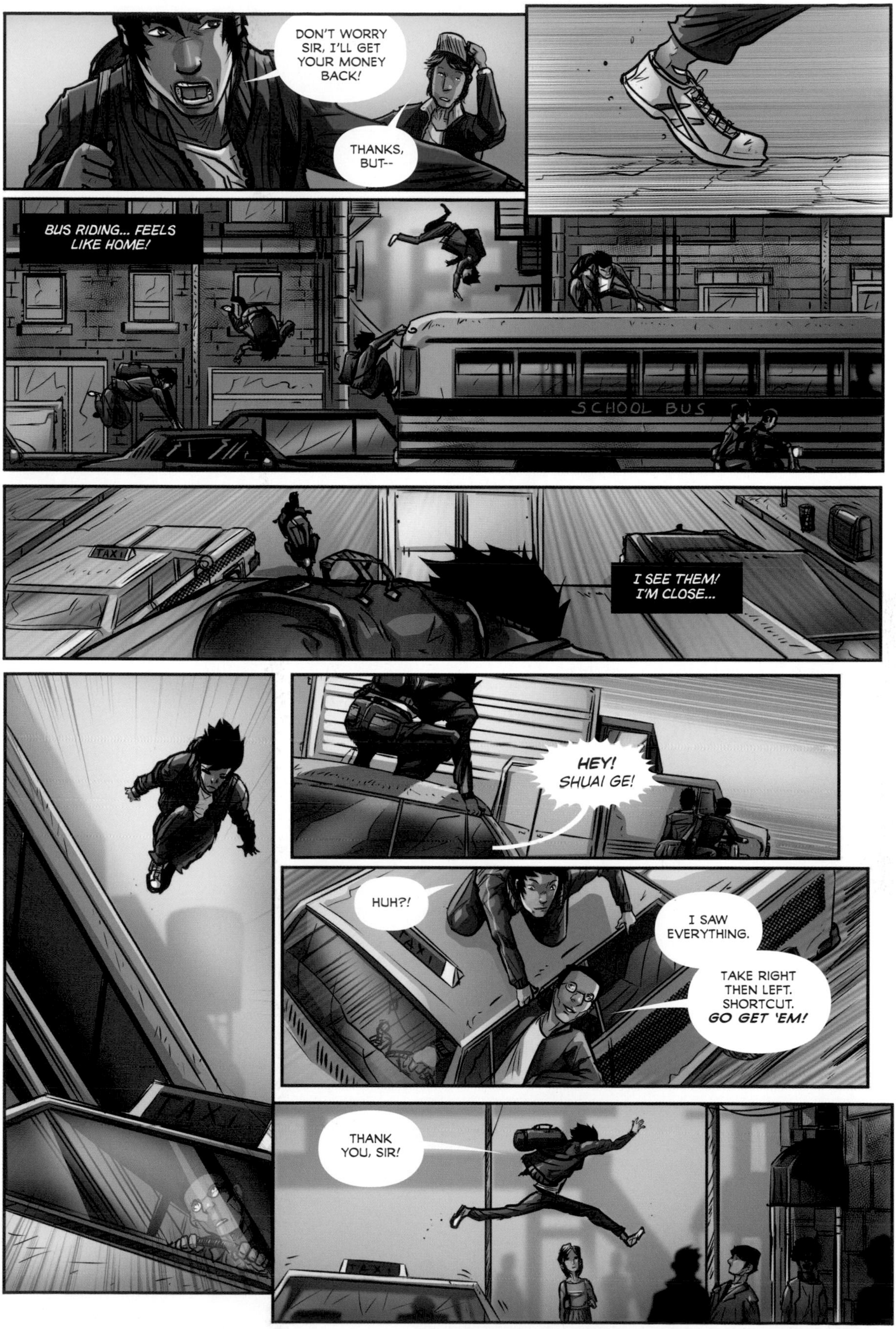
DON'T WORRY SIR, I'LL GET YOUR MONEY BACK!
THANKS, BUT--
BUS RIDING... FEELS LIKE HOME!
SCHOOL BUS
TAXI
I SEE THEM! I'M CLOSE...
HEY! SHUAI GE!
HUH?!
I SAW EVERYTHING.
TAKE RIGHT THEN LEFT. SHORTCUT. GO GET 'EM!
THANK YOU, SIR!

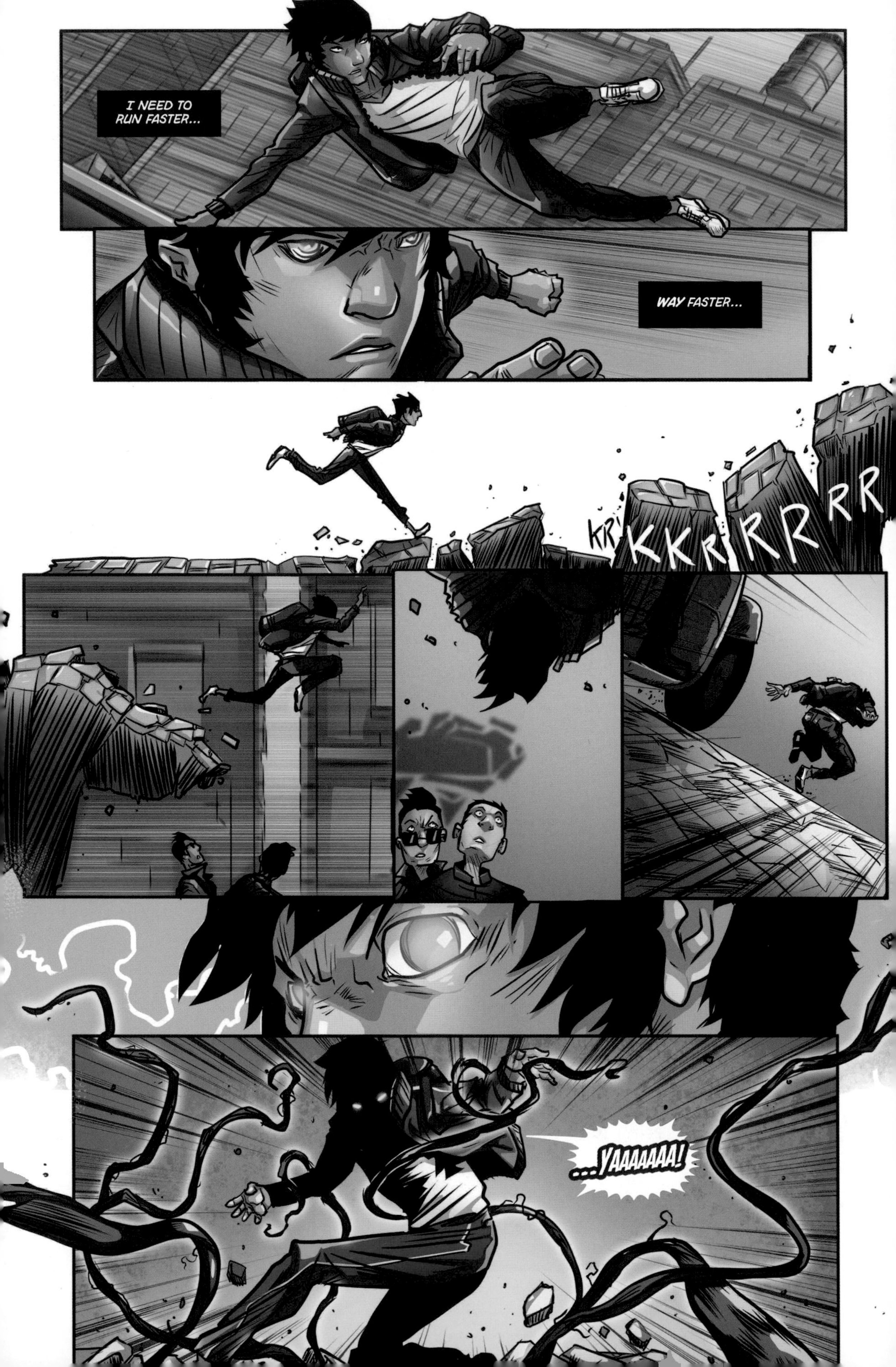

I NEED TO RUN FASTER...
WAY FASTER...
KR KKRRRRRR
...YAAAAAAA!

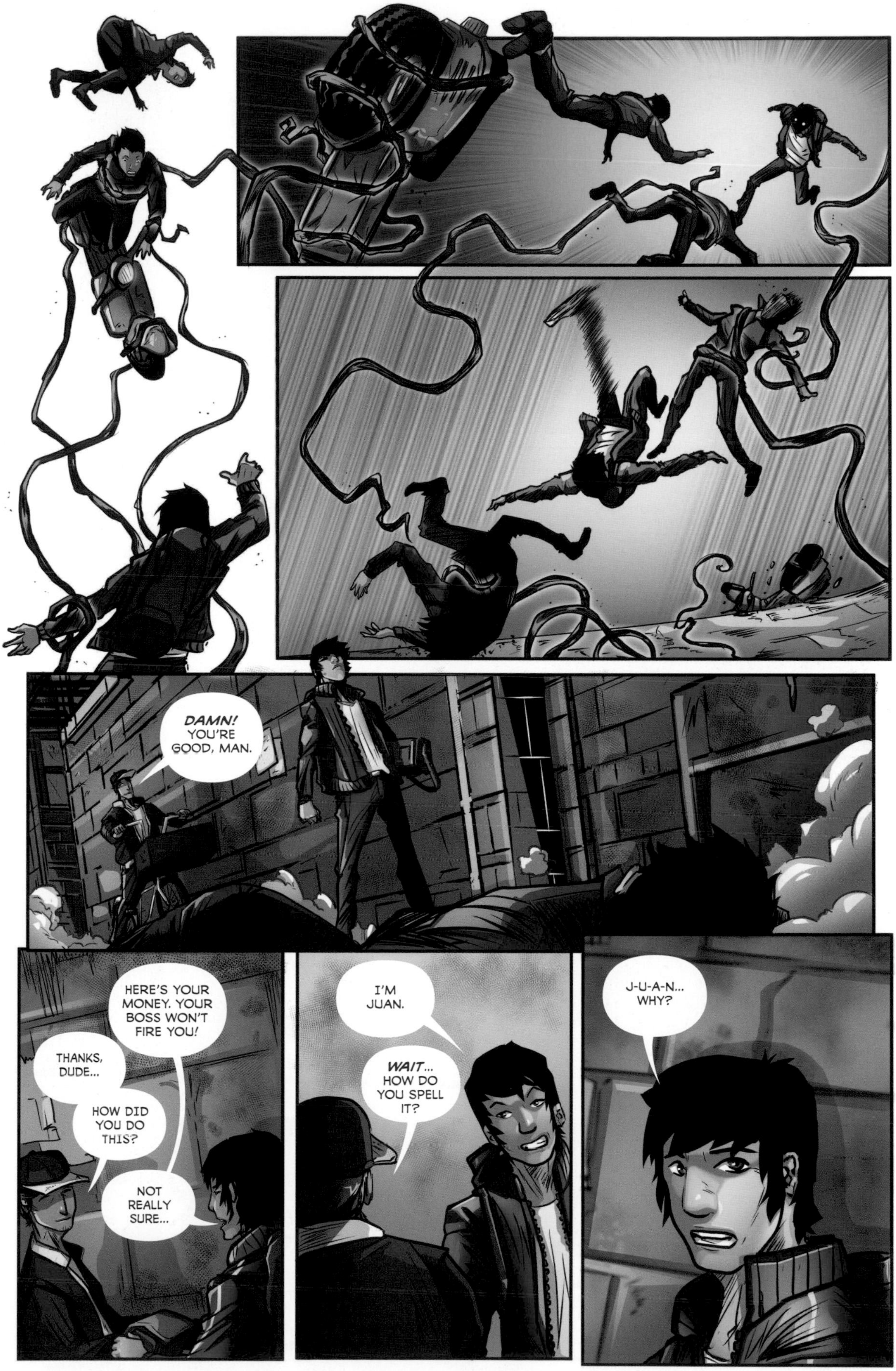
DAMN! YOU'RE GOOD, MAN.
HERE'S YOUR MONEY. YOUR BOSS WON'T FIRE YOU!
THANKS, DUDE...
HOW DID YOU DO THIS?
NOT REALLY SURE...
I'M JUAN.
WAIT... HOW DO YOU SPELL IT?
J-U-A-N... WHY?

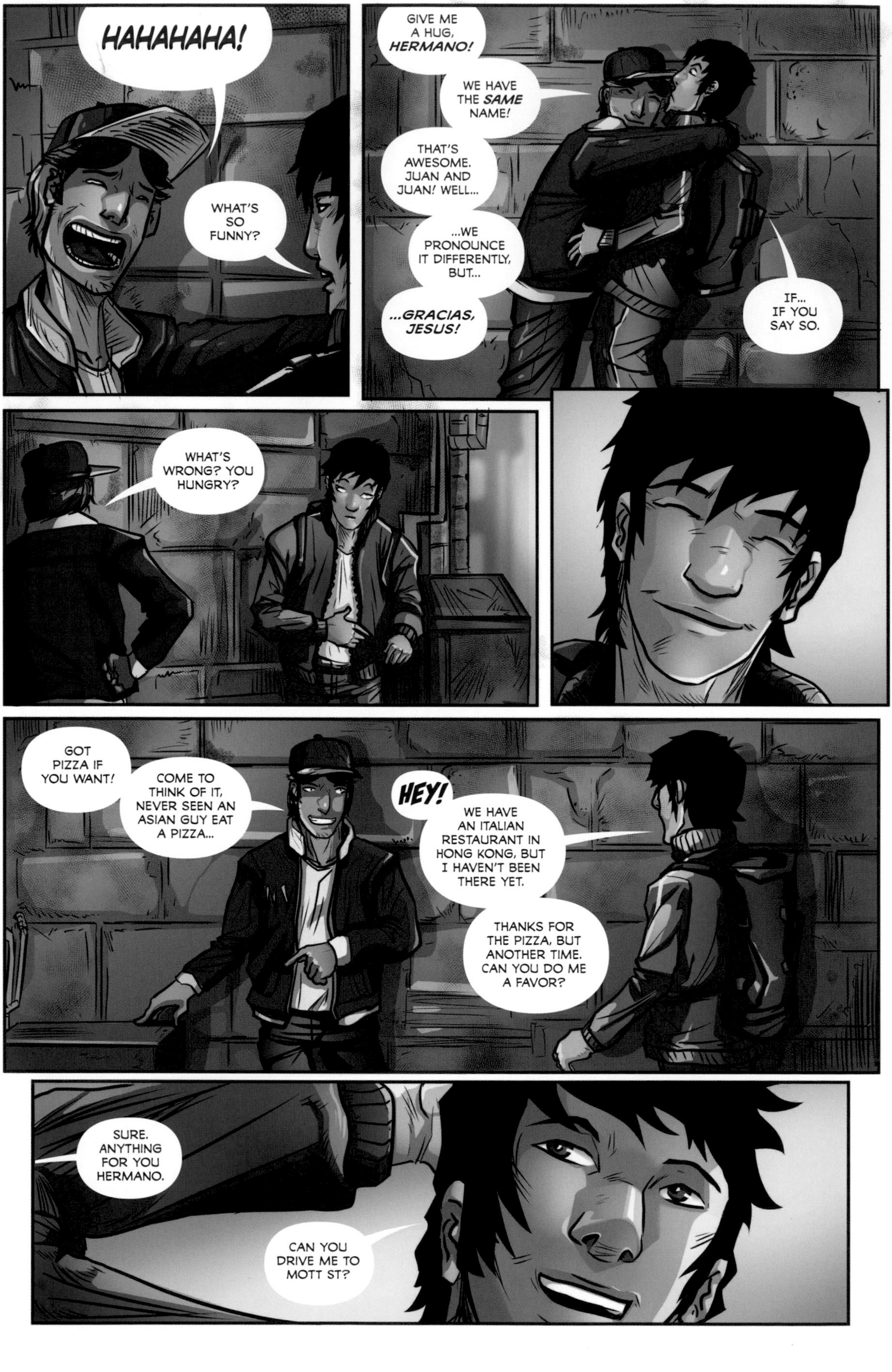
HAHAHAHA!
WHAT'S SO FUNNY?
GIVE ME A HUG, **HERMANO!**
WE HAVE THE **SAME** NAME!
THAT'S AWESOME. JUAN AND JUAN! WELL...
...WE PRONOUNCE IT DIFFERENTLY, BUT...
...GRACIAS, JESUS!
IF... IF YOU SAY SO.
WHAT'S WRONG? YOU HUNGRY?
GOT PIZZA IF YOU WANT!
COME TO THINK OF IT, NEVER SEEN AN ASIAN GUY EAT A PIZZA...
HEY!
WE HAVE AN ITALIAN RESTAURANT IN HONG KONG, BUT I HAVEN'T BEEN THERE YET.
THANKS FOR THE PIZZA, BUT ANOTHER TIME. CAN YOU DO ME A FAVOR?
SURE. ANYTHING FOR YOU HERMANO.
CAN YOU DRIVE ME TO MOTT ST?

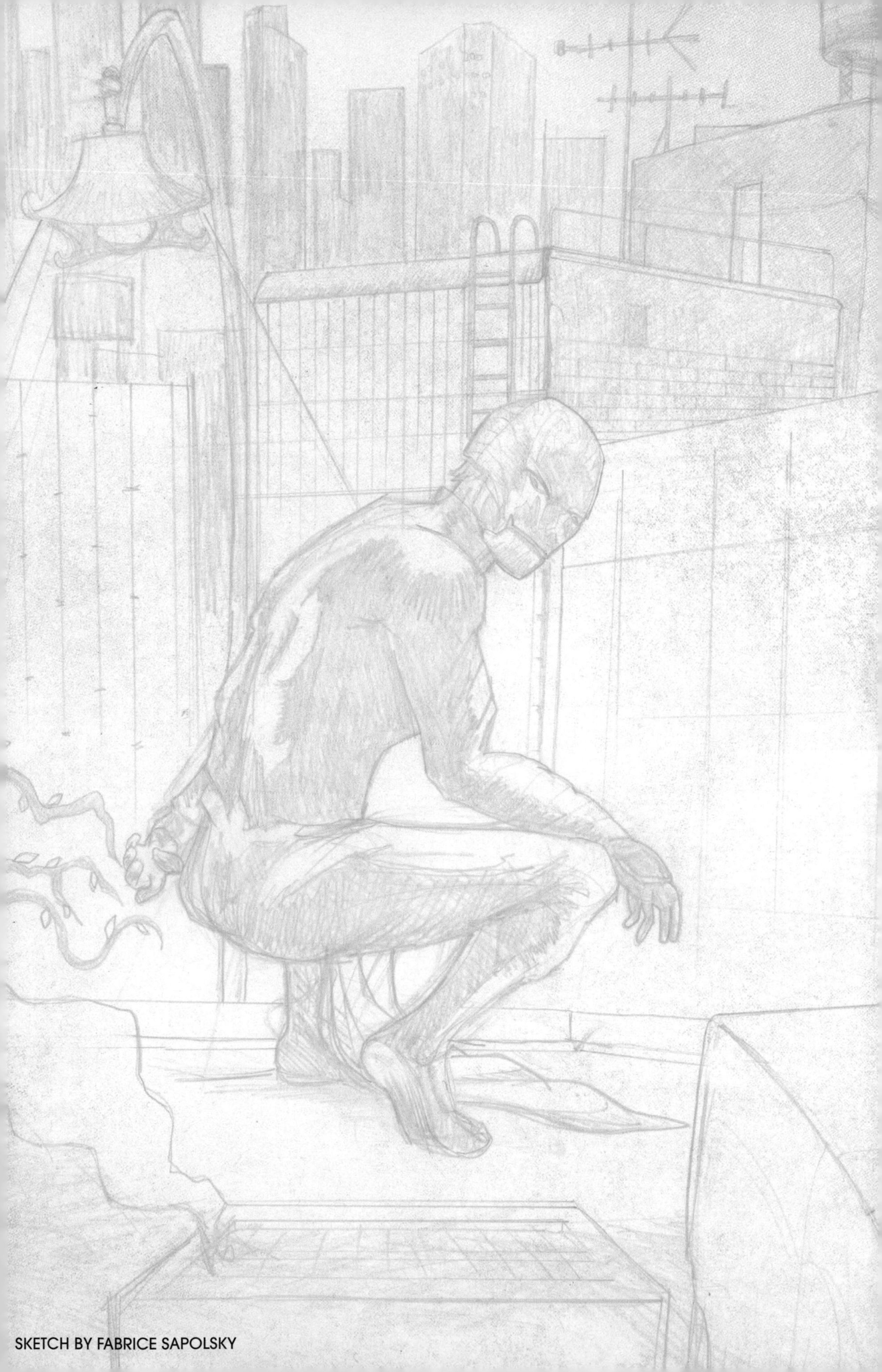

SKETCH BY FABRICE SAPOLSKY

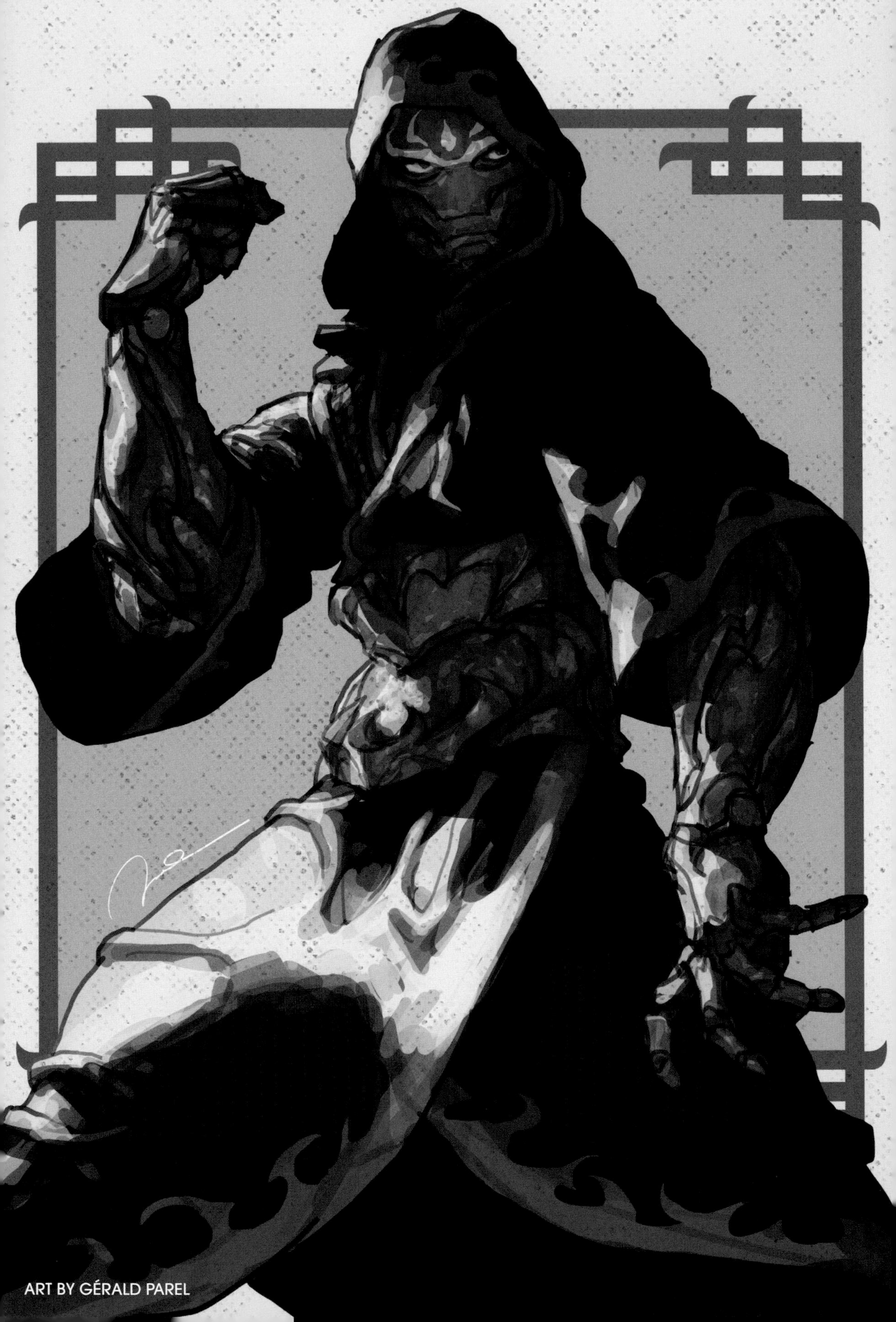

ART BY GÉRALD PAREL

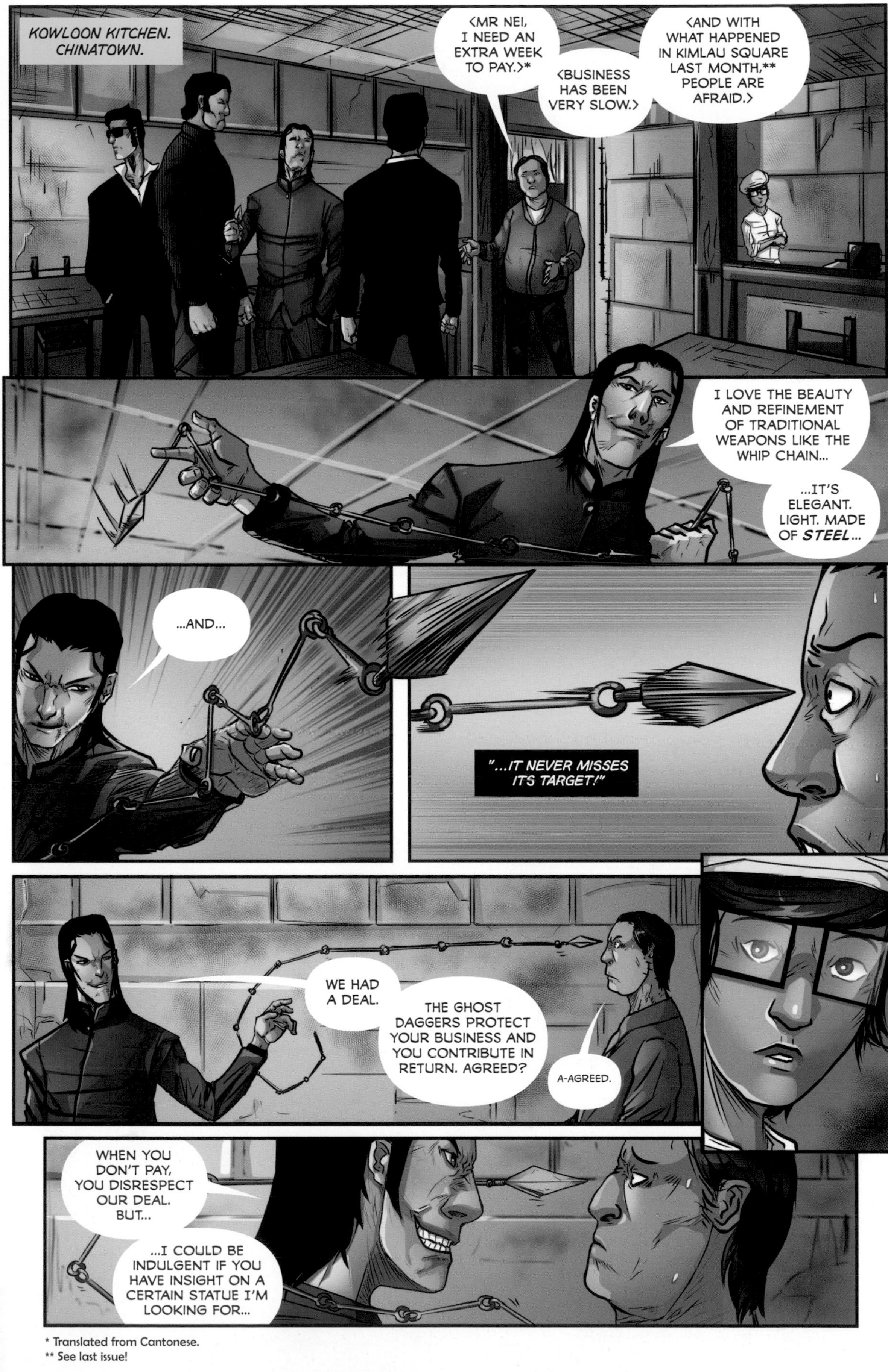
KOWLOON KITCHEN. CHINATOWN.
<MR NEI, I NEED AN EXTRA WEEK TO PAY.>*
<BUSINESS HAS BEEN VERY SLOW.>
<AND WITH WHAT HAPPENED IN KIMLAU SQUARE LAST MONTH,** PEOPLE ARE AFRAID.>
I LOVE THE BEAUTY AND REFINEMENT OF TRADITIONAL WEAPONS LIKE THE WHIP CHAIN...
...IT'S ELEGANT. LIGHT. MADE OF STEEL...
...AND...
"...IT NEVER MISSES ITS TARGET!"
WE HAD A DEAL.
THE GHOST DAGGERS PROTECT YOUR BUSINESS AND YOU CONTRIBUTE IN RETURN. AGREED?
A-AGREED.
WHEN YOU DON'T PAY, YOU DISRESPECT OUR DEAL. BUT...
...I COULD BE INDULGENT IF YOU HAVE INSIGHT ON A CERTAIN STATUE I'M LOOKING FOR...

* Translated from Cantonese.

** See last issue!

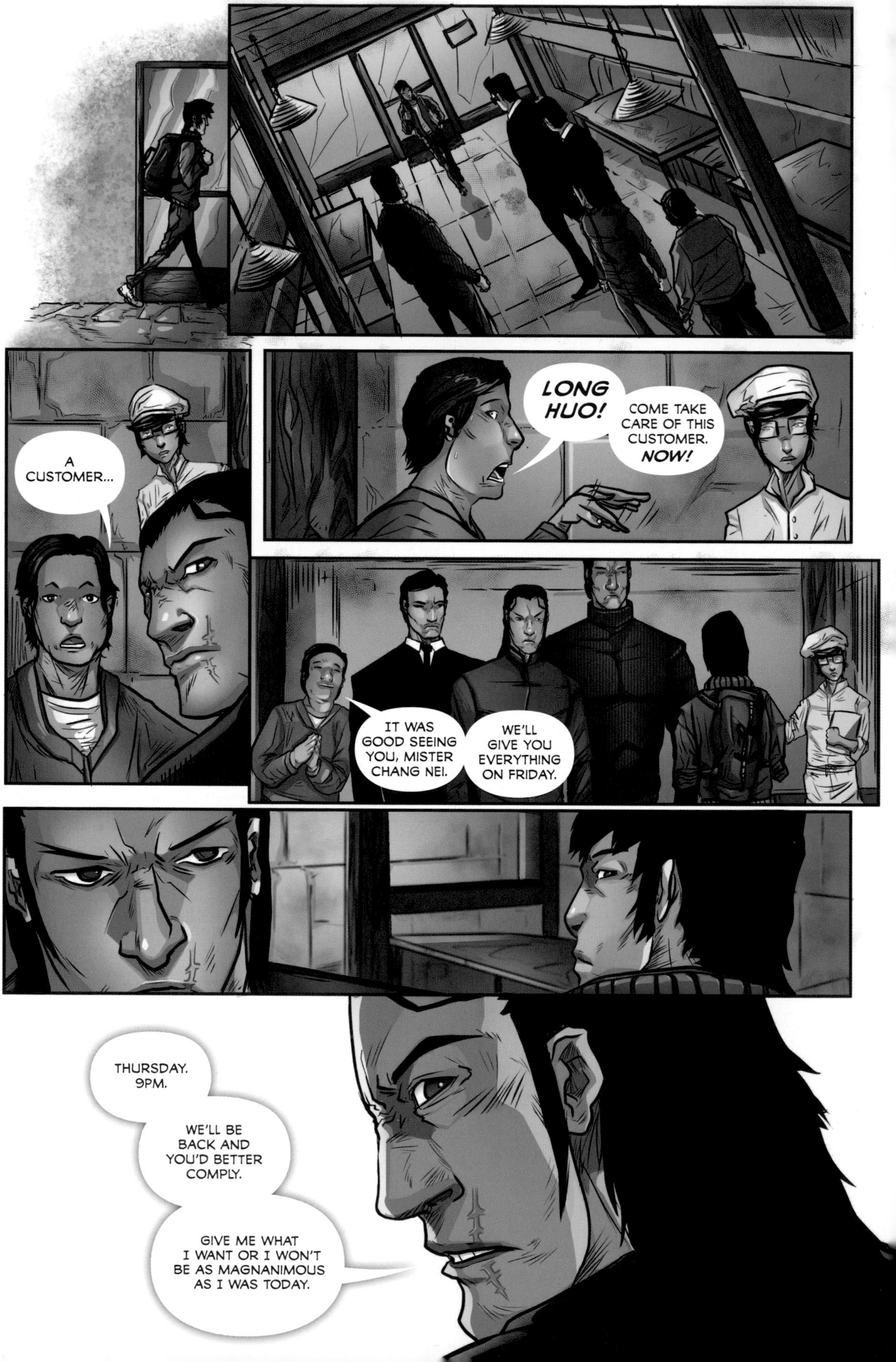
A CUSTOMER...
LONG HUO!
COME TAKE CARE OF THIS CUSTOMER. NOW!
IT WAS GOOD SEEING YOU, MISTER CHANG NEI.
WE'LL GIVE YOU EVERYTHING ON FRIDAY.
THURSDAY. 9PM.
WE'LL BE BACK AND YOU'D BETTER COMPLY.
GIVE ME WHAT I WANT OR I WON'T BE AS MAGNANIMOUS AS I WAS TODAY.

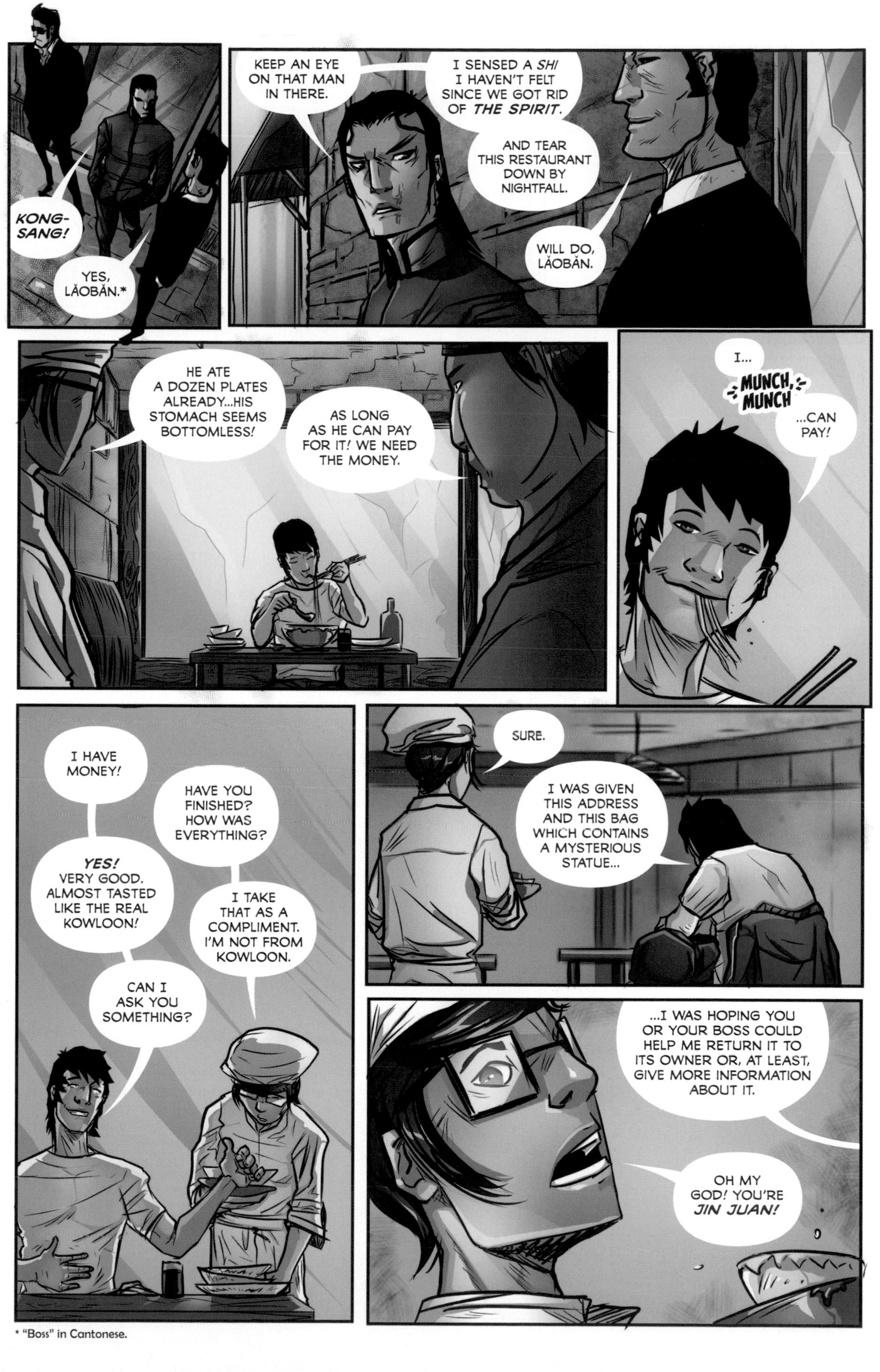
KONG-SANG!
YES, LǍOBǍN.*
KEEP AN EYE ON THAT MAN IN THERE.
I SENSED A SHI I HAVEN'T FELT SINCE WE GOT RID OF THE SPIRIT.
AND TEAR THIS RESTAURANT DOWN BY NIGHTFALL.
WILL DO, LǍOBǍN.
HE ATE A DOZEN PLATES ALREADY...HIS STOMACH SEEMS BOTTOMLESS!
AS LONG AS HE CAN PAY FOR IT! WE NEED THE MONEY.
I...
MUNCH, MUNCH
...CAN PAY!
I HAVE MONEY!
HAVE YOU FINISHED? HOW WAS EVERYTHING?
YES! VERY GOOD. ALMOST TASTED LIKE THE REAL KOWLOON!
I TAKE THAT AS A COMPLIMENT. I'M NOT FROM KOWLOON.
CAN I ASK YOU SOMETHING?
SURE.
I WAS GIVEN THIS ADDRESS AND THIS BAG WHICH CONTAINS A MYSTERIOUS STATUE...
...I WAS HOPING YOU OR YOUR BOSS COULD HELP ME RETURN IT TO ITS OWNER OR, AT LEAST, GIVE MORE INFORMATION ABOUT IT.
OH MY GOD! YOU'RE JIN JUAN!

* "Boss" in Cantonese.

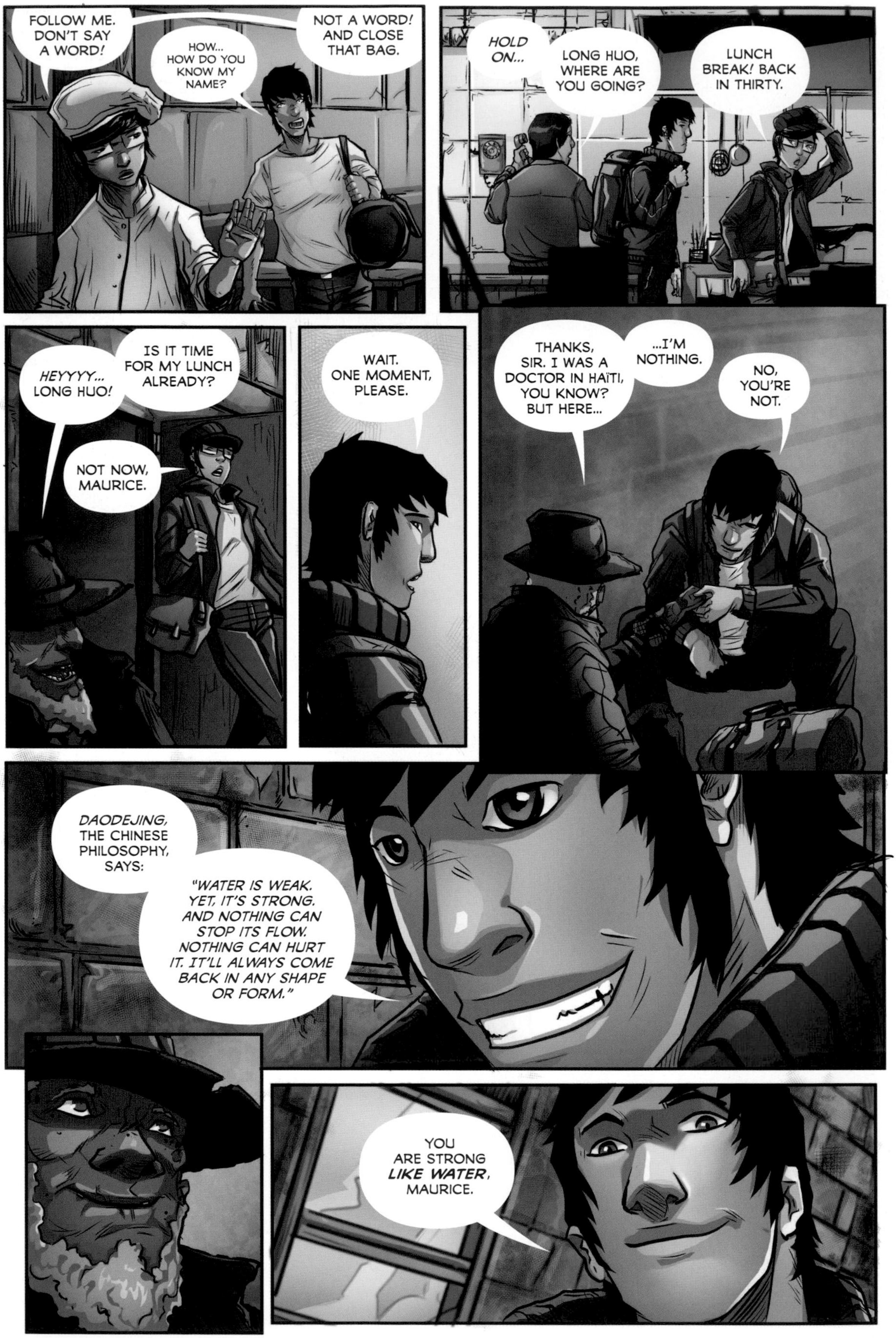
FOLLOW ME. DON'T SAY A WORD!
HOW... HOW DO YOU KNOW MY NAME?
NOT A WORD! AND CLOSE THAT BAG.
HOLD ON...
LONG HUO, WHERE ARE YOU GOING?
LUNCH BREAK! BACK IN THIRTY.
HEYYYY... LONG HUO!
IS IT TIME FOR MY LUNCH ALREADY?
NOT NOW, MAURICE.
WAIT. ONE MOMENT, PLEASE.
THANKS, SIR. I WAS A DOCTOR IN HAÏTI, YOU KNOW? BUT HERE...
...I'M NOTHING.
NO, YOU'RE NOT.
DAODEJING, THE CHINESE PHILOSOPHY, SAYS:
"WATER IS WEAK. YET, IT'S STRONG. AND NOTHING CAN STOP ITS FLOW. NOTHING CAN HURT IT. IT'LL ALWAYS COME BACK IN ANY SHAPE OR FORM."
YOU ARE STRONG LIKE WATER, MAURICE.

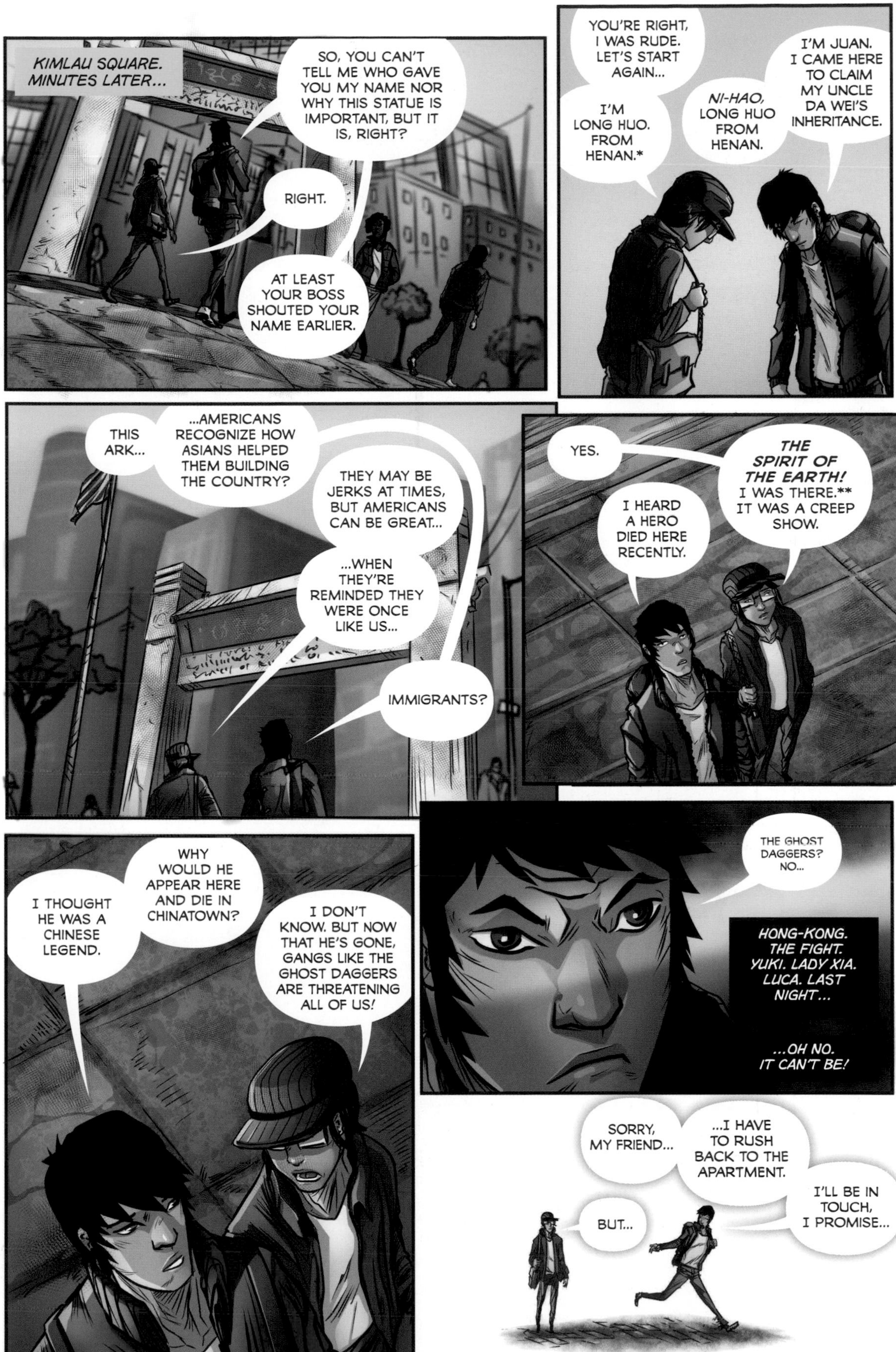
KIMLAU SQUARE. MINUTES LATER...
SO, YOU CAN'T TELL ME WHO GAVE YOU MY NAME NOR WHY THIS STATUE IS IMPORTANT, BUT IT IS, RIGHT?
RIGHT.
AT LEAST YOUR BOSS SHOUTED YOUR NAME EARLIER.
YOU'RE RIGHT, I WAS RUDE. LET'S START AGAIN...
I'M LONG HUO. FROM HENAN.*
NI-HAO, LONG HUO FROM HENAN.
I'M JUAN. I CAME HERE TO CLAIM MY UNCLE DA WEI'S INHERITANCE.
THIS ARK...
...AMERICANS RECOGNIZE HOW ASIANS HELPED THEM BUILDING THE COUNTRY?
THEY MAY BE JERKS AT TIMES, BUT AMERICANS CAN BE GREAT...
...WHEN THEY'RE REMINDED THEY WERE ONCE LIKE US...
IMMIGRANTS?
YES.
THE SPIRIT OF THE EARTH! I WAS THERE.** IT WAS A CREEP SHOW.
I HEARD A HERO DIED HERE RECENTLY.
I THOUGHT HE WAS A CHINESE LEGEND.
WHY WOULD HE APPEAR HERE AND DIE IN CHINATOWN?
I DON'T KNOW. BUT NOW THAT HE'S GONE, GANGS LIKE THE GHOST DAGGERS ARE THREATENING ALL OF US!
THE GHOST DAGGERS? NO...
HONG-KONG. THE FIGHT. YUKI. LADY XIA. LUCA. LAST NIGHT...
...OH NO. IT CAN'T BE!
SORRY, MY FRIEND...
...I HAVE TO RUSH BACK TO THE APARTMENT.
BUT...
I'LL BE IN TOUCH, I PROMISE...

* Henan is a chinese province. Its capital is Kaifeng.
** Still in Intertwined #3

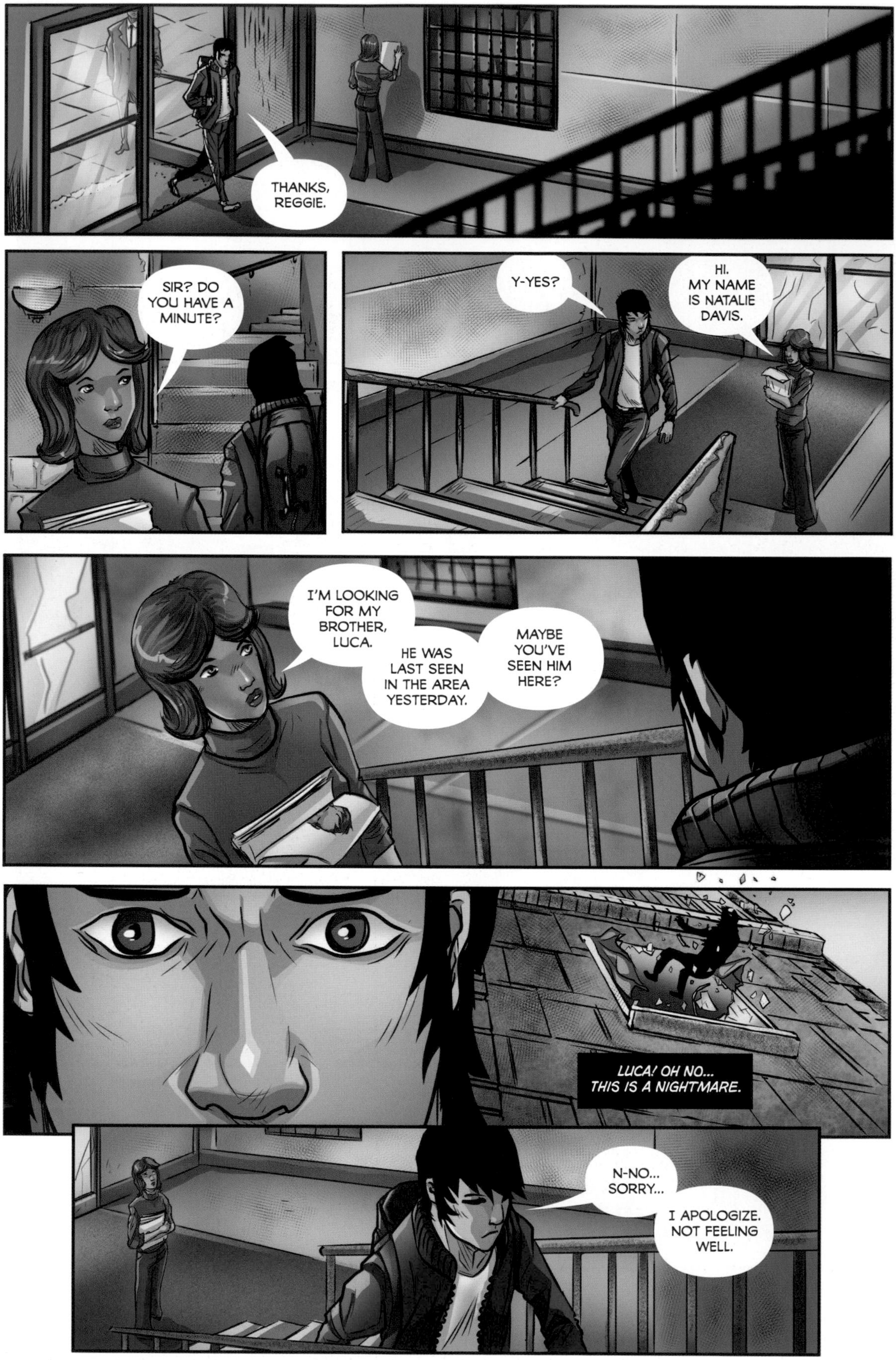
THANKS, REGGIE.
SIR? DO YOU HAVE A MINUTE?
Y-YES?
HI. MY NAME IS NATALIE DAVIS.
I'M LOOKING FOR MY BROTHER, LUCA.
HE WAS LAST SEEN IN THE AREA YESTERDAY.
MAYBE YOU'VE SEEN HIM HERE?
LUCA! OH NO... THIS IS A NIGHTMARE.
N-NO... SORRY...
I APOLOGIZE. NOT FEELING WELL.

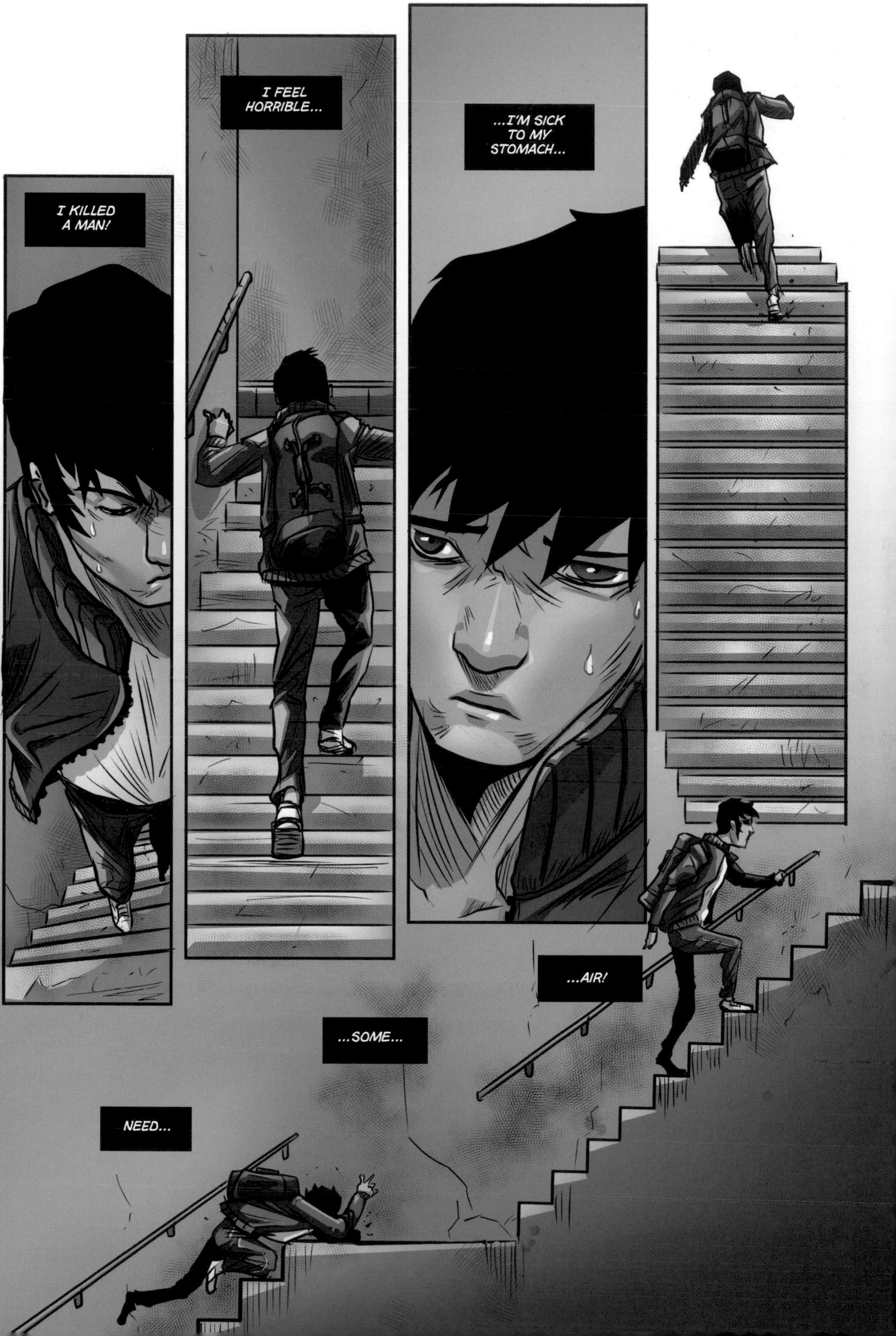
I KILLED A MAN!
I FEEL HORRIBLE...
...I'M SICK TO MY STOMACH...
NEED...
...SOME...
...AIR!

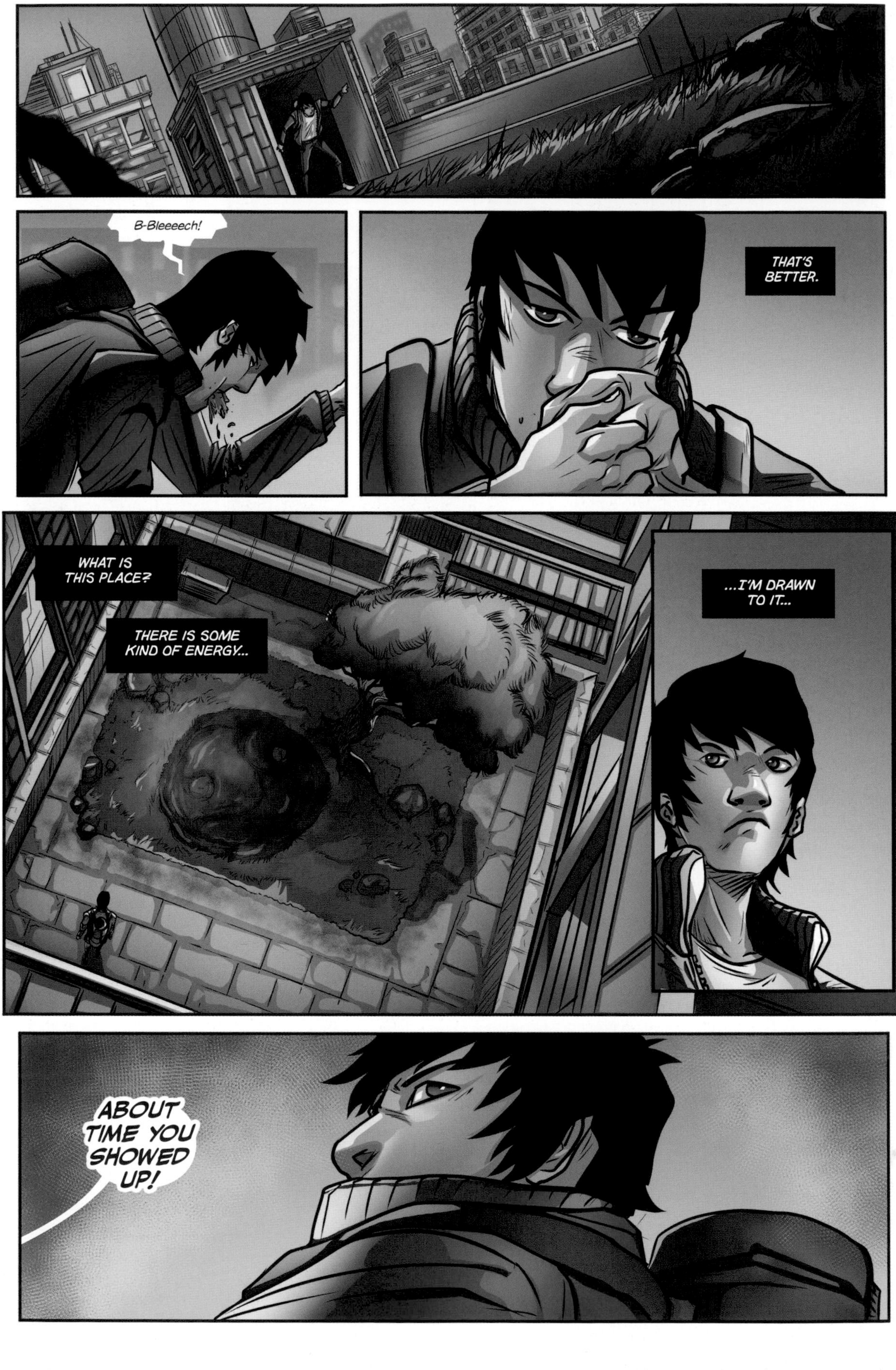
B-Bleeeech!
THAT'S BETTER.
WHAT IS THIS PLACE?
THERE IS SOME KIND OF ENERGY...
...I'M DRAWN TO IT...
ABOUT TIME YOU SHOWED UP!

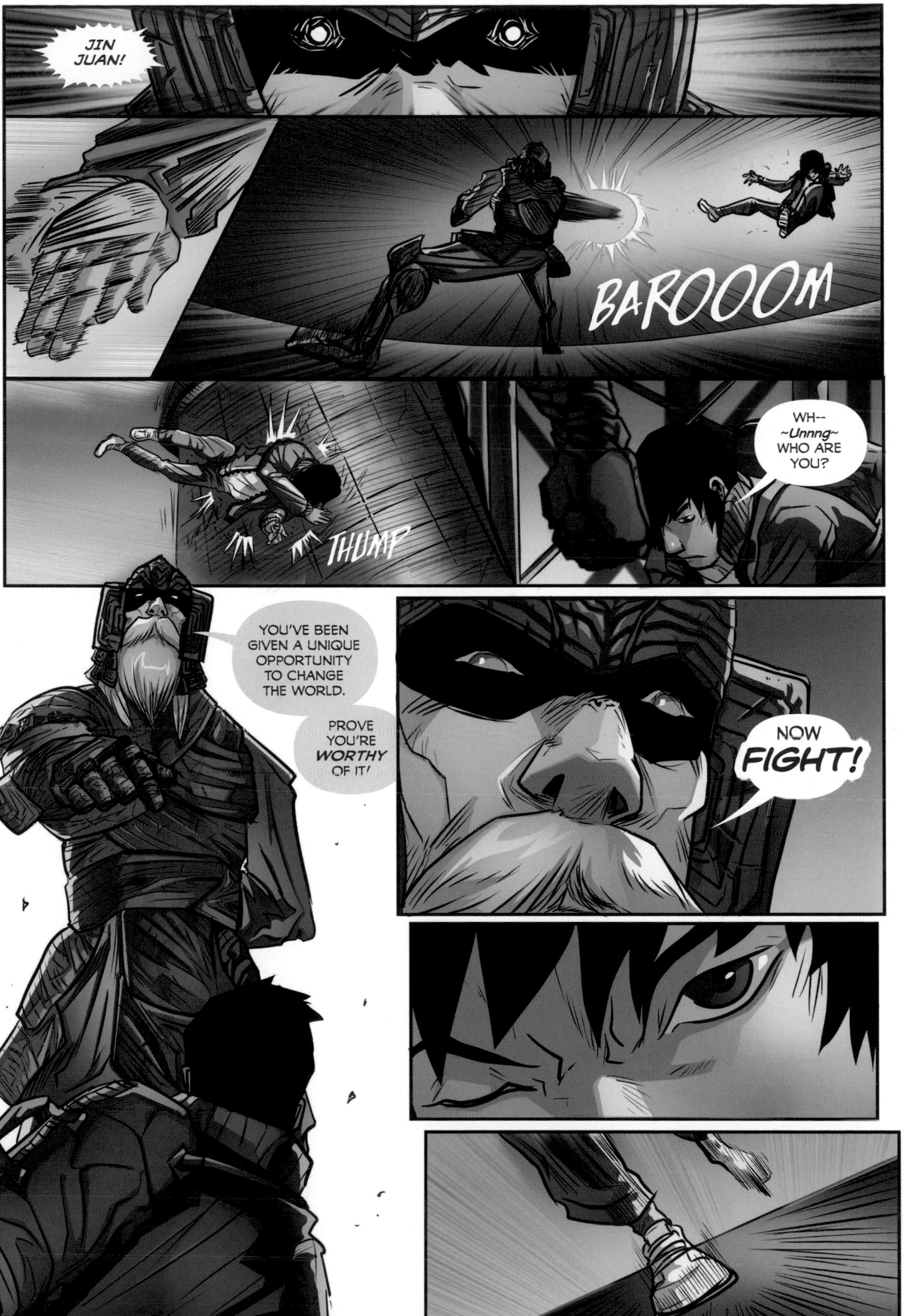
JIN JUAN!
BAROOOM
THUMP
WH-- ~Unnng~ WHO ARE YOU?
YOU'VE BEEN GIVEN A UNIQUE OPPORTUNITY TO CHANGE THE WORLD.
PROVE YOU'RE WORTHY OF IT!
NOW FIGHT!

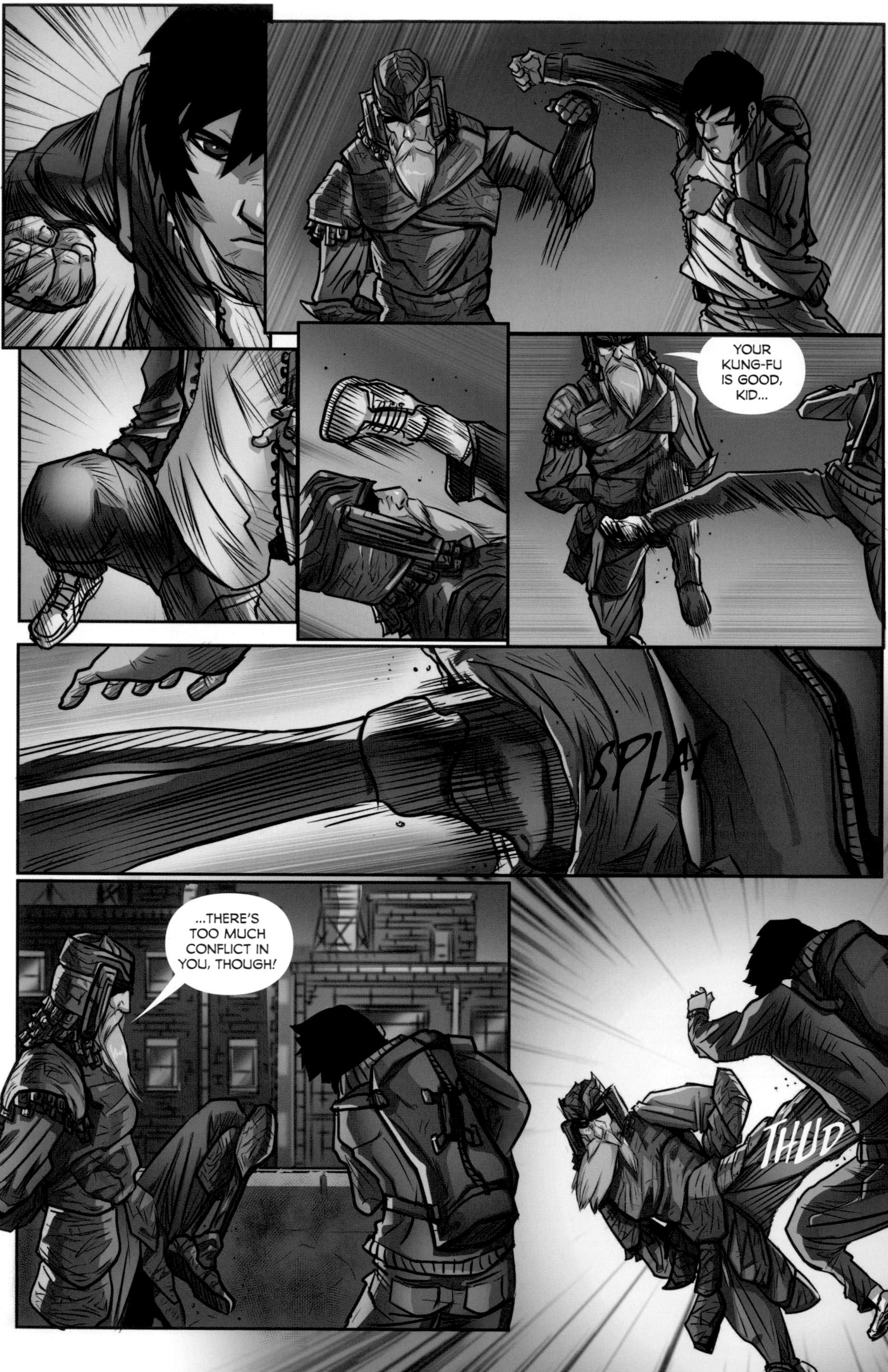
YOUR KUNG-FU IS GOOD, KID...
SPLAT
...THERE'S TOO MUCH CONFLICT IN YOU, THOUGH!
THUD

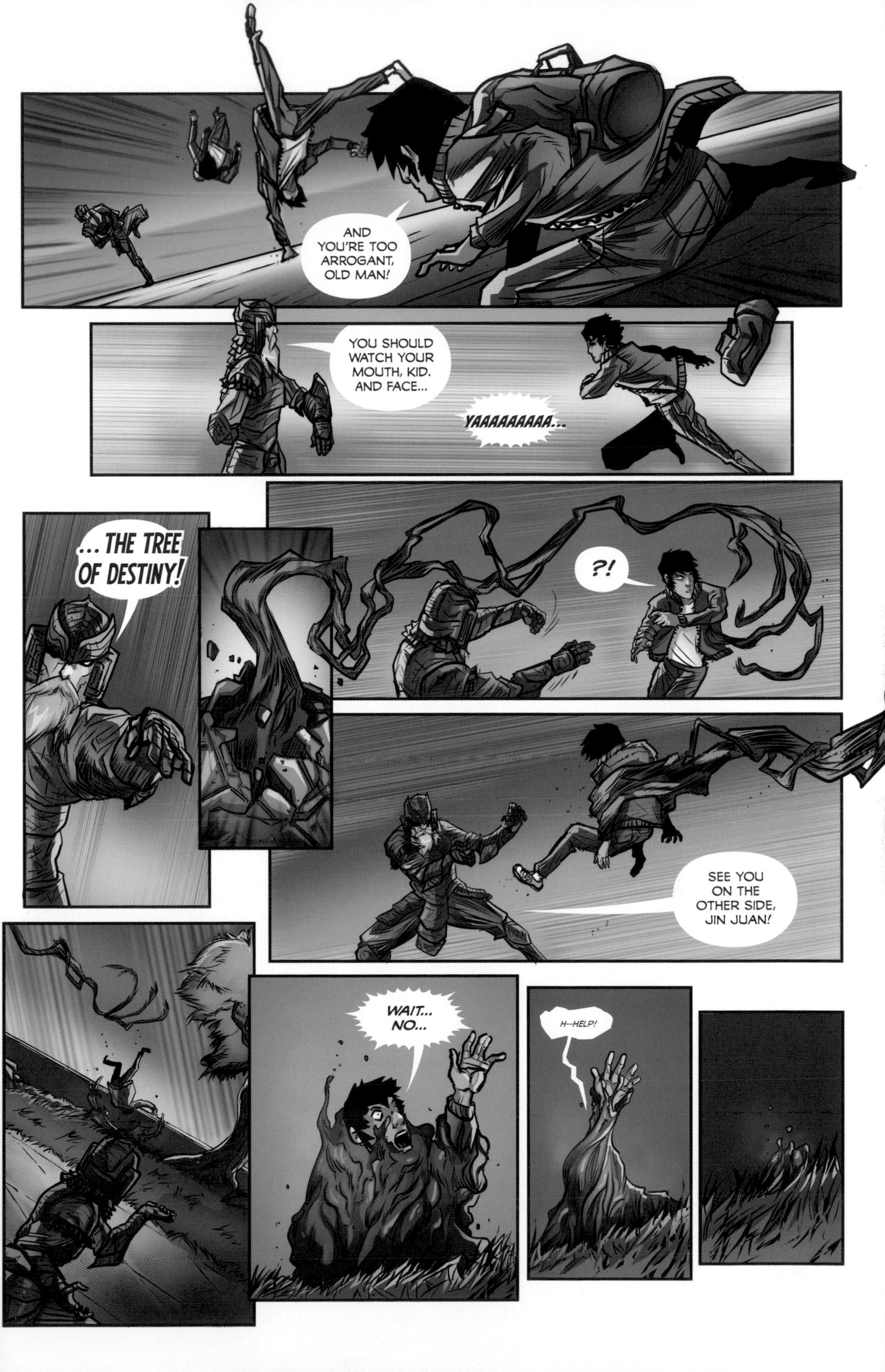
AND YOU'RE TOO ARROGANT, OLD MAN!
YOU SHOULD WATCH YOUR MOUTH, KID. AND FACE...
YAAAAAAAAA...
...THE TREE OF DESTINY!
?!
SEE YOU ON THE OTHER SIDE, JIN JUAN!
WAIT... NO...
H--HELP!

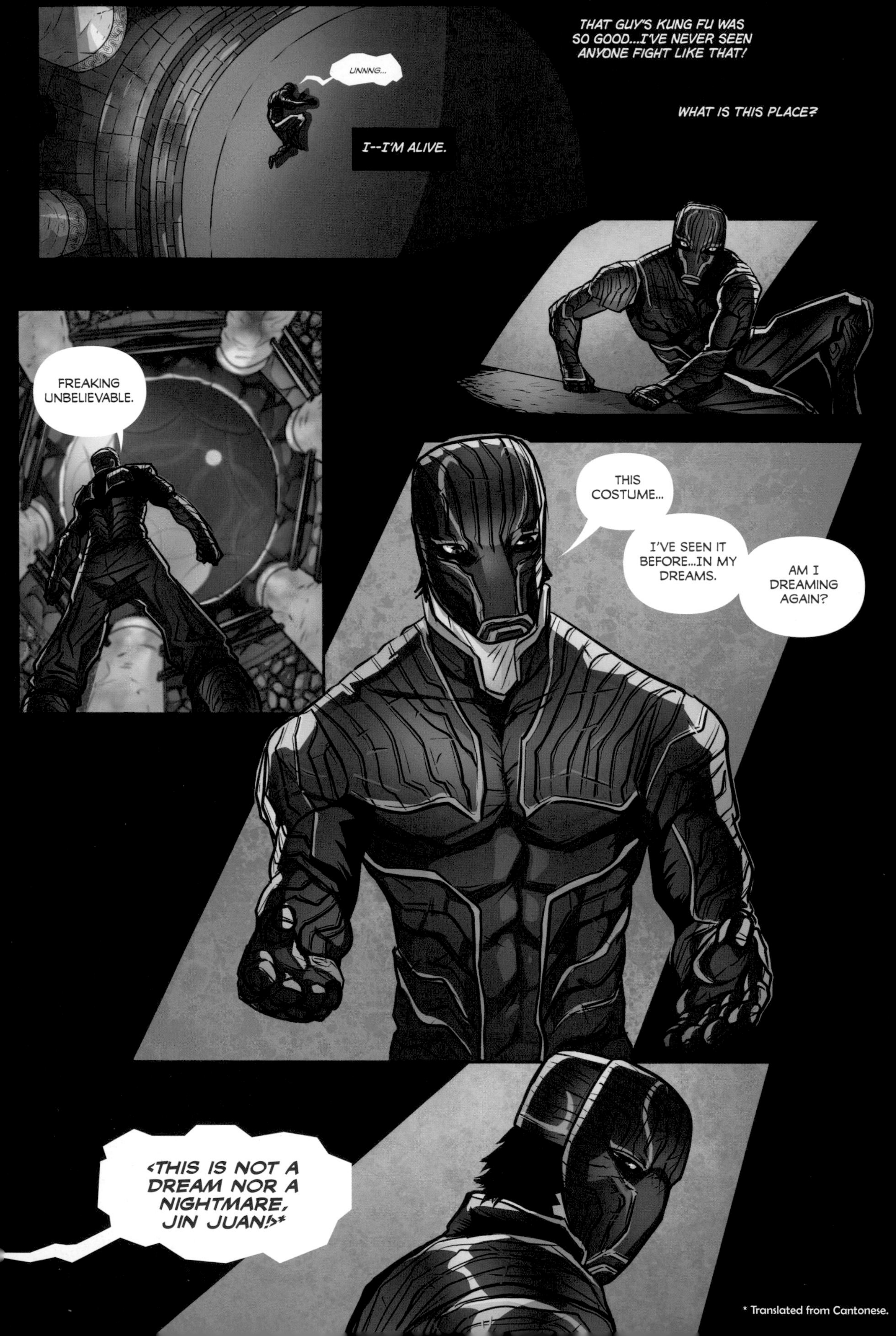
UNNNG...
I--I'M ALIVE.
THAT GUY'S KUNG FU WAS SO GOOD...I'VE NEVER SEEN ANYONE FIGHT LIKE THAT!
WHAT IS THIS PLACE?
FREAKING UNBELIEVABLE.
THIS COSTUME...
I'VE SEEN IT BEFORE...IN MY DREAMS.
AM I DREAMING AGAIN?
‹THIS IS NOT A DREAM NOR A NIGHTMARE, JIN JUAN!›*

* Translated from Cantonese.

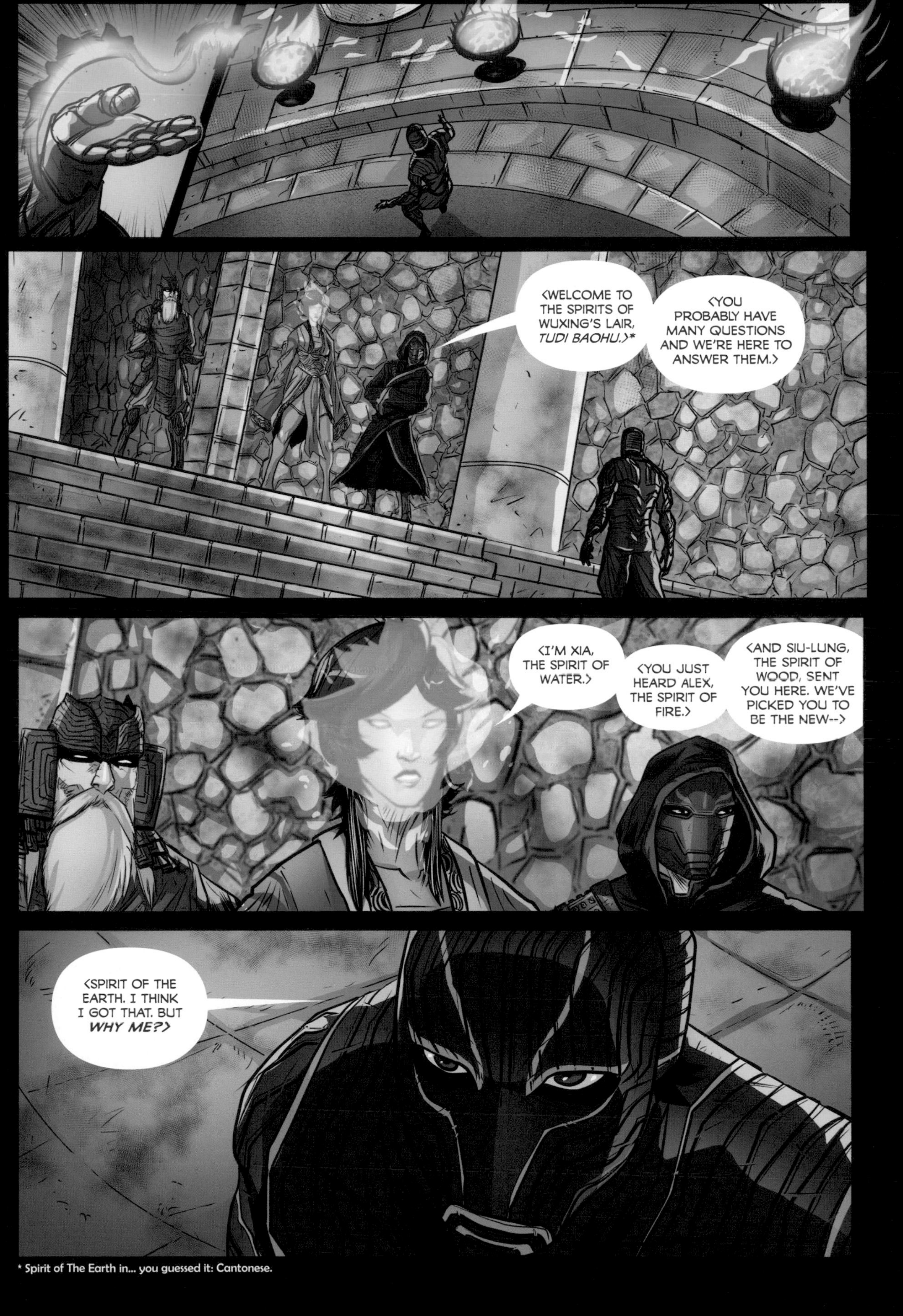
<WELCOME TO THE SPIRITS OF WUXING'S LAIR, *TUDI BAOHU.*>*
<YOU PROBABLY HAVE MANY QUESTIONS AND WE'RE HERE TO ANSWER THEM.>
<I'M XIA, THE SPIRIT OF WATER.>
<YOU JUST HEARD ALEX, THE SPIRIT OF FIRE.>
<AND SIU-LUNG, THE SPIRIT OF WOOD, SENT YOU HERE. WE'VE PICKED YOU TO BE THE NEW-->
<SPIRIT OF THE EARTH. I THINK I GOT THAT. BUT ***WHY ME?***>

* Spirit of The Earth in... you guessed it: Cantonese.

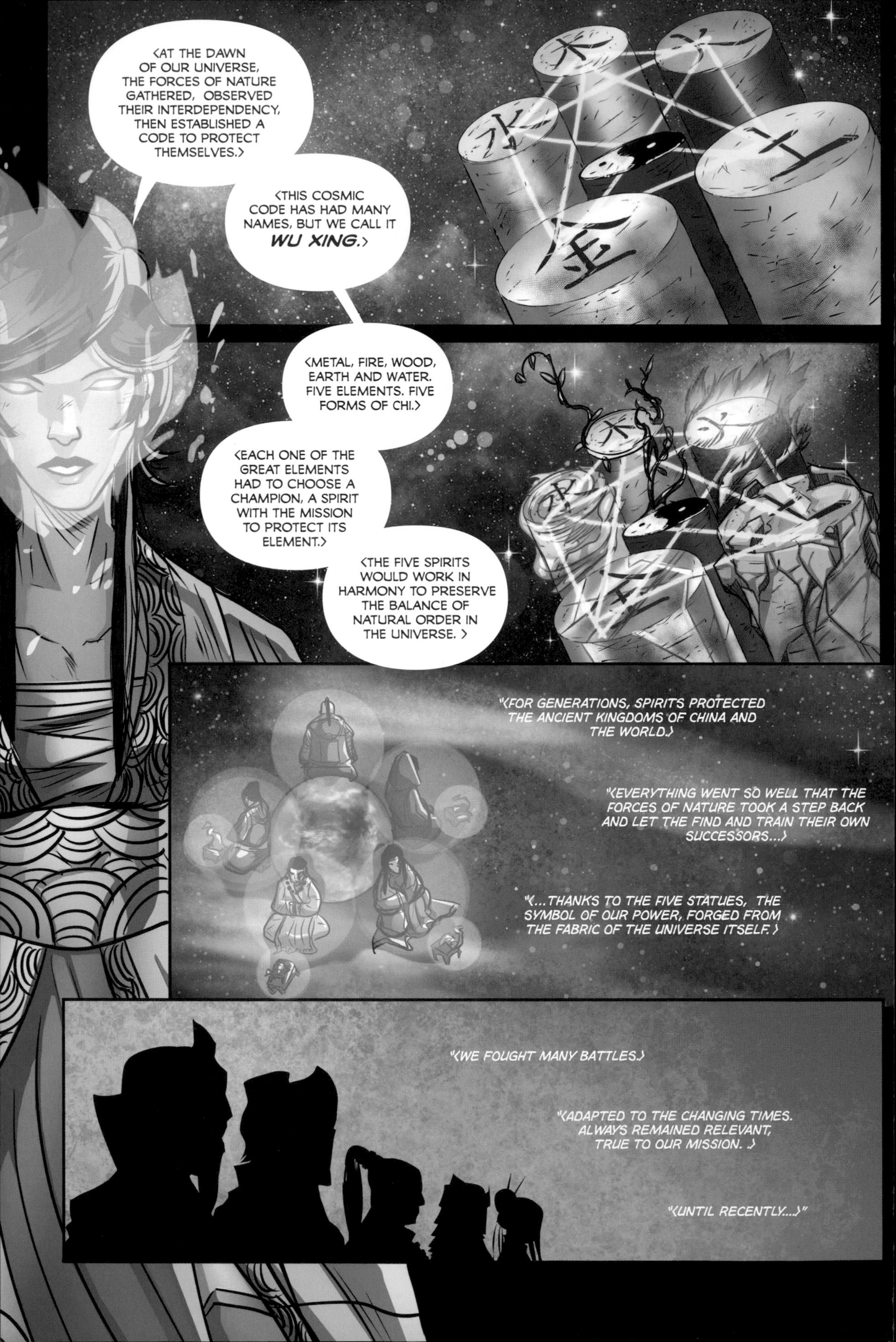

<AT THE DAWN OF OUR UNIVERSE, THE FORCES OF NATURE GATHERED, OBSERVED THEIR INTERDEPENDENCY, THEN ESTABLISHED A CODE TO PROTECT THEMSELVES.>
<THIS COSMIC CODE HAS HAD MANY NAMES, BUT WE CALL IT ***WU XING***.>
<METAL, FIRE, WOOD, EARTH AND WATER. FIVE ELEMENTS. FIVE FORMS OF CHI.>
<EACH ONE OF THE GREAT ELEMENTS HAD TO CHOOSE A CHAMPION, A SPIRIT WITH THE MISSION TO PROTECT ITS ELEMENT.>
<THE FIVE SPIRITS WOULD WORK IN HARMONY TO PRESERVE THE BALANCE OF NATURAL ORDER IN THE UNIVERSE. >
"<FOR GENERATIONS, SPIRITS PROTECTED THE ANCIENT KINGDOMS OF CHINA AND THE WORLD.>
"<EVERYTHING WENT SO WELL THAT THE FORCES OF NATURE TOOK A STEP BACK AND LET THE FIND AND TRAIN THEIR OWN SUCCESSORS...>
"<...THANKS TO THE FIVE STATUES, THE SYMBOL OF OUR POWER, FORGED FROM THE FABRIC OF THE UNIVERSE ITSELF. >
"<WE FOUGHT MANY BATTLES.>
"<ADAPTED TO THE CHANGING TIMES. ALWAYS REMAINED RELEVANT, TRUE TO OUR MISSION. .>
"<UNTIL RECENTLY...>"

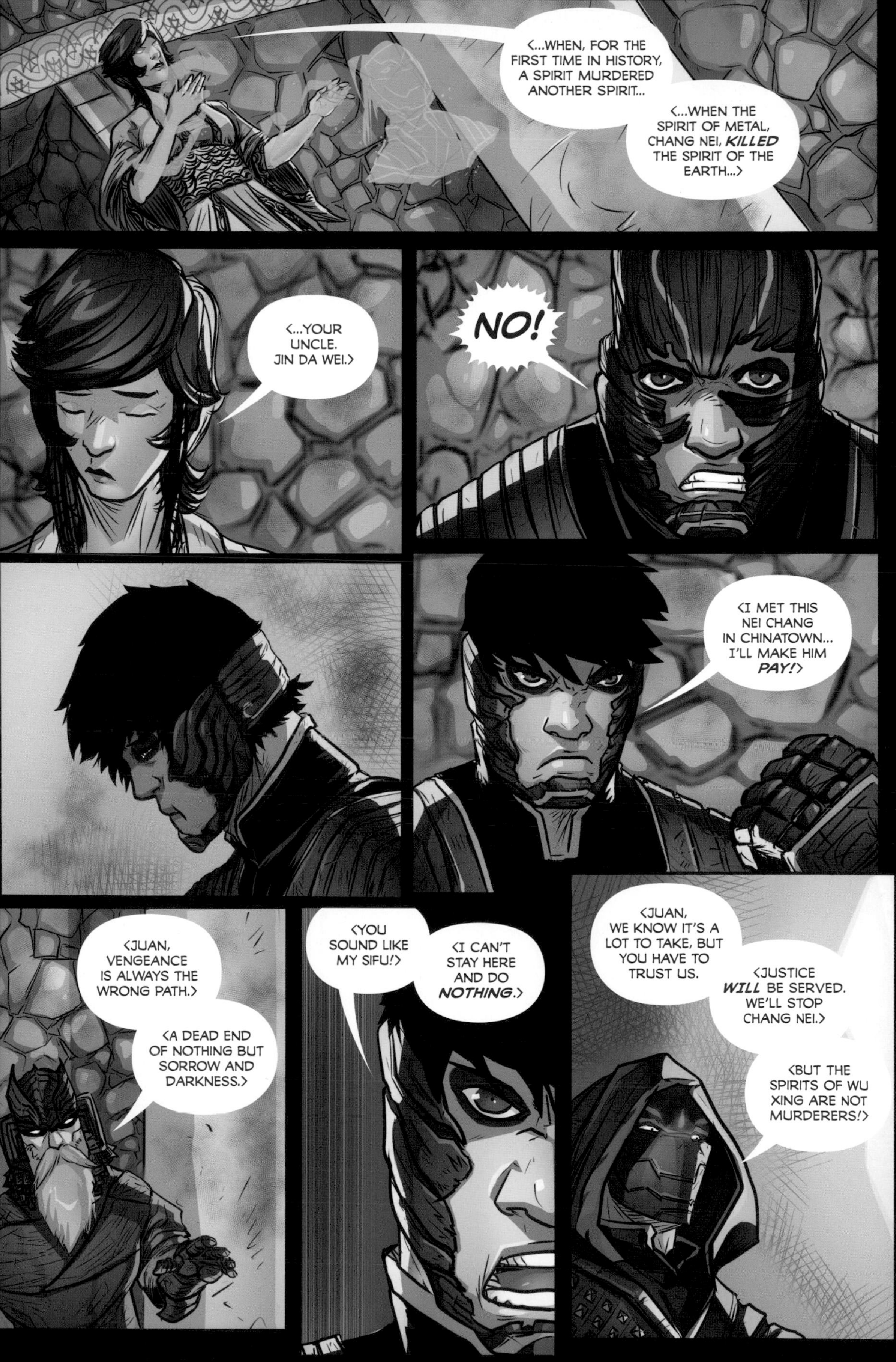

<...WHEN, FOR THE FIRST TIME IN HISTORY, A SPIRIT MURDERED ANOTHER SPIRIT...
<...WHEN THE SPIRIT OF METAL, CHANG NEI, ***KILLED*** THE SPIRIT OF THE EARTH...>
<...YOUR UNCLE. JIN DA WEI.>
NO!
<I MET THIS NEI CHANG IN CHINATOWN... I'LL MAKE HIM ***PAY!***>
<JUAN, VENGEANCE IS ALWAYS THE WRONG PATH.>
<A DEAD END OF NOTHING BUT SORROW AND DARKNESS.>
<YOU SOUND LIKE MY SIFU!>
<I CAN'T STAY HERE AND DO ***NOTHING***.>
<JUAN, WE KNOW IT'S A LOT TO TAKE, BUT YOU HAVE TO TRUST US.
<JUSTICE ***WILL*** BE SERVED. WE'LL STOP CHANG NEI.>
<BUT THE SPIRITS OF WU XING ARE NOT MURDERERS!>

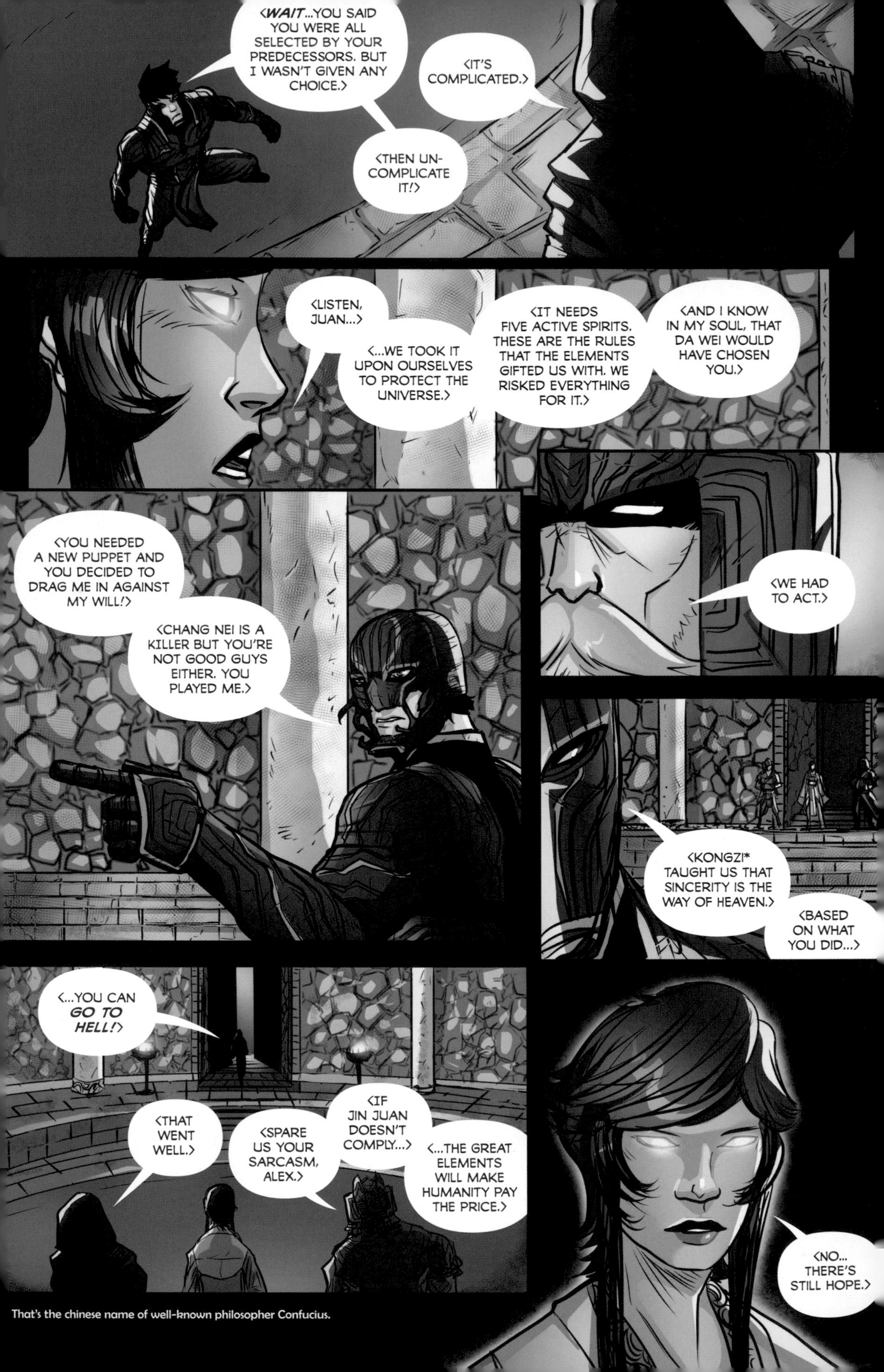
<*WAIT*...YOU SAID YOU WERE ALL SELECTED BY YOUR PREDECESSORS. BUT I WASN'T GIVEN ANY CHOICE.>
<IT'S COMPLICATED.>
<THEN UN-COMPLICATE IT!>
<LISTEN, JUAN...>
<...WE TOOK IT UPON OURSELVES TO PROTECT THE UNIVERSE.>
<IT NEEDS FIVE ACTIVE SPIRITS. THESE ARE THE RULES THAT THE ELEMENTS GIFTED US WITH. WE RISKED EVERYTHING FOR IT.>
<AND I KNOW IN MY SOUL, THAT DA WEI WOULD HAVE CHOSEN YOU.>
<WE HAD TO ACT.>
<YOU NEEDED A NEW PUPPET AND YOU DECIDED TO DRAG ME IN AGAINST MY WILL!>
<CHANG NEI IS A KILLER BUT YOU'RE NOT GOOD GUYS EITHER. YOU PLAYED ME.>
<KONGZI!* TAUGHT US THAT SINCERITY IS THE WAY OF HEAVEN.>
<BASED ON WHAT YOU DID...>
<...YOU CAN ***GO TO HELL!***>
<THAT WENT WELL.>
<SPARE US YOUR SARCASM, ALEX.>
<IF JIN JUAN DOESN'T COMPLY...>
<...THE GREAT ELEMENTS WILL MAKE HUMANITY PAY THE PRICE.>
<NO... THERE'S STILL HOPE.>

That's the chinese name of well-known philosopher Confucius.

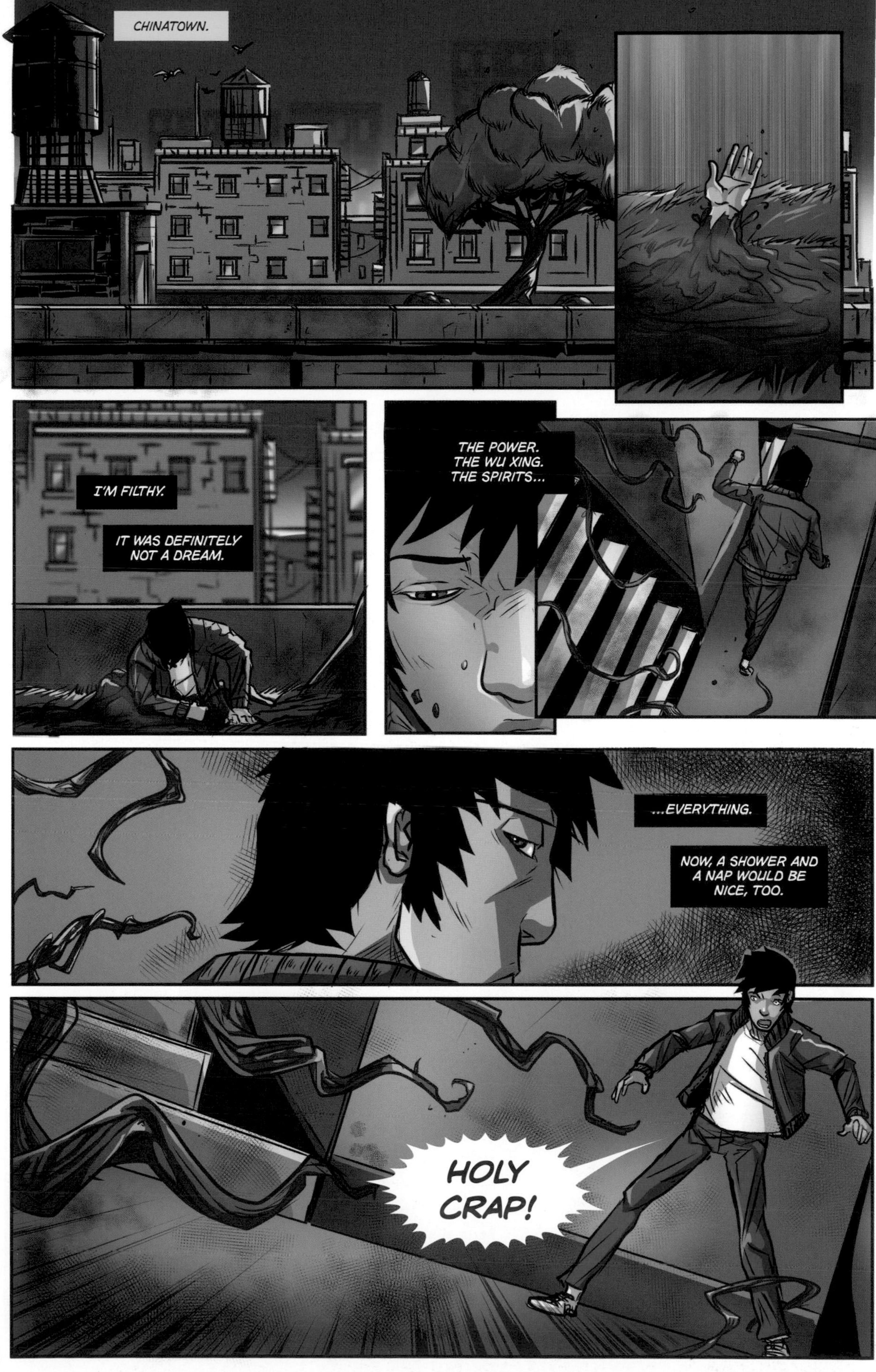
CHINATOWN.
I'M FILTHY.
IT WAS DEFINITELY NOT A DREAM.
THE POWER. THE WU XING. THE SPIRITS...
...EVERYTHING.
NOW, A SHOWER AND A NAP WOULD BE NICE, TOO.
HOLY CRAP!

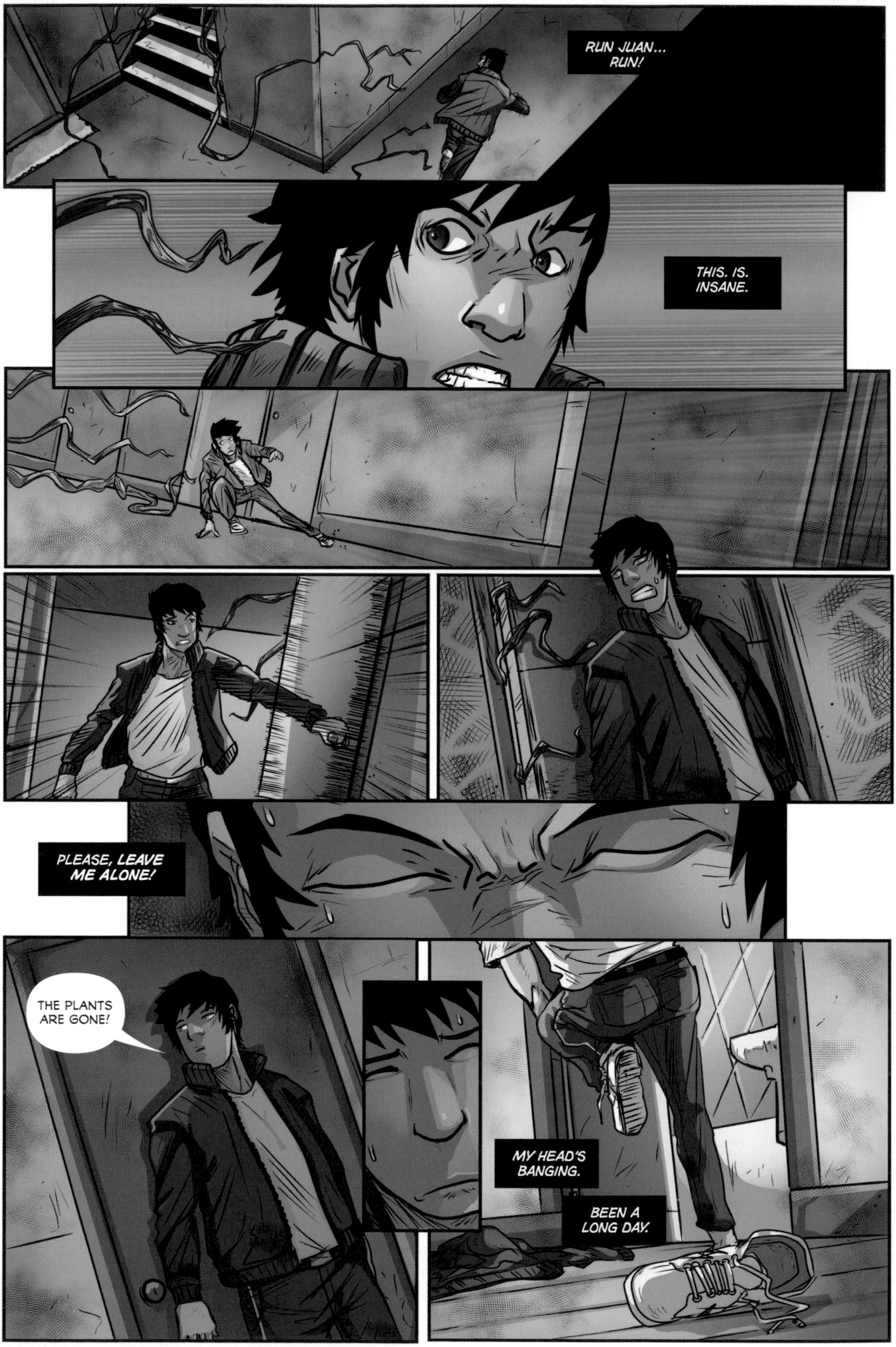
RUN JUAN... RUN!
THIS. IS. INSANE.
PLEASE, LEAVE ME ALONE!
THE PLANTS ARE GONE!
MY HEAD'S BANGING.
BEEN A LONG DAY.

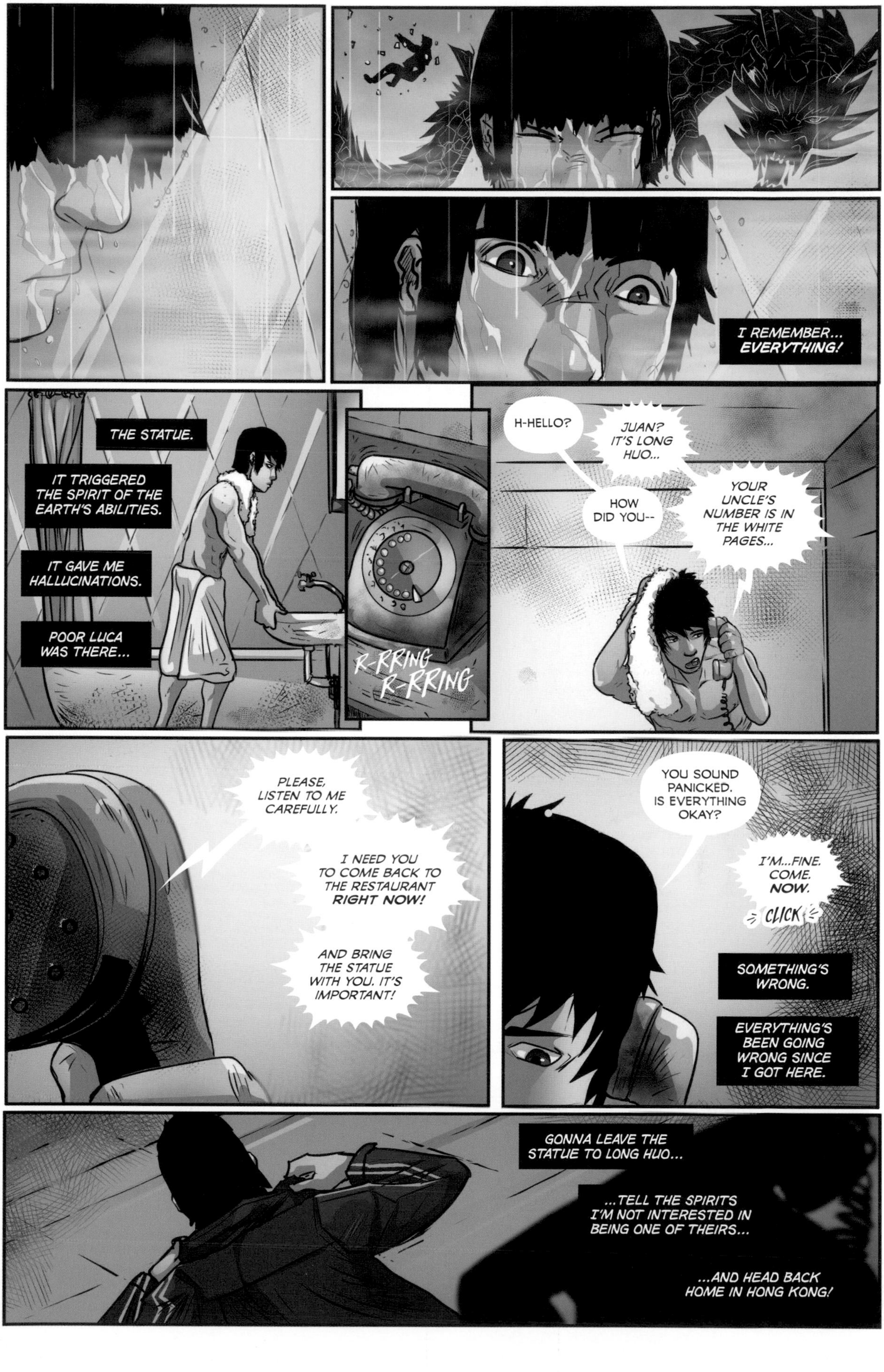
I REMEMBER... EVERYTHING!
THE STATUE.
IT TRIGGERED THE SPIRIT OF THE EARTH'S ABILITIES.
IT GAVE ME HALLUCINATIONS.
POOR LUCA WAS THERE...
R-RRING R-RRING
H-HELLO?
JUAN? IT'S LONG HUO...
HOW DID YOU--
YOUR UNCLE'S NUMBER IS IN THE WHITE PAGES...
PLEASE, LISTEN TO ME CAREFULLY.
I NEED YOU TO COME BACK TO THE RESTAURANT RIGHT NOW!
AND BRING THE STATUE WITH YOU. IT'S IMPORTANT!
YOU SOUND PANICKED. IS EVERYTHING OKAY?
I'M...FINE. COME. NOW.
CLICK
SOMETHING'S WRONG.
EVERYTHING'S BEEN GOING WRONG SINCE I GOT HERE.
GONNA LEAVE THE STATUE TO LONG HUO...
...TELL THE SPIRITS I'M NOT INTERESTED IN BEING ONE OF THEIRS...
...AND HEAD BACK HOME IN HONG KONG!

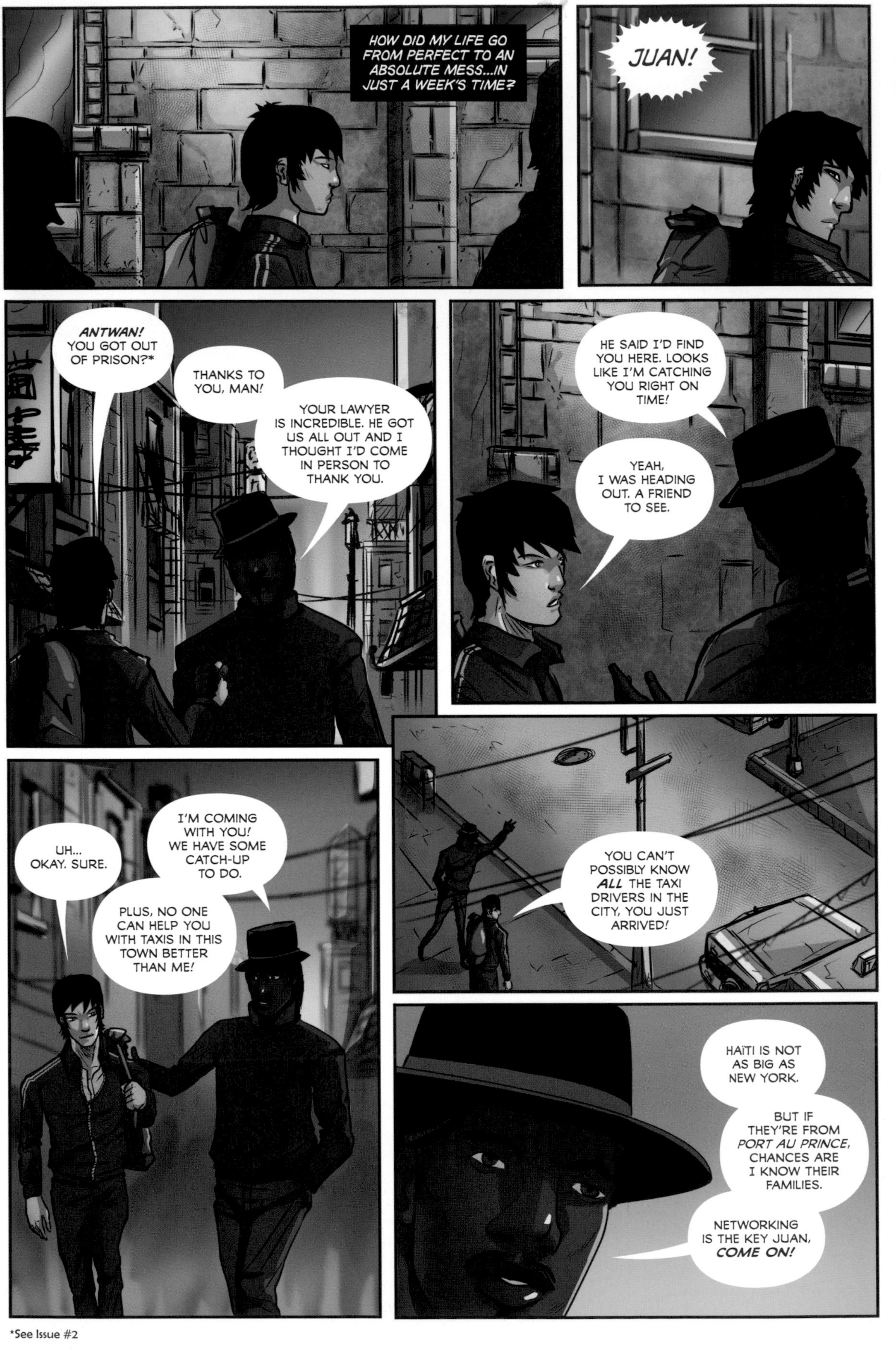
HOW DID MY LIFE GO FROM PERFECT TO AN ABSOLUTE MESS...IN JUST A WEEK'S TIME?
JUAN!
ANTWAN! YOU GOT OUT OF PRISON?*
THANKS TO YOU, MAN!
YOUR LAWYER IS INCREDIBLE. HE GOT US ALL OUT AND I THOUGHT I'D COME IN PERSON TO THANK YOU.
HE SAID I'D FIND YOU HERE. LOOKS LIKE I'M CATCHING YOU RIGHT ON TIME!
YEAH, I WAS HEADING OUT. A FRIEND TO SEE.
UH... OKAY. SURE.
I'M COMING WITH YOU! WE HAVE SOME CATCH-UP TO DO.
PLUS, NO ONE CAN HELP YOU WITH TAXIS IN THIS TOWN BETTER THAN ME!
YOU CAN'T POSSIBLY KNOW ALL THE TAXI DRIVERS IN THE CITY, YOU JUST ARRIVED!
HAÏTI IS NOT AS BIG AS NEW YORK.
BUT IF THEY'RE FROM PORT AU PRINCE, CHANCES ARE I KNOW THEIR FAMILIES.
NETWORKING IS THE KEY JUAN, COME ON!

*See Issue #2

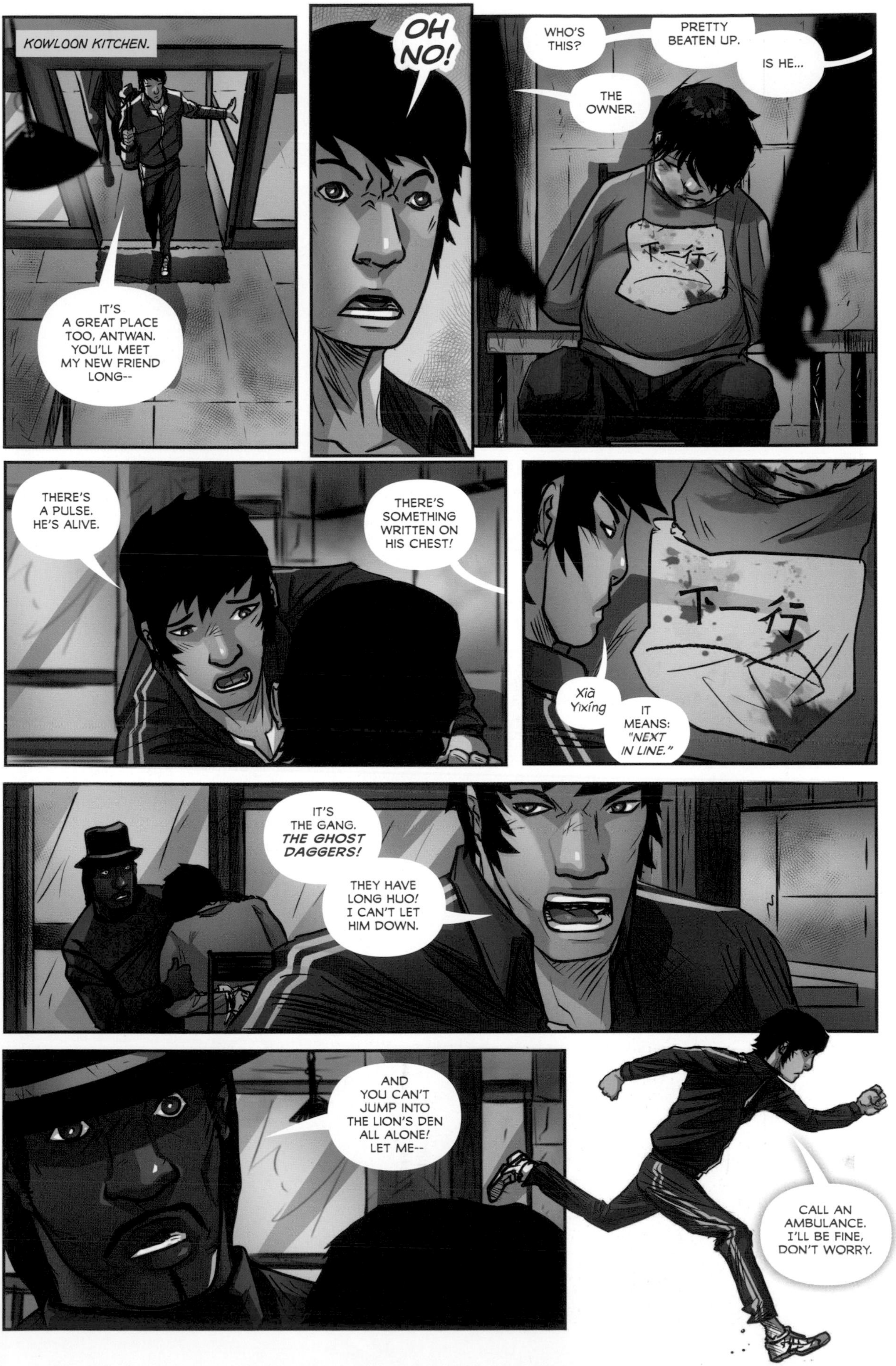
KOWLOON KITCHEN.
IT'S A GREAT PLACE TOO, ANTWAN. YOU'LL MEET MY NEW FRIEND LONG--
OH NO!
WHO'S THIS?
PRETTY BEATEN UP.
IS HE...
THE OWNER.
下一行
THERE'S A PULSE. HE'S ALIVE.
THERE'S SOMETHING WRITTEN ON HIS CHEST!
下一行
Xià Yixíng
IT MEANS: "NEXT IN LINE."
IT'S THE GANG. THE GHOST DAGGERS!
THEY HAVE LONG HUO! I CAN'T LET HIM DOWN.
AND YOU CAN'T JUMP INTO THE LION'S DEN ALL ALONE! LET ME--
CALL AN AMBULANCE. I'LL BE FINE, DON'T WORRY.

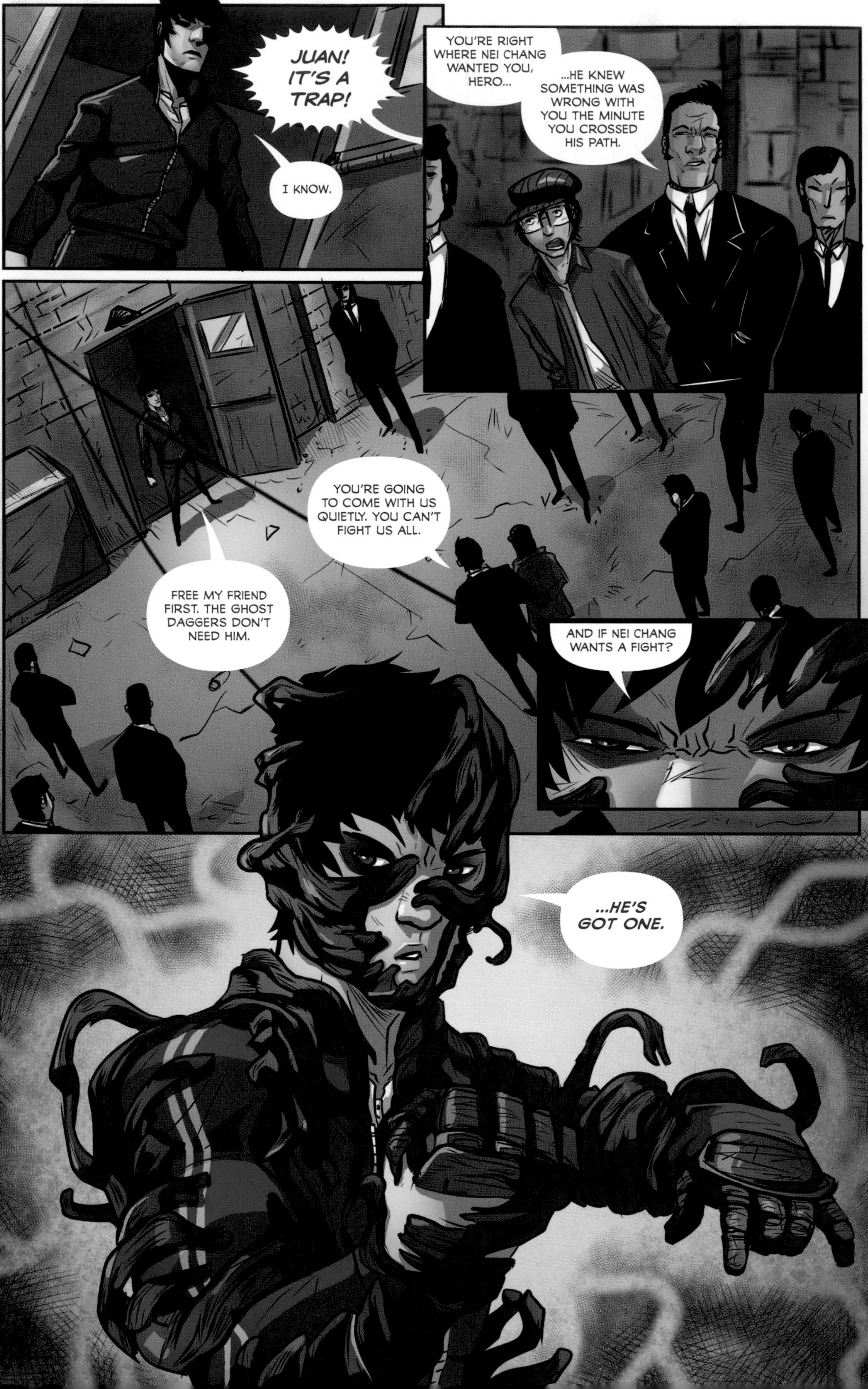
JUAN! IT'S A TRAP!
I KNOW.
YOU'RE RIGHT WHERE NEI CHANG WANTED YOU, HERO...
...HE KNEW SOMETHING WAS WRONG WITH YOU THE MINUTE YOU CROSSED HIS PATH.
YOU'RE GOING TO COME WITH US QUIETLY. YOU CAN'T FIGHT US ALL.
FREE MY FRIEND FIRST. THE GHOST DAGGERS DON'T NEED HIM.
AND IF NEI CHANG WANTS A FIGHT?
...HE'S GOT ONE.

INTERTWINED BEHIND THE SCENES

INTERTWINED
FABRICE SAPOLSKY
FRED PHAM CHUONG
A KUNG-FU NOIR
COMIC BOOK SERIES
CONTACT: FABRICESAPOLSKY@GMAIL.COM
PARENTAL ADVISORY EXPLICIT COMICS

INTERTWINED

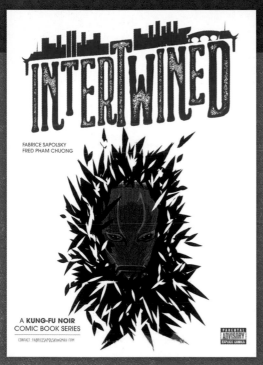

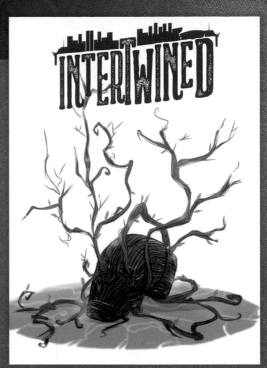

ABOVE: When pitching to publishers, different things were tried to draw attention at first glance. Fred drew these two pieces before Fabrice and him finally settled on the one on the left, the "Lion King" one. Looks like it worked.

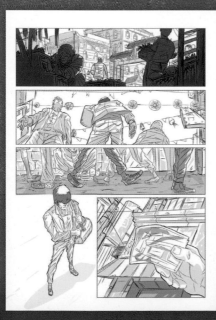

FRED'S TEST PAGES

When Fabrice recruited Fred, he put him to the test! Here are the first two pages that he drew to convince Fabrice he was the only guy for the job. And he knocked it out of the park.

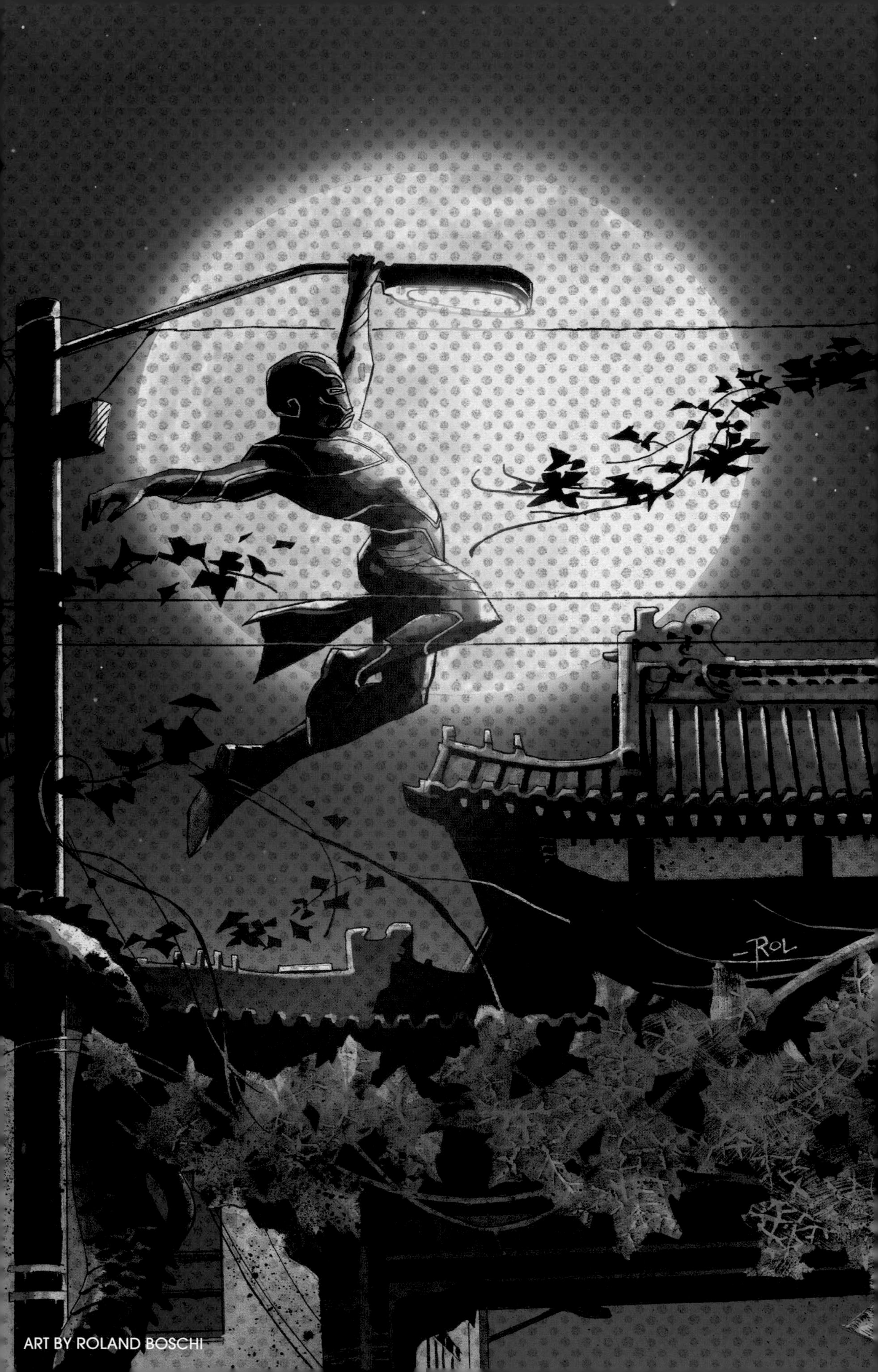
-ROL

ART BY ROLAND BOSCHI

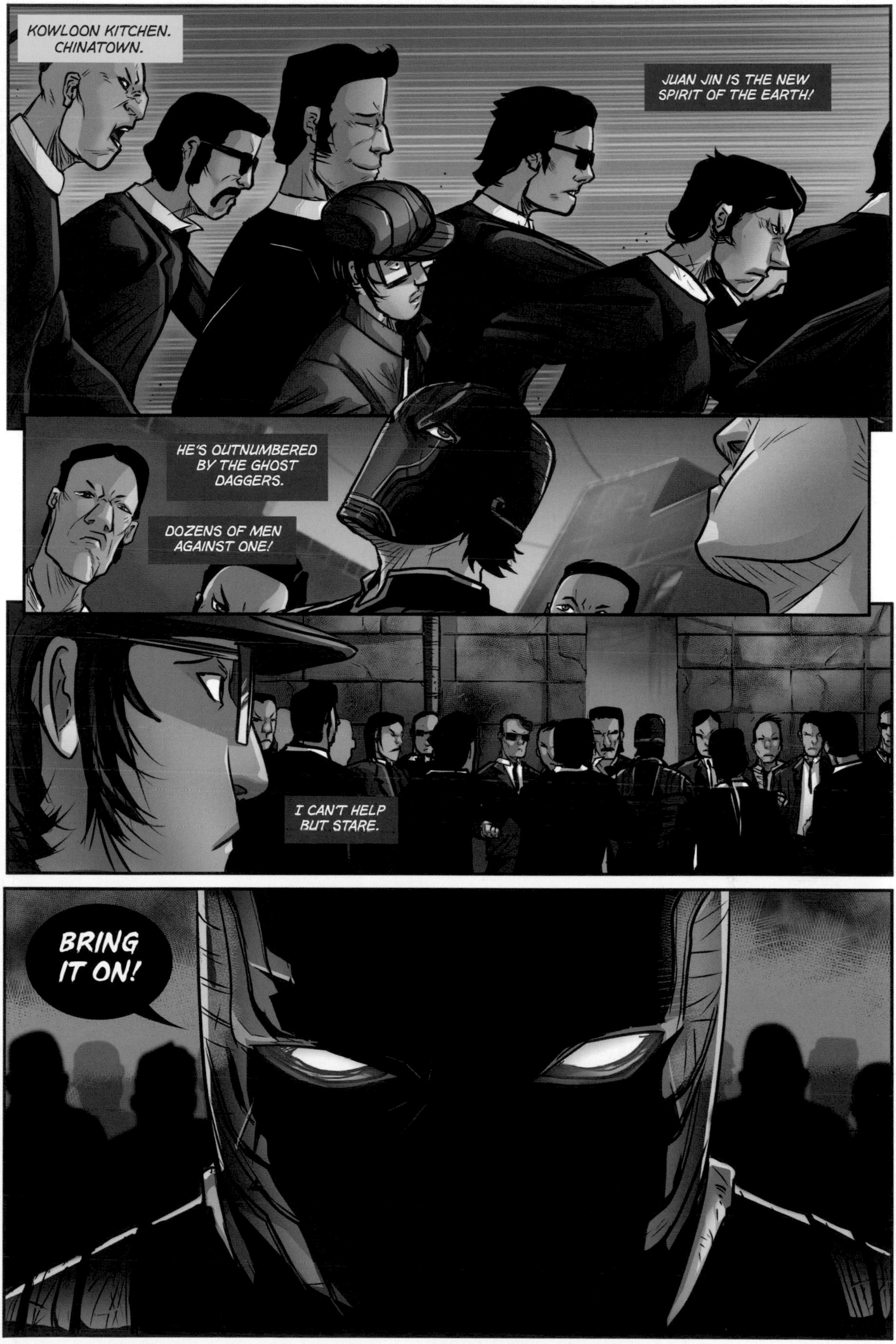
KOWLOON KITCHEN. CHINATOWN.
JUAN JIN IS THE NEW SPIRIT OF THE EARTH!
HE'S OUTNUMBERED BY THE GHOST DAGGERS.
DOZENS OF MEN AGAINST ONE!
I CAN'T HELP BUT STARE.
BRING IT ON!

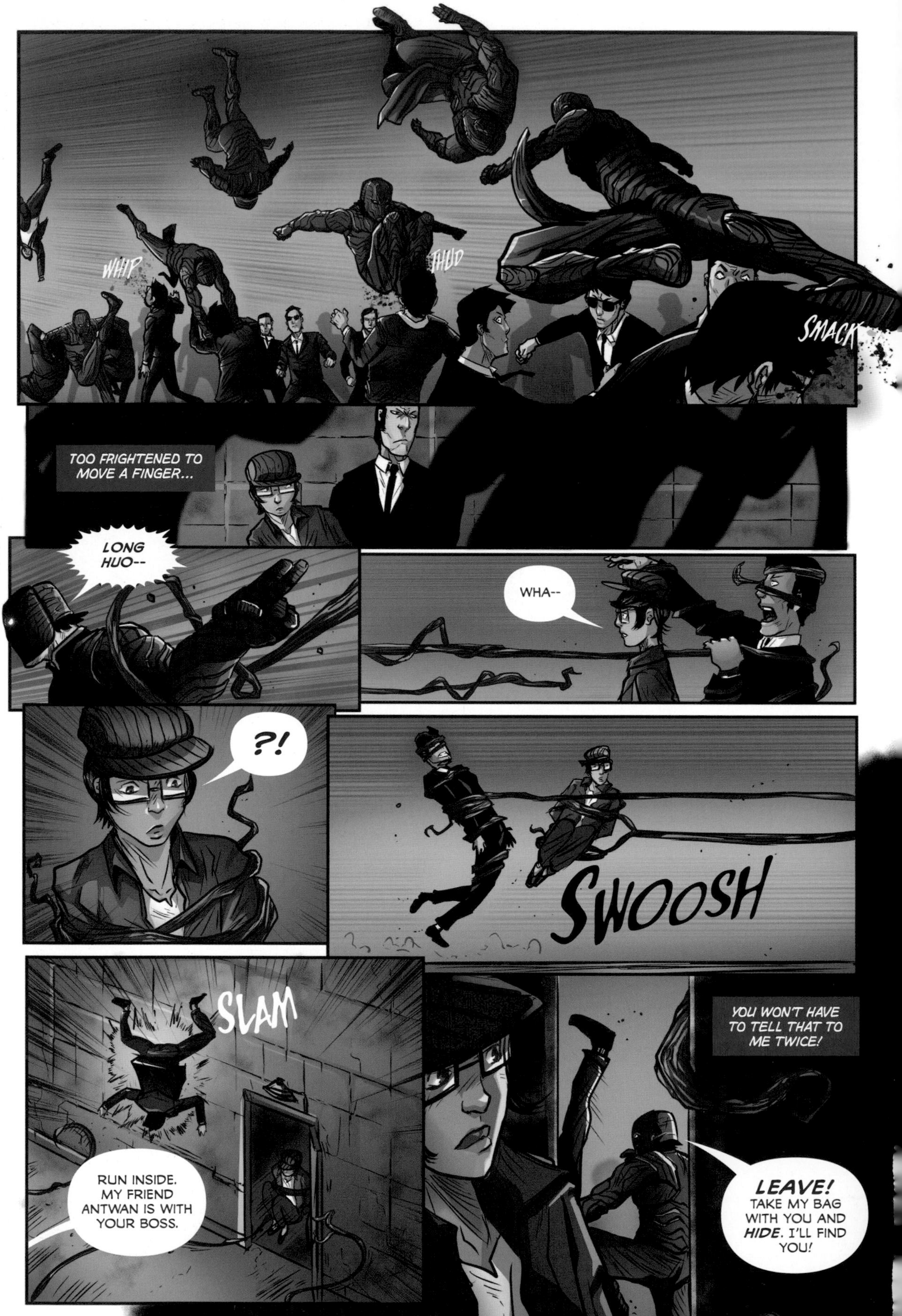
WHIP
THUD
SMACK
TOO FRIGHTENED TO MOVE A FINGER...
LONG HUO--
WHA--
?!
SWOOSH
SLAM
RUN INSIDE. MY FRIEND ANTWAN IS WITH YOUR BOSS.
YOU WON'T HAVE TO TELL THAT TO ME TWICE!
LEAVE! TAKE MY BAG WITH YOU AND HIDE. I'LL FIND YOU!

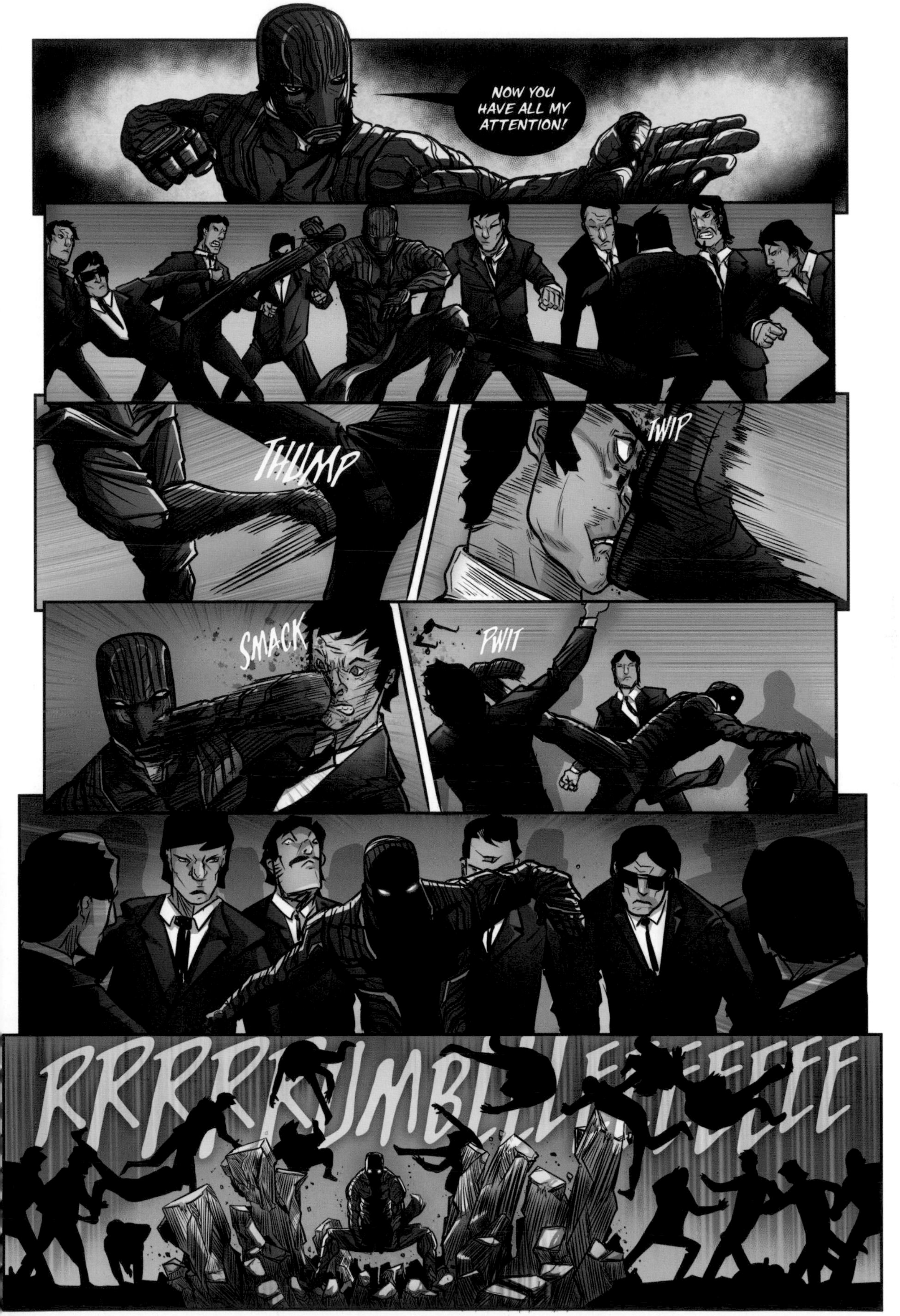
NOW YOU HAVE ALL MY ATTENTION!
THUMP
TWIP
SMACK
PWIT
RRRRRUMBLLLLEEEEEE

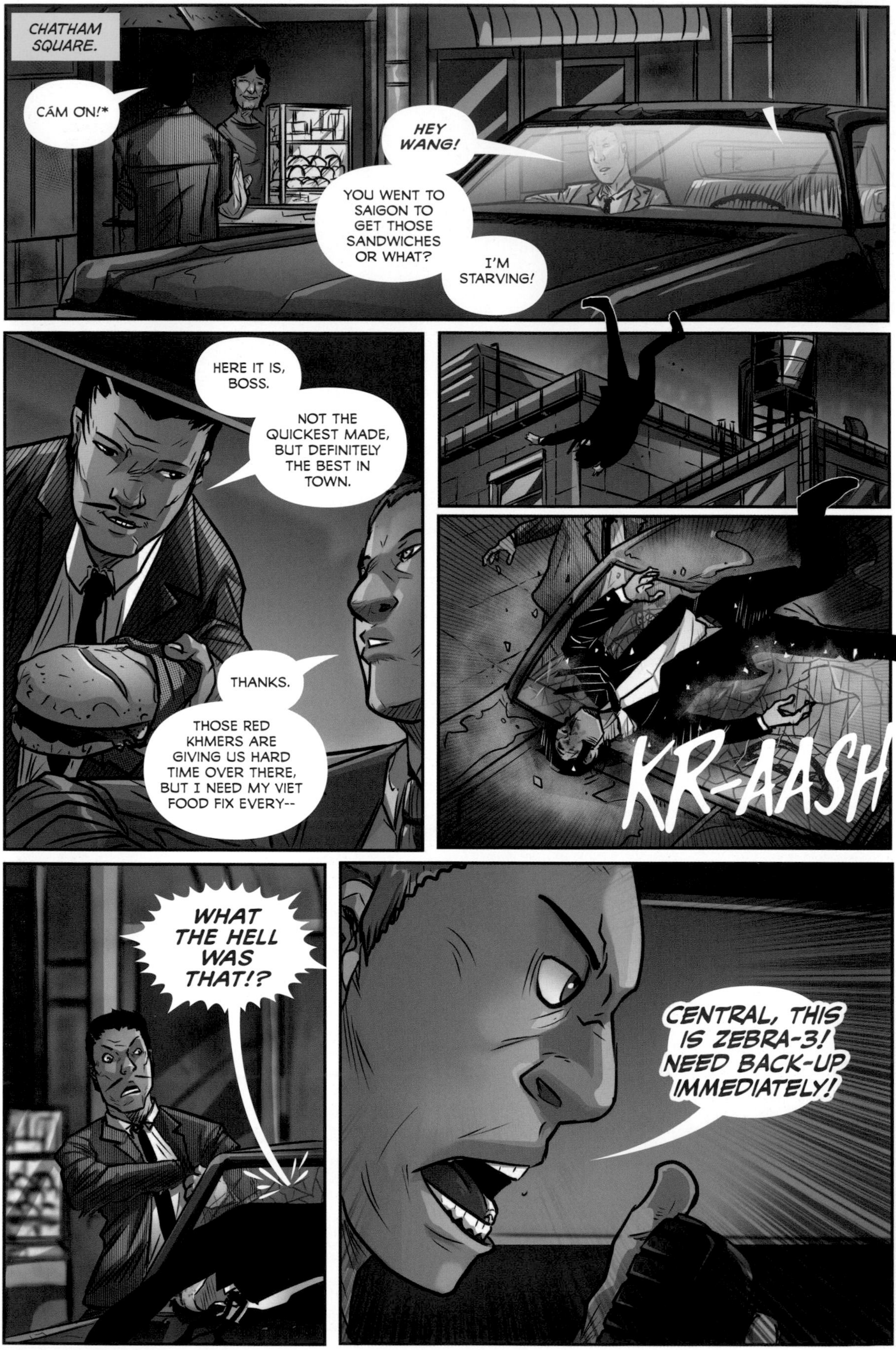
CHATHAM SQUARE.
CẢM ƠN!*
HEY WANG!
YOU WENT TO SAIGON TO GET THOSE SANDWICHES OR WHAT?
I'M STARVING!
HERE IT IS, BOSS.
NOT THE QUICKEST MADE, BUT DEFINITELY THE BEST IN TOWN.
THANKS.
THOSE RED KHMERS ARE GIVING US HARD TIME OVER THERE, BUT I NEED MY VIET FOOD FIX EVERY--
KR-AASH
WHAT THE HELL WAS THAT!?
CENTRAL, THIS IS ZEBRA-3! NEED BACK-UP IMMEDIATELY!

* Thank you in vietnamese

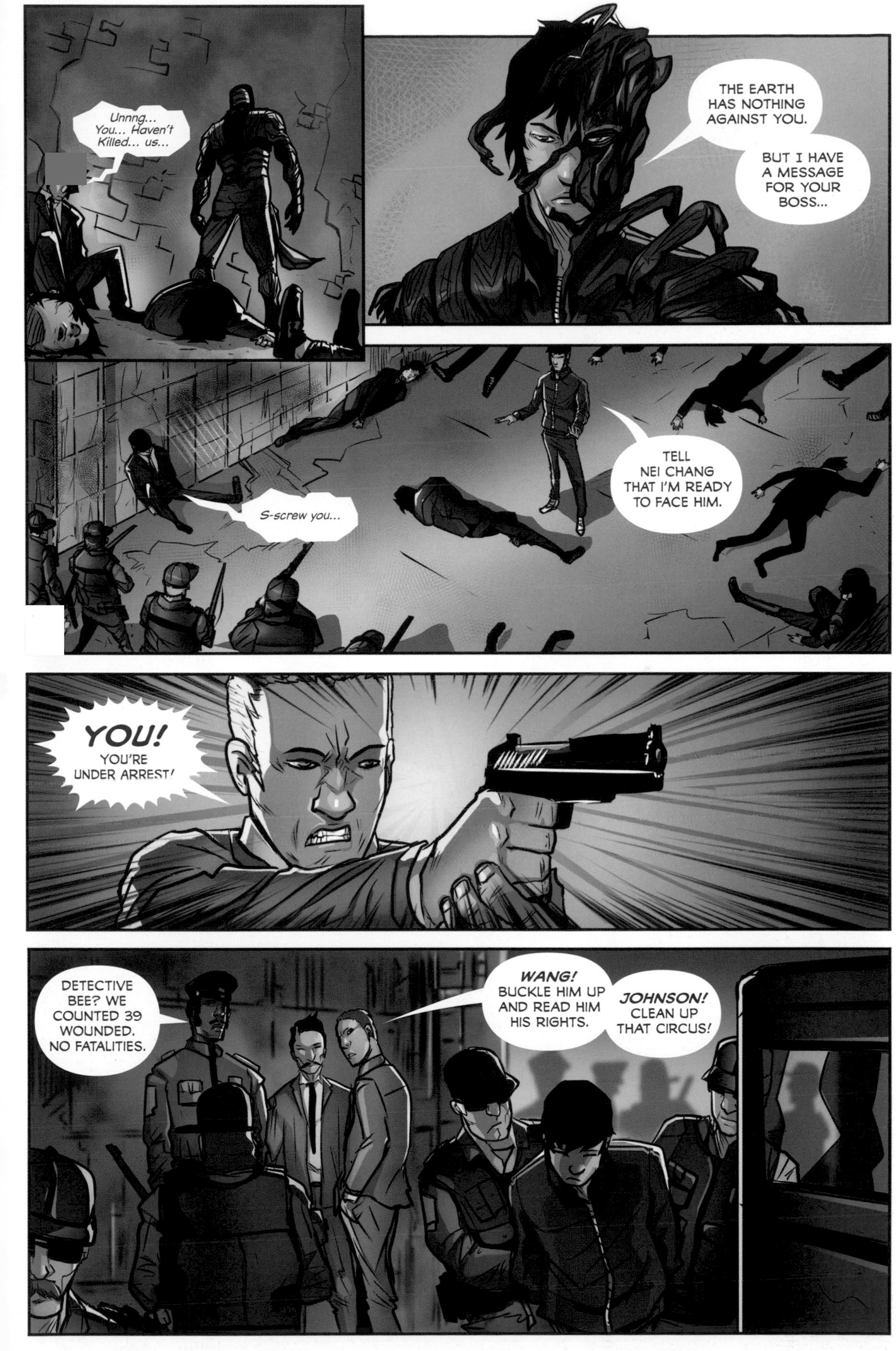
Unnng... You... Haven't Killed... us...
THE EARTH HAS NOTHING AGAINST YOU.
BUT I HAVE A MESSAGE FOR YOUR BOSS...
S-screw you...
TELL NEI CHANG THAT I'M READY TO FACE HIM.
YOU! YOU'RE UNDER ARREST!
DETECTIVE BEE? WE COUNTED 39 WOUNDED. NO FATALITIES.
WANG! BUCKLE HIM UP AND READ HIM HIS RIGHTS.
JOHNSON! CLEAN UP THAT CIRCUS!

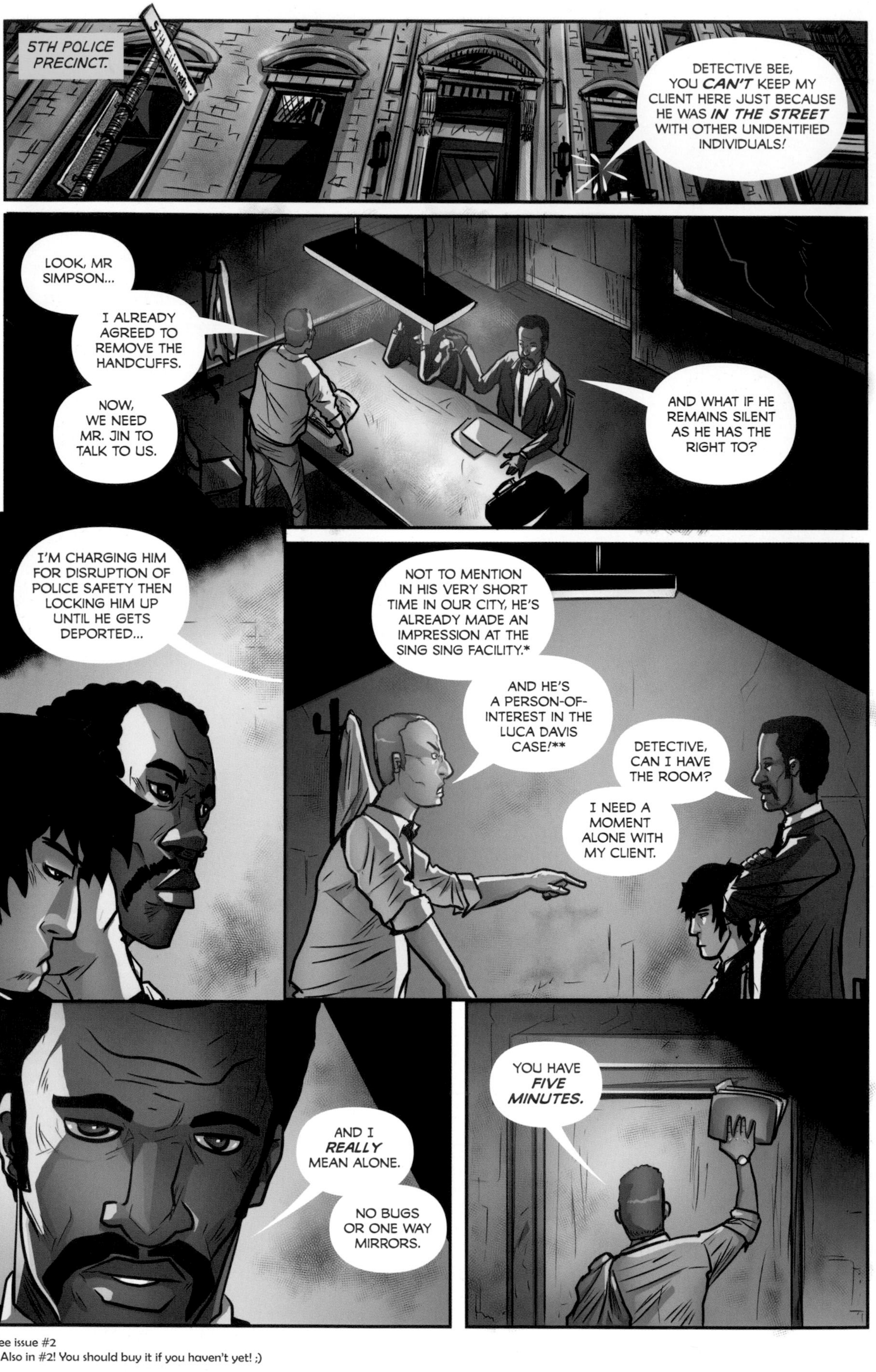
5TH POLICE PRECINCT.
DETECTIVE BEE, YOU CAN'T KEEP MY CLIENT HERE JUST BECAUSE HE WAS IN THE STREET WITH OTHER UNIDENTIFIED INDIVIDUALS!
LOOK, MR SIMPSON...
I ALREADY AGREED TO REMOVE THE HANDCUFFS.
NOW, WE NEED MR. JIN TO TALK TO US.
AND WHAT IF HE REMAINS SILENT AS HE HAS THE RIGHT TO?
I'M CHARGING HIM FOR DISRUPTION OF POLICE SAFETY THEN LOCKING HIM UP UNTIL HE GETS DEPORTED...
NOT TO MENTION IN HIS VERY SHORT TIME IN OUR CITY, HE'S ALREADY MADE AN IMPRESSION AT THE SING SING FACILITY.*
AND HE'S A PERSON-OF-INTEREST IN THE LUCA DAVIS CASE!**
DETECTIVE, CAN I HAVE THE ROOM?
I NEED A MOMENT ALONE WITH MY CLIENT.
AND I REALLY MEAN ALONE.
NO BUGS OR ONE WAY MIRRORS.
YOU HAVE FIVE MINUTES.

*See issue #2
** Also in #2! You should buy it if you haven't yet! ;)

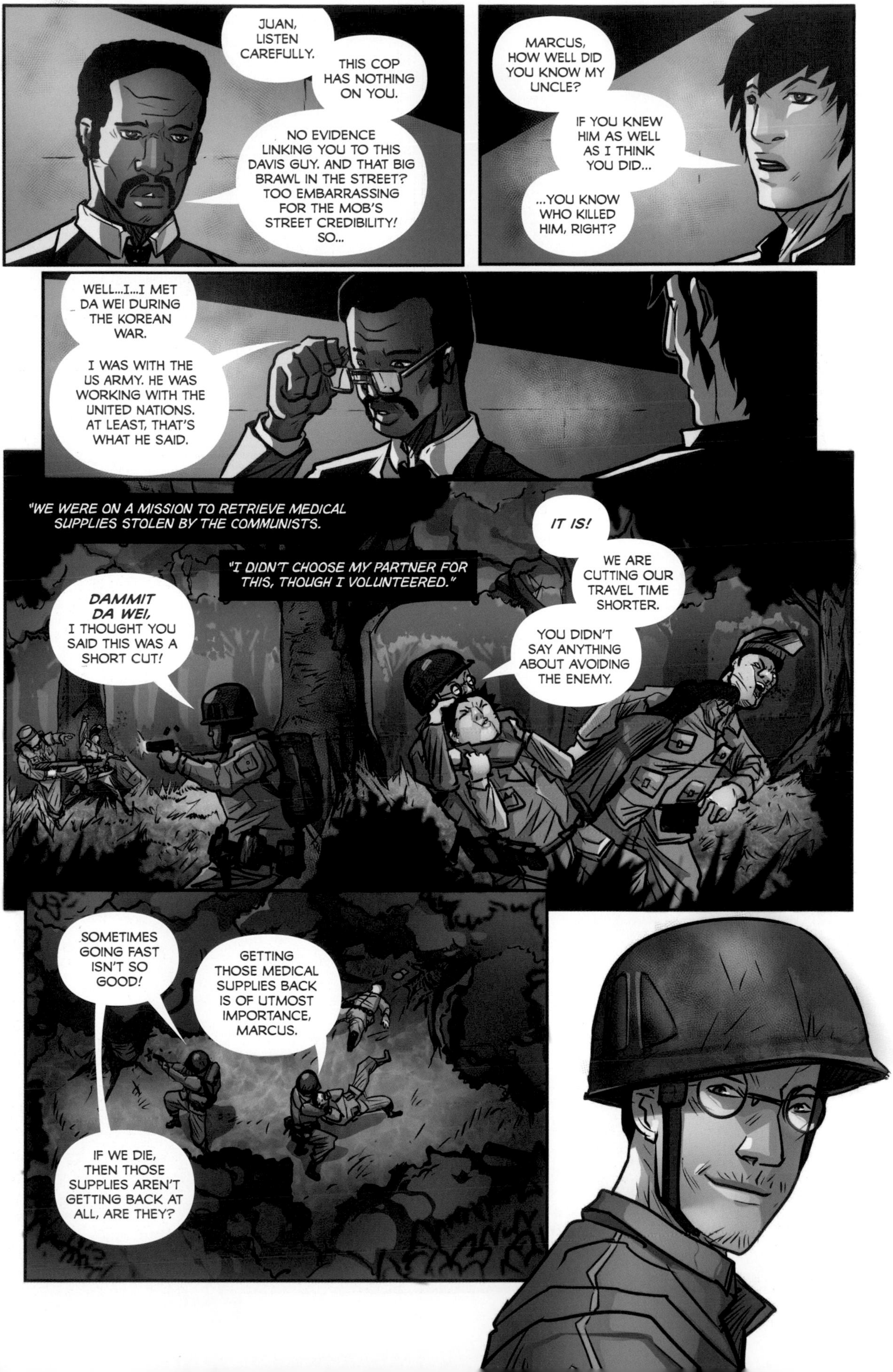
JUAN, LISTEN CAREFULLY.
THIS COP HAS NOTHING ON YOU.
NO EVIDENCE LINKING YOU TO THIS DAVIS GUY. AND THAT BIG BRAWL IN THE STREET? TOO EMBARRASSING FOR THE MOB'S STREET CREDIBILITY! SO...
MARCUS, HOW WELL DID YOU KNOW MY UNCLE?
IF YOU KNEW HIM AS WELL AS I THINK YOU DID...
...YOU KNOW WHO KILLED HIM, RIGHT?
WELL...I...I MET DA WEI DURING THE KOREAN WAR.
I WAS WITH THE US ARMY. HE WAS WORKING WITH THE UNITED NATIONS. AT LEAST, THAT'S WHAT HE SAID.
"WE WERE ON A MISSION TO RETRIEVE MEDICAL SUPPLIES STOLEN BY THE COMMUNISTS.
"I DIDN'T CHOOSE MY PARTNER FOR THIS, THOUGH I VOLUNTEERED."
DAMMIT DA WEI, I THOUGHT YOU SAID THIS WAS A SHORT CUT!
IT IS!
WE ARE CUTTING OUR TRAVEL TIME SHORTER.
YOU DIDN'T SAY ANYTHING ABOUT AVOIDING THE ENEMY.
SOMETIMES GOING FAST ISN'T SO GOOD!
GETTING THOSE MEDICAL SUPPLIES BACK IS OF UTMOST IMPORTANCE, MARCUS.
IF WE DIE, THEN THOSE SUPPLIES AREN'T GETTING BACK AT ALL, ARE THEY?

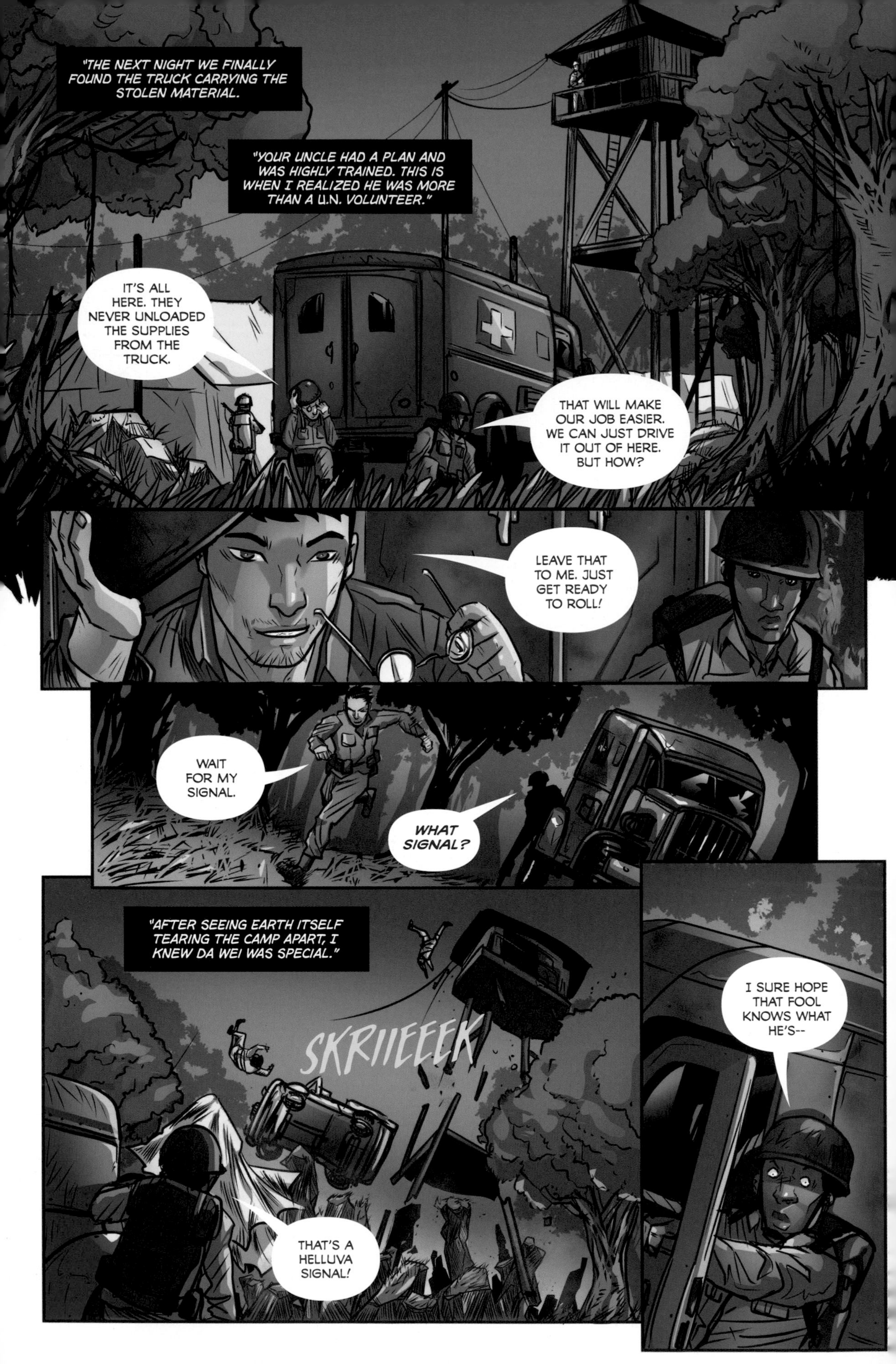
"THE NEXT NIGHT WE FINALLY FOUND THE TRUCK CARRYING THE STOLEN MATERIAL.
"YOUR UNCLE HAD A PLAN AND WAS HIGHLY TRAINED. THIS IS WHEN I REALIZED HE WAS MORE THAN A U.N. VOLUNTEER."
IT'S ALL HERE. THEY NEVER UNLOADED THE SUPPLIES FROM THE TRUCK.
THAT WILL MAKE OUR JOB EASIER. WE CAN JUST DRIVE IT OUT OF HERE. BUT HOW?
LEAVE THAT TO ME. JUST GET READY TO ROLL!
WAIT FOR MY SIGNAL.
WHAT SIGNAL?
"AFTER SEEING EARTH ITSELF TEARING THE CAMP APART, I KNEW DA WEI WAS SPECIAL."
SKRIIEEEK
THAT'S A HELLUVA SIGNAL!
I SURE HOPE THAT FOOL KNOWS WHAT HE'S--

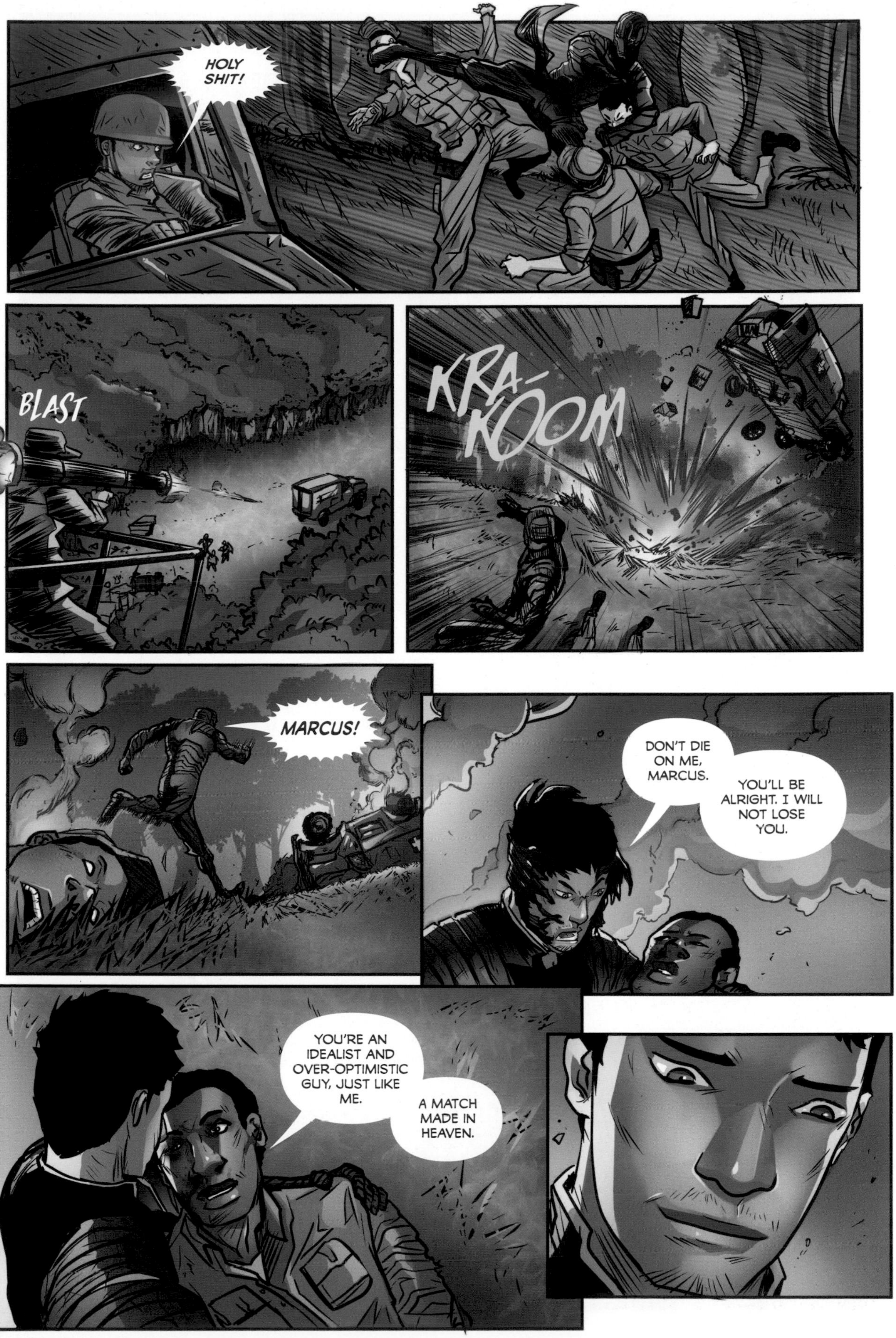
HOLY SHIT!
BLAST
KRA-KOOM
MARCUS!
DON'T DIE ON ME, MARCUS.
YOU'LL BE ALRIGHT. I WILL NOT LOSE YOU.
YOU'RE AN IDEALIST AND OVER-OPTIMISTIC GUY, JUST LIKE ME.
A MATCH MADE IN HEAVEN.

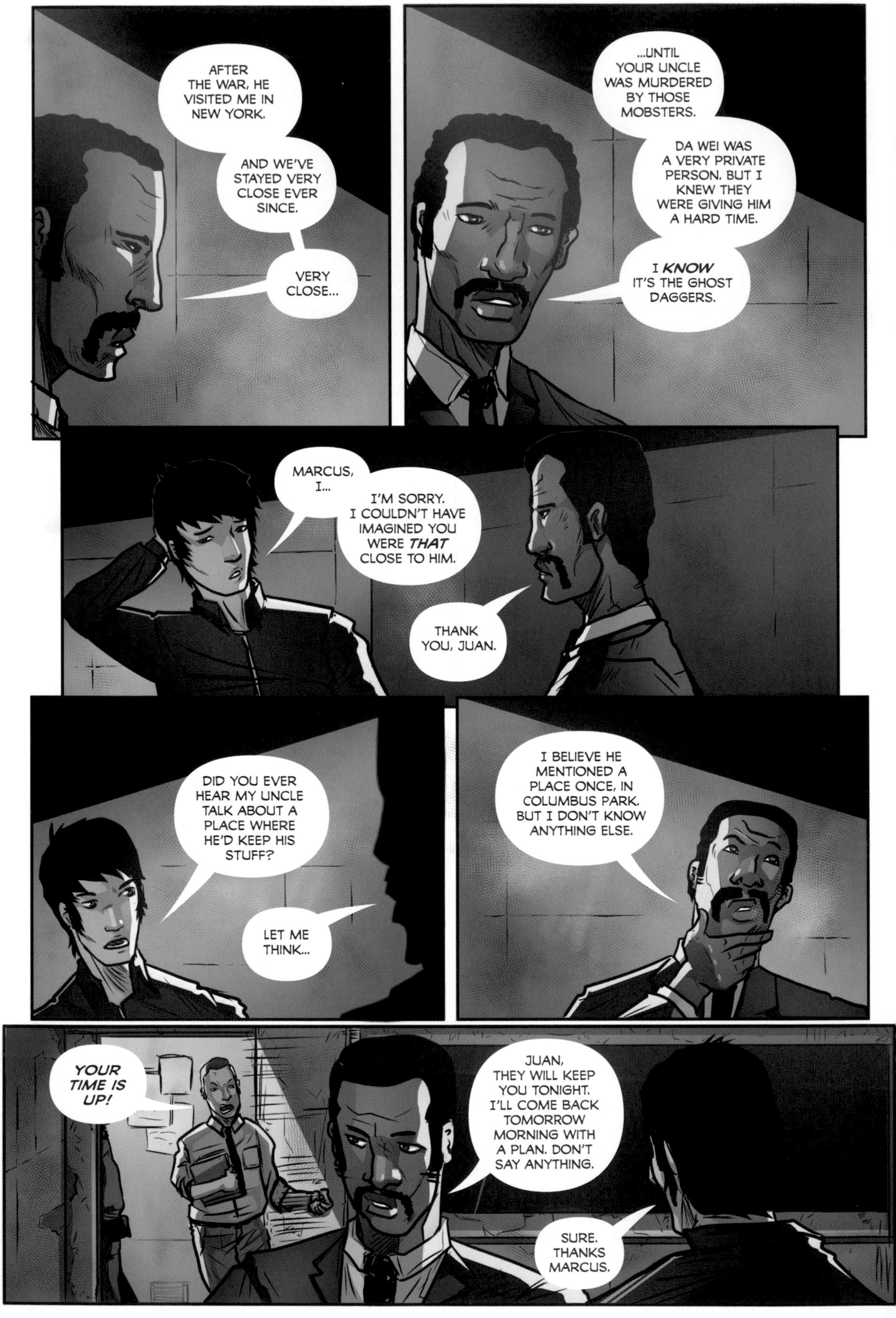
AFTER THE WAR, HE VISITED ME IN NEW YORK.
AND WE'VE STAYED VERY CLOSE EVER SINCE.
VERY CLOSE...
...UNTIL YOUR UNCLE WAS MURDERED BY THOSE MOBSTERS.
DA WEI WAS A VERY PRIVATE PERSON. BUT I KNEW THEY WERE GIVING HIM A HARD TIME.
I *KNOW* IT'S THE GHOST DAGGERS.
MARCUS, I...
I'M SORRY. I COULDN'T HAVE IMAGINED YOU WERE *THAT* CLOSE TO HIM.
THANK YOU, JUAN.
DID YOU EVER HEAR MY UNCLE TALK ABOUT A PLACE WHERE HE'D KEEP HIS STUFF?
LET ME THINK...
I BELIEVE HE MENTIONED A PLACE ONCE, IN COLUMBUS PARK. BUT I DON'T KNOW ANYTHING ELSE.
YOUR TIME IS UP!
JUAN, THEY WILL KEEP YOU TONIGHT. I'LL COME BACK TOMORROW MORNING WITH A PLAN. DON'T SAY ANYTHING.
SURE. THANKS MARCUS.

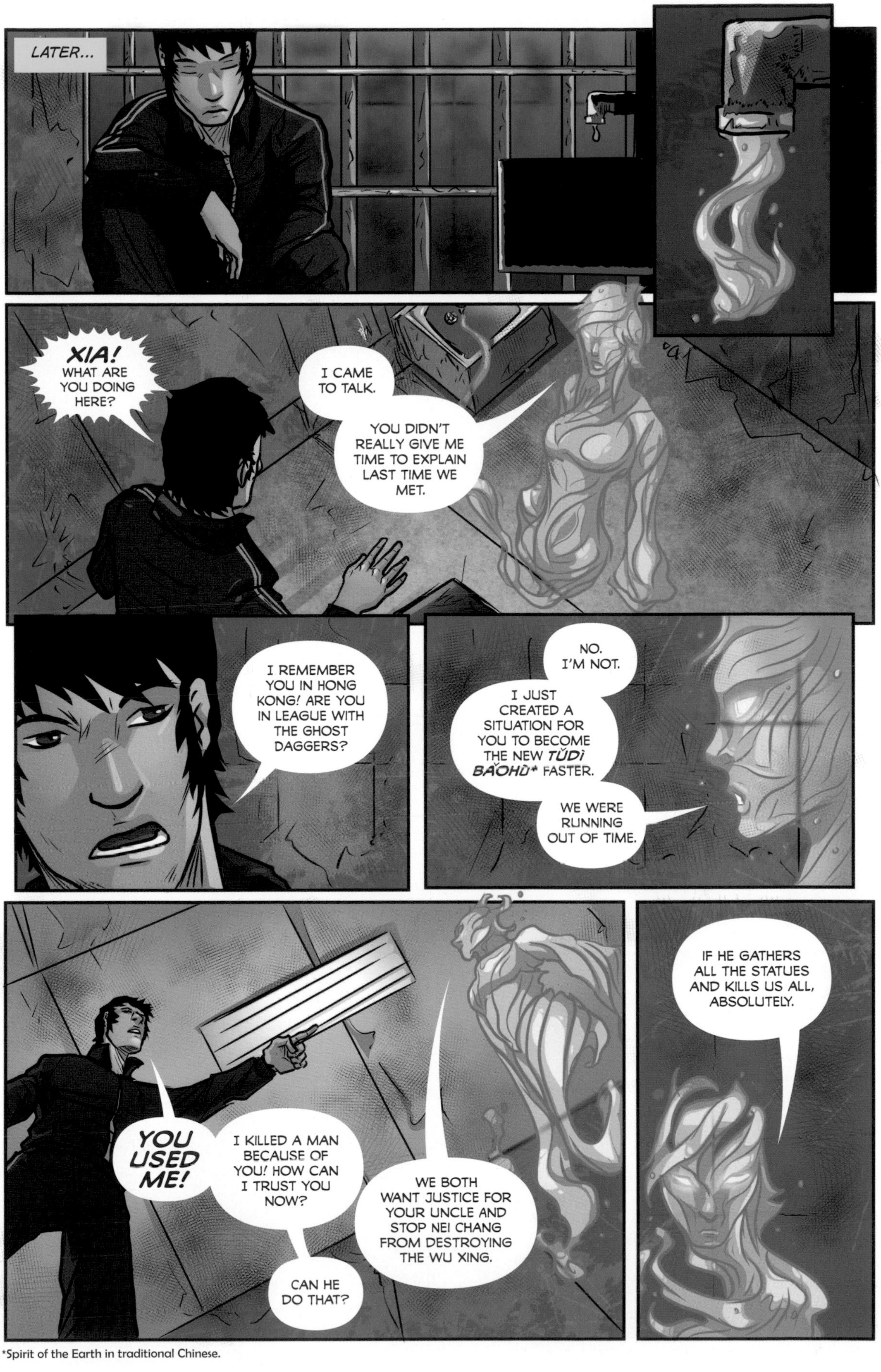
LATER...
XIA! WHAT ARE YOU DOING HERE?
I CAME TO TALK.
YOU DIDN'T REALLY GIVE ME TIME TO EXPLAIN LAST TIME WE MET.
I REMEMBER YOU IN HONG KONG! ARE YOU IN LEAGUE WITH THE GHOST DAGGERS?
NO. I'M NOT.
I JUST CREATED A SITUATION FOR YOU TO BECOME THE NEW TǓDÌ BǍOHÙ* FASTER.
WE WERE RUNNING OUT OF TIME.
YOU USED ME!
I KILLED A MAN BECAUSE OF YOU! HOW CAN I TRUST YOU NOW?
WE BOTH WANT JUSTICE FOR YOUR UNCLE AND STOP NEI CHANG FROM DESTROYING THE WU XING.
CAN HE DO THAT?
IF HE GATHERS ALL THE STATUES AND KILLS US ALL, ABSOLUTELY.

*Spirit of the Earth in traditional Chinese.

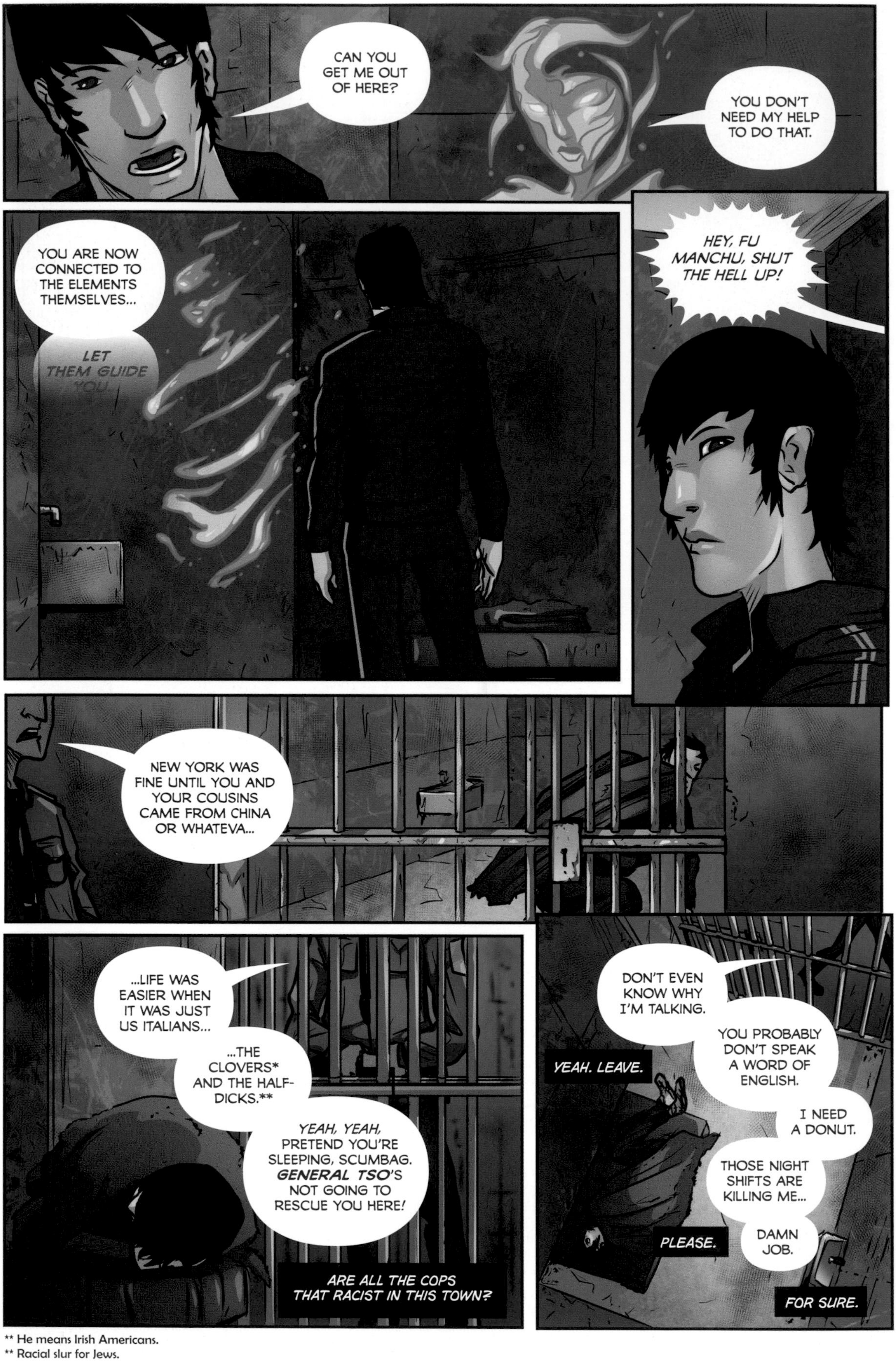
CAN YOU GET ME OUT OF HERE?
YOU DON'T NEED MY HELP TO DO THAT.
YOU ARE NOW CONNECTED TO THE ELEMENTS THEMSELVES...
LET THEM GUIDE YOU...
HEY, FU MANCHU, SHUT THE HELL UP!
NEW YORK WAS FINE UNTIL YOU AND YOUR COUSINS CAME FROM CHINA OR WHATEVA...
...LIFE WAS EASIER WHEN IT WAS JUST US ITALIANS...
...THE CLOVERS* AND THE HALF-DICKS.**
YEAH, YEAH, PRETEND YOU'RE SLEEPING, SCUMBAG. GENERAL TSO'S NOT GOING TO RESCUE YOU HERE!
ARE ALL THE COPS THAT RACIST IN THIS TOWN?
DON'T EVEN KNOW WHY I'M TALKING.
YEAH. LEAVE.
YOU PROBABLY DON'T SPEAK A WORD OF ENGLISH.
I NEED A DONUT.
THOSE NIGHT SHIFTS ARE KILLING ME...
PLEASE.
DAMN JOB.
FOR SURE.

** He means Irish Americans.
** Racial slur for Jews.

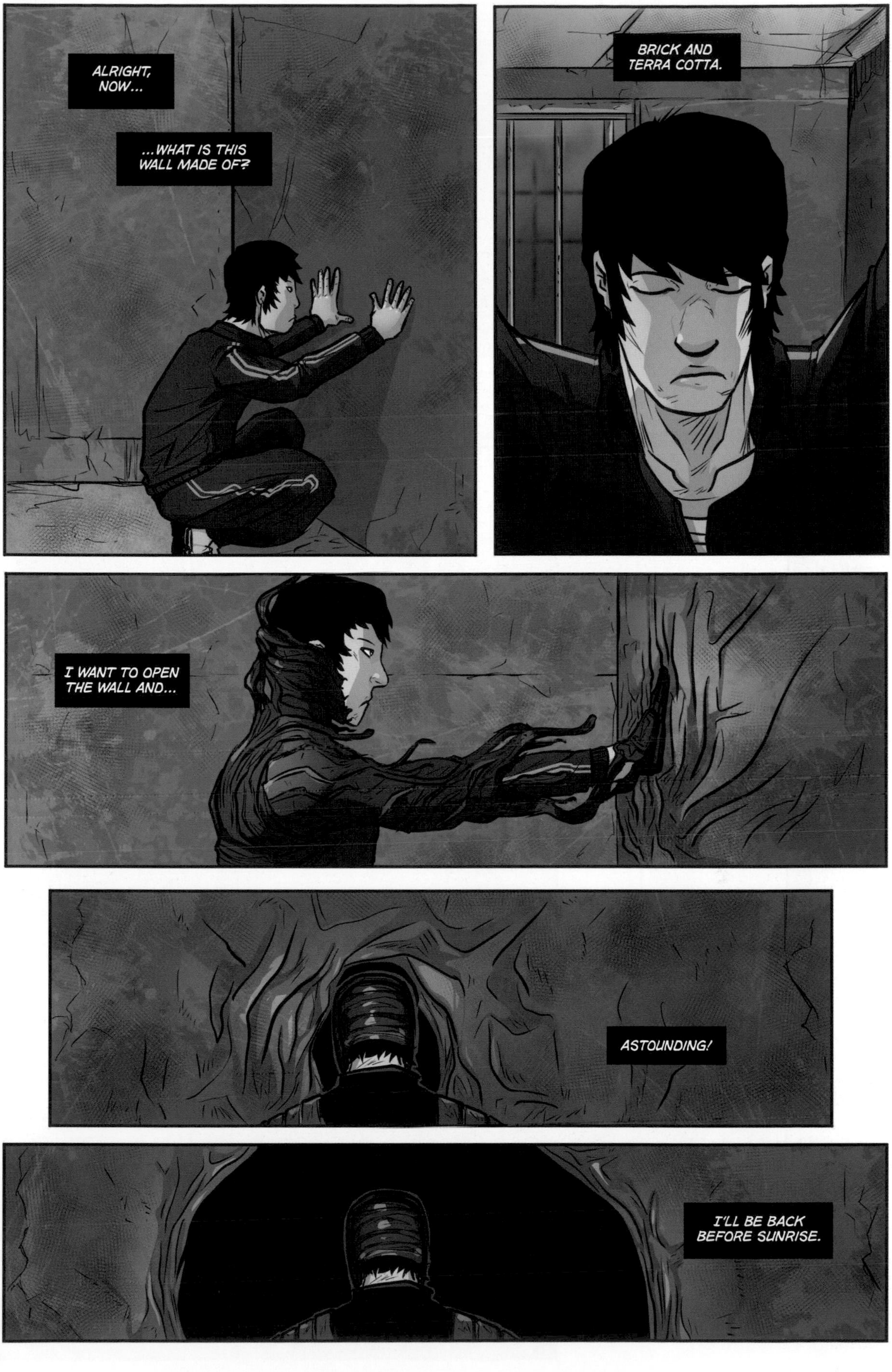
ALRIGHT, NOW...
...WHAT IS THIS WALL MADE OF?
BRICK AND TERRA COTTA.
I WANT TO OPEN THE WALL AND...
ASTOUNDING!
I'LL BE BACK BEFORE SUNRISE.

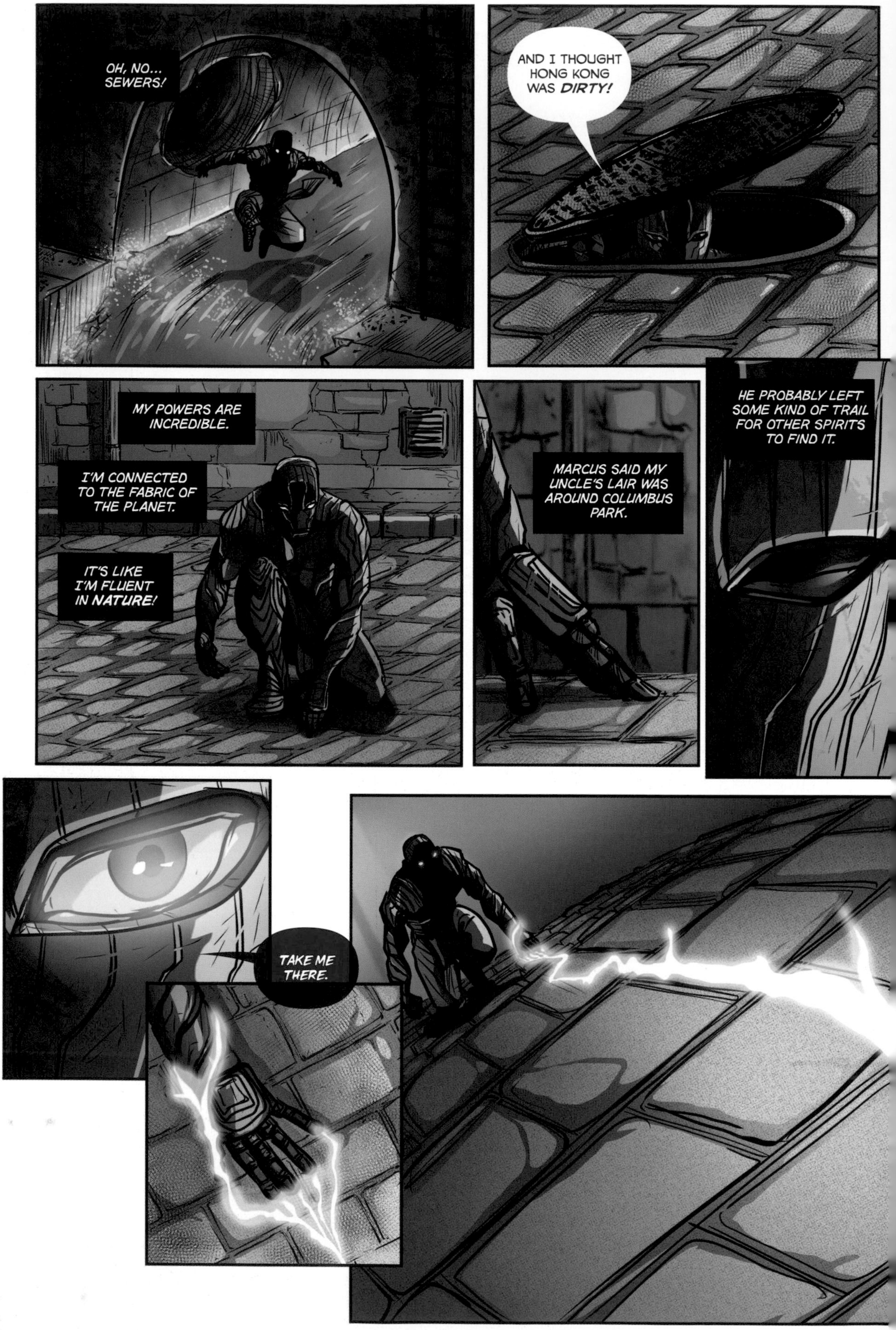
OH, NO... SEWERS!
AND I THOUGHT HONG KONG WAS DIRTY!
MY POWERS ARE INCREDIBLE.
I'M CONNECTED TO THE FABRIC OF THE PLANET.
IT'S LIKE I'M FLUENT IN NATURE!
MARCUS SAID MY UNCLE'S LAIR WAS AROUND COLUMBUS PARK.
HE PROBABLY LEFT SOME KIND OF TRAIL FOR OTHER SPIRITS TO FIND IT.
TAKE ME THERE.

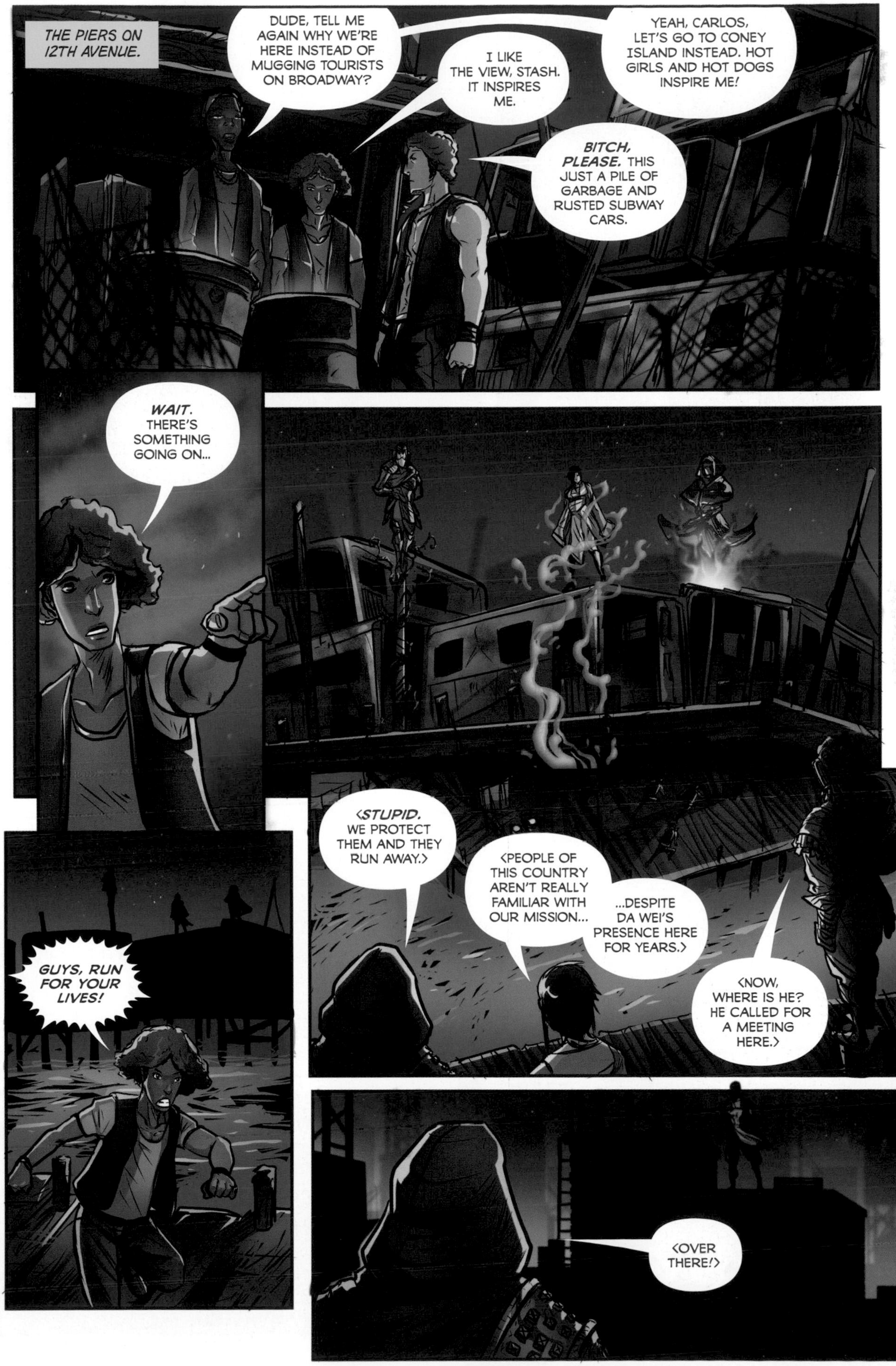
THE PIERS ON 12TH AVENUE.
DUDE, TELL ME AGAIN WHY WE'RE HERE INSTEAD OF MUGGING TOURISTS ON BROADWAY?
I LIKE THE VIEW, STASH. IT INSPIRES ME.
YEAH, CARLOS, LET'S GO TO CONEY ISLAND INSTEAD. HOT GIRLS AND HOT DOGS INSPIRE ME!
BITCH, PLEASE. THIS JUST A PILE OF GARBAGE AND RUSTED SUBWAY CARS.
WAIT. THERE'S SOMETHING GOING ON...
GUYS, RUN FOR YOUR LIVES!
<STUPID. WE PROTECT THEM AND THEY RUN AWAY.>
<PEOPLE OF THIS COUNTRY AREN'T REALLY FAMILIAR WITH OUR MISSION...
...DESPITE DA WEI'S PRESENCE HERE FOR YEARS.>
<NOW, WHERE IS HE? HE CALLED FOR A MEETING HERE.>
<OVER THERE!>

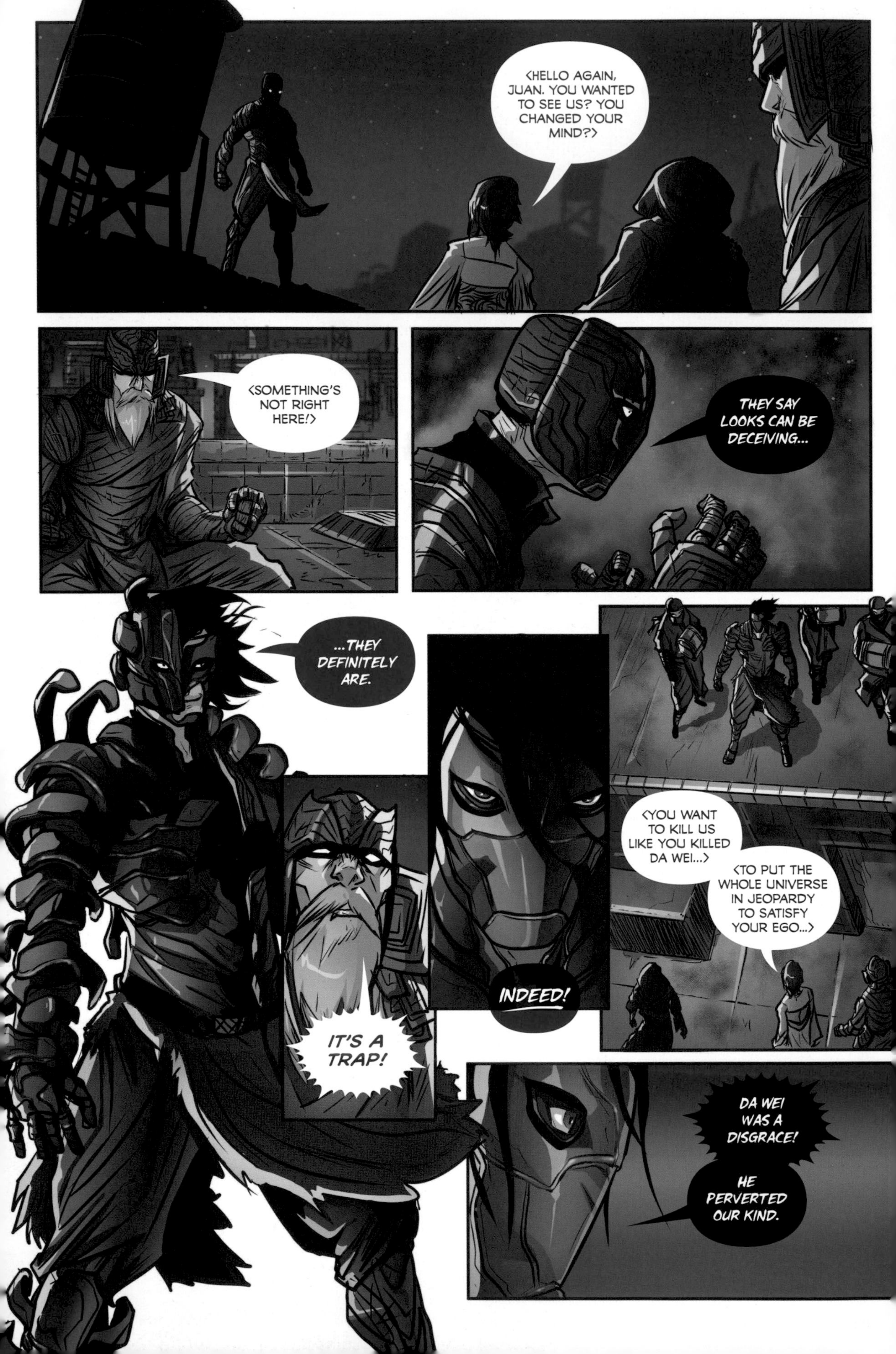

<HELLO AGAIN, JUAN. YOU WANTED TO SEE US? YOU CHANGED YOUR MIND?>
<SOMETHING'S NOT RIGHT HERE!>
THEY SAY LOOKS CAN BE DECEIVING...
...THEY DEFINITELY ARE.
IT'S A TRAP!
INDEED!
<YOU WANT TO KILL US LIKE YOU KILLED DA WEI...>
<TO PUT THE WHOLE UNIVERSE IN JEOPARDY TO SATISFY YOUR EGO...>
DA WEI WAS A DISGRACE!
HE PERVERTED OUR KIND.

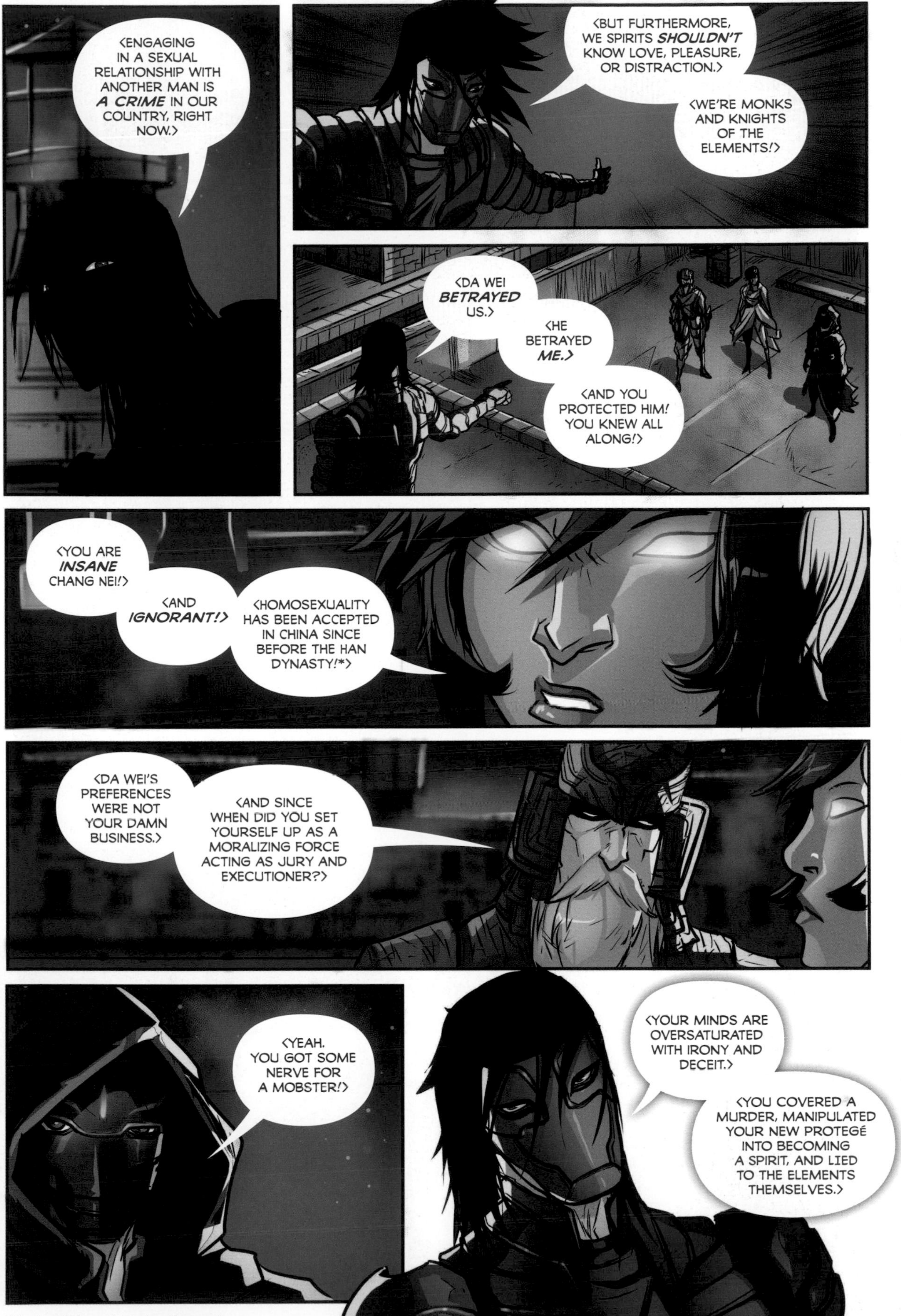
<ENGAGING IN A SEXUAL RELATIONSHIP WITH ANOTHER MAN IS *A CRIME* IN OUR COUNTRY, RIGHT NOW.>
<BUT FURTHERMORE, WE SPIRITS ***SHOULDN'T*** KNOW LOVE, PLEASURE, OR DISTRACTION.>
<WE'RE MONKS AND KNIGHTS OF THE ELEMENTS!>
<DA WEI ***BETRAYED*** US.>
<HE BETRAYED ***ME.>***
<AND YOU PROTECTED HIM! YOU KNEW ALL ALONG!>
<YOU ARE ***INSANE*** CHANG NEI!>
<AND ***IGNORANT!>***
<HOMOSEXUALITY HAS BEEN ACCEPTED IN CHINA SINCE BEFORE THE HAN DYNASTY!*>
<DA WEI'S PREFERENCES WERE NOT YOUR DAMN BUSINESS.>
<AND SINCE WHEN DID YOU SET YOURSELF UP AS A MORALIZING FORCE ACTING AS JURY AND EXECUTIONER?>
<YEAH. YOU GOT SOME NERVE FOR A MOBSTER!>
<YOUR MINDS ARE OVERSATURATED WITH IRONY AND DECEIT.>
<YOU COVERED A MURDER, MANIPULATED YOUR NEW PROTEGÉ INTO BECOMING A SPIRIT, AND LIED TO THE ELEMENTS THEMSELVES.>

* That's 206BC-220 AD... a long time ago!

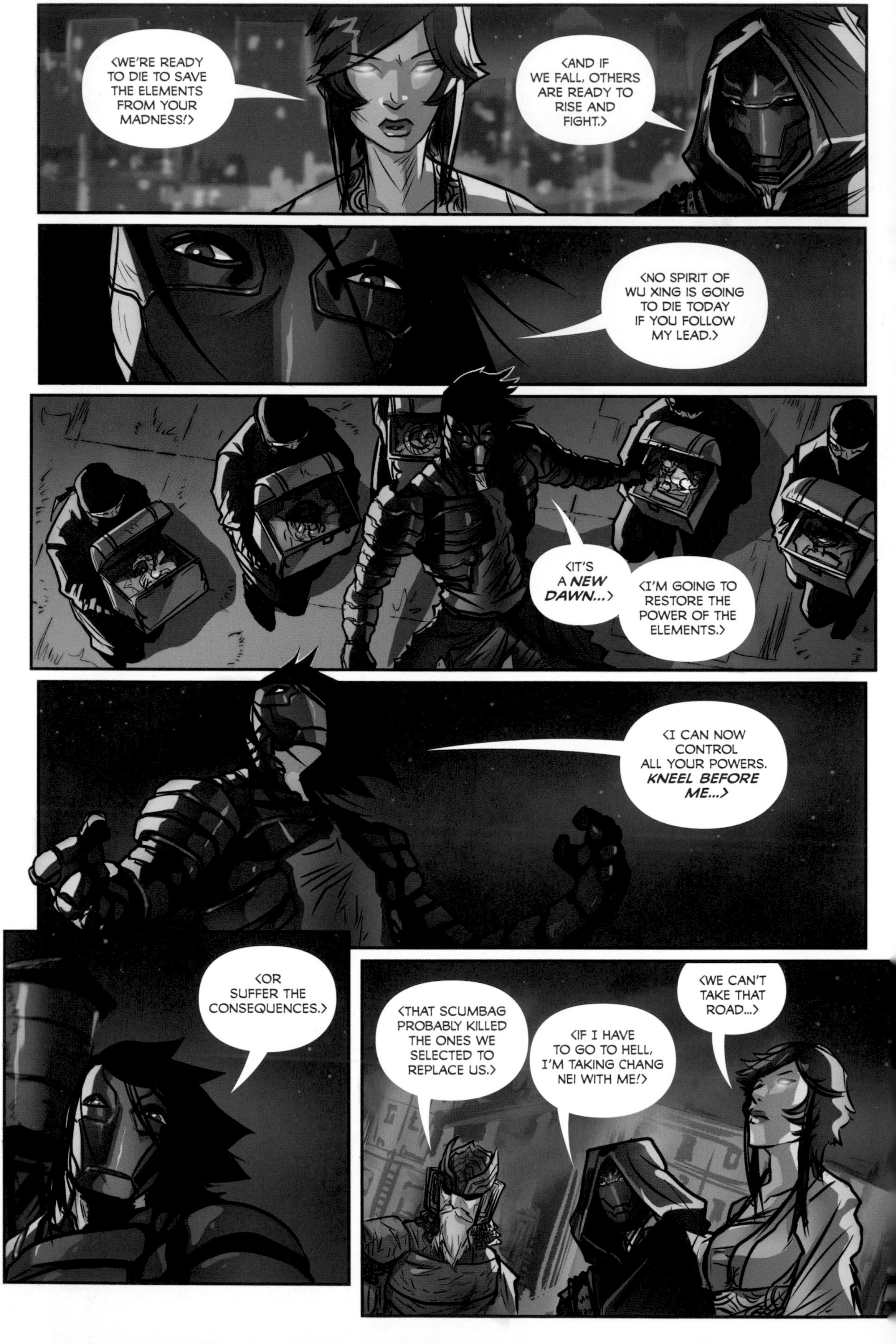
<WE'RE READY TO DIE TO SAVE THE ELEMENTS FROM YOUR MADNESS!>
<AND IF WE FALL, OTHERS ARE READY TO RISE AND FIGHT.>
<NO SPIRIT OF WU XING IS GOING TO DIE TODAY IF YOU FOLLOW MY LEAD.>
<IT'S A NEW DAWN...>
<I'M GOING TO RESTORE THE POWER OF THE ELEMENTS.>
<I CAN NOW CONTROL ALL YOUR POWERS. KNEEL BEFORE ME...>
<OR SUFFER THE CONSEQUENCES.>
<THAT SCUMBAG PROBABLY KILLED THE ONES WE SELECTED TO REPLACE US.>
<IF I HAVE TO GO TO HELL, I'M TAKING CHANG NEI WITH ME!>
<WE CAN'T TAKE THAT ROAD...>

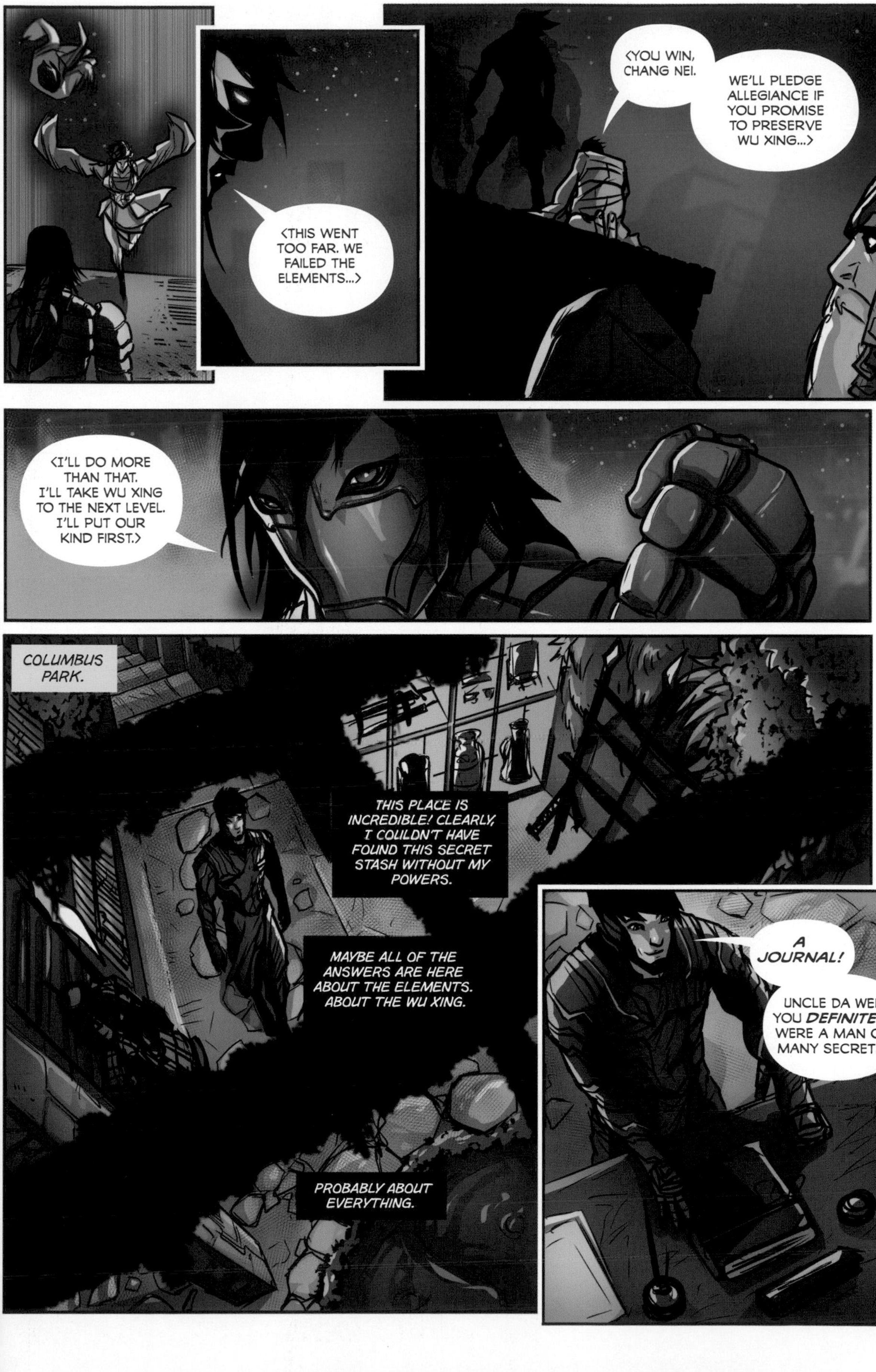

<THIS WENT TOO FAR. WE FAILED THE ELEMENTS...>
<YOU WIN, CHANG NEI.
WE'LL PLEDGE ALLEGIANCE IF YOU PROMISE TO PRESERVE WU XING...>
<I'LL DO MORE THAN THAT. I'LL TAKE WU XING TO THE NEXT LEVEL. I'LL PUT OUR KIND FIRST.>
COLUMBUS PARK.
THIS PLACE IS INCREDIBLE! CLEARLY, I COULDN'T HAVE FOUND THIS SECRET STASH WITHOUT MY POWERS.
MAYBE ALL OF THE ANSWERS ARE HERE ABOUT THE ELEMENTS. ABOUT THE WU XING.
PROBABLY ABOUT EVERYTHING.
A JOURNAL!
UNCLE DA WEI, YOU *DEFINITELY* WERE A MAN OF MANY SECRETS.

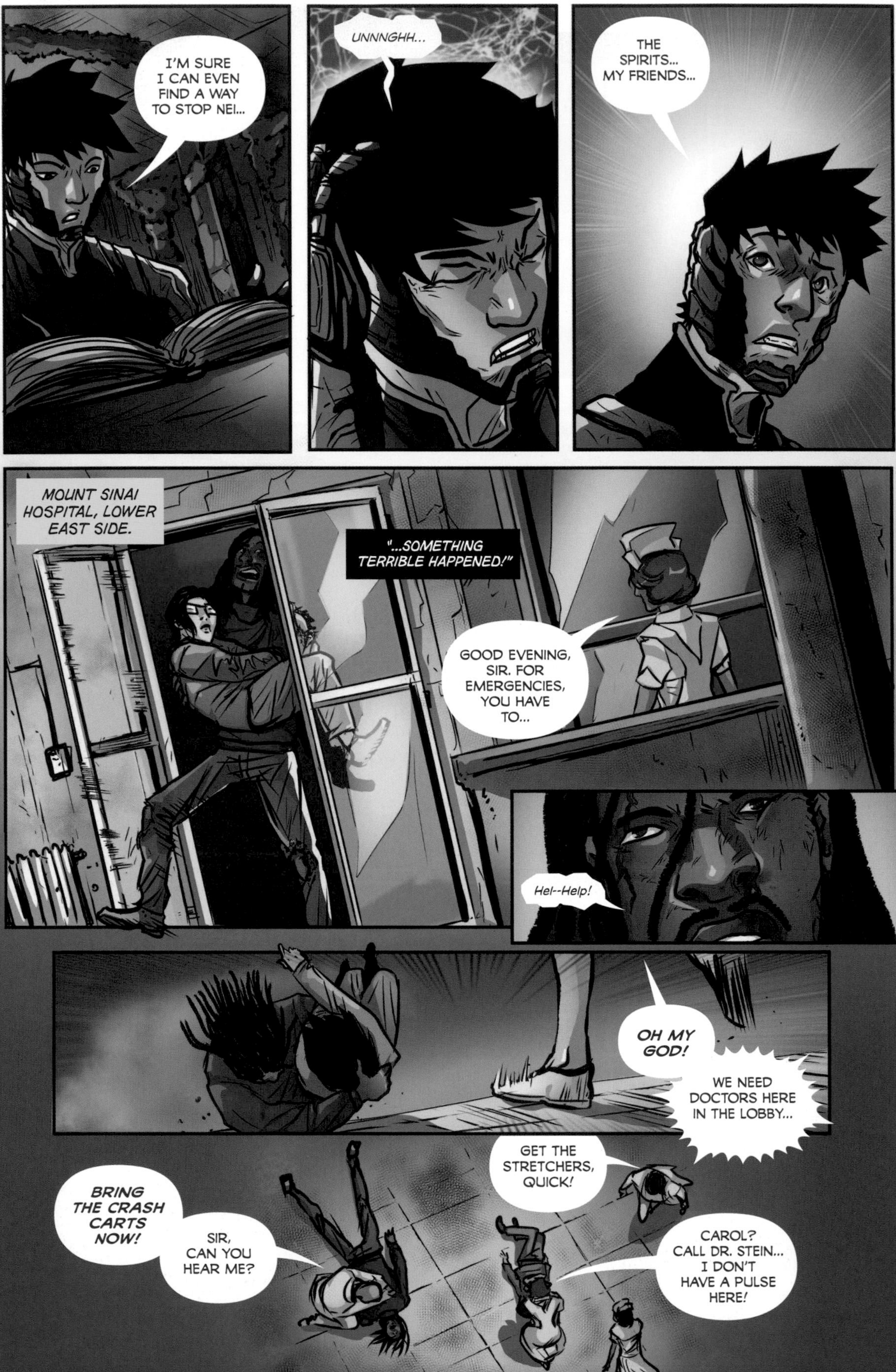
I'M SURE I CAN EVEN FIND A WAY TO STOP NEI...
UNNNGHH...
THE SPIRITS... MY FRIENDS...
MOUNT SINAI HOSPITAL, LOWER EAST SIDE.
"...SOMETHING TERRIBLE HAPPENED!"
GOOD EVENING, SIR. FOR EMERGENCIES, YOU HAVE TO...
Hel--Help!
OH MY GOD!
WE NEED DOCTORS HERE IN THE LOBBY...
BRING THE CRASH CARTS NOW!
SIR, CAN YOU HEAR ME?
GET THE STRETCHERS, QUICK!
CAROL? CALL DR. STEIN... I DON'T HAVE A PULSE HERE!

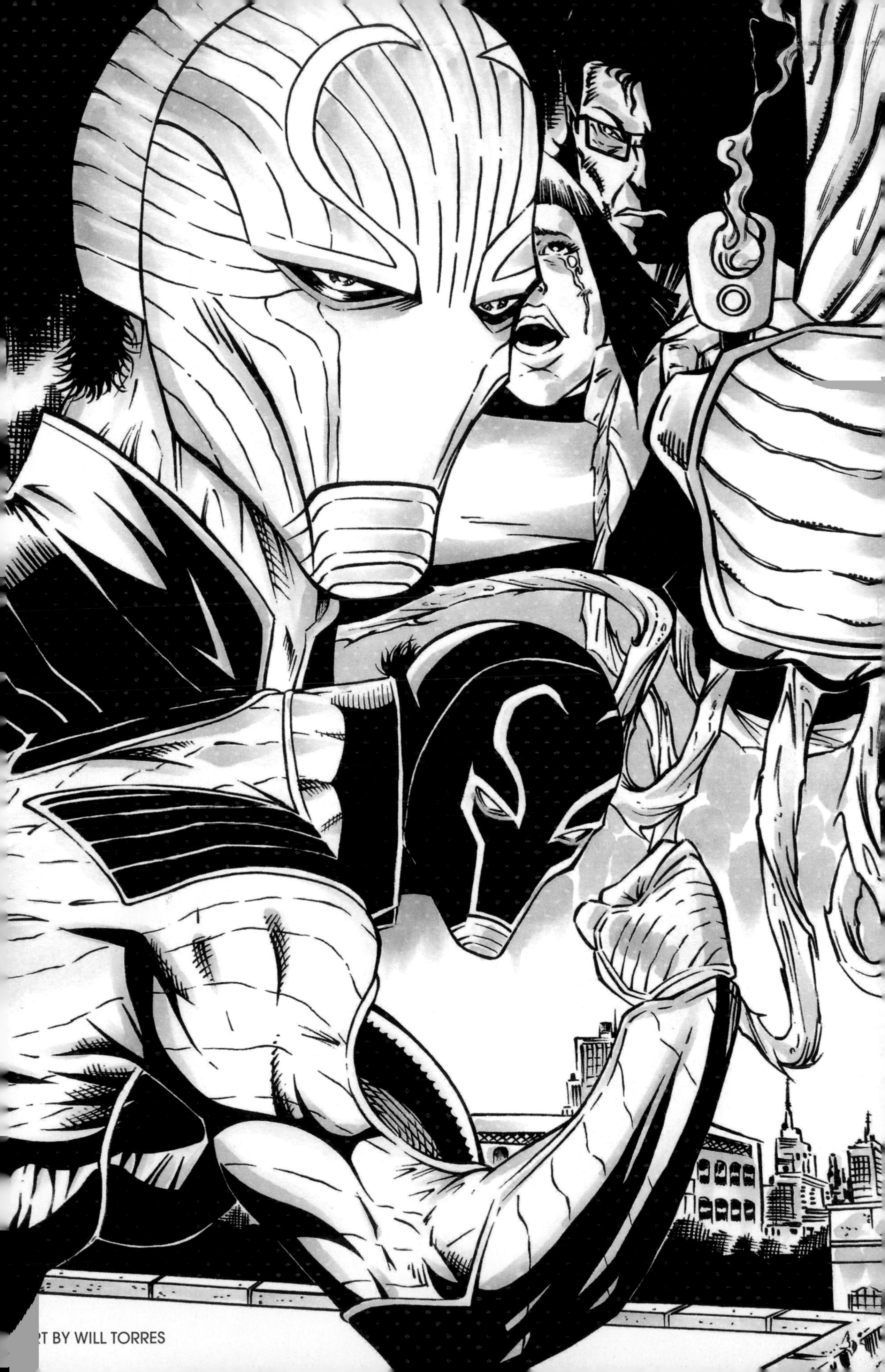

RT BY WILL TORRES

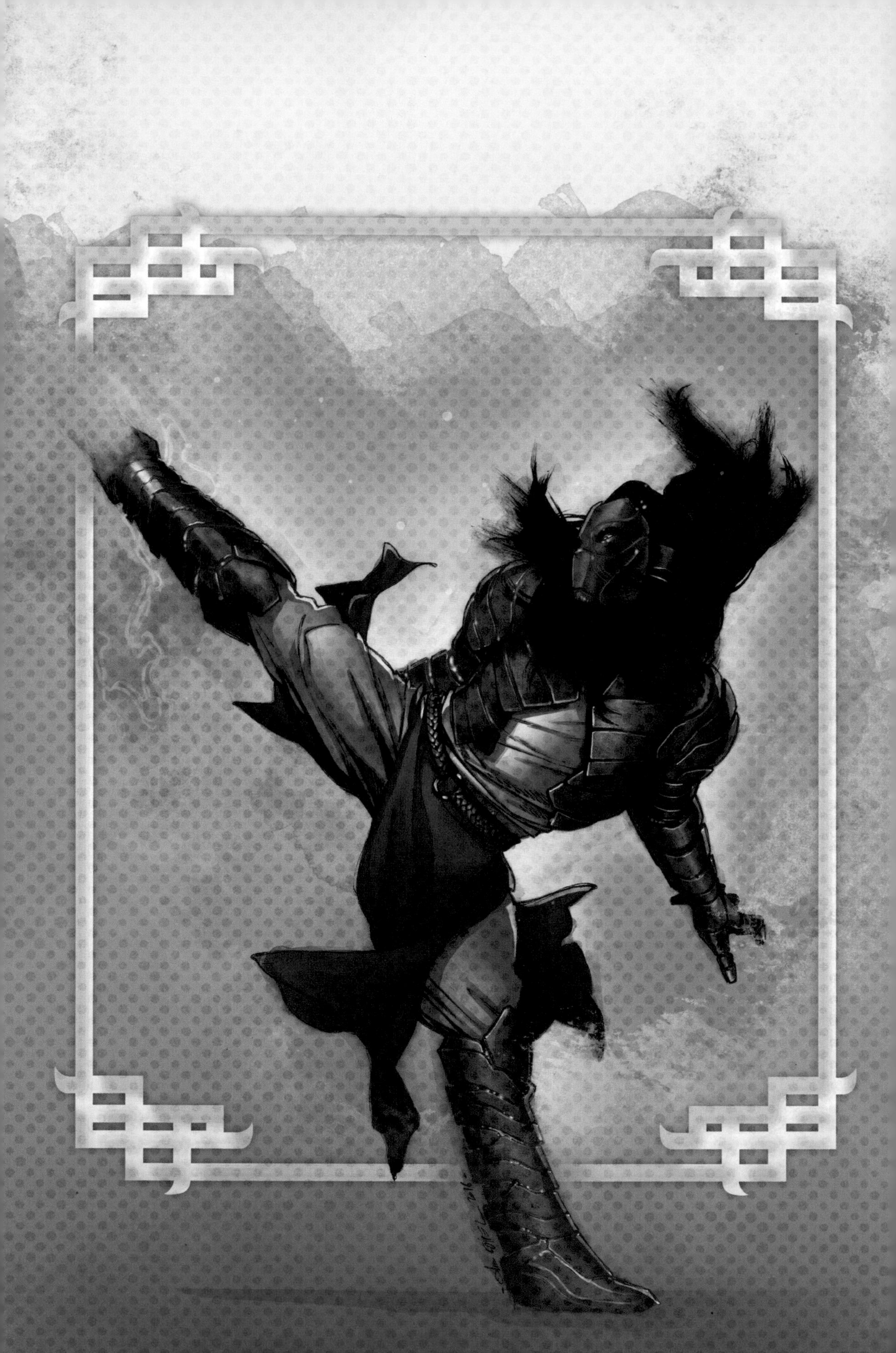

ART BY OLIVIER COIPEL

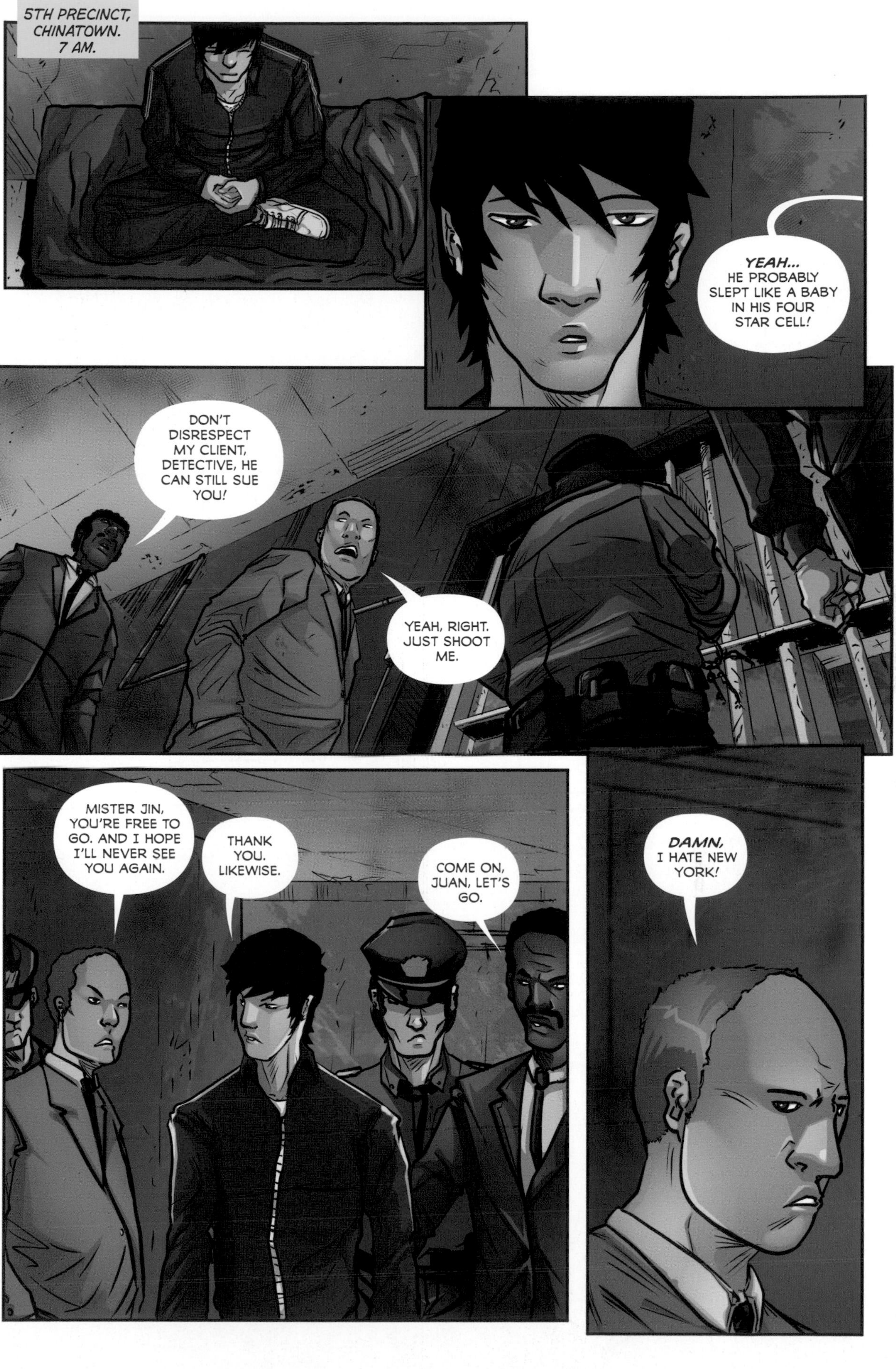
5TH PRECINCT, CHINATOWN. 7 AM.
YEAH... HE PROBABLY SLEPT LIKE A BABY IN HIS FOUR STAR CELL!
DON'T DISRESPECT MY CLIENT, DETECTIVE, HE CAN STILL SUE YOU!
YEAH, RIGHT. JUST SHOOT ME.
MISTER JIN, YOU'RE FREE TO GO. AND I HOPE I'LL NEVER SEE YOU AGAIN.
THANK YOU. LIKEWISE.
COME ON, JUAN, LET'S GO.
DAMN, I HATE NEW YORK!

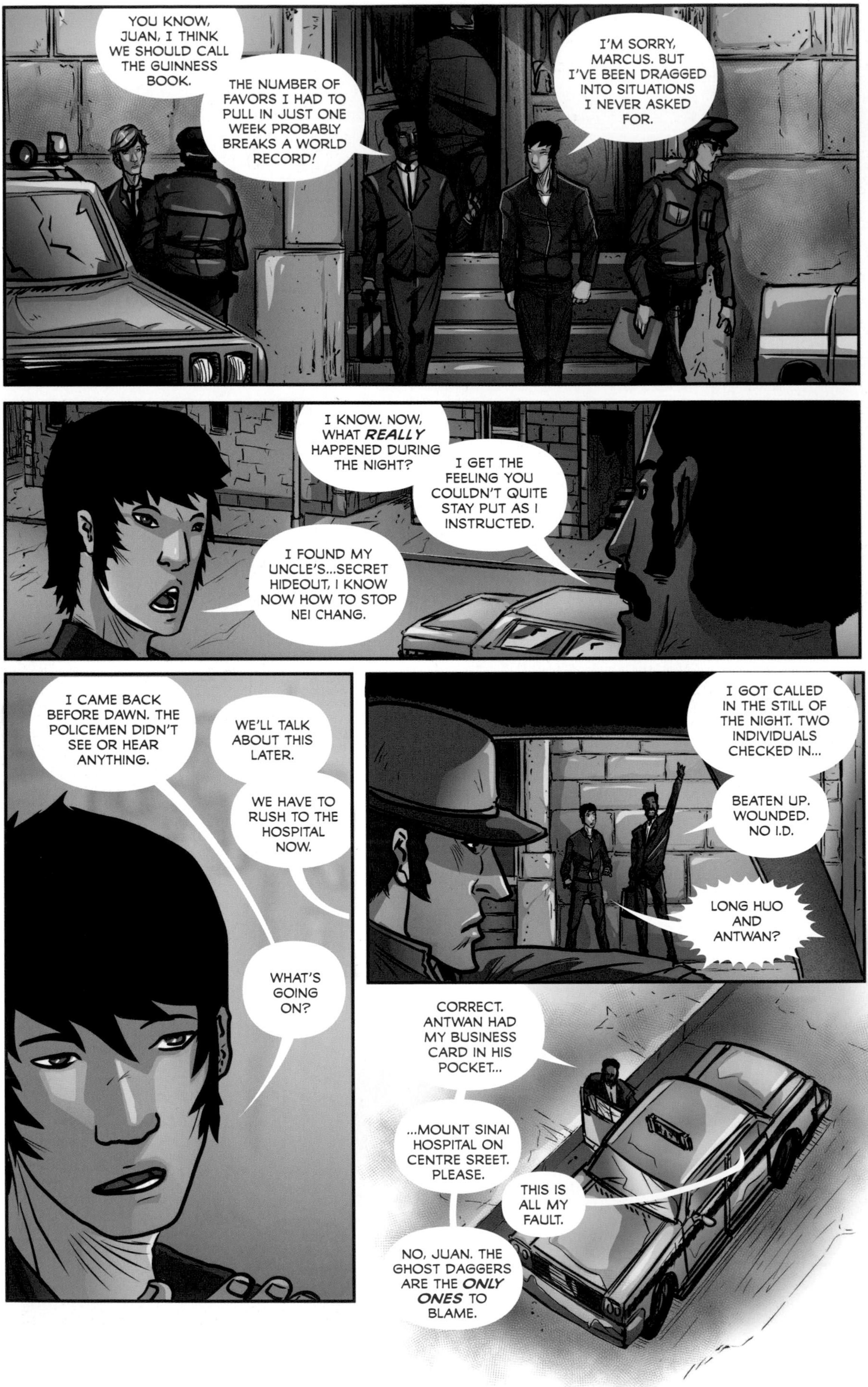
YOU KNOW, JUAN, I THINK WE SHOULD CALL THE GUINNESS BOOK.
THE NUMBER OF FAVORS I HAD TO PULL IN JUST ONE WEEK PROBABLY BREAKS A WORLD RECORD!
I'M SORRY, MARCUS. BUT I'VE BEEN DRAGGED INTO SITUATIONS I NEVER ASKED FOR.
I KNOW. NOW, WHAT *REALLY* HAPPENED DURING THE NIGHT?
I GET THE FEELING YOU COULDN'T QUITE STAY PUT AS I INSTRUCTED.
I FOUND MY UNCLE'S...SECRET HIDEOUT, I KNOW NOW HOW TO STOP NEI CHANG.
I CAME BACK BEFORE DAWN. THE POLICEMEN DIDN'T SEE OR HEAR ANYTHING.
WE'LL TALK ABOUT THIS LATER.
WE HAVE TO RUSH TO THE HOSPITAL NOW.
WHAT'S GOING ON?
I GOT CALLED IN THE STILL OF THE NIGHT. TWO INDIVIDUALS CHECKED IN...
BEATEN UP. WOUNDED. NO I.D.
LONG HUO AND ANTWAN?
CORRECT. ANTWAN HAD MY BUSINESS CARD IN HIS POCKET...
...MOUNT SINAI HOSPITAL ON CENTRE SREET. PLEASE.
THIS IS ALL MY FAULT.
NO, JUAN. THE GHOST DAGGERS ARE THE *ONLY ONES* TO BLAME.

HI. I'M MARCUS SIMPSON, ATTORNEY AT LAW. I'M LOOKING FOR MY CLIENTS.

TWO MEN. ONE HAITIAN, BLACK AND AN ASIAN... NO I.D.

GOOD MORNING. I SEE WHO YOU'RE TALKING ABOUT...

"...WE'RE NOT TAILORED TO HANDLE E.R. SITUATIONS HERE, BUT DR. STEIN TOOK CARE OF THEM."

I'M DR. STEIN. YOUR CLIENTS WERE BADLY WOUNDED.

ARE THEY DOCUMENTED OR EVEN INSURED?

WE JUST NEED SOME DISCRETION.

MONEY IS NOT A PROBLEM.

WE CAN TALK PRIVATELY IN MY OFFICE. FOLLOW ME.

YOUR OFFICE IS... AN OPERATION ROOM?

I'M A *SURGEON*, WHAT DID YOU EXPECT?

PLEASE, DR. STEIN, WHAT'S THE SITUATION?

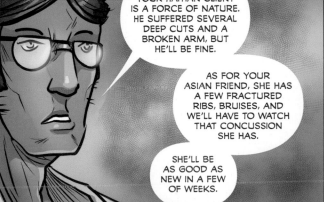

YOUR HAITIAN CLIENT IS A FORCE OF NATURE. HE SUFFERED SEVERAL DEEP CUTS AND A BROKEN ARM, BUT HE'LL BE FINE.

AS FOR YOUR ASIAN FRIEND, SHE HAS A FEW FRACTURED RIBS, BRUISES, AND WE'LL HAVE TO WATCH THAT CONCUSSION SHE HAS.

SHE'LL BE AS GOOD AS NEW IN A FEW OF WEEKS.

SHE?

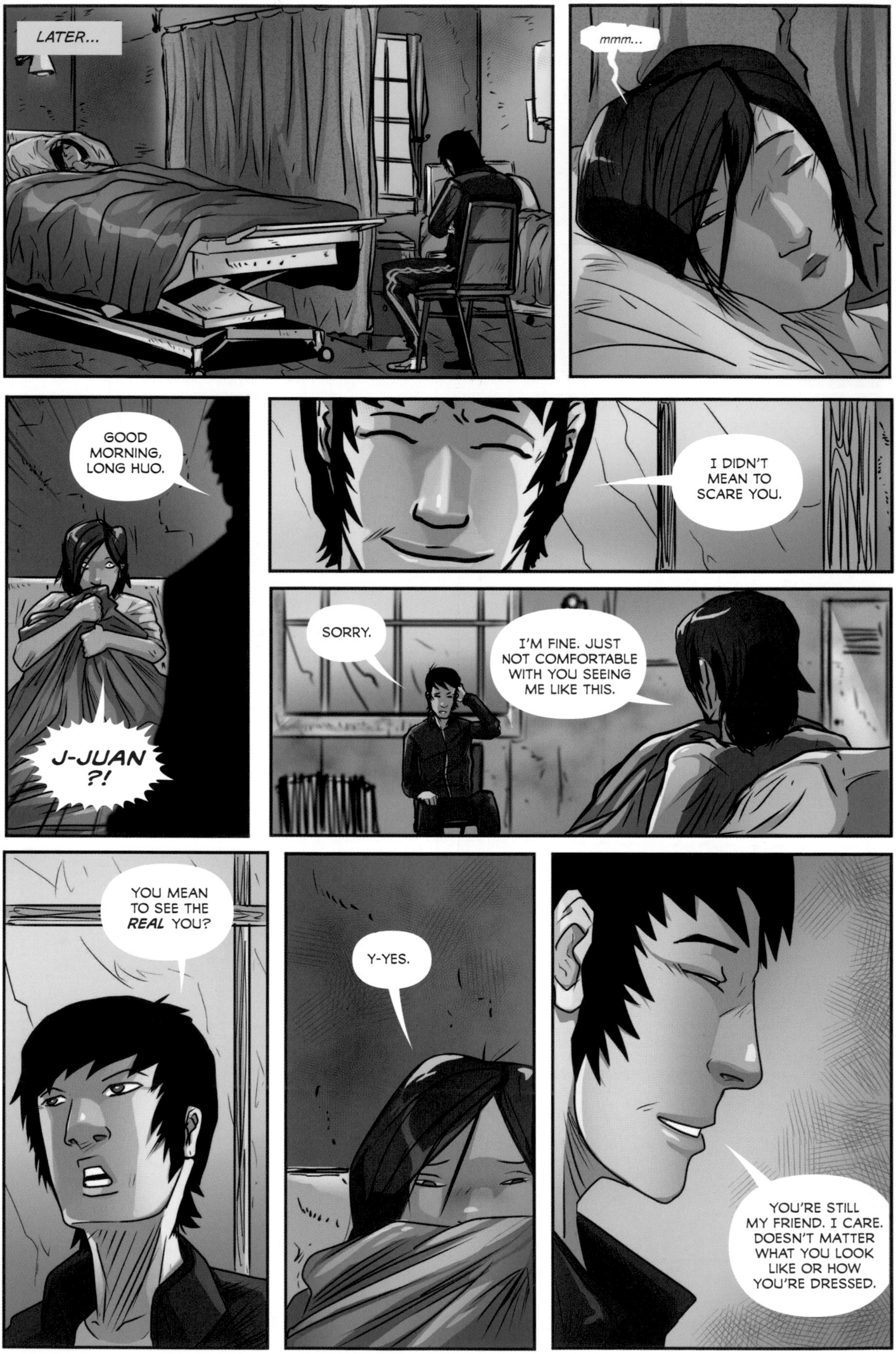
LATER...
mmm...
GOOD MORNING, LONG HUO.
J-JUAN ?!
I DIDN'T MEAN TO SCARE YOU.
SORRY.
I'M FINE. JUST NOT COMFORTABLE WITH YOU SEEING ME LIKE THIS.
YOU MEAN TO SEE THE *REAL* YOU?
Y-YES.
YOU'RE STILL MY FRIEND. I CARE. DOESN'T MATTER WHAT YOU LOOK LIKE OR HOW YOU'RE DRESSED.

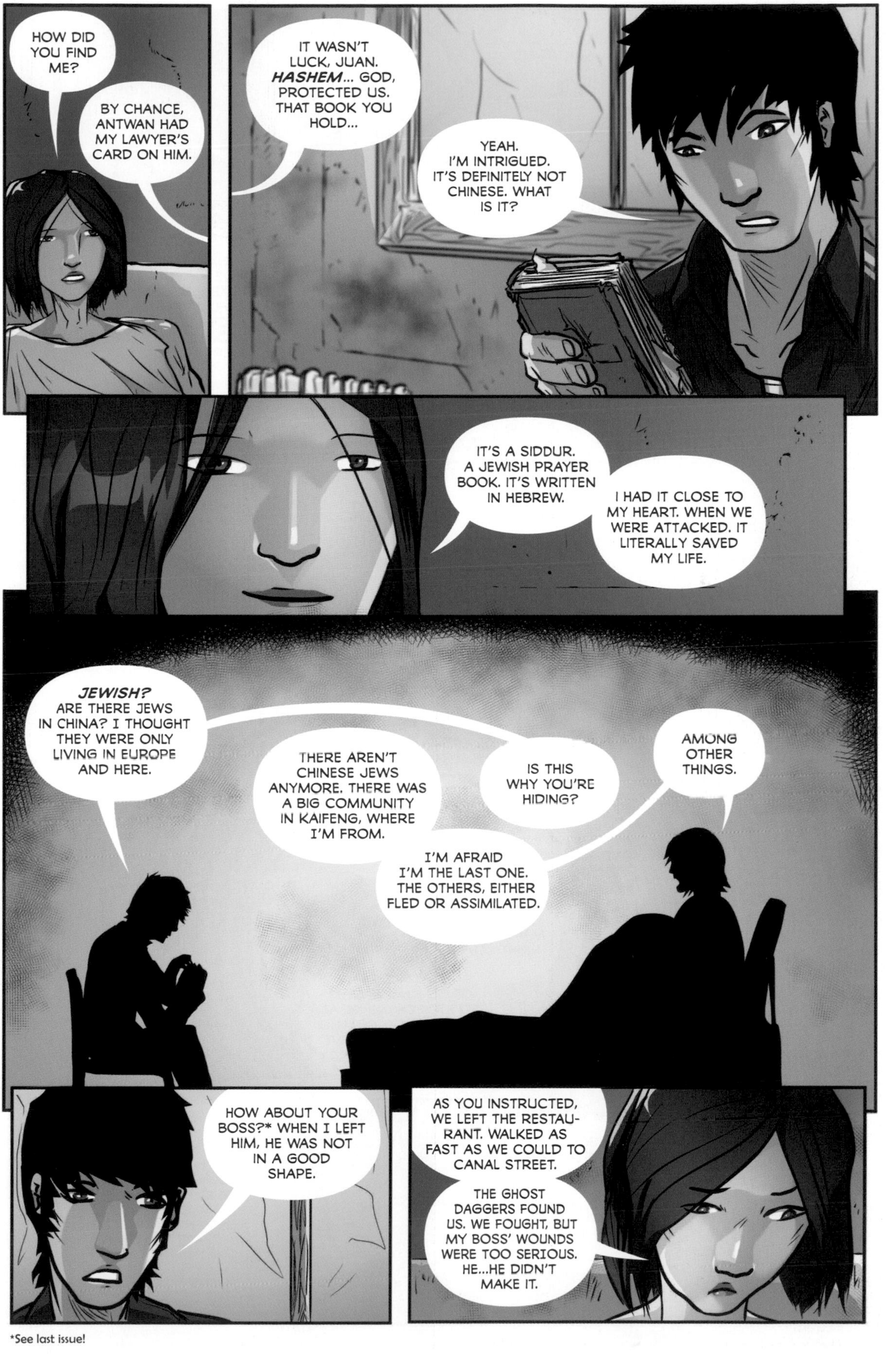
HOW DID YOU FIND ME?
BY CHANCE, ANTWAN HAD MY LAWYER'S CARD ON HIM.
IT WASN'T LUCK, JUAN. *HASHEM*... GOD, PROTECTED US. THAT BOOK YOU HOLD...
YEAH. I'M INTRIGUED. IT'S DEFINITELY NOT CHINESE. WHAT IS IT?
IT'S A SIDDUR. A JEWISH PRAYER BOOK. IT'S WRITTEN IN HEBREW.
I HAD IT CLOSE TO MY HEART. WHEN WE WERE ATTACKED. IT LITERALLY SAVED MY LIFE.
JEWISH? ARE THERE JEWS IN CHINA? I THOUGHT THEY WERE ONLY LIVING IN EUROPE AND HERE.
THERE AREN'T CHINESE JEWS ANYMORE. THERE WAS A BIG COMMUNITY IN KAIFENG, WHERE I'M FROM.
I'M AFRAID I'M THE LAST ONE. THE OTHERS, EITHER FLED OR ASSIMILATED.
IS THIS WHY YOU'RE HIDING?
AMONG OTHER THINGS.
HOW ABOUT YOUR BOSS?* WHEN I LEFT HIM, HE WAS NOT IN A GOOD SHAPE.
AS YOU INSTRUCTED, WE LEFT THE RESTAU-RANT. WALKED AS FAST AS WE COULD TO CANAL STREET.
THE GHOST DAGGERS FOUND US. WE FOUGHT, BUT MY BOSS' WOUNDS WERE TOO SERIOUS. HE...HE DIDN'T MAKE IT.

*See last issue!

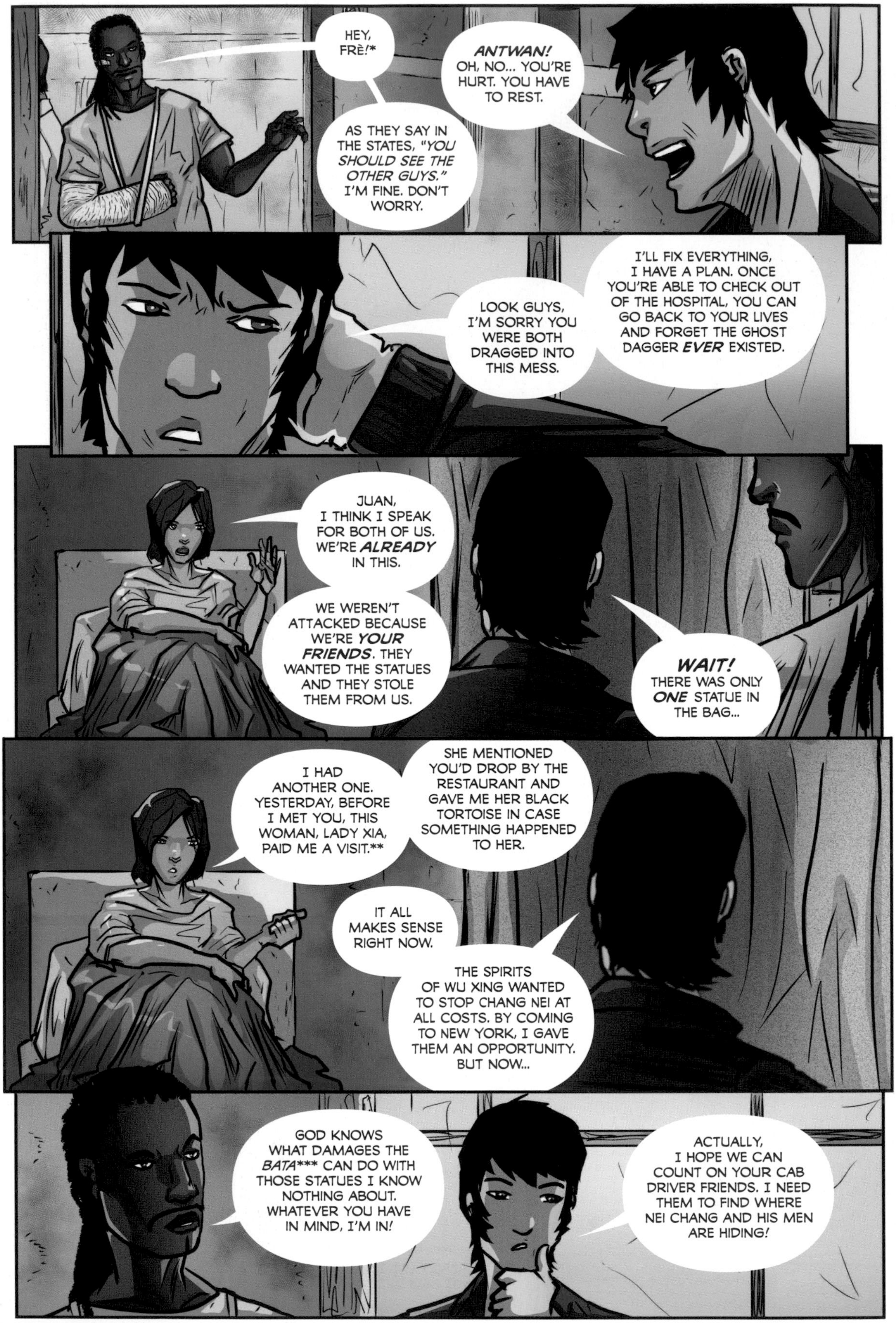
HEY, FRÈ!*
AS THEY SAY IN THE STATES, "YOU SHOULD SEE THE OTHER GUYS." I'M FINE. DON'T WORRY.
ANTWAN! OH, NO... YOU'RE HURT. YOU HAVE TO REST.
LOOK GUYS, I'M SORRY YOU WERE BOTH DRAGGED INTO THIS MESS.
I'LL FIX EVERYTHING, I HAVE A PLAN. ONCE YOU'RE ABLE TO CHECK OUT OF THE HOSPITAL, YOU CAN GO BACK TO YOUR LIVES AND FORGET THE GHOST DAGGER EVER EXISTED.
JUAN, I THINK I SPEAK FOR BOTH OF US. WE'RE ALREADY IN THIS.
WE WEREN'T ATTACKED BECAUSE WE'RE YOUR FRIENDS. THEY WANTED THE STATUES AND THEY STOLE THEM FROM US.
WAIT! THERE WAS ONLY ONE STATUE IN THE BAG...
I HAD ANOTHER ONE. YESTERDAY, BEFORE I MET YOU, THIS WOMAN, LADY XIA, PAID ME A VISIT.**
SHE MENTIONED YOU'D DROP BY THE RESTAURANT AND GAVE ME HER BLACK TORTOISE IN CASE SOMETHING HAPPENED TO HER.
IT ALL MAKES SENSE RIGHT NOW.
THE SPIRITS OF WU XING WANTED TO STOP CHANG NEI AT ALL COSTS. BY COMING TO NEW YORK, I GAVE THEM AN OPPORTUNITY. BUT NOW...
GOD KNOWS WHAT DAMAGES THE BATA*** CAN DO WITH THOSE STATUES I KNOW NOTHING ABOUT. WHATEVER YOU HAVE IN MIND, I'M IN!
ACTUALLY, I HOPE WE CAN COUNT ON YOUR CAB DRIVER FRIENDS. I NEED THEM TO FIND WHERE NEI CHANG AND HIS MEN ARE HIDING!

* "Hey Brother" in Haitian Creole.
** That happened in issue #3 folks
*** "Bastard", in Creole too.

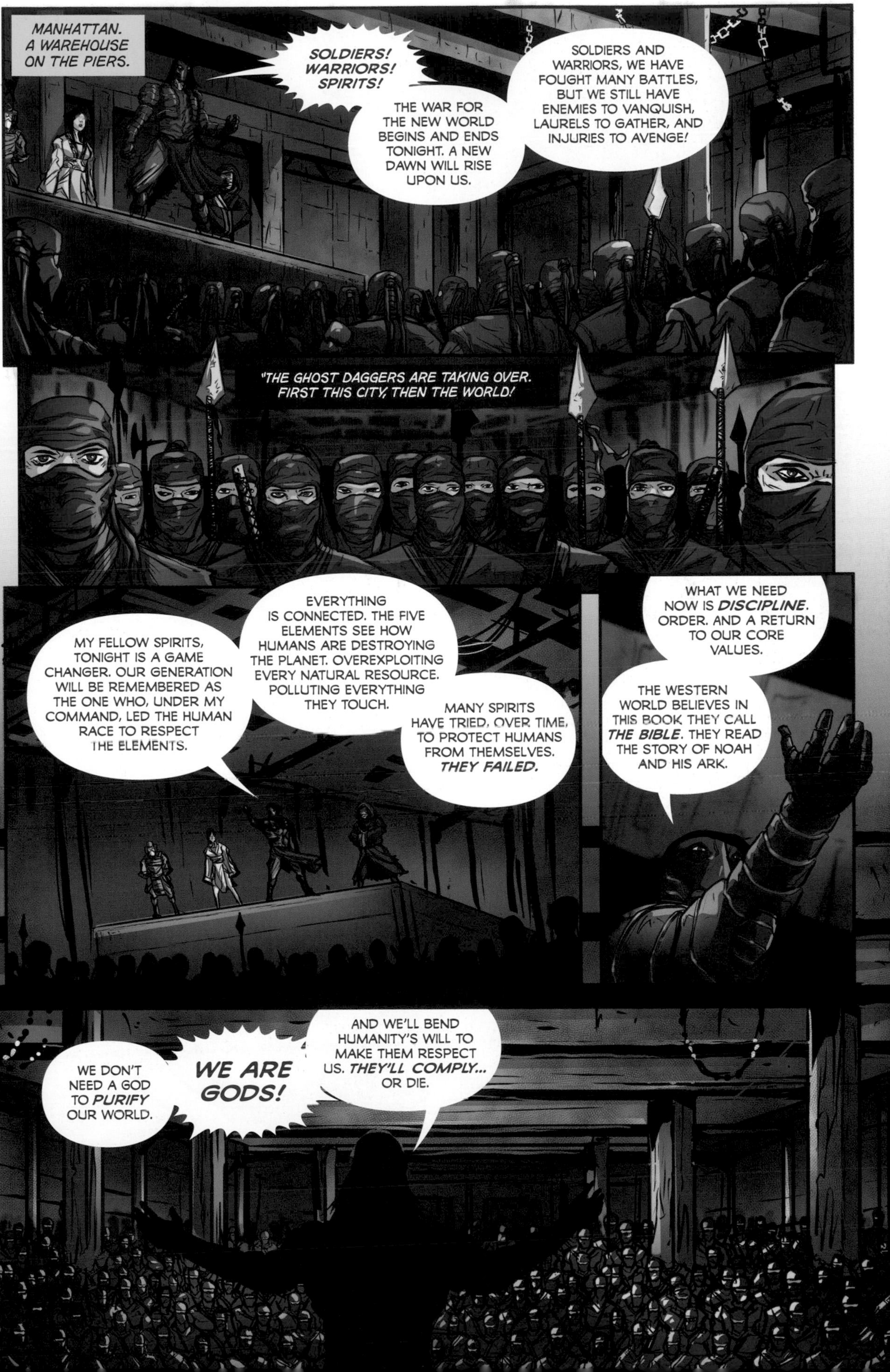
MANHATTAN. A WAREHOUSE ON THE PIERS.
SOLDIERS! WARRIORS! SPIRITS!
THE WAR FOR THE NEW WORLD BEGINS AND ENDS TONIGHT. A NEW DAWN WILL RISE UPON US.
SOLDIERS AND WARRIORS, WE HAVE FOUGHT MANY BATTLES, BUT WE STILL HAVE ENEMIES TO VANQUISH, LAURELS TO GATHER, AND INJURIES TO AVENGE!
"THE GHOST DAGGERS ARE TAKING OVER. FIRST THIS CITY, THEN THE WORLD!
MY FELLOW SPIRITS, TONIGHT IS A GAME CHANGER. OUR GENERATION WILL BE REMEMBERED AS THE ONE WHO, UNDER MY COMMAND, LED THE HUMAN RACE TO RESPECT THE ELEMENTS.
EVERYTHING IS CONNECTED. THE FIVE ELEMENTS SEE HOW HUMANS ARE DESTROYING THE PLANET. OVEREXPLOITING EVERY NATURAL RESOURCE. POLLUTING EVERYTHING THEY TOUCH.
MANY SPIRITS HAVE TRIED, OVER TIME, TO PROTECT HUMANS FROM THEMSELVES. THEY FAILED.
WHAT WE NEED NOW IS DISCIPLINE. ORDER. AND A RETURN TO OUR CORE VALUES.
THE WESTERN WORLD BELIEVES IN THIS BOOK THEY CALL THE BIBLE. THEY READ THE STORY OF NOAH AND HIS ARK.
WE DON'T NEED A GOD TO PURIFY OUR WORLD.
WE ARE GODS!
AND WE'LL BEND HUMANITY'S WILL TO MAKE THEM RESPECT US. THEY'LL COMPLY... OR DIE.

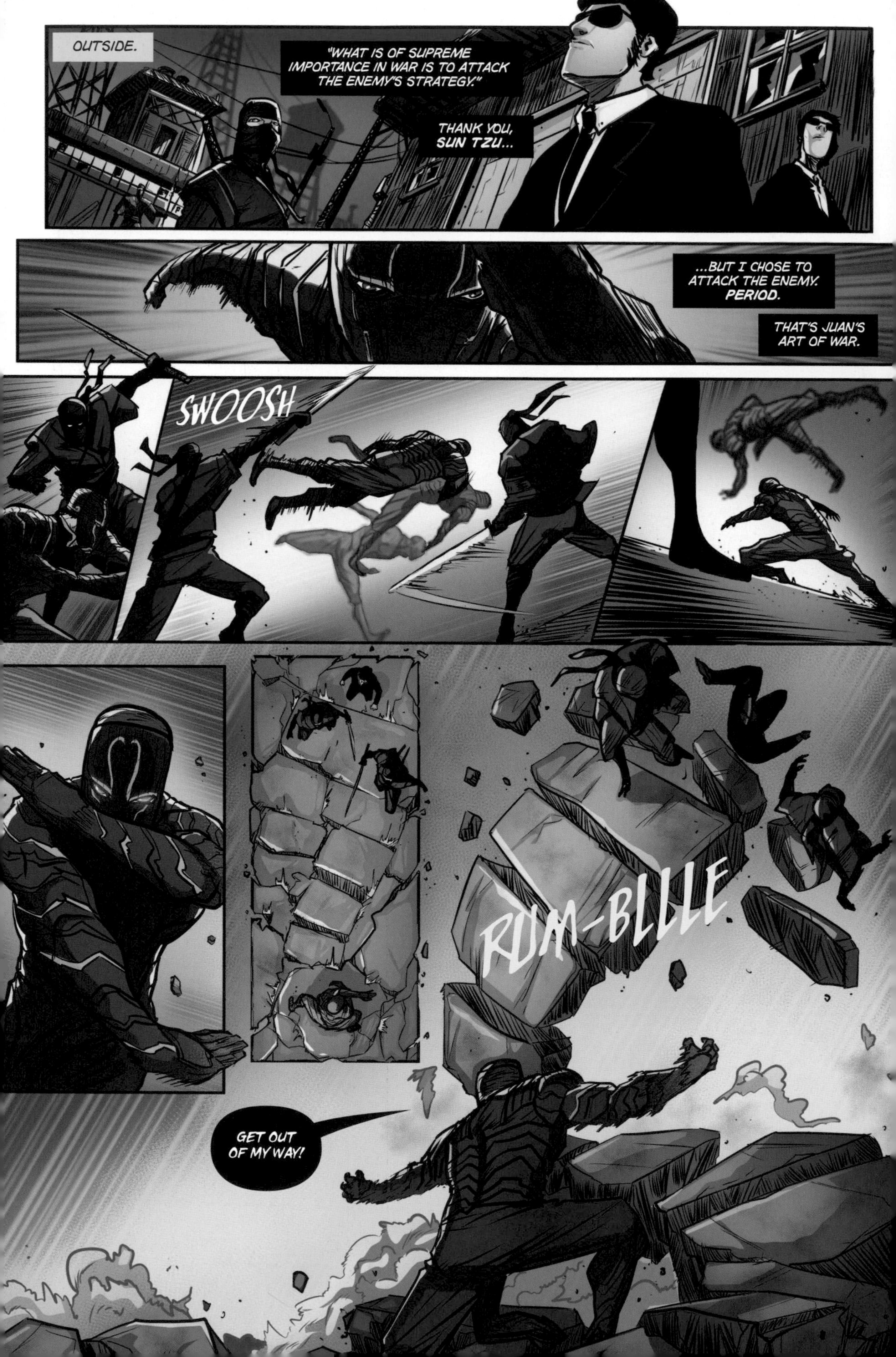
OUTSIDE.
"WHAT IS OF SUPREME IMPORTANCE IN WAR IS TO ATTACK THE ENEMY'S STRATEGY."
THANK YOU, SUN TZU...
...BUT I CHOSE TO ATTACK THE ENEMY. PERIOD.
THAT'S JUAN'S ART OF WAR.
SWOOSH
RUM-BLLLE
GET OUT OF MY WAY!

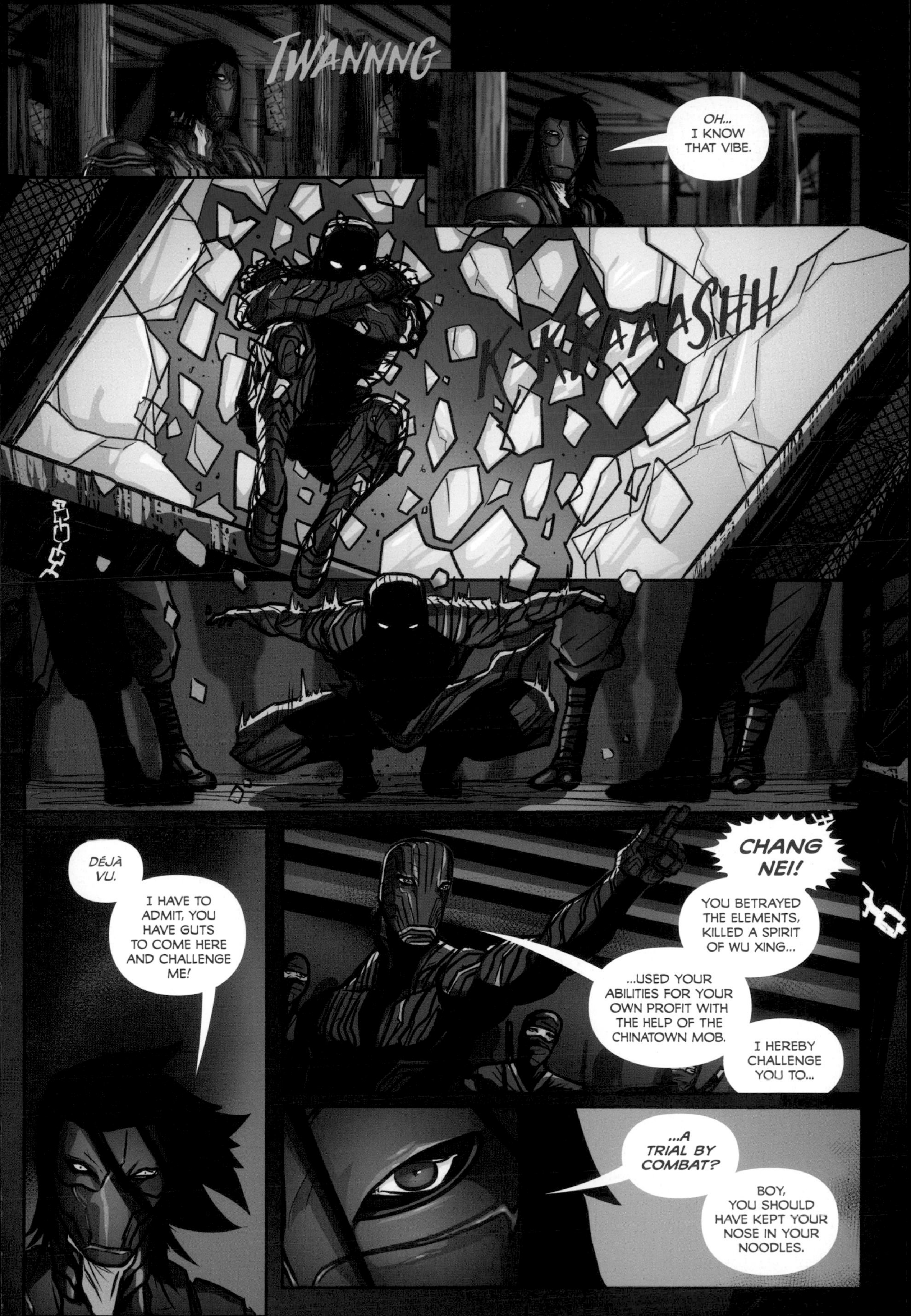
TWANNNG
OH... I KNOW THAT VIBE.
K-KRAAASHH
DÉJÀ VU.
I HAVE TO ADMIT, YOU HAVE GUTS TO COME HERE AND CHALLENGE ME!
CHANG NEI!
YOU BETRAYED THE ELEMENTS, KILLED A SPIRIT OF WU XING...
...USED YOUR ABILITIES FOR YOUR OWN PROFIT WITH THE HELP OF THE CHINATOWN MOB.
I HEREBY CHALLENGE YOU TO...
...A TRIAL BY COMBAT?
BOY, YOU SHOULD HAVE KEPT YOUR NOSE IN YOUR NOODLES.

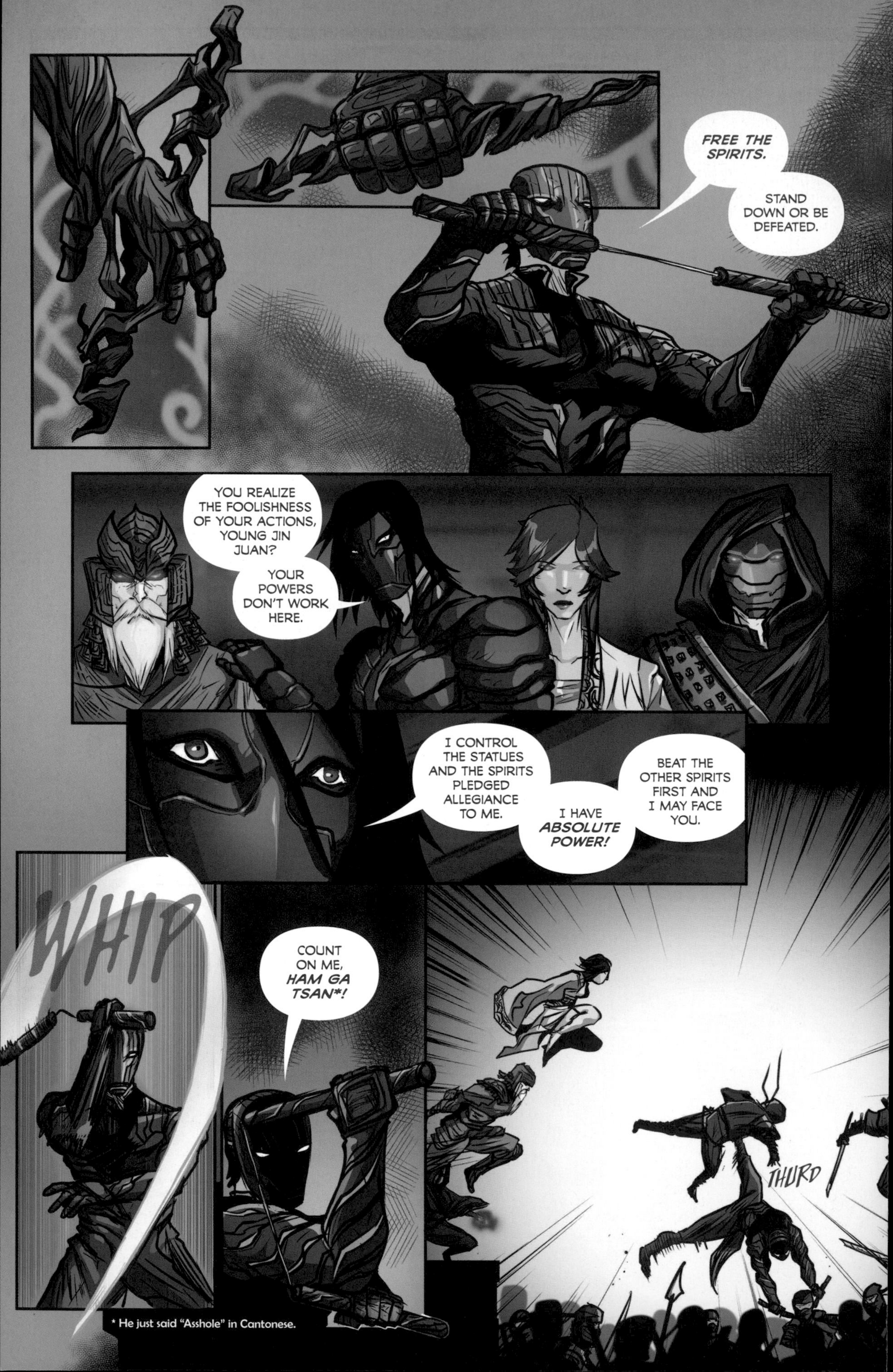
FREE THE SPIRITS.
STAND DOWN OR BE DEFEATED.
YOU REALIZE THE FOOLISHNESS OF YOUR ACTIONS, YOUNG JIN JUAN?
YOUR POWERS DON'T WORK HERE.
I CONTROL THE STATUES AND THE SPIRITS PLEDGED ALLEGIANCE TO ME.
I HAVE ABSOLUTE POWER!
BEAT THE OTHER SPIRITS FIRST AND I MAY FACE YOU.
WHIP
COUNT ON ME, HAM GA TSAN*!
THURD
* He just said "Asshole" in Cantonese.

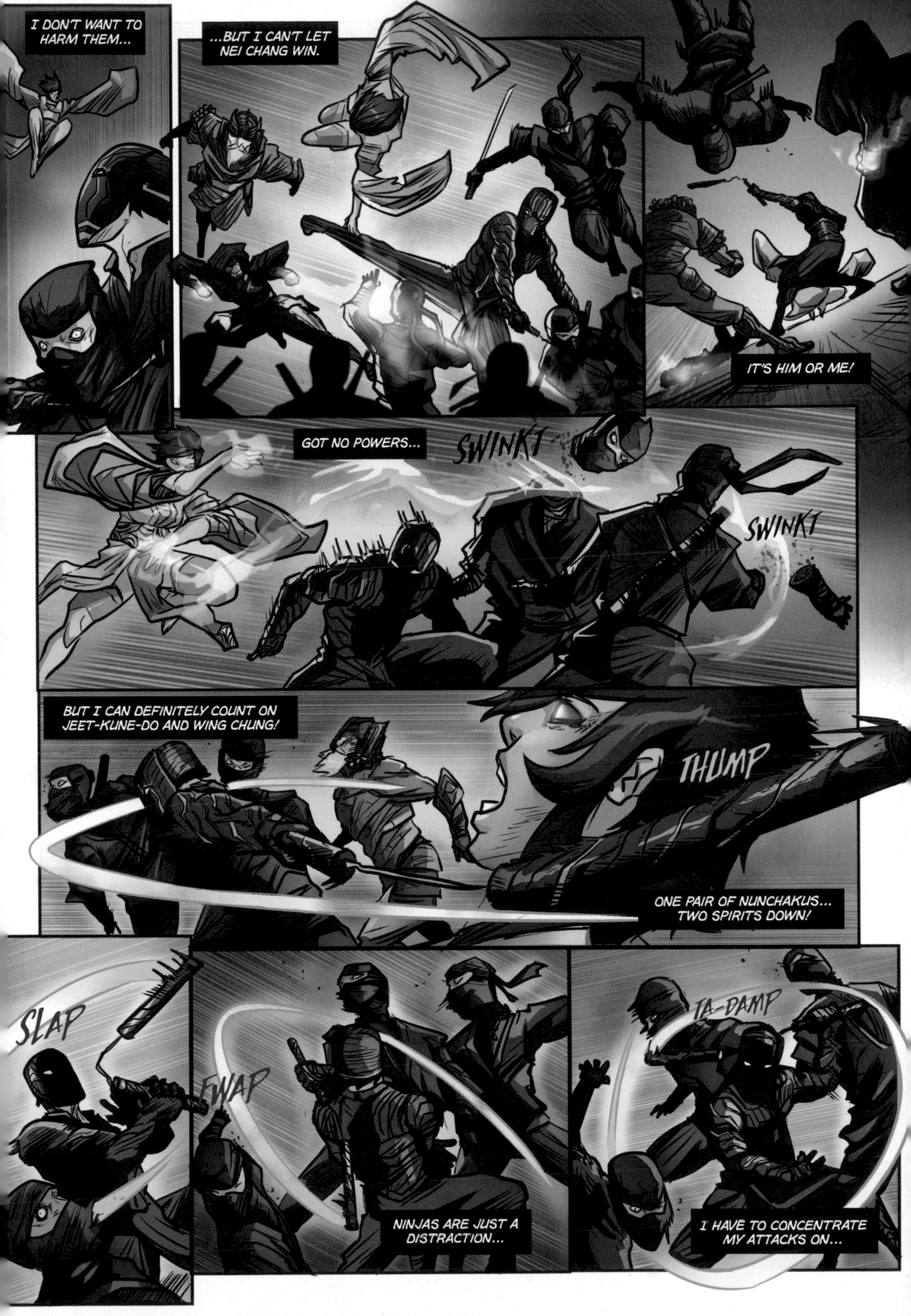
I DON'T WANT TO HARM THEM...
...BUT I CAN'T LET NEI CHANG WIN.
IT'S HIM OR ME!
GOT NO POWERS...
SWINKT
SWINKT
BUT I CAN DEFINITELY COUNT ON JEET-KUNE-DO AND WING CHUNG!
THUMP
ONE PAIR OF NUNCHAKUS... TWO SPIRITS DOWN!
SLAP
FWAP
NINJAS ARE JUST A DISTRACTION...
TA-DAMP
I HAVE TO CONCENTRATE MY ATTACKS ON...

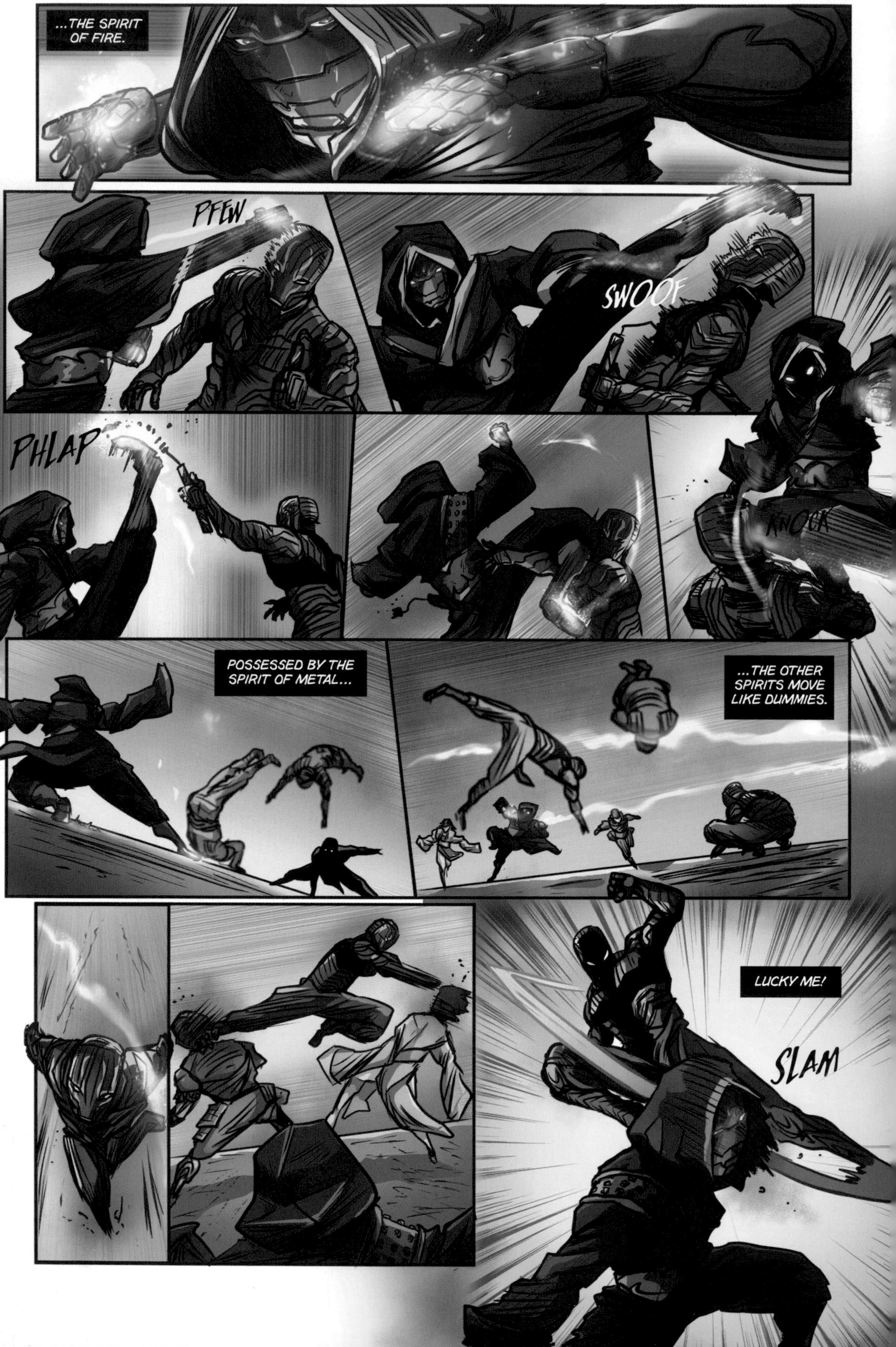
...THE SPIRIT OF FIRE.
PFEW
SWOOF
PHLAP
KNOCK
POSSESSED BY THE SPIRIT OF METAL...
...THE OTHER SPIRITS MOVE LIKE DUMMIES.
LUCKY ME!
SLAM

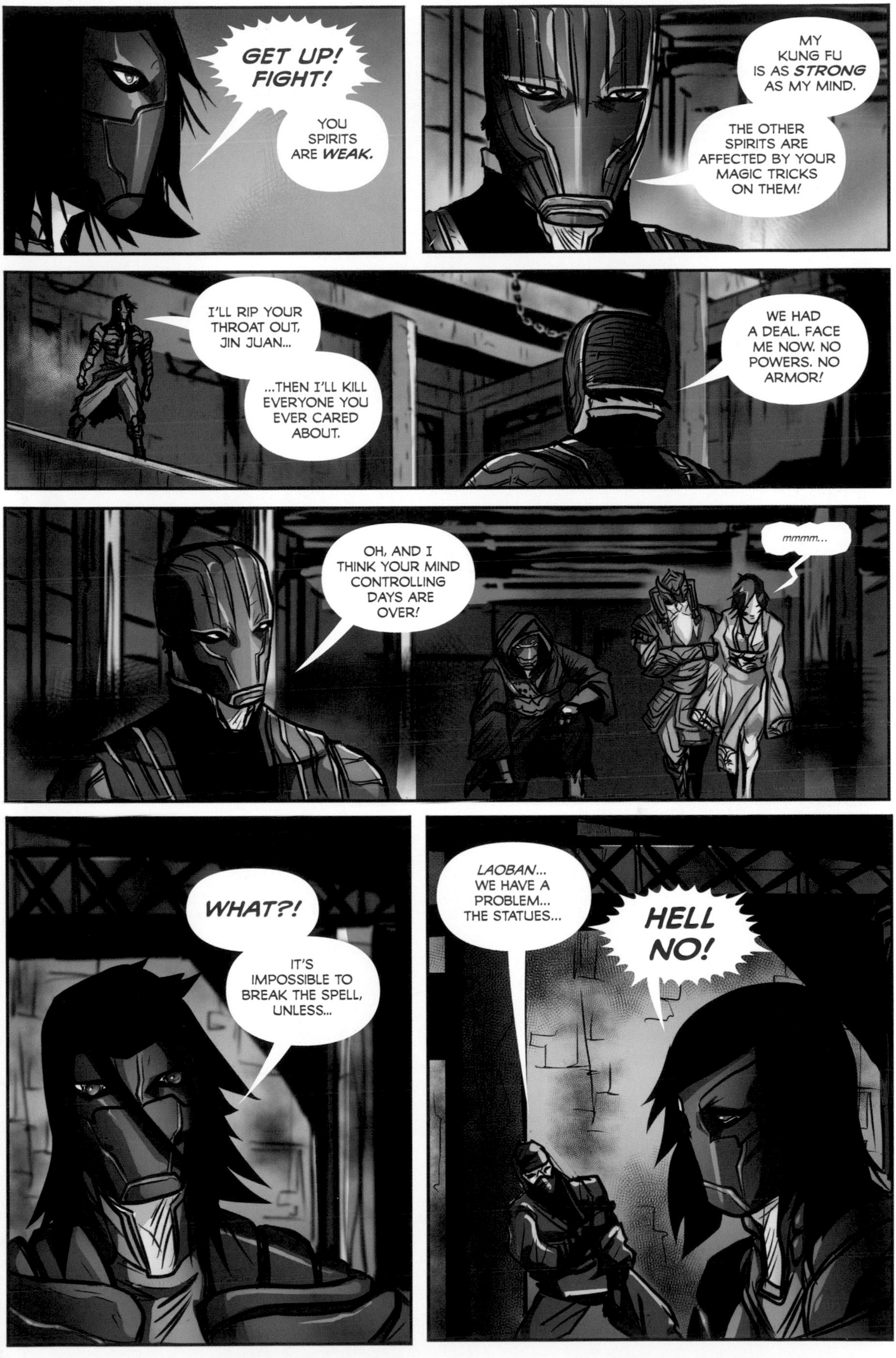
GET UP! FIGHT!
YOU SPIRITS ARE *WEAK.*
MY KUNG FU IS AS *STRONG* AS MY MIND.
THE OTHER SPIRITS ARE AFFECTED BY YOUR MAGIC TRICKS ON THEM!
I'LL RIP YOUR THROAT OUT, JIN JUAN...
...THEN I'LL KILL EVERYONE YOU EVER CARED ABOUT.
WE HAD A DEAL. FACE ME NOW. NO POWERS. NO ARMOR!
OH, AND I THINK YOUR MIND CONTROLLING DAYS ARE OVER!
mmmm...
WHAT?!
IT'S IMPOSSIBLE TO BREAK THE SPELL, UNLESS...
LAOBAN... WE HAVE A PROBLEM... THE STATUES...
HELL NO!

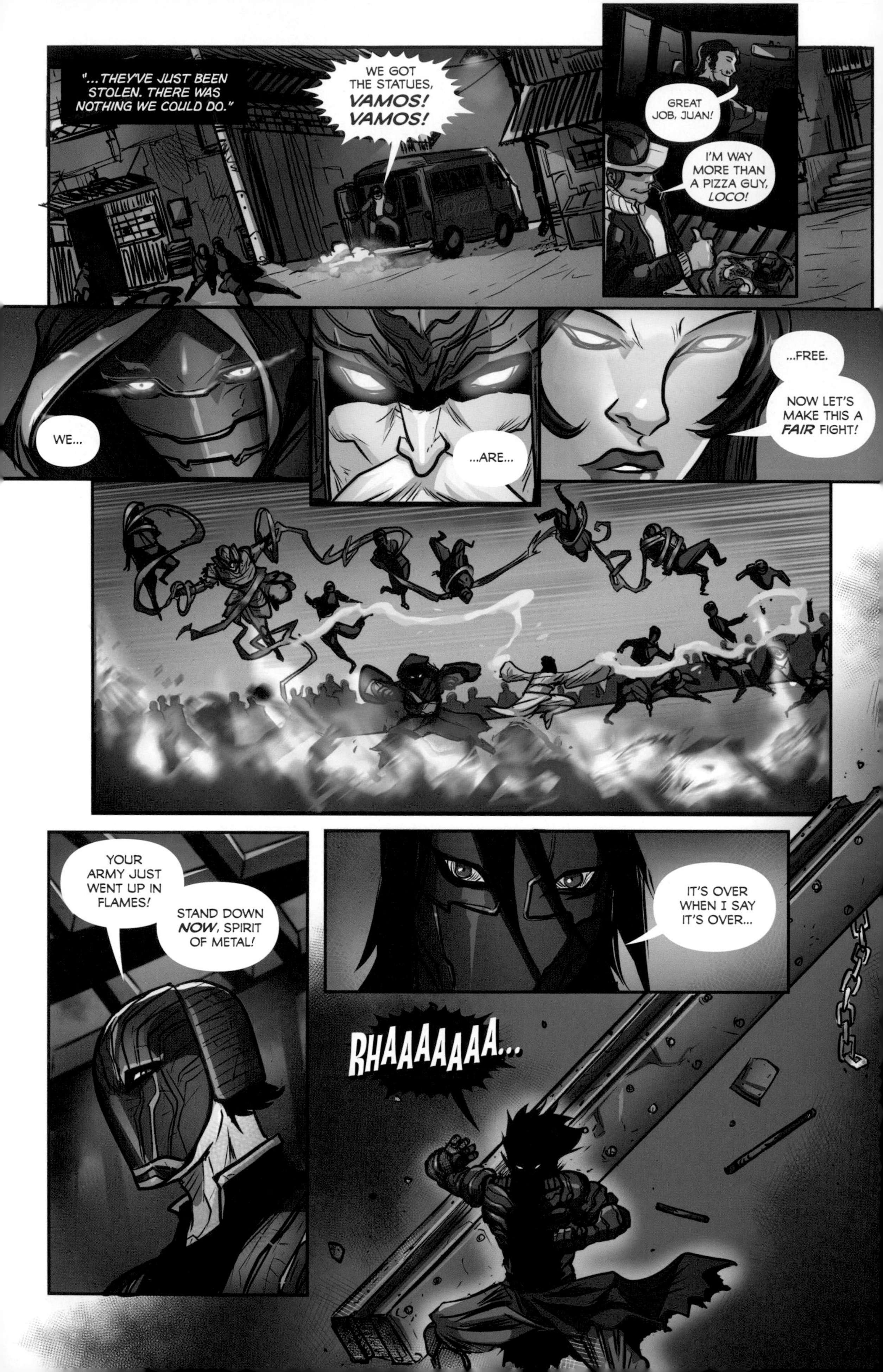
"...THEY'VE JUST BEEN STOLEN. THERE WAS NOTHING WE COULD DO."
WE GOT THE STATUES, VAMOS! VAMOS!
GREAT JOB, JUAN!
I'M WAY MORE THAN A PIZZA GUY, LOCO!
WE...
...ARE...
...FREE.
NOW LET'S MAKE THIS A FAIR FIGHT!
YOUR ARMY JUST WENT UP IN FLAMES!
STAND DOWN NOW, SPIRIT OF METAL!
IT'S OVER WHEN I SAY IT'S OVER...
RHAAAAAAA...

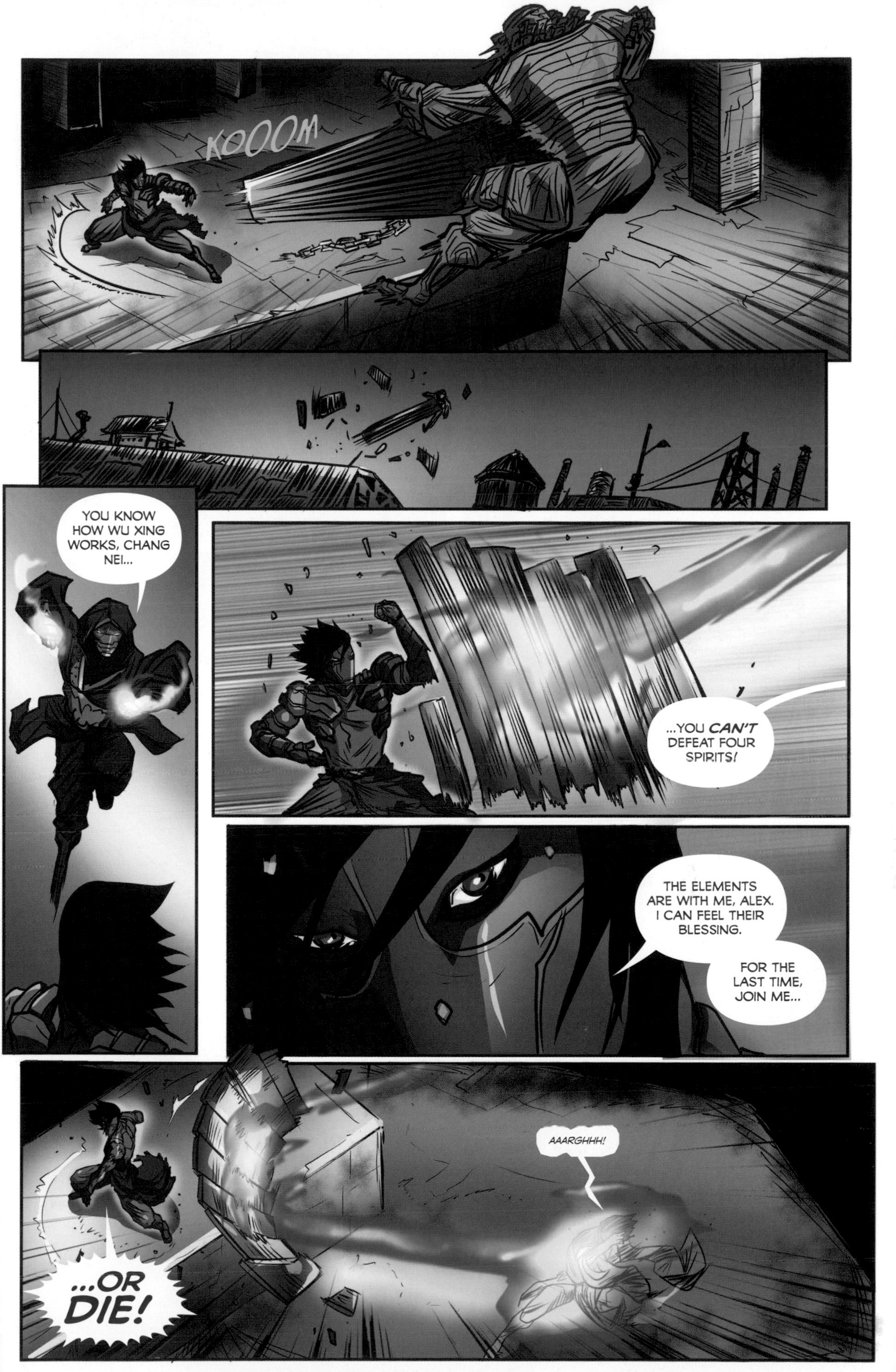
KOOOM
YOU KNOW HOW WU XING WORKS, CHANG NEI...
...YOU *CAN'T* DEFEAT FOUR SPIRITS!
THE ELEMENTS ARE WITH ME, ALEX. I CAN FEEL THEIR BLESSING.
FOR THE LAST TIME, JOIN ME...
...OR DIE!
AAARGHHH!

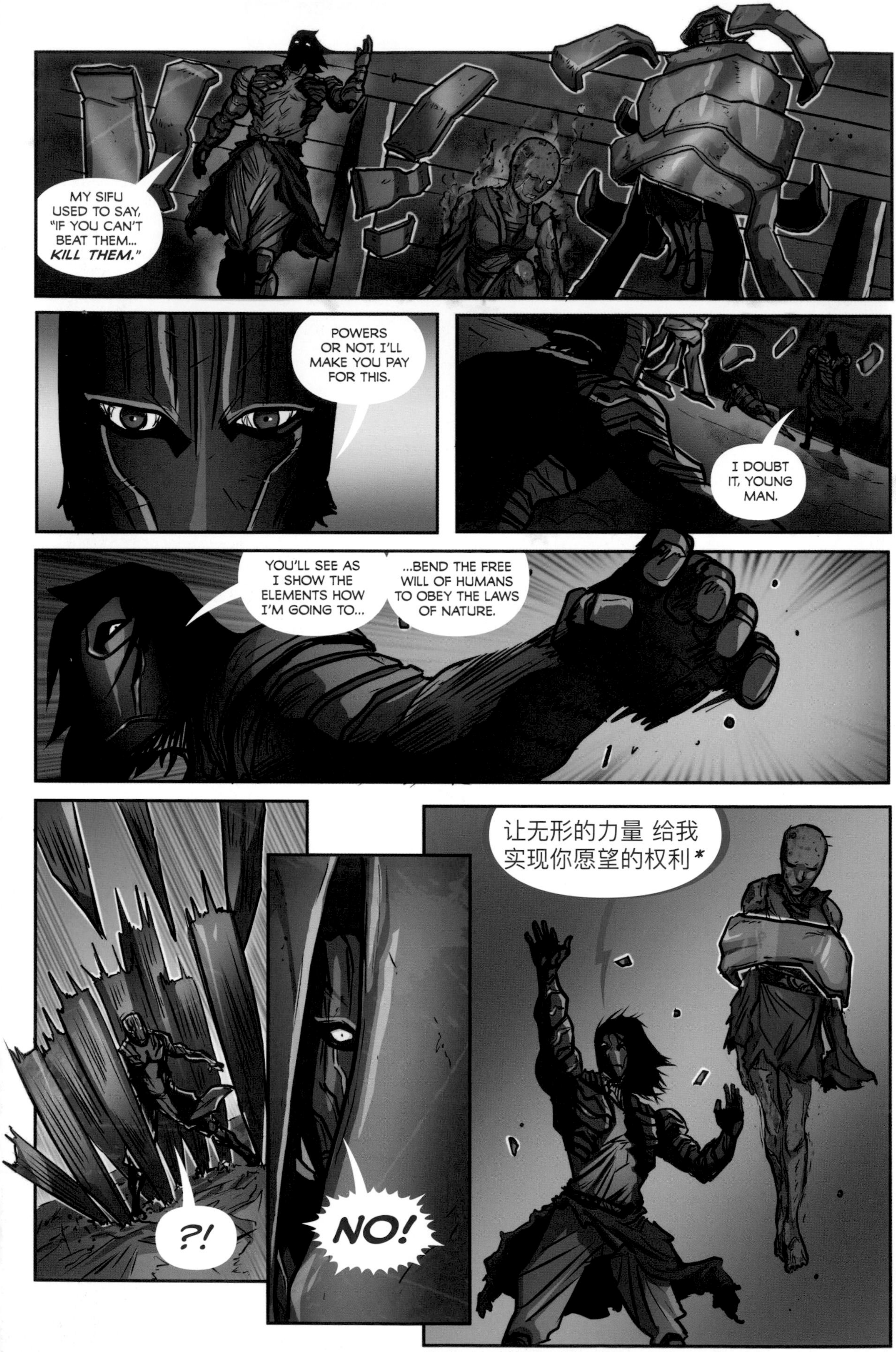
MY SIFU USED TO SAY, "IF YOU CAN'T BEAT THEM... *KILL THEM.*"
POWERS OR NOT, I'LL MAKE YOU PAY FOR THIS.
I DOUBT IT, YOUNG MAN.
YOU'LL SEE AS I SHOW THE ELEMENTS HOW I'M GOING TO...
...BEND THE FREE WILL OF HUMANS TO OBEY THE LAWS OF NATURE.
?!
NO!
让无形的力量 给我实现你愿望的权利*

*By the power of the Great Elements, give me the strength to fulfill my destiny.

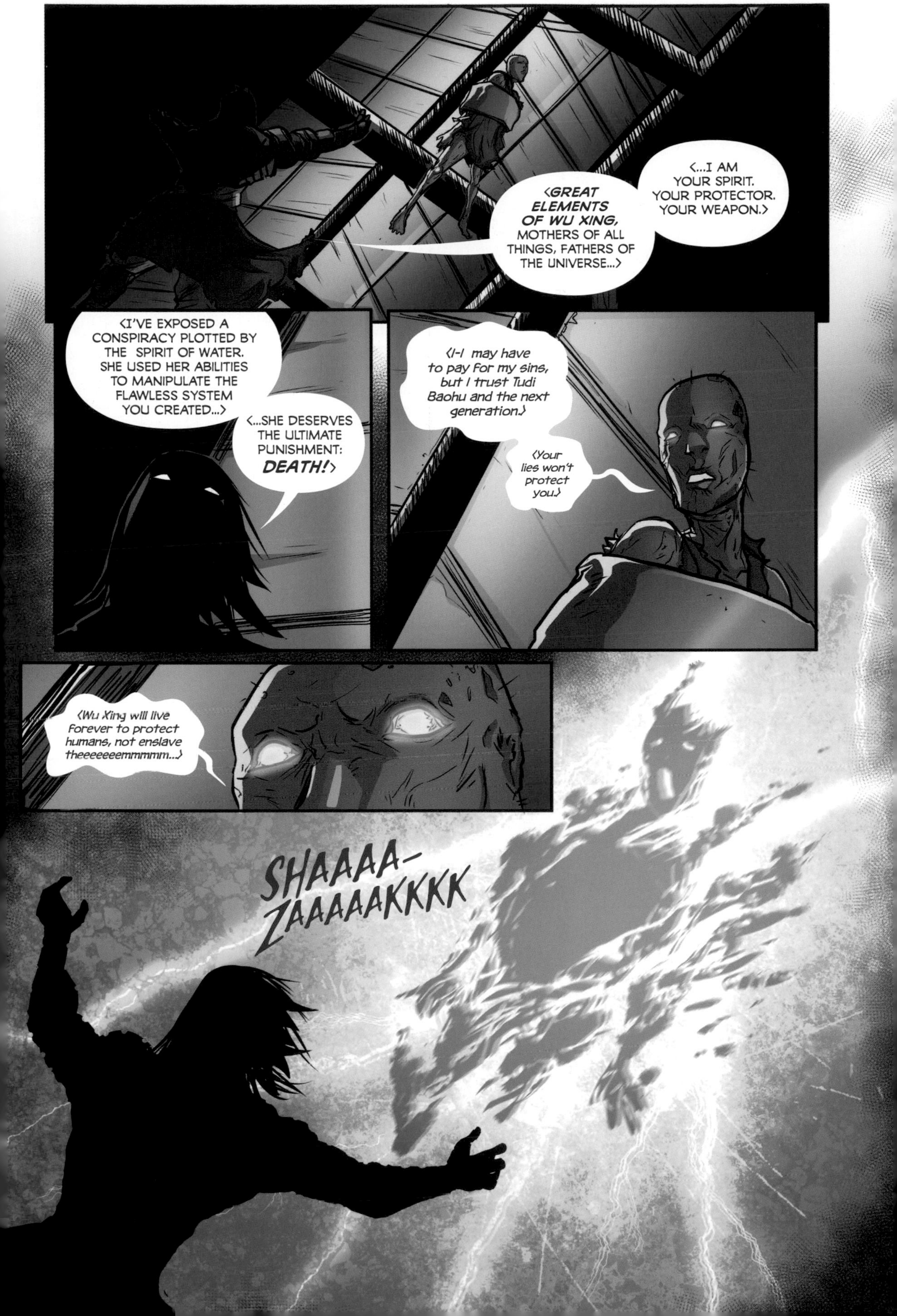

<GREAT ELEMENTS OF WU XING, MOTHERS OF ALL THINGS, FATHERS OF THE UNIVERSE...>
<...I AM YOUR SPIRIT. YOUR PROTECTOR. YOUR WEAPON.>
<I'VE EXPOSED A CONSPIRACY PLOTTED BY THE SPIRIT OF WATER. SHE USED HER ABILITIES TO MANIPULATE THE FLAWLESS SYSTEM YOU CREATED...>
<...SHE DESERVES THE ULTIMATE PUNISHMENT: DEATH!>
<I-I may have to pay for my sins, but I trust Tudi Baohu and the next generation.>
<Your lies won't protect you.>
<Wu Xing will live forever to protect humans, not enslave theeeeeeemmmmm...>
SHAAAA-ZAAAAAKKKK

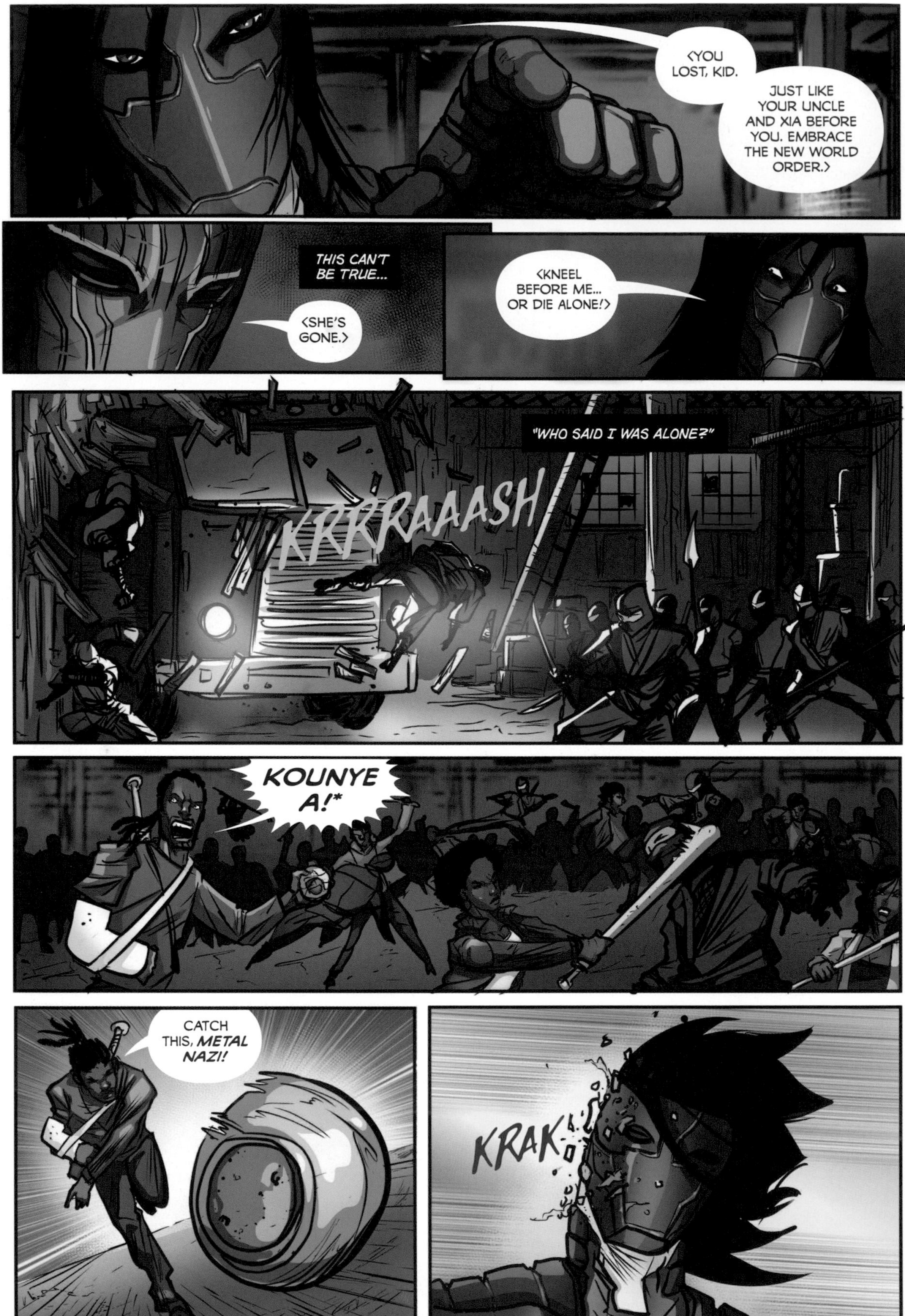
<YOU LOST, KID.
JUST LIKE YOUR UNCLE AND XIA BEFORE YOU. EMBRACE THE NEW WORLD ORDER.>
THIS CAN'T BE TRUE...
<SHE'S GONE.>
<KNEEL BEFORE ME... OR DIE ALONE!>
"WHO SAID I WAS ALONE?"
KRRRAAASH
KOUNYE A!*
CATCH THIS, METAL NAZI!
KRAK

*He just said "Now!" in Haitian Creole.

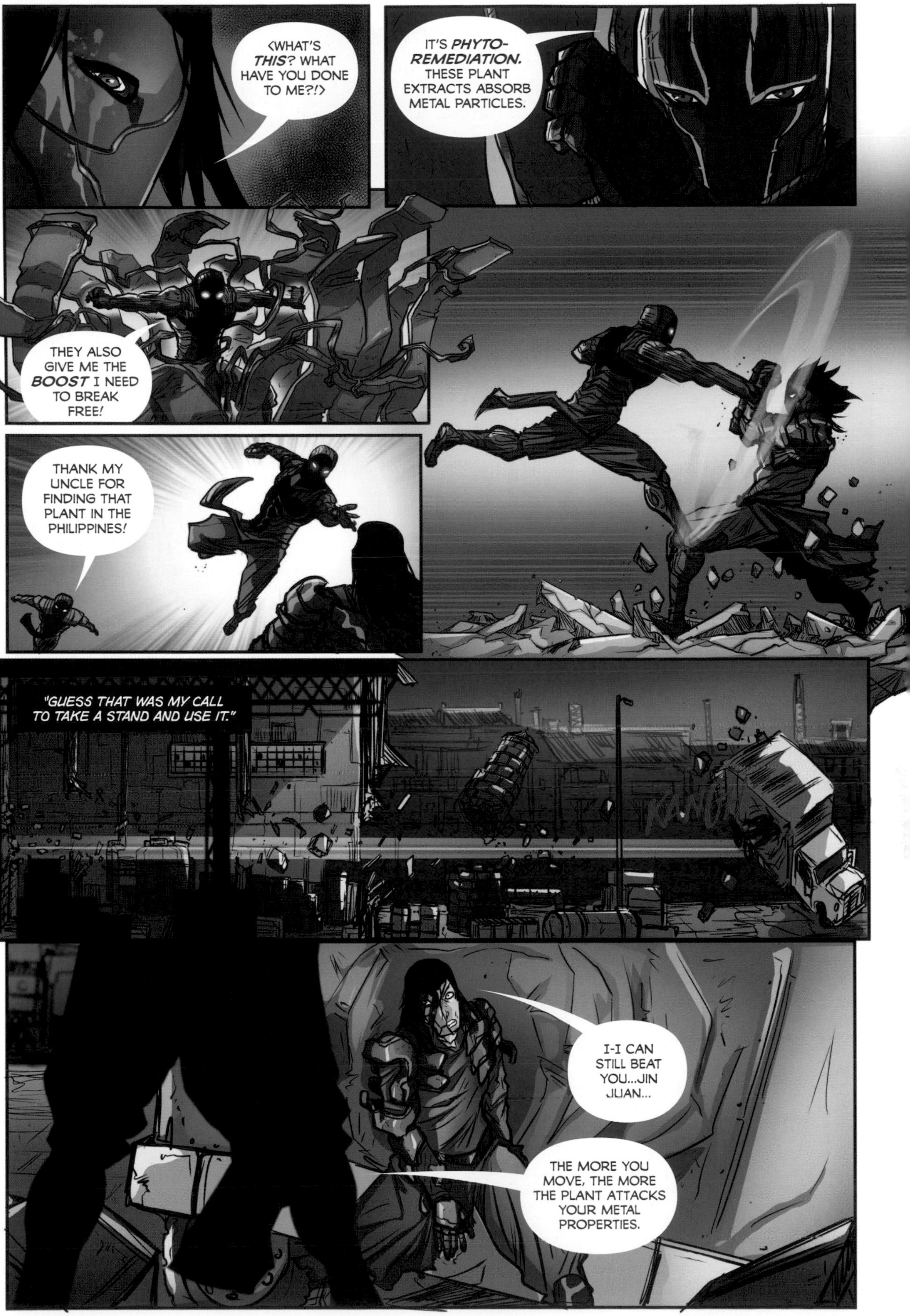

<WHAT'S THIS? WHAT HAVE YOU DONE TO ME?!>
IT'S PHYTO-REMEDIATION. THESE PLANT EXTRACTS ABSORB METAL PARTICLES.
THEY ALSO GIVE ME THE BOOST I NEED TO BREAK FREE!
THANK MY UNCLE FOR FINDING THAT PLANT IN THE PHILIPPINES!
"GUESS THAT WAS MY CALL TO TAKE A STAND AND USE IT."
I-I CAN STILL BEAT YOU...JIN JUAN...
THE MORE YOU MOVE, THE MORE THE PLANT ATTACKS YOUR METAL PROPERTIES.

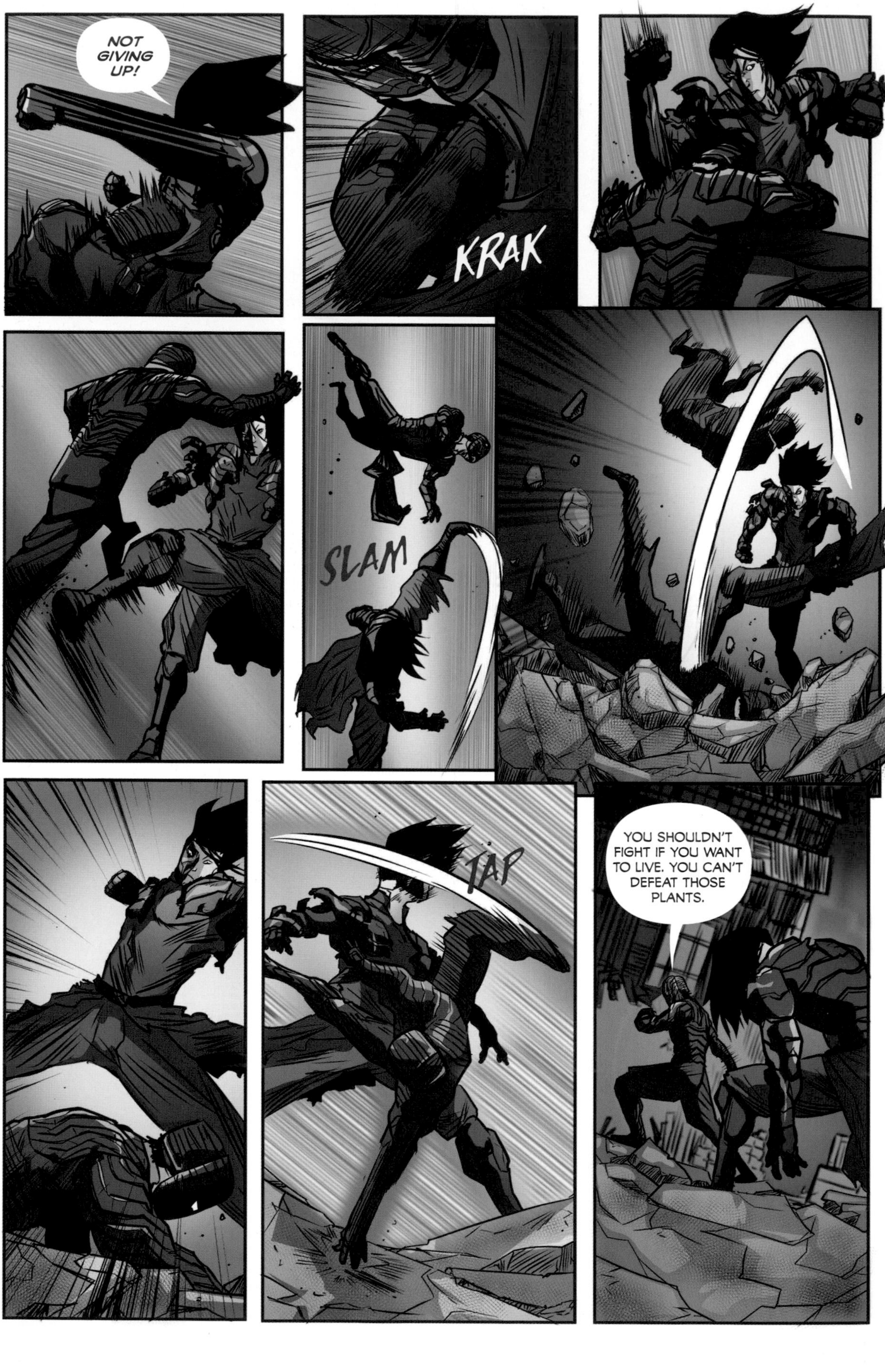
NOT GIVING UP!
KRAK
SLAM
TAP
YOU SHOULDN'T FIGHT IF YOU WANT TO LIVE. YOU CAN'T DEFEAT THOSE PLANTS.

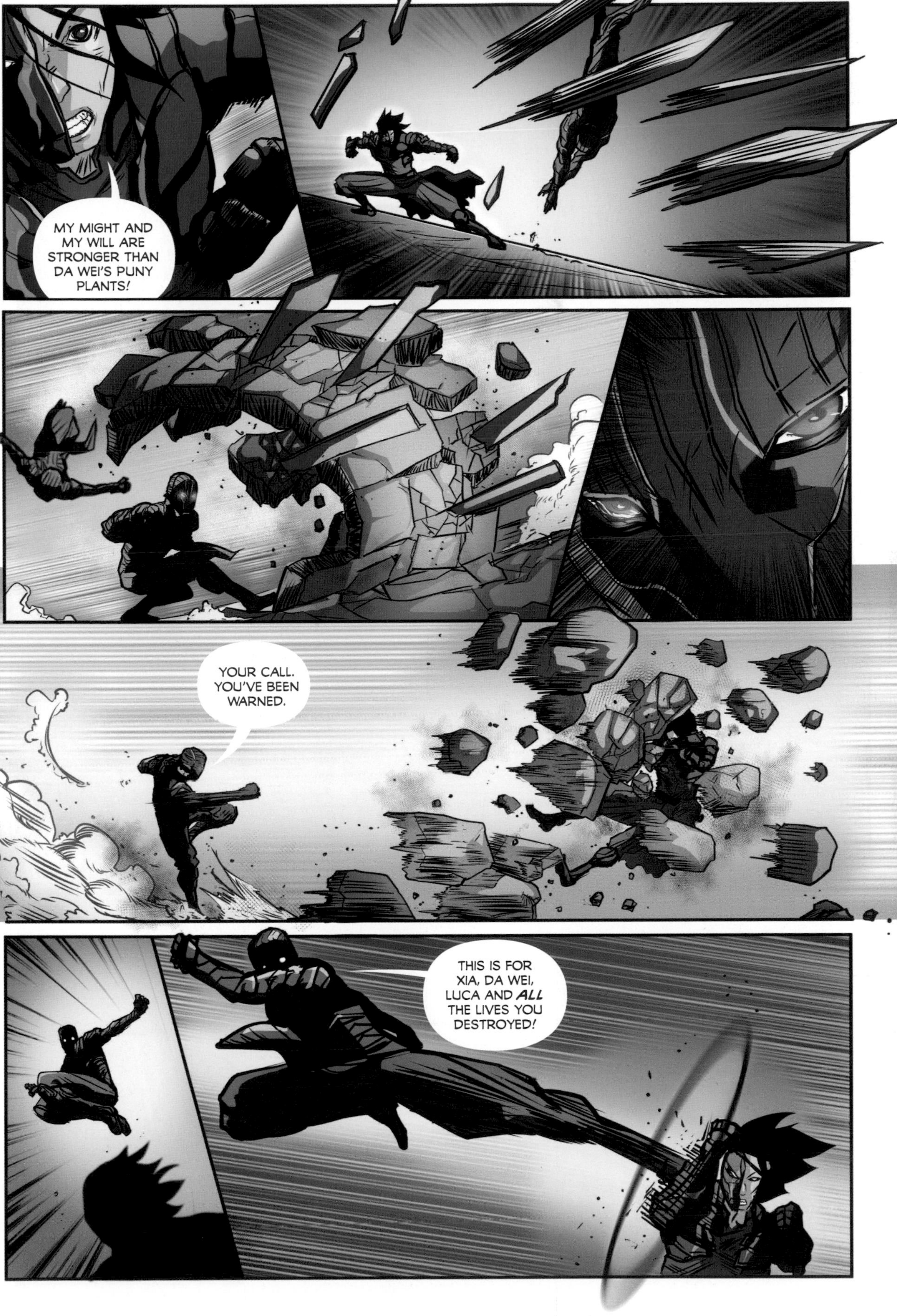
MY MIGHT AND MY WILL ARE STRONGER THAN DA WEI'S PUNY PLANTS!
YOUR CALL. YOU'VE BEEN WARNED.
THIS IS FOR XIA, DA WEI, LUCA AND *ALL* THE LIVES YOU DESTROYED!

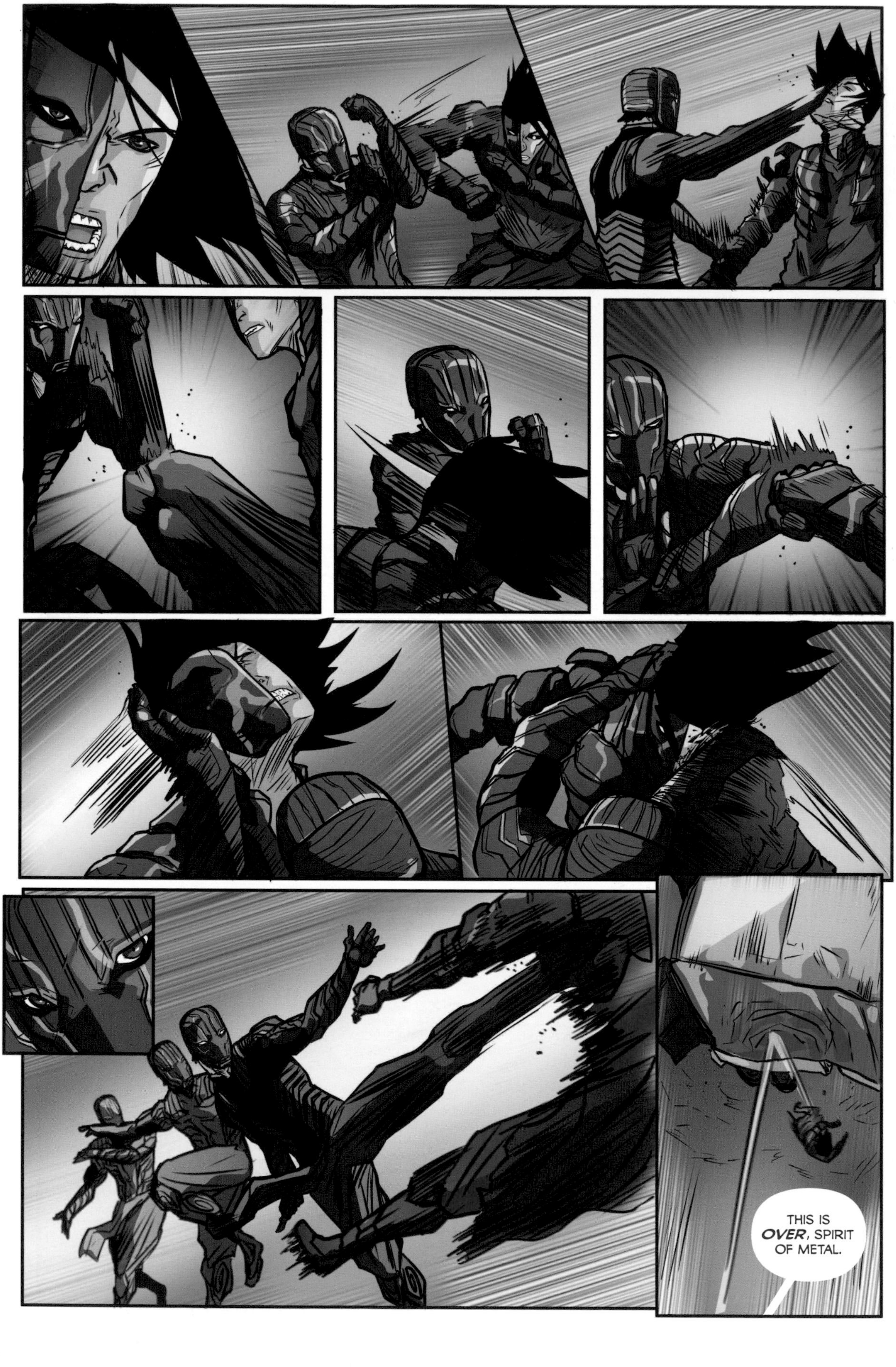
THIS IS **OVER**, SPIRIT OF METAL.

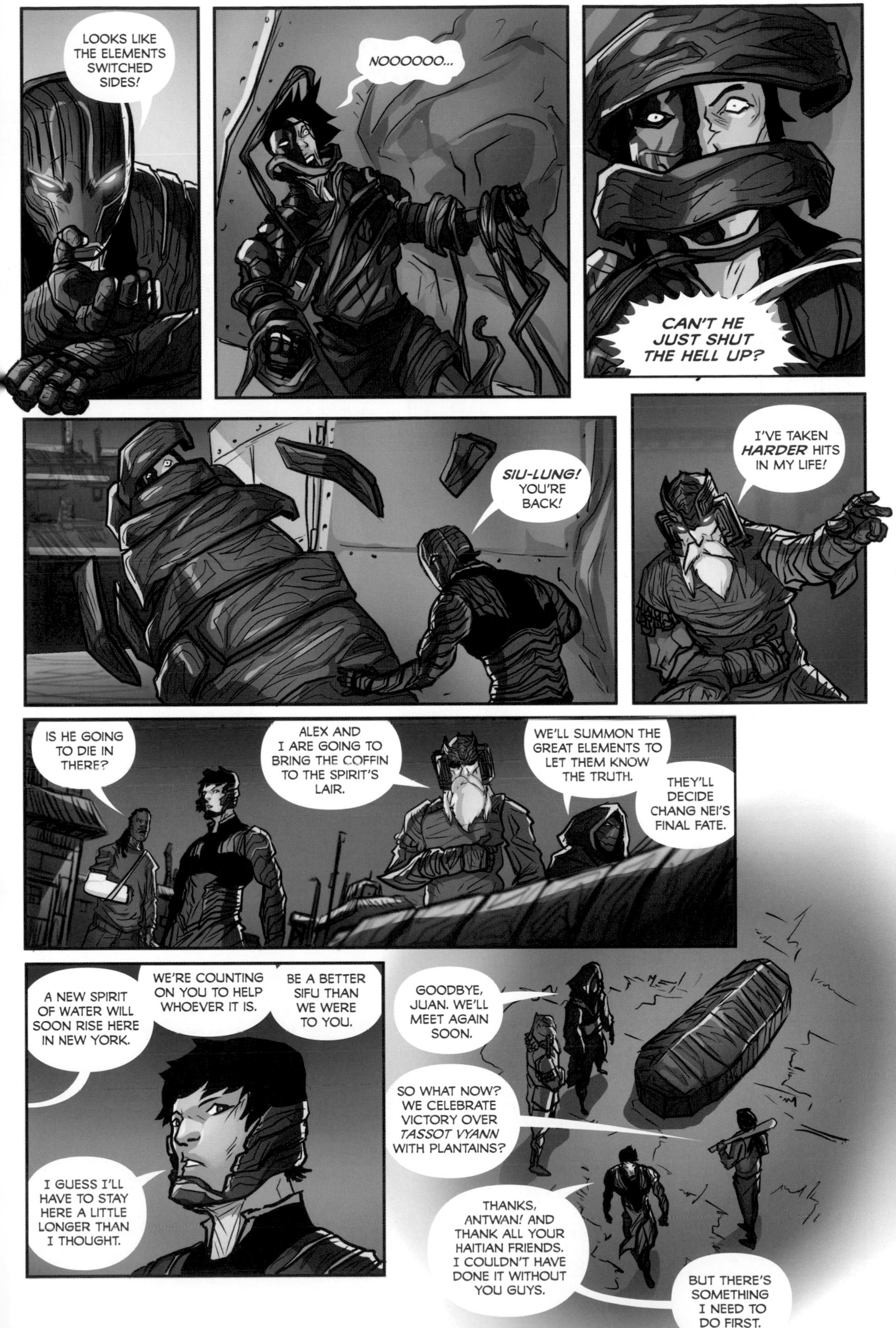
LOOKS LIKE THE ELEMENTS SWITCHED SIDES!
NOOOOOO...
CAN'T HE JUST SHUT THE HELL UP?
SIU-LUNG! YOU'RE BACK!
I'VE TAKEN HARDER HITS IN MY LIFE!
IS HE GOING TO DIE IN THERE?
ALEX AND I ARE GOING TO BRING THE COFFIN TO THE SPIRIT'S LAIR.
WE'LL SUMMON THE GREAT ELEMENTS TO LET THEM KNOW THE TRUTH.
THEY'LL DECIDE CHANG NEI'S FINAL FATE.
A NEW SPIRIT OF WATER WILL SOON RISE HERE IN NEW YORK.
WE'RE COUNTING ON YOU TO HELP WHOEVER IT IS.
BE A BETTER SIFU THAN WE WERE TO YOU.
I GUESS I'LL HAVE TO STAY HERE A LITTLE LONGER THAN I THOUGHT.
GOODBYE, JUAN. WE'LL MEET AGAIN SOON.
SO WHAT NOW? WE CELEBRATE VICTORY OVER TASSOT VYANN WITH PLANTAINS?
THANKS, ANTWAN! AND THANK ALL YOUR HAITIAN FRIENDS. I COULDN'T HAVE DONE IT WITHOUT YOU GUYS.
BUT THERE'S SOMETHING I NEED TO DO FIRST.

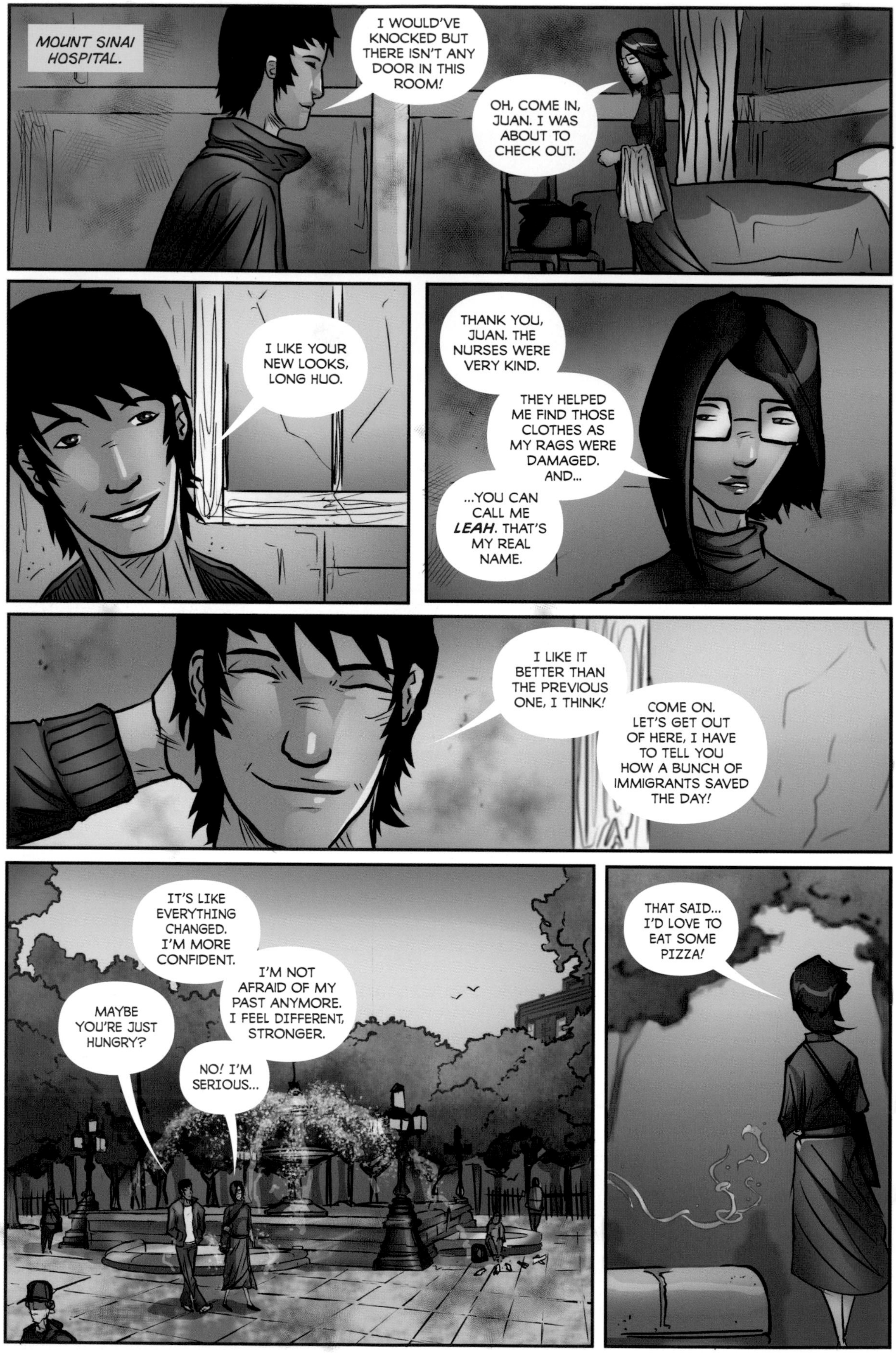
MOUNT SINAI HOSPITAL.
I WOULD'VE KNOCKED BUT THERE ISN'T ANY DOOR IN THIS ROOM!
OH, COME IN, JUAN. I WAS ABOUT TO CHECK OUT.
I LIKE YOUR NEW LOOKS, LONG HUO.
THANK YOU, JUAN. THE NURSES WERE VERY KIND.
THEY HELPED ME FIND THOSE CLOTHES AS MY RAGS WERE DAMAGED. AND...
...YOU CAN CALL ME LEAH. THAT'S MY REAL NAME.
I LIKE IT BETTER THAN THE PREVIOUS ONE, I THINK!
COME ON. LET'S GET OUT OF HERE, I HAVE TO TELL YOU HOW A BUNCH OF IMMIGRANTS SAVED THE DAY!
IT'S LIKE EVERYTHING CHANGED. I'M MORE CONFIDENT.
I'M NOT AFRAID OF MY PAST ANYMORE. I FEEL DIFFERENT, STRONGER.
MAYBE YOU'RE JUST HUNGRY?
NO! I'M SERIOUS...
THAT SAID... I'D LOVE TO EAT SOME PIZZA!

"We're growing up together, the human race. And we've discovered a lot of things that we didn't know. We're finding our way. Instead of thinking about doomsday all the time, think about how beautiful the world is. We're all together, and together we're getting wiser."
-- Yoko Ono

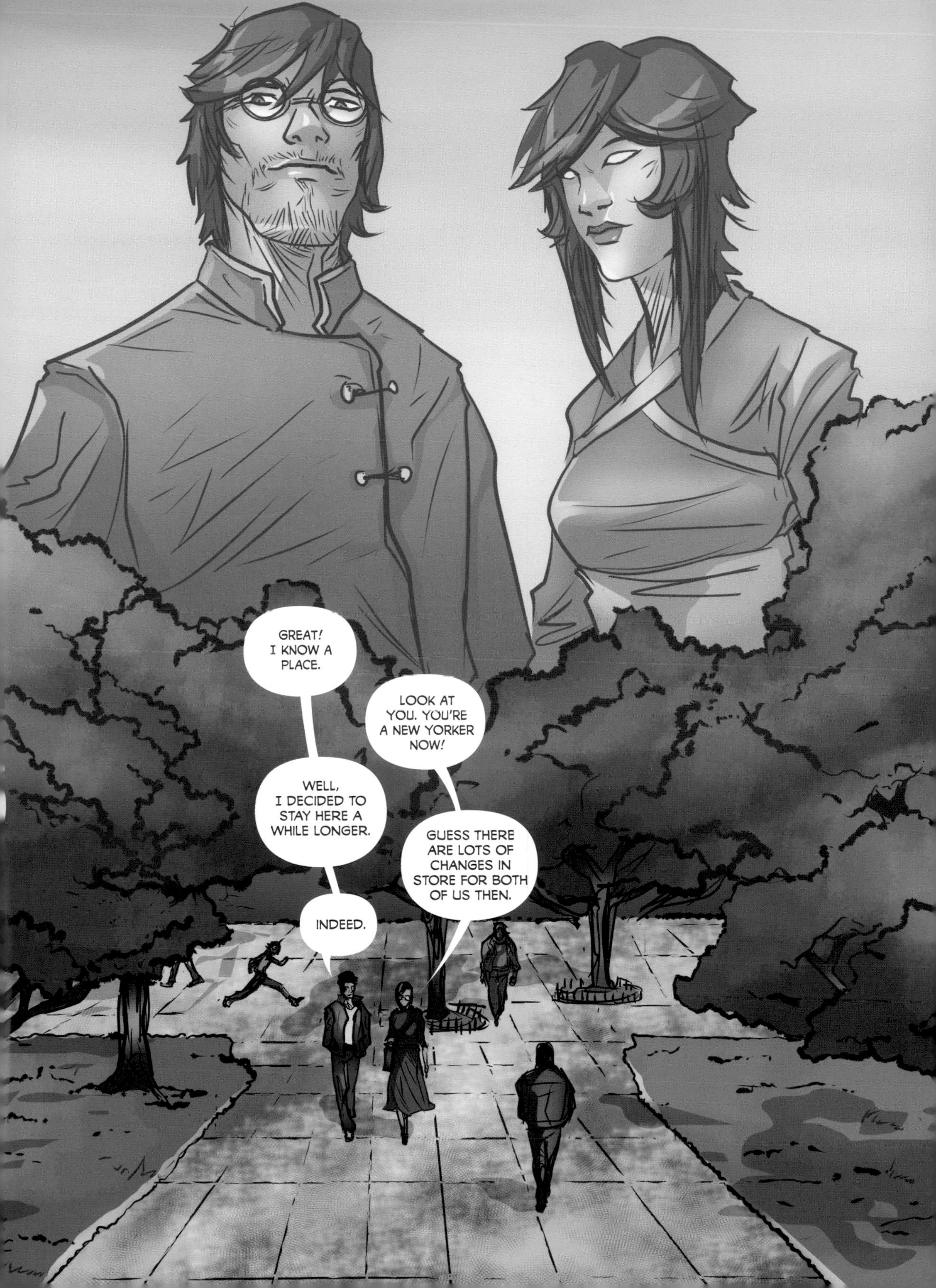

GREAT! I KNOW A PLACE.
LOOK AT YOU. YOU'RE A NEW YORKER NOW!
WELL, I DECIDED TO STAY HERE A WHILE LONGER.
GUESS THERE ARE LOTS OF CHANGES IN STORE FOR BOTH OF US THEN.
INDEED.

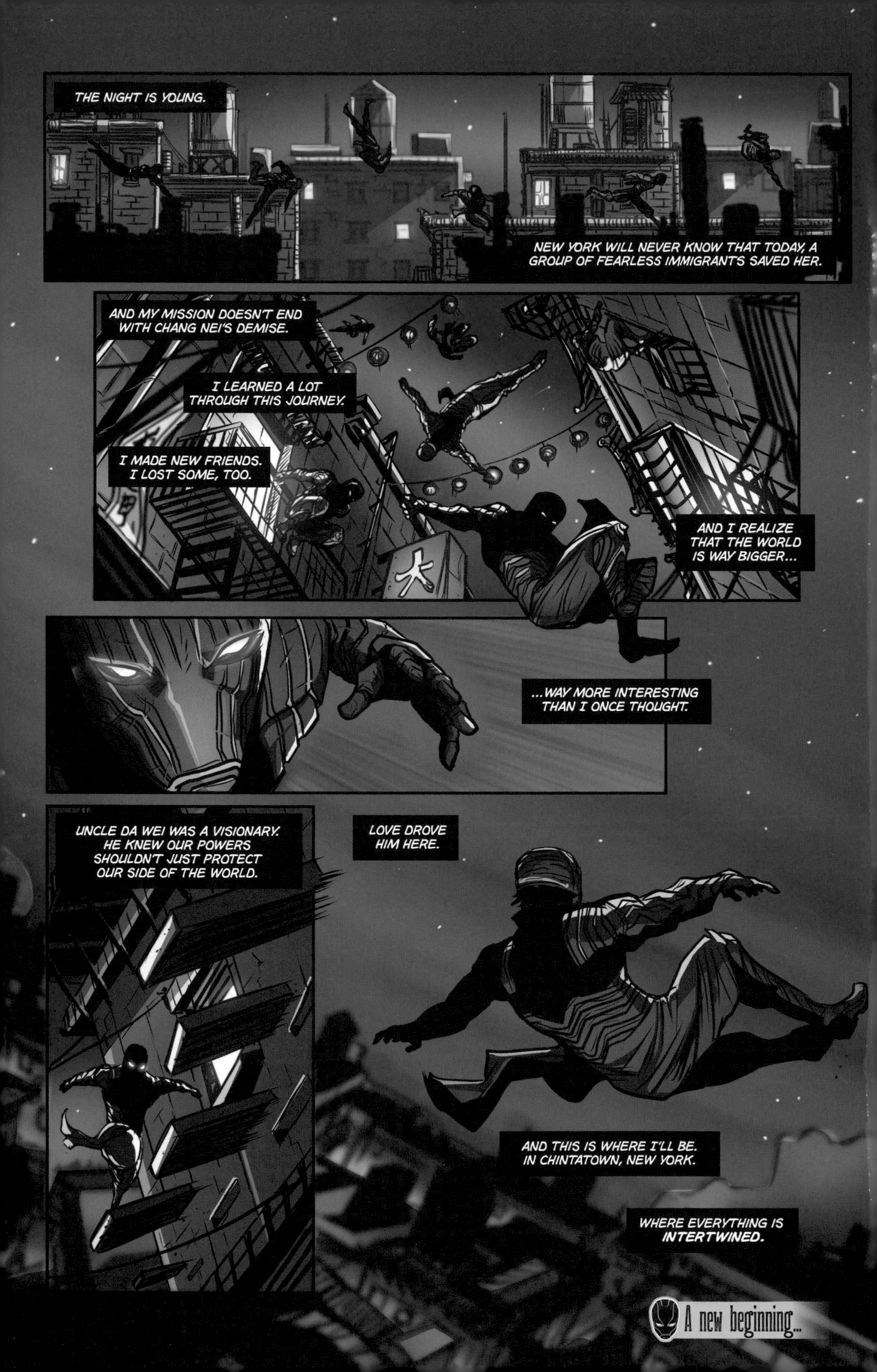
THE NIGHT IS YOUNG.
NEW YORK WILL NEVER KNOW THAT TODAY, A GROUP OF FEARLESS IMMIGRANTS SAVED HER.
AND MY MISSION DOESN'T END WITH CHANG NEI'S DEMISE.
I LEARNED A LOT THROUGH THIS JOURNEY.
I MADE NEW FRIENDS. I LOST SOME, TOO.
大
AND I REALIZE THAT THE WORLD IS WAY BIGGER...
...WAY MORE INTERESTING THAN I ONCE THOUGHT.
UNCLE DA WEI WAS A VISIONARY. HE KNEW OUR POWERS SHOULDN'T JUST PROTECT OUR SIDE OF THE WORLD.
LOVE DROVE HIM HERE.
AND THIS IS WHERE I'LL BE. IN CHINTATOWN, NEW YORK.
WHERE EVERYTHING IS INTERTWINED.
A new beginning...

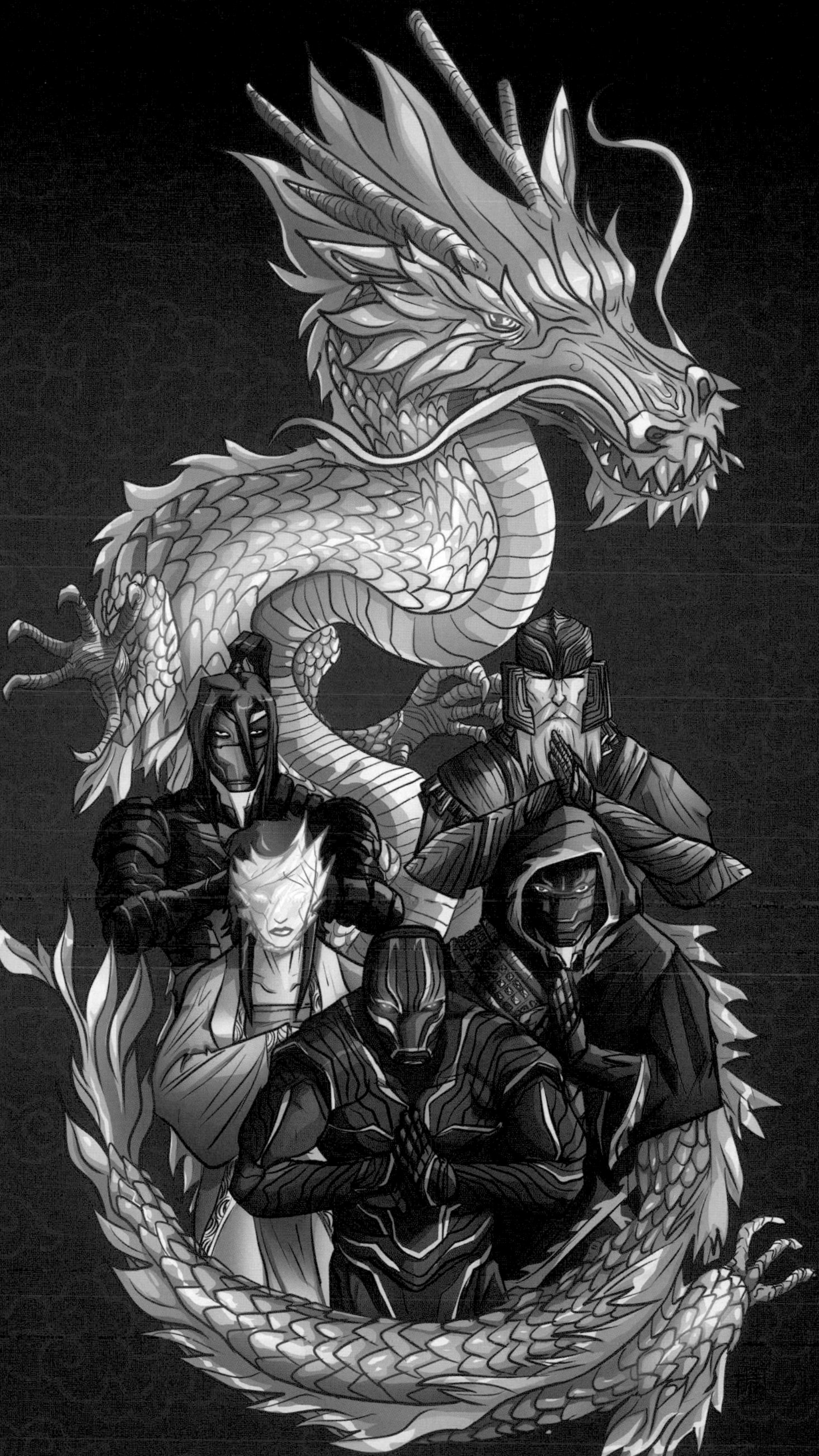

The Spirits of Wu Xing will be back...

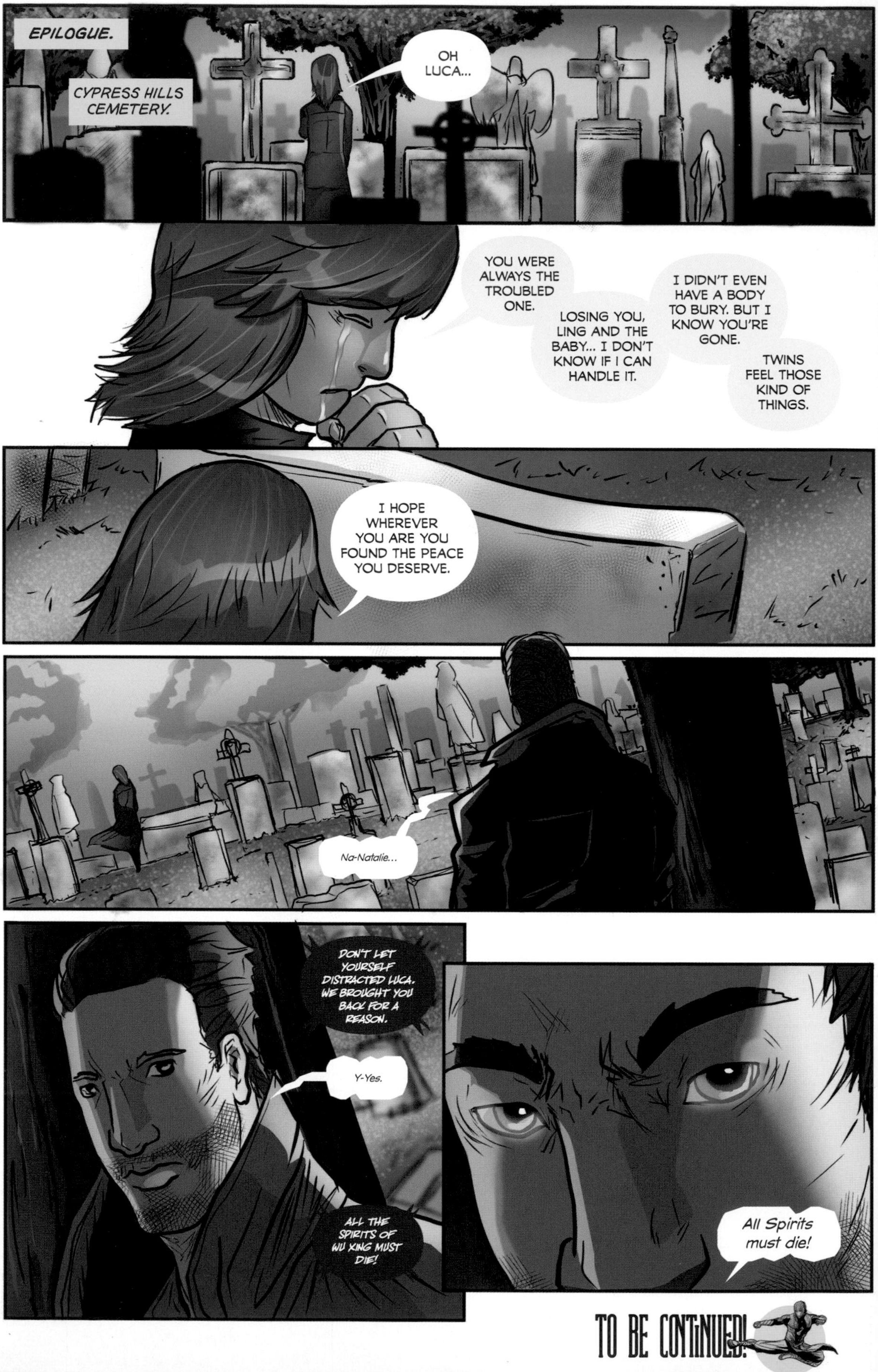
EPILOGUE.
CYPRESS HILLS CEMETERY.
OH LUCA...
YOU WERE ALWAYS THE TROUBLED ONE.
LOSING YOU, LING AND THE BABY... I DON'T KNOW IF I CAN HANDLE IT.
I DIDN'T EVEN HAVE A BODY TO BURY. BUT I KNOW YOU'RE GONE.
TWINS FEEL THOSE KIND OF THINGS.
I HOPE WHEREVER YOU ARE YOU FOUND THE PEACE YOU DESERVE.
Na-Natalie...
DON'T LET YOURSELF DISTRACTED LUCA. WE BROUGHT YOU BACK FOR A REASON.
Y-Yes.
ALL THE SPIRITS OF WU XING MUST DIE!
All Spirits must die!
TO BE CONTINUED!